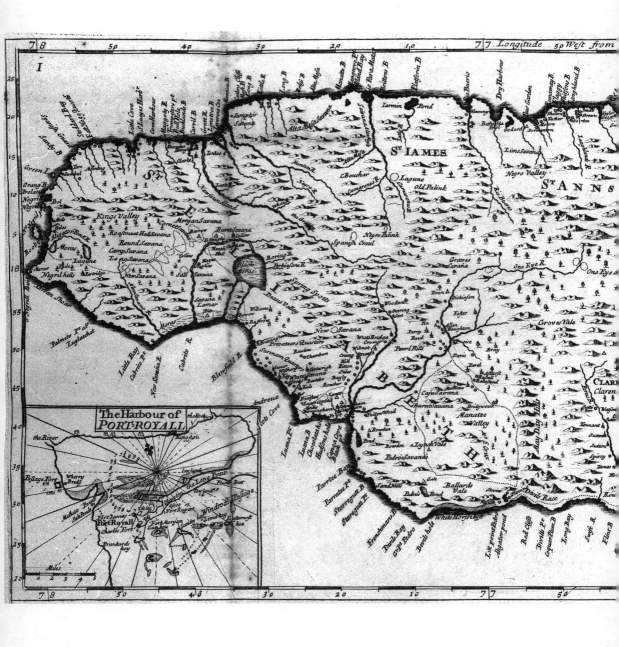

The Harbour of
PORT-ROYALL

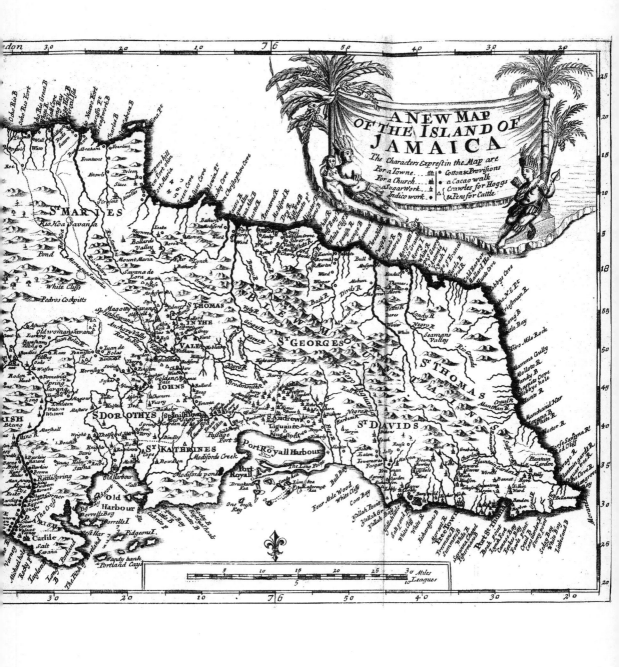

A NEW MAP OF THE ISLAND OF JAMAICA

The Characters Exprest in the Map are
For a Towne . . . . ▦ . . . . . Cotton & Provisions
For a Church . . . . ⛪ . . . . . a Cacao walk
a Sugar Work . . . . ● . . . . . Crawles for Hoggs
Indico work . . . . ● . . . . . & Pens for Cattle

On the Account in the 'Golden Age': Piracy and the Americas, 1670–1726

ON THE ACCOUNT IN THE 'GOLDEN AGE'

Piracy and the Americas, 1670–1726

JOSEPH GIBBS

sussex
ACADEMIC
PRESS

Brighton • Chicago • Toronto

2 4 6 8 10 9 7 5 3 1

First published 2014 in Great Britain by
SUSSEX ACADEMIC PRESS
PO Box 139
Eastbourne BN24 9BP

and in the United States of America by
SUSSEX ACADEMIC PRESS
920 NE 58th Avenue, Suite 300
Portland, Oregon 97213-3786

and in Canada by
SUSSEX ACADEMIC PRESS (CANADA)
1108/115 Antibes Drive,
Toronto, Ontario M2R 2Y9

British Library Cataloguing in Publication Data
A CIP catalogue record for this book is available from the British Library.

Library of Congress Cataloging-in-Publication Data
Applied for.

Paperback ISBN 978-1-84519-617-2

MIX
Paper from
responsible sources
FSC® C013056

Typeset and designed by Sussex Academic Press, Brighton & Eastbourne.
Printed by TJ International, Padstow, Cornwall.
This book is printed on acid-free paper.

Contents

List of Illustrations   vii

Introduction   viii

1   "For the most of his Majesties Honor and Service, and the safety of Jamaica" – The buccaneers, Henry Morgan, and the sack of Panamá (1670–1671)   1

2   "Through insuperable Difficulties" – Bartholomew Sharp's buccaneer campaign (1680–1682)   20

3   "Those vile Remains of that abominable Crew" – Samuel Bellamy and the wreck of the *Whydah* (1717)   54

4   "A sort of People, who may be truly called Enemies to Mankind" – The *Boston News-Letter* covers the era of Blackbeard (1717–1719)   101

5   "Like a parcel of Furies" – Bartholomew Roberts captures the *Samuel* (1720)   122

6   "Profligate, cursing and swearing much, and very ready and willing to do any Thing on Board" – The trial of Ann Bonny and Mary Read (1720)   130

7   "All the Barbarity imaginable" – Edward Low, George Lowther, and associates (1722–1725)   138

8   "Such Bad Company" – Edward Low and Francis Spriggs as seen by prisoners Philip Ashton and Nicholas Merritt (1722–1724)   178

9   "Hung up in Chains" – William Fly and the end of the Golden Age (1726)   208

Bibliography   230

Index   236

List of Illustrations

Cover illustrations: Front – "The Combatants Cut and Slashed with Savage Fury" (Howard Pyle); back – "The Buccaneer was a Picturesque Fellow" (Howard Pyle).

Endpapers: Etching from Sir Hans Sloane, *A Voyage to the Islands Madera, Barbados, Nieves, S. Christophers and Jamaica . . .* (Courtesy of the LuEsther T. Mertz Library of The New York Botanical Garden, Bronx, New York).

Images listed below without acknowledgment are in the public domain; if no artist's name is cited, artist is unknown. In other cases, the author and publisher gratefully acknowledge those named for permission to reproduce copyright material.

Chapter 1

"The Buccaneer was a Picturesque Fellow" (Howard Pyle). 2

Port Royal Harbour, Jamaica, from Sir Hans Sloane, *A Voyage to the Islands Madera, Barbados, Nieves, S. Christophers and Jamaica . . .* (Courtesy of the LuEsther T. Mertz Library of The New York Botanical Garden, Bronx, New York). 4

"Sir Henry Morgan – Buccaneer" (J.N. Marchand). 5

"The Sacking of Panama" (Howard Pyle). 18

Chapter 2

William Dampier (Thomas Murray). 20

"The Buccaneers" (Frank Brangwyn). 21

A brigantine. 29

"So the Treasure Was Divided" (Howard Pyle). 38

"Capture of the Galleon" (Howard Pyle). 49

Chapter 3

"Preparing for the Mutiny" (N.C. Wyeth). 61

A pirate marooned on a desert island (Howard Pyle). 67

Map of the Caribbean, from Sir Hans Sloane, *A Voyage to the Islands Madera, Barbados, Nieves, S. Christophers and Jamaica* . . . (Courtesy of the LuEsther T. Mertz Library of The New York Botanical Garden, Bronx, New York). 74

The Jolly Roger (Richard H. Rodgers). 82

Chapter 4

"Blackbeard in Smoke and Flame" (Frank Schoonover). 102

Blackbeard and Stede Bonnet (George Varian). 104

"New York as it appeared in about 1690" (Howard Pyle). 110

"The Combatants Cut and Slashed with Savage Fury" (Howard Pyle). 116

Blackbeard's death (George Varian). 118

Stowing the outer jib. 120

Chapter 5

Bartholomew Roberts. 123

Royal Fortune and *Ranger* in the Whydah Road. 127

Roberts' crew carousing. 128

Chapter 6

Mary Read. 131

Chapter 7

Edward Low. 139

George Lowther. 140

Chapter 8

Pirate armed with cutlass and pistols (Howard Pyle). 180

Reveling on deck. 185

Eighteenth century English warship. 187

Chapter 9

Chase scene (George Varian). 222

Introduction

Buccaneer Captain Bartholomew Sharp, whose memoir of ravaging part of Spanish America in the early 1680s appears herein, was among the first mariners on record to speak of *going on the account*.[1] The phrase, according to a work published in the early 1700s, was recognized as being "a Term among the Pyrates, which speaks their Profession."[2] It is unclear exactly how it was derived, but as it can be read as equating piracy with a business arrangement, or with obtaining goods on credit, a wry sense of humor may have been involved.[3]

Something similar may have been afoot when late 19th century writers began applying the words *golden age* to piracy. "Whoever first dubbed the period the 'Golden Age of Piracy' clearly did so with their tongue firmly in their cheek," a modern maritime historian observed. "The irony was certainly lost on those who had fallen victim to men like Blackbeard, 'Black Bart' Roberts or Charles Vane."[4]

However unlikely, the term endured. Today a reference to the Golden Age invokes piracy in the Caribbean and Atlantic – sometimes further afield – in an era that began (depending on the historian) sometime between 1650–1716, and ended by about 1725–1730.[5] Certainly the period was golden in the sense that some sea rovers operating in these years struck it especially rich, often by stealing treasures European states were themselves wrenching from their overseas colonies. But the term may also be understood in a literary sense of richness, for contemporary chroniclers detailed episodes and characters that still resonate with modern audiences fascinated by piracy in the Age of Sail.

With that said, Golden Age piracy has at times been presented in ways far removed from what appear to have been its realities. The modern historian C.R. Pennell remarked at how "the common perception of seventeenth- and eighteenth-century pirates came to be rooted in a mixture of romanticization and (sometimes intentional) misrepresentation." Even some books long considered authoritative have undergone sharp historiographical criticism. In the last century, serious academic

---

1   See the introduction to Chapter 2.
2   Schonhorn, ed., *General History*, 585.
3   *Oxford English Dictionary*, I:85–86.
4   Konstam, *Piracy*, 151. For an early (1894) reference to piracy having a *golden age*, see Powell, "A Pirate's Paradise," 23.
5   For examples of discussions of the time frame the term *Golden Age* covers, see Baer, *British Piracy*, I:x; Konstam, *Piracy*, 150–154; Schonhorn, ed., *General History*, 701; and Rediker, *Villains of All Nations*, 8.

efforts competed for attention with publications that "straddled the difficult ground between scholarship and popular writing . . . and that line has been blurred ever since." Further muddying the water, a trend continued among some writers (and later, filmmakers) to sanitize and sentimentalize pirates for mass audiences. As Pennell observed tellingly of some late 19th and early 20th century literary works, this could only be done when the subjects "were safely in the past and they could be seen as attractive figures. That is not possible or desirable with the pirates of our own time. They have not, of course, been romanticized. . . . They are no one's heroes, except perhaps their own."[6]

Many observers in the Golden Age would have voiced similar sentiments. Consider how an article in a 1726 newspaper described the arrival in a Curaçao courtroom of a gang of captured pirates, led by their captain, Philip Lyne. It is a stark report that conjures an ugly and bloody scene, even striving to convey the unpleasant atmosphere in the courtroom.

> The way they went to be Tryed was thus, the Commander went at the Head, with about 20 other Pirates, with their Black Silk Flagg before them, with the Representation of a Man in full Proportion, with a Cutlas in one Hand, and a Pistol in the other Extended; as they were much wounded, & no care taken in Dressing, they were very offensive, and Stank as they went along, particularly Line the Commander, he had one Eye Shot out, which with part of his Nose, hung down on his Face; . . .[7]

Seafarers of the period knew that falling into the hands of such a crew could mean more than financial loss. Merchant captains might fare especially badly, especially if they had a reputation for harshness. But pirates could abuse and kill common sailors as well. The above-mentioned Philip Lyne, for example, "confessed upon his Tryil, that he had killed 37 Masters of Vessels, besides Foremast Men, during the Time of his Piracy."[8] Under any circumstances it was a violent era on either side of the law. In one historian's words, "the frequency and intensity of buccaneer brutality was a symptom of the age. . . . Men who became pirates had been raised on what seem today to be instances of inexplicably cruel practices carried out regularly by local and national authorities in England and in the West Indies."[9]

These observations are borne out in many writings of the period, which like the newspaper article quoted above present a sharp view of a time when pirates were anything but a novelty. They also frequently offer more textured and nuanced visions of episodes and characters than those encountered in entertainment media, or even

6 Pennell, "Brought to Book: Reading about Pirates," in Pennell, ed., *Bandits at Sea*, 5.
7 "Philadelphia, Feb. 22," *Boston Gazette*, 28 March 1726, 2.
8 From "Philadelphia, Feb. 22," *Boston Gazette*, 28 March 1726, 2. See also Rediker, *Villains of All Nations*, 83–102; and Leeson, *Invisible Hook*, 107–133.
9 Burg, *Sodomy and the Perception of Evil*, 165–166.

some nonfiction books. Accordingly, modern maritime scholars (including the authors of some thoughtful, well-documented mainstream works) emphasize such first-hand accounts and other contemporary primary sources free from later embellishment. Some are doubtlessly flawed, contradictory, incomplete, and otherwise problematic, and like all centuries-old data require careful handling. But used appropriately they may help lead one closer to complex and/or long-overlooked realities of historical piracy.

In that vein, this book aims to present to modern readers a sampling of such original, English-language accounts of piracy in the Americas in the late 17th and early 18th centuries. The contents are drawn from materials including official reports, newspapers, monographs, and trial records. All stand on their own as historical texts; some help flesh out people and events of their times; many help illuminate, or bring different perspectives to, parts of long-influential book-length histories of their period. They are rendered with annotations meant to guide general readers through many of the geographical, historical, legal, literary, and nautical references of a past era.

ooooo

The essence of *maritime piracy* is that of robbery at sea, with or without violence. It was distinguished from *privateering*, in which mariners, in time of war, acquired government commissions that permitted them to attack an enemy. The line between piracy and privateering could be a fine one, and two chapters herein address instances in which the Caribbean *boucaniers* of the later 1600s crossed it. One involves the report of Henry Morgan, who in 1670–71 led a largely English buccaneer force off the water and onto an ordeal-filled march across the isthmus of Panamá. Though they operated as privateers (with official support from Jamaica's governor) during a time of hostilities, Morgan's amphibious campaign came at a time when Spain and England were officially at peace. Nonetheless, Morgan would eventually receive a knighthood for his actions, being seen at the English court merely as (in one historian's words) a "young buccaneer who exceeded his commission."[10] About a decade later the aforementioned Bartholomew Sharp also landed in trouble with London for a while (before being pardoned) for his role in a grueling, chaotic buccaneer trek against Spanish America, undertaken ostensibly on behalf of an indigenous Central American nation. His report, parts of which underscore the quasi-democratic if ill-disciplined nature of the buccaneers, appears in Chapter 2.

Other chapters include newspaper sources about later characters and events, some famous (or infamous) in the annals of Caribbean and Atlantic piracy, and provide views all the more engaging for their unvarnished quality: details of Blackbeard's career and

---

10 Williams, *Captains Outrageous*, x–xi.

his bloody demise; an account of Bartholomew Roberts' crew sacking a ship off Newfoundland; and glimpses of the dreaded Edward Low and company. Additional information comes in excerpts from court documents of the piracy trials of the survivors of Samuel Bellamy's company; of Ann Bonny and Mary Read; and of Captains Charles Harris and William Fly and their crews. Also appearing are particulars of life aboard pirate vessels, related in some cases by those who regained their freedom after being forced to serve aboard them in some capacity.

Being "forced" was a reality, and some of the following chapters contain references to the practice of coercing captives into pirate crews. Those who survived a pirate encounter often published details of crewmen being compelled to join their captors, to aid their later vindication; samples of such "advertisements" appear herein. Some scholars have concluded that genuine acts of impressment were probably rare, in part because such men were a security threat.[11] Others have noted that forced men might eventually sign pirate articles "voluntarily and with good grace, otherwise they would slave away without hopes of a share in the booty and never be allowed ashore."[12] Regardless, to claim forced status was perhaps the only courtroom defense possible for those the authorities captured aboard a suspect vessel. Many accused alongside Captain Stede Bonnet claimed at their 1718 trial that they were in his pirate crew against their will.[13] The tactic worked for some, failed for others. Even being forced was not necessarily a good-enough excuse in some eyes. The judge at the Bonnet trial remarked that one of the accused "was threatened to be made a slave of; though indeed he had been better made a slave than go a pirating."[14] Puritan clergyman Cotton Mather told a convicted pirate who maintained he had been forced: "Better have died a Martyr by the cruel Hands of your Brethren, than have become one of their Brethren."[15] At the trial of Bonnet and his men, Attorney General Richard Allen called piracy "a crime so odious and horrid in all its circumstances, that those who have treated on that subject have been at a loss for words and terms to stamp a sufficient ignominy upon it."[16]

Yet it is important to note that some mariners in the period might well turn to piracy, like some on land might turn to crime, out of a sense of desperation. As scholar Marcus Rediker has pointed out, severe maltreatment was frequently the norm in naval and merchant service, and sailors had little hope of redress.[17] Moreover, the legal system of the time was a hurried and, by modern standards, very imperfect process. "Most trials lasted no more than one or two days, even when twenty or thirty prisoners were

---

11 See Leeson, *Invisible Hook*, 134–155.
12 Williams, *Captains Outrageous*, 161–162.
13 *Trials of Major Stede Bonnet and Thirty-three Others*, in Cobbett, Howell, and Howell, *State Trials*, XV:1269.
14 *Trials of Major Stede Bonnet and Thirty-three Others*, in Cobbett, Howell, and Howell, *State Trials*, XV:1281.
15 Mather, *Instructions to the Living*, 17.
16 *Trials of Major Stede Bonnet and Thirty-three Others*, in Cobbett, Howell, and Howell, *State Trials*, XV:1243.
17 See Rediker, *Villains of All Nations*, 154 and passim; and Rediker, *Between the Devil and the Deep Blue Sea*, esp. 254–287.

involved," noted historian David Cordingly.[18] Excerpts from trial documents that appear in the following chapters affirm that while suspects might spend months rotting in jail, colonial courts operated rapidly once proceedings began.

ooooo

As with its predecessor *On the Account: Piracy and the Americas, 1766–1835*, this volume makes no pretense to being a comprehensive omnibus of source documents; nor is it a stand-alone piracy history. Rather it is intended to make a selection of contemporary texts on the subject approachable to modern, general readers. Note that analyses of the causes and phenomena of piracy itself awaited the rise of later scholarship, although some contemporary writers made attempts.[19] Additionally, a book this size can only sample the number of sources available. Space limitations meant that some well-known pirates of the era are unrepresented herein. Henry Every, Thomas Tew, and William Kidd, for example, had links to the Americas (which is the thematic basis of this volume and its predecessor), but were left out as their best-known exploits occurred in far-distant waters. Production realities also restricted the chapter on Ann Bonny and Mary Read to just the report of their own trial, although the rare document from which it is excerpted also included accounts of court proceedings against male contemporaries such as Jack Rackam and Charles Vane.

Generally the transcriptions are faithful to the originals but are not facsimiles.[20] Capitalization, including irregularities and variations within an individual text itself, is largely reproduced as it first appeared; brackets show instances where it was changed during editing. Bracketed ellipses [. . .] or editor's notes indicate when material was deleted or paraphrased. Paragraph break symbols [¶] appear when sections of text were cut into shorter elements.

The principal problem facing the editor involved spelling and grammar. The documents presented here originated much earlier than those in *On the Account* and contained infinitely more candidates for correction, not to mention instances of inconsistent spelling (including individuals' names) in the same source. To avoid adding extraordi-

---

18 "There were no doubt practical reasons for hurrying things along. Following the Act of 1700 which authorized the setting up of Vice-Admiralty Courts in the colonies, it was usual for the colonial governor to preside over pirate trials, assisted by a group of local worthies and the captains of naval ships stationed in the area. The governors had many other duties to attend to, the captains would have been reluctant to leave their ships for more than a few days, and prominent citizens and merchants would have wanted to get back to their businesses and their estates. But the principal reason for the pace of the proceedings was the absence of arguments for the defense. In accordance with the usual practice of the day, the accused men had no legal representation and had to conduct their own defense. Since the majority of men on trial were seamen with little or no education, they were ill equipped to make a good case" (Cordingly, *Under the Black Flag*, 228).

19 Baer, *British Piracy*, I:xxxiv. Broad modern and often interdisciplinary treatments of piracy and its causes may be found in some of the works cited in the footnotes and bibliography herein. For a comprehensive survey circa 2001 of academic studies of historical piracy (an area which, in English at least, is more than a century old) see Pennell, "Brought to Book: Reading about Pirates," in Pennell, ed., *Bandits at Sea*, 3–24.

20 Texts that influenced the transcription and editing process here included Boyd, ed., *Papers of Thomas Jefferson*, I: xxv–xxxviii; Schonhorn, ed., *General History*, xli–xlii; and Stevens and Burg, *Editing Historical Documents*.

nary editorial clutter, it was decided to "forgive" archaic, obsolete, and/or phonetically acceptable spellings from which the proper meaning could reasonably be inferred. Thus, alongside occasional instances of erratic grammar, readers may encounter renderings such as *antient* for ancient, *cutlas* or *cutlash* for cutlass, *entituled* for entitled, *flower* for flour, *goal* for gaol (i.e., jail), *mony* for money, *murther* for murder, *reer* for rear, *spick* for spike, and of course *pyrate* for pirate. Variant spellings for names of persons, vessels and places were also left intact. When adjustment was felt necessary for clarity's sake, an attempt was made to leave the original form deducible. Changes involving only the addition of characters were placed in brackets, such as "no[t]," etc.; surplus characters or words were deleted using a strikethrough and superscripted brackets, such as "~~[of]~~," etc. The word *sic* in brackets was used on rare occasions; more often, troublesome words and terms were addressed in footnotes. The results no doubt reflect imperfect judgment in some cases, but the system adopted does have benefits of consistency of approach, while hopefully still being respectful to the original documents.

Except for quotation marks and hyphens, punctuation issues were generally silently remedied, as were some run-on and broken words. Other silent emendations imposed throughout were:

- Replacement of the archaic "long s" (ſ) with the modern s, so that words such as *Maſſachuſetts* became "Massachusetts."
- Replacement of dashes used to end sentences (rather than introduce incidental remarks) with periods; the first word in the following sentence was capitalized if necessary.
- Standardization of multiple short dashes [---] into a single long dash [–].
- Elimination of excessive highlighting, such as capitalization and italicization. However, vessel and publication names were italicized regardless of how they originally appeared.

To better delineate the editor's modifications to the texts, brackets appearing in the originals were replaced with parentheses. Brackets also indicate short additions to the text when clarification did not require a separate annotation.

Besides specific works cited, the annotations made extensive use of many "common knowledge" sources. These included standard reference works such as *Merriam Webster's Biographical, Collegiate,* and *Geographical* dictionaries; the *Columbia Gazetteer of the World* edited by Saul Cohen; and the Google maps website. Manuel Schonhorn's edited version of the *General History* and the notes sections of Joel H. Baer's four-volume *British Piracy in the Golden Age* were also valuable in clarifying obscure place names in the original texts.

The documents herein convey insight not only about acts of piracy, their perpetrators, and their victims, but often also about the journalism, court procedures, and attitudes of their time. They should be read and appreciated in that context. While at times an editor's note may intervene to move a story forward, these texts are largely left to speak for themselves. In them, modern readers will get a sense of piracy's Golden Age from those who experienced it at first hand. Occasionally the genuine words of an authentic pirate will ring through as well.

ooooo

My first thanks is reserved for the editors and staff of Sussex Academic Press, to whom I am grateful for their enthusiasm and support for this volume and its predecessor. For the third consecutive book I also find myself acknowledging the help and knowledge of John Frayler, retired historian at the Salem (Massachusetts) Maritime National Historic Site, and author of many accomplished monographs. I am also grateful for the kind advice of Dr. Rodney Carlisle, Professor Emeritus of Rutgers University; and Dr. Manuel Schonhorn, Professor Emeritus of Southern Illinois University.

Many other people and institutions also helped with the making of this volume and its predecessor over many years of gathering data, either by contributing their time or by providing access to their general holdings, special collections, microfilms, and other resources. They include the American Antiquities Society; the Boston Public Library; the British Library (special thanks to Jackie Browne and Jovita Callueng of permissions); Guildhall Library, London; Dover Publications (special thanks to Joann Schwendemann); the Library of Congress; the Library Company of Philadelphia; the Mariners' Museum, Newport News, Virginia; the Massachusetts Historical Society; the G.W. Blunt Library of Mystic Seaport, Connecticut; the National Archives of the United Kingdom (special thanks to Paul Johnson, Hugh Alexander, and Judy Nokes); the National Archives and Records Administration of the United States; the LuEsther T. Mertz Library of The New York Botanical Garden (special thanks to Marie Long); the New York Public Library; the Rhode Island Historical Society; and the libraries of the following institutions of higher education: Ball State University, Boston College (special thanks to Elliot Brandow), Boston University (special thanks to Barbara Maratos), Brandeis University, Harvard University, the University of Illinois, Indiana University, the University of Oklahoma, Princeton University, Temple University (special thanks to Andrew Diamond), and the University of Tennessee. The staff of the library of the American University of Sharjah was especially helpful, particularly Librarian Daphne Flanagan and her colleagues Scott Carlson, Saad Farooqi, Zaineb Habib, Alya Kattan, Mary Ann Nash, and Amar Zahra; my AUS colleagues Dr. Victoria Amador, Anna Marie Castillo, Dr. Kevin Gray, and Dr. Hania Nashef also provided valuable support. Finally, I send my love and thanks to my wife Tanya and sons Michael and Brian for their love and enormous patience.

With those acknowledgements given, please note that any errors herein are the author's responsibility.

1

"For the most of his Majesties Honor and Service, and the safety of Jamaica" – The buccaneers, Henry Morgan, and the sack of Panamá (1670–1671)

The Caribbean buccaneers were a multi-national mix of adventurers, renegades, and refugees who, despite a general Spanish opposition to their presence, settled on and established their own colonies in parts of the West Indies in the 1600s.[1] Mostly Dutch, English, and French, their origins were as hunter-traders, and from the indigenous Carib people they acquired skills in salting and smoking meat. "The meat was hung in strips over a frame of green sticks, and dried above a fire fed with animal bones and hide trimmings. Both the wooden grating and the place where the curing was done were called by the Carib name of *boucan*, and the hunters engaged in this work became known as *boucaniers*."[2] By the mid-1600s many *boucaniers* had turned to the sea and drifted into privateering, an activity which occasionally brought them ashore for the purposes of raiding enemy settlements.

Legitimate privateering occurred in a time of war, when privately owned vessels with government-issued commissions or letters of marque might seek to capture enemy shipping, while following strict regulations as to conduct and the disposal of prizes.[3] But whether the buccaneers' activities constituted privateering or piracy was sometimes vague, as the status of peace, war, and alliance among European players in the Caribbean was fluid. Official word from Europe took months to arrive in the colonies, where governors were capable of acting on their own initiative. These circumstances tended to work to the

---

1   "The buccaneer was the English-derived sea rover of the region, the filibuster or *flibustier* the French-derived, although the English often used buccaneer to refer to all West Indian sea rovers, as did the French with filibuster" (Little, *Sea Rover's Practice*, 10). The term *flibustier* itself represented a French effort to pronounce the English word "freebooter," a synonym for pirate (Williams, *Captains Outrageous*, 123). For historical background, see Haring, *The Buccaneers*, 57–84.
2   Jack Beeching, introduction to Exquemelin, *Buccaneers of America*, 9; see also Exquemelin's description on 58–59. The term *barbecue* "is from the Haitian *barbacoa*, another name for the *boucan*. ... By the turn of the eighteenth century the English term for *boucanned* pork, or roasted or broiled pork, was *barbecued pig*, while dried or lightly smoked meat was *jerk* or *jerked beef* (or pork)" (Little, *Sea Rover's Practice*, 248–249).
3   A contemporary discussion is contained in Justice, *General Treatise of the Dominion and Laws of the Sea*, 461–472, reproduced in Baer, *British Piracy*, III:355–366.

"The Buccaneer was a Picturesque Fellow" (Howard Pyle).

disadvantage of Spain. In Angus Konstam's words, "the English governors of Jamaica and Barbados, the French governors of Tortuga and Martinique, and the Dutch governors of St. Eustatis and Curaçao all adopted the expedient policy that, while wars might come and go between their three powers, the Spanish would always remain the enemy. Therefore, unless direct orders came from Europe, the Spanish were regarded as fair game. This meant that Dutch, English and French buccaneers tended to work together, regardless of the political situation at home."[4] Alexandre Exquemelin, who later wrote of his own experiences among the buccaneers in the 1660s and 1670s, classified them simply as "pirates – for I don't know what other name they deserve, as they were not backed by any prince."[5]

They were also tough. In his book, eventually translated into English as *Bucaniers of America*, Exquemelin recounted how in one battle, a comrade pulled an arrow out of his shoulder, put it in his musket barrel, set it alight, and fired it back. At another time the famished buccaneers ate leather: "They beat the leather between two stones at the water's edge, made it wet, and scraped off the hair while it was soft. Then, having roasted it on hot embers, they cut it up in small pieces which they swallowed whole." These remarkably resilient characters had high standards of loyalty to one another, practiced forms of communal democracy, and resisted class distinctions. Buccaneer captains, for instance, had "no better fare than the meanest on board. If they notice he has better food, the men bring the dish from their own mess and exchange it for the captain's." Before setting out on a voyage they would "resolve by common vote where they shall cruise," and set down agreements on share-outs and compensation for those wounded in action – a forerunner of the "articles" of later pirate companies. Yet they were also habitually violent and cruel. They so ill-used the indigenous people that one hitherto friendly tribe became their implacable enemies. Exquemelin, himself a former indentured servant, held that "there is more comfort in three years on a galley than one in the service of a *boucanier*."[6]

Jamaica, which the English captured from Spain in 1655, became the center of much buccaneer activity, especially after the island's administrators turned to them for security after navy ships went home in 1660. However, Jamaica's location encouraged attacks on Spanish shipping irrespective of peace or war, and loot arriving in Port Royal was warmly welcomed. As England sought to improve relations with Spain, in 1664 Sir Thomas Modyford was named governor with instructions to curb the buccaneers' activities, but after initial efforts he let the matter slide. Cracking down on them was uneconomical, "privateering then being the great business and concern of the island," as the author of a later history of Jamaica expressed it. Moreover, doing so hindered efforts meant to defend the island by using the buccaneer captains, who gainfully employed many of the English convicts being sent in droves to help settle Jamaica.[7]

---

4   Konstam, *Piracy*, 108. See also Haring, *The Buccaneers*, 131–132.
5   Exquemelin, *Buccaneers of America*, 67.
6   Exquemelin, *Buccaneers of America*, 55, 70–71, 72, 181, 187–188, 209.
7   Haring, *The Buccaneers*, 120–128; Williams, *Captains Outrageous*, 124–125; Long, *History of Jamaica*, I:14.

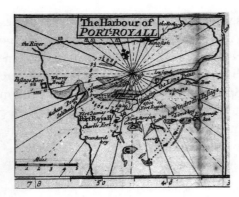

An early 1700s map of Port Royal Harbour, Jamaica; much of Port Royal was destroyed in a 1692 earthquake (Detail from "A New Map of the Island of Jamaica," from Sir Hans Sloane, *A Voyage to the Islands Madera, Barbados, Nieves, S. Christophers and Jamaica . . .* [London: B. M., 1707 and 1725]). Courtesy of the LuEsther T. Mertz Library of The New York Botanical Garden, Bronx, New York.)

By the late 1660s, the Jamaica-based buccaneers were under the command of Welsh soldier and privateer captain Henry Morgan, who had possibly arrived as part of the invasion force of 1655.[8] Some measure of Morgan may be gleaned from a letter he sent the governor of Panamá after sacking the Spanish settlement of Portobello in 1668. Morgan had demanded 350,000 pesos (or pieces of eight) in return for not burning the city, an offer the governor refused. To his letter, Morgan responded:

> Although your letter does not deserve a reply, since you call me a corsair, nevertheless I write you these few lines to ask you to come quickly. We are waiting for you with great pleasure and we have powder and ball with which to receive you. If you do not come very soon, we will, with the favour of God and our arms, come and visit you in Panama. Now, it is our intention to garrison the castles and keep them for the King of England, my master, who, since he had a mind to seize them, has also a mind to keep them. And since I do not believe that you have sufficient men to fight with me tomorrow, I will order all the poor prisoners to be freed so that they may go to help you.[9]

As author Peter Earle observed, this "was written by a man who had no commission to invade Spanish territory and at a time when a treaty of peace and friendship had recently been signed between the two nations."[10]

Both sides, it must be noted, could violate whatever agreements were being signed an ocean away. Two years later, and with a new, fragile treaty between England and Spain in place, Morgan led a force of 1,400 buccaneers – it has been described effectively as a "pirate army" – on a campaign that culminated in the sacking of Panamá.[11] Undertaken with Modyford's support, and in fear of a Spanish invasion of Jamaica, this was largely a land-based affair rather than a maritime one, and as such offered opportu-

---

8 Earle, *Sack of Panamá*, 46–47.
9 Quoted in Earle, *Sack of Panamá*, 71.
10 Earle, *Sack of Panamá*, 72.
11 Talty, *Empire of Blue Water*, 230. For an analysis of the treaty situation at the time of Morgan's operation, see Baer, *British Piracy*, I:51–53.

"Sir Henry Morgan – Buccaneer" (J.N. Marchand).

nities to sack and re-provision along the way.[12] It was also an ordeal-filled effort that faced a variety of challenges, and in this context, Morgan's success speaks well of his generalship.[13] But Exquemelin, who accompanied Morgan, would later damn his leader's excesses, charging that the admiral-general and those under his command indulged in an orgy of burning, torture, and rape following the fall of Panamá. Having been part of the venture, Exquemelin has credibility, but some historians have questioned his total veracity and reliability, noting that Exquemelin and many of the buccaneers felt Morgan had cheated them out of loot at Panamá.[14]

The following excerpt presents Morgan's own report of the Panamá campaign, as transcribed by his secretary, John Peeke; the text occasionally shifts in voice from the first- to the third-person. The straightforward account contains no references to torture or other cruelty on the part of the buccaneers. It may well have, however, been prepared in response to concern that, even with Modyford's backing, the expedition had crossed a line with London. Morgan would in fact be sent back to England as a prisoner, although he would eventually be exonerated and knighted. He was, in one historian's words, "made much of at the court of Charles II, where ready money and a certain brutal dash went a long way," and the buccaneer admiral-general would return to Jamaica in triumph.[15]

Sir Henry Morgan would later round off his successes by winning a libel suit against Exquemelin's English-language publishers over the book's depiction of Morgan's conduct and background.[16] Earle contended that Exquemelin had indeed gone "out of his way to blacken the Admiral's name and to give him a reputation which is not sustained even by the Spanish evidence."[17] Writing of a later reprinting of Morgan's report on the Panamá operation, historian Joel H. Baer observed that: "Accusations of torture, rape and 'low' parentage aside, Morgan's version of events is less colourful and perhaps more accurate than that of Exquemelin, especially concerning the command structure of the buccaneer troops and amount of their winnings."[18]

ooooo

---

12 Pope, *Harry Morgan's Way*, 153.

13 For assessments of Morgan's leadership qualities, see, for example, Little, *History's Greatest Pirates*, 90–91; and Pope, *Harry Morgan's Way*, 260.

14 See, for example, Earle, *Sack of Panamá*, 251–252. Author Terry Breverton called Exquemelin "one of the first proponents of 'niche marketing,' with variants for different nationalities – in the Spanish edition, the Spanish were heroes, and the like in the French edition" (*Admiral Sir Henry Morgan*, 5).

15 Beeching, introduction to Exquemelin, *Buccaneers of America*, 17.

16 Little, *History's Greatest Pirates*, 101; and Breverton, *Admiral Sir Henry Morgan*, 100–102.

17 Earle, *Sack of Panamá*, 252.

18 "He estimates the plunder at about £30,000 . . . while Exquemelin gives 200 pesos (£50) a share for the ordinary buccaneers, amounting to a total of at least £50,000, assuming 1,000 men of the original 1,400 lived to take a share. However, because we do not know the actual number of shares, nor whether the estimates encompass specie only or include ransom money and the value of other forms of booty, these figures are unreliable" (Baer, *British Piracy*, I:103). Baer in this case was writing about the "summarized and rephrased" version of Morgan's report published by Philip Ayres in *Voyages and Adventures*.

From "Sir Henry Morgan's Voyage to Panama, 1670," in *The Present State of Jamaica with the Life of the Great Columbus the First Discoverer: To which is added, an Account of Sir H. Morgan's Voyage to, and Famous Siege and Taking of Panama* (London: Thomas Malthus, 1683), 74-94.[19]

[Prologue and Preparations]

A true Account and Relation of this last Expedition against the Spaniard, by vertue of a Commission given unto H. Morgan[20] by his Excel. Sir Tho. Modyford,[21] Governour General of His Majesties Island of Jamaica, with the advice and approbation of His Majesties Honourable Council fully Assembled, the prosecution of which I humbly here present.

His Commission bearing date the 22 of July 1670, the tenour of which was to fight with, take, or destroy all the Ships that I should meet withal belonging to the subjects of his Catholick Majesty in the American Seas, as also to Land on the Island of Cuba, attempt the City of St. Jago[22] upon the said Island, if himself and the Commanders find it feazible, and farther more to Land in any of the Dominions of his said Catholique Majesty in America, and to attempt, take, or surprize by force of Arms any of his said Catholique Majesties Cities, Towns, Forts, or Fortresses where he should by any intelligences be advised that they were storing up or making Magazines of Arms, Ammunition, or Provisions, or levying any men for the propagating or maintaining of this War against his Majesties Island of Jamaica.

1670. In order whereunto they sailed from Port-Royal[23] the 14th of August, with 11 Sail of Vessels, and 600 men, and having rounded the Island, we arrived at the Isle of

---

19   © British Library Board (shelf mark G.7089). Used with permission.
20   Henry Morgan "was born in 1635 at Llanrhymney, Glamorgan, of parents who evidently were prosperous yeomen, hopeful of one day being considered gentry. One uncle, Thomas Morgan, became General Monck's second-in-command, and served as governor of the island of Jersey. Another uncle, Colonel Edward Morgan, who happened in the Civil War to have taken the royalist side, went into exile in the Caribbean, and became a soldier once more, in Jamaica." By the start of the Second Dutch War (1665) Henry Morgan was an established Jamaica-based buccaneer and shipowner (Beeching, introduction to Exquemelin, *Buccaneers of America*, 14–15).
21   Sir Thomas Modyford (1620?–1679) served as governor of Jamaica from 1664–1671.
22   I.e., to attempt to capture St. Jago, or Santiago, Cuba. "St. Jago is the capital of half the island, and has a resident governor and a bishop. Most of its commerce is with the Canary Islands, where it sends sugar, tobacco and hides from its subordinate towns. Although protected by a fort, this city has been plundered by buccaneers from Jamaica and Tortuga" (Exquemelin, *Buccaneers of America*, 128). Morgan probably accompanied English naval officer and buccaneer commander Christopher Myngs when a force under his command attacked it in 1662 (Konstam, *Piracy*, 126; and Cordingly, *Under the Black Flag*, 44).
23   Originally called Cagway, the Jamaican capital Port Royal rapidly became the center of English buccaneering, given its position near the Spanish Main, its spacious harbor, merchants (and their backers) happy to trade in stolen goods, and authorities who not only ignored lawlessness but "actively encouraged the buccaneers to plunder from the Spanish, regardless of whether England and Spain were at war." By the time of Morgan's raid on Panamá, Port Royal contained about 6,000 inhabitants, and was second only to Boston as the most prosperous settlement in the Americas. A fifth of its buildings were said to be "'brothels, gaming houses, taverns and grog shops'" (Konstam, *Piracy*, 113–116).

Ash,[24] the place of Rendezvous, the 2 of September following, from whence we having no Advice of the course of the Enemy or their design, we dispatched away Vice Admiral Collier[25] the sixth of the same Month, with six Sail of Vessels, and 350 men, to go for the Course of the Main[26] to get Prisoners for Intelligence for the better stearing our Course and managing our design, for the most of his Majesties Honor and Service, and the safety of Jamaica.

[Editor's Note: In early 1670 Portuguese Captain Manoel Rivera Pardal, commanding the Spanish privateer *San Pedro y la Fama*, began a series of operations against the English. Having attacked English towns in the Cayman Islands, off Cuba he took an English privateer conveying a message of goodwill from Modyford to the local governor. Rivera subsequently landed a force on the Jamaican coast at Montego Bay and burned a settlement.[27] As the new campaign against the Spanish got underway, Morgan would learn that one of his officers had captured the *San Pedro y la Fama*, with its captain dying in the engagement.]

The last of September arrived to us at the Isle of Ash, Capt. John Morris,[28] who brought with him Imanuel Rivera's Vessel of eight Guns, who burnt the Coast of Jamaica, having taken him on the Coast of Cuba, and in her three original Commissions, 2 of which they sent his Excellency; the 7th of October following so violent a Storm happened in the Harbour that drove all the Fleet ashore except the Admiral's Vessel, then consisting of 11 Sail; all of which, except three, were got off again and made serviceable.

In this Month arrived here three French Vessels, and conditioned to sail under our Flag, and in November arrived seven sail more from Jamaica.[29] Now being of force

---

24 Isla Vaca or Île à Vache (Island of Cows), off the coast of modern Haiti.
25 Edward Collier, Morgan's second-in-command on the expedition. He had earlier captured at Île à Vache the French pirate *Le Cerf Volant* which would become Morgan's flagship *Satisfaction* (Pope, *Harry Morgan's Way*, 181). On this intelligence-gathering mission Collier would earn "a much worse reputation than Morgan" regarding the use of torture, with three of his captives "reported to have died as a result of his attentions" (Earle, *Sack of Panama*, 148).
26 The Spanish Main. "In theory, this term referred to the northern coastline of the South American mainland – the region Spanish settlers called the Tierra Firme, or 'dry land.' However, the term 'main,' or sea, was soon extended far beyond these coastal waters, and by the mid-16th century it had become synonymous with anywhere in the Caribbean basin. After all, the Spanish regarded the whole area as theirs, so calling the waters and coastline of the Caribbean basin the 'Spanish Sea' was no exaggeration" (Konstam, *Piracy*, 39).
27 Earle, *Sack of Panama*, 135–138; Talty, *Empire of Blue Water*, 184–189.
28 John Morris was a Jamaica landowner who, in command of the eight-gun privateer *Dolphin*, earlier accompanied Christopher Myngs in his raids against the Spanish. He would receive the title of major during the land campaign against Panamá. Of the *Dolphin* and other vessels in the buccaneering fleet: "Her dimensions are not known, but she is unlikely to have been more than fifty feet long on deck, with a beam of about sixteen feet – the size of a large fishing smack or shrimper. Many of the privateers were much smaller, simply large open boats decked over forward to provide shelter for the crews and a comparatively dry place to store provisions. Fitted with a single mast, they could be rowed in calms or to manoeuver among cays" (Pope, *Harry Morgan's Way*, 86, 107, 153, 208; see also Baer, *British Piracy*, I:367).

enough to attempt St. Jago, we examined some of our own men, who had been lately there Prisoners; and also those Spaniards that were taken in Imanuel Rivera's:[30] One of our men in particular, Captain Richard Powell, Captain of the Prize that was Rivera's Ship, who had not been above 30 daies from St. Jago, declared that time of year being Winter, and being but one landing place, and that strongly fortified, it was impossible for us to attempt that place without the hazard of the whole Party and the certain loss of the most, if not all our Vessels, by foul weather; all the knowing Prisoners examined, affirming the same, upon which we relinquished that Design.

The 20th of the same Month Vice Admiral Collier returned from the Main with good quantities of provisions, and two of the Enemies Vessels, one of which called the *Galerdeene*[31] was assistant to Rivera's in the burning of the Coast of Jamaica, and in her were 38 Prisoners, who the 29th of the same Month were examined, and what was said by two of the most sensiblest of them reduc'd into English is as followeth:

Nov. the 29, 1670

The Deposition of Marcus de Cuba, Spaniard, Master Pilot[32] of the *Galerdeene* Prize, born at the Grand Canaries,[33] aged 47 years or thereabouts, being disposeth[34] saith,

That he did see the People at Carthagena[35] Listed and all in Arms offensive against the English. And farther saith, that several Spanish Ships have had and

---

29 "Morgan's two squadrons sailing for Panama had each a different set of colors. One flew the 'royal flag' or union flag at the mainmast, the 'Parliamentary' ensign of a white cross on a red field at the stern, and the union jack at the bowsprit. The other flew the 'white flag, though English' – probably St. George's Cross – at the mainmast, a white ensign with 'four small red squares in one of the quarters' (perhaps a white cross on a red field in the canton, the reverse of the red ensign), and the union jack at the bow" (Little, *Sea Rover's Practice*, 114).

30 I.e., taken prisoner in Manoel Rivera Pardal's *San Pedro y la Fama*.

31 The 80–ton, 10–gun *Galliardena* was a Spanish privateer operating with Manoel Rivera Pardal, which Collier captured after taking and ransoming the town of Rìo de la Hacha (Pope, *Harry Morgan's Way*, 228–230).

32 "*Pilot*, the officer who superintends the navigation, either upon the sea-coast or on the main ocean. It is, however, more particularly applied by our mariners to the person charged with the direction of a ship's course, on, or near the sea-coast, and into the roads, bays, rivers, havens, &c within his respective district" (Falconer, *Universal Dictionary*, n.p.).

33 Gran Canaria, one of the Canary Islands off the northwest coast of Africa.

34 I.e., be deposed, to give formal testimony under oath (Nolfi, *Legal Terminology Explained*, 256).

35 "The City of Carthagena lies on a Bay by the Sea side, built on a Sand, but to Landward it is very boggy. It is in length about three-quarters of a mile, and not full half a mile in breadth. 'Tis walled all round with a thick stone wall of about four and twenty foot high, with Bastions built with Orillons, in some parts, in others they are plain: But has neither Grass nor Ramparts. The Guns which are in number one hundred twenty six, are most Brass and Copper, and lie upon the Parapets, and looking over the tops of the walls, without either Battlements, or common Baskets, to blind them. In the wall are three Gates; one to the South called San Domingo; one to the North East, called Santa Catalina, and one to the East, which goes to the Harbour, and into the Country. This City nevertheless is not strong, for there is neither Castle, nor any considerable place of strength in it; and moreover to the North West, which is the Bay, those winds have made in the wall three great Breaches, which may be entred with ease. ... Their Souldiers are Armed (for Fire Arms) only with match Locks, in the use of which they are likewise very unexpert" (from "The Relation of Colonel Beeston, his Voyage to Carthagena, for adjusting the Peace made in Spain, for the West-Indies, &c.," in Ayres, *Voyages and Adventures*, 169–170).

now have Commissions from the president of Panama, named (Don Juan Perez de Gusman)[36] and that they have taken several Englishmen, and that the last Spaniard have by the said President great incouragement against the Island of Jamaica, and the more by reason of a Fleet fitted out of old Spain for those parts, under the Command and Conduct of one (Don Alonso[37]) and further saith not.

Sworn the day and year above written *Coram*.[38]

Henry Morgan, and the rest of the Officers of the Fleet.

ooooo

Nov. 29, 1670

The Deposition of Lucas Peroz, a Seaman,[39] born at Palma,[40] aged 31 years or thereabouts, being disposeth saith,

That he did see the People at Carthagena, some of them in Arms, others Listing of themselves; and two Ships ready fitted against Jamaica, one with 18, and the other 12 Guns; and also that the President of Panama hath granted several Commissions against the English, by vertue of which, several English Ships hath been taken, and further saith not.

Sworn the day and year above written *Coram*.

Morgan and the rest of the Officers of the Fleet.

---

36 Don Juan Pérez de Guzmán was President of the Audiencia of Panamá and Governor and Captain-General of the province of Tierra Firme. According to author Peter Earle, he "was a loyal and intensely religious servant of the Spanish Crown, 'a man of much courage and good will, but very little fortune.' He had been born in Seville in 1618, and had seen a considerable variety of military service in Milan and in the royal fleet before becoming interim Governor of Cartagena in the late 1650s and Governor of Puerto Rico from 1661 to 1664. He had arrived in Panamá to take up his present post … in January 1665. The Audiencia of Panamá was the smallest and least populated jurisdiction in the Spanish colonial empire, but its defence was absolutely vital to the maintenance of that empire and, indeed, of Spain herself. For it was here, at the narrowest part of the isthmus of Central America, that the immense wealth of the silver mines of Peru was exchanged for the much coveted manufactured goods of Europe." Despite the inadequacy of some Spanish resistance to Morgan, Earle wrote that "An old man in Panamá, who had seen fourteen presidents come and go, said that Don Juan did more for the defence of the Kingdom in the year of 1670 than the other thirteen had done in the past half-century, and this is not far from the truth" (Earle, *Sack of Panamá*, 17–18, 128).
37 Don Alonzo de Campos y Espinosa, operating a fleet of five vessels, with orders to eradicate pirates along the Spanish-held coasts (Talty, *Empire of Blue Water*, 86, 158–166).
38 Latin for "before."
39 "*Seaman, homme de mer*, a mariner or person trained in the exercise of fixing the machinery of a ship, and applying it to the purposes of navigation. The principal articles required in a common sailor to intitle him to the full wages, are, that he can steer, sound, and manage the sails by extending, reefing [i.e., shortening], and furling them, as occasion requires. When he is expert at these exercises, his skill in all other matters relative to his employment is taken for granted" (Falconer, *Universal Dictionary*, n.p.).
40 One of the Canary Islands bears this name, as does (among other places) a city on the Spanish island of Majorca.

Upon December the 22d [*sic* – 2nd] Commanded all the Captains on board me[41] being 37 in number, and demanded their advice what place was fittest to attain for His Majesties Honour, and preservation of Jamaica; and to put the greater curb to the Insolencies of the Enemy; in answer to which they all unanimously agreed on Panama, as by their resolutions under their hand in these words appears.[42]

On Board the *Satisfaction* Frigat,[43] Dec. 2, 1670.

Honoured Sir,

We having seriously considered of what place may prove advantageous for the safety of the English, and more especially for the security of his Majesty's Island of Jamaica, to prevent the Invasion of the Spaniards, it being referred by the rest of the Commanders in the Fleet in General to us whose Names are here under written, to pitch upon a place that we thought might be most feazable and just to take for the good of Jamaica, and Honour of our Nation; do all of us conclude it stands most for the good of Jamaica, and safety of us all to take Panama, the President thereof having granted several Commissions against the English, to the great anoyance of Jamaica and our Merchant Men, as by the Oaths of two Spaniards, have been made most evidently appear.

This is the Judgment and Resolution of

Lieutenant Col. Joseph Bradley,[44]
Richard Norman,[45]
Thomas Harrison,
Robert Delander, [46]

---

41 Morgan's flagship was the 22–gun *Satisfaction*, originally the French pirate *Le Cerf Volant*, which Collier had captured at Île à Vache (Pope, *Harry Morgan's Way*, 180–181, 219, 221).

42 For observations on the choice of Panamá as a target, see Baer, *British Piracy*, I:367, and Talty, *Empire of Blue Water*, 203–204). According to Exquemelin's description of Panamá, "There were about 2,000 houses in the city belonging to prosperous merchants, and about 3,000 ordinary dwellings, together with stables for the pack animals which carried silver across country to the north coast. In the suburbs were orchards and gardens, full of fruit trees and vegetables" (*Buccaneers of America*, 197).

43 A *frigate*, according to the 1771 edition of William Falconer's nautical dictionary, was "in the navy, a light nimble ship built for the purposes of sailing swiftly. These vessels mount from twenty to thirty-eight guns, and are esteemed excellent cruizers." The related-term *frigate-built* "implies the disposition of the decks of such merchant ships as have a descent of four or five steps from the quarter-deck and fore castle into the waist, in contra-distinction to those whose decks are on a continued line for the whole length of the ship, which are called galley-built" (Falconer, *Universal Dictionary*, n.p.).

44 Bradley had commanded the seventy-ton vessel *Mayflower* within the buccaneer fleet (Talty, *Empire of Blue Water*, 194).

45 Captain Richard Norman had been part of the 1669 Morgan-led raid on Maracaibo, in command of the ten-gun privateer *Lily*; he "assumed the rank of major once he stepped on shore." He would later assume command of the buccaneer force at Chagres following Bradley's fatal wounding (Pope, *Harry Morgan's Way*, 231, 246).

46 Delander had earlier spent time in a Cuban prison, the Havana authorities allowing him to enter the port for repairs but then seizing his vessel (Pope, *Harry Morgan's Way*, 184).

John Harmonson,

John Galoone,

John Pyne,

Dego Moleene,[47]

Vice Admiral Ed. Collier, [48]

Lawrence Prince,[49]

John Morris,

Thomas Rogers,[50]

Cha. Swan,[51]

Hen. Wills,

Richard Ludbury,

Clement Simmons.

To Henry Morgan Esq; Admiral and Commander in Chief of His Majesties Fleet belonging to the Island of Jamaica, for this present Expedition.

To the which the Admiral consented, and having called the captains again on Board to consult of the manner of carrying on that attempt, and whereby to find Prisoners to be guides for Panama, it was voted that Providence being the King's Antient propriety, and most of the people there being sent from Panama, that no place could be more fit.[52]

---

47 "Diego" commanded the 10–gun, 80–ton *St.John* in the buccaneer fleet (Breverton, *Admiral Sir Henry Morgan*, 58). Little identified this captain as "Diego the Mulatto" (*History's Greatest Pirates*, 82).

48 Jamaica landowner Collier received the title of colonel as the buccaneers' campaign moved from water to land (Pope, *Harry Morgan's Way*, 232, 261).

49 A Jamaica landowner and planter, Prince had earlier served on Christopher Myngs' operations against the Spanish in command of the four-gun, 50–ton privateer vessel *Pearl*, its armament later upped to ten guns. On land with the buccaneers, Prince held the rank of lieutenant colonel, then colonel (Pope, *Harry Morgan's Way*, 86, 208, 219, 232, 265).

50 Rogers commanded the 12-gun privateer *Gift*. He provided some of the evidence that led to Morgan's expedition against Panamá, this occurring when he captured a Spanish vessel that had attacked him, and among the prisoners "found an English renegade who had adopted Spanish nationality and religion and lived in Cartagena. On questioning him, Rogers was startled to be told that 'war against Jamaica' had been proclaimed in Cartagena" (Pope, *Harry Morgan's Way*, 215, 231).

51 "After paying shares, Charles Swan became the leader of a disaffected faction that plotted to seize Morgan's ships and cruise the South Seas for prey. Swan returned to Panama in 1685 with the second wave of buccaneers, but when their plan to take the fabled 'plate fleet' from Lima collapsed, he sailed to the Philippines piloted by William Dampier. The latter's famous book, *A New Voyage Round the World* (London, 1697) tells of Swan's deteriorating mental stability that ended in mutiny and his abandonment on Mindanao where he was murdered by natives in 1687" (Baer, *British Piracy*, I:367).

52 "Providence and its smaller sister island, Santa Catalina, had been one of the first English colonies in the Americas, settled by Puritans from Bermuda and England in 1630. They lay almost halfway between Port Royal and the Spanish town of Portobelo, where the silver fleets came to fetch the king's treasure every year" (Talty, *Empire of Blue Water*, 79–80). In 1641 the Spanish captured them and expelled the English settlers (Rowland, "Spanish Occupation of the Island of Old Providence," 299–300).

[Providence, Chagres, and Venta Cruce]

December the 8th we sailed, and the 14th arrived at Providence by 8 of the Clock in the morning, and by two in the Afternoon were possessed of the great Island without resistance; the 15th, sent a Summons to the Governour to deliver the little Island, who willingly submitted to that he might have good Quarters, and Transportation to any part of the Main, which was granted and duly performed; but four of his Souldiers took up Arms with us, and became our Guides; and by them understanding the Castle of Changra[53] blocked our way, the Admiral called a Councel of all the chief Captains, where it was determined to attain the Castle of Changra; and forthwith there was dispatched 470 men in 3 Ships, under the Command of Lieutenant Col. Joseph Bradly, with 3 Captains and 4 Lieutenants, and upon the 27th were safely landed within four Miles of the Castle by twelve of the Clock, and by two had made their approach one of the other, and by three into Trenches where they continued fighting till eight the next Morning, and then had [*sic* – would have] returned *re infecta*,[54] if in playing [◦◦] their Granadoes,[55] they had not by good fortune set a Guard-house on fire that stood upon the Walls, which caused a breach, where our men couragiously stormed,[56] and the Enemy as bravely defended it to the last Man, refusing Quarters, which cost them the lives of 360 men, and of our side was lost 30 out-right, one Capt. and one Lieutenant, and 76 wounded, whereof the brave Bradly was one, with two Lieutenants, who died within ten daies after their wounds, to the grief of himself[57] and all in general.

Jan. 2 the Adm. arrived with the whole Fleet, and understood that the Enemy lay with Forces to endeavour the taking of the Castle, whereupon he gave order for the Fleet

---

53 Exquemelin described the "fortress San Lorenzo de Chagre" as "standing on a high mountain at the mouth of the river. The summit is intersected by a moat, a good thirty feet deep, which can be crossed at one place only, where there is a drawbridge. The fortress is surrounded by strong palisades, filled in with earth. Four bastions command the landward side, and two face the sea. To the south, the mountain is so steep it is impossible to climb, and to the north lies the river. A tower, mounted with eight cannon, defends the entry of the river, and somewhat lower down are two more batteries, each with six cannon, defending the river banks" (*Buccaneers of America*, 180).

54 With the project unfinished.

55 "The Grenado is a kind of little bomb of the same character as a four pound bullet; it weighs about two pounds, being charged with four or five ounces of powder. Grenadoes are thrown from the tops by the hands of the seamen. They have a touch-hole in the same manner as a bomb, and a fuse of the same composition. ... The sailor fires the fuse with a match, and throws the grenado as he is directed: the powder being inflamed, the shell instantly bursts into splinters that kill or maim whomsoever they reach on the decks of the enemy. As this machine cannot be thrown by hand above fifteen or sixteen fathoms [a fathom being six feet], the ship must be pretty near to render it useful in battle." From *Engagement*, in Falconer, *Universal Dictionary* (n.p.).

56 Don Juan Pérez de Guzmán would report that the day-long battle resulted in the killing of two hundred buccaneers, and that the defenders repulsed "above six Assaults, until the English taking advantage of the night, and by the help of their Fire-balls set on Fire the Fortifications, because the outsides were of Wood. They likewise burnt the Castellan's or Gouvernour's House, being thatched with Palm, and consumed all the good Arms within. There was Killed above half the People, the Lieutenant also and the Castellan, who all had behaved themselves with great Valour, and had it not been for the Fire, the Enemy had never gained it" (as translated in Ayres, *Voyages and Adventures*, 146–147).

57 Morgan.

to follow him into the Harbor, but had the ill fortune to be cast away [in] the Ship that he was in, and four more, but saved the men;[58] the rest being come in fell to preparing to go up the River, where they understood the Enemy had entrenched themselves, and had six several retreating Breastworks upon the River.

Whereupon the Adm. gave order that 7 Sail of lesser Vessels should be rigged to go up the River, and filled them with Men and great Guns; and left to Guard the Castle and the Ships 300 men, under the Command of Captain Richard Norman. Monday the 9th we began our march, 1,400 men[59] in the said 7 Vessels, and 36 Boats and Cannons.

Upon the 12th Instant we got to the first Entrenchment, where the Enemy had lately quitted it, and set all on Fire, as they did all the rest, without striking a stroke for it,[60] and there was forced to leave our Ships and Boats with 200 men to Guard them under the Command of Captain Robert Delander, and betook ourselves to the wild Woods, where was no path for 24 Miles, but what we cut. The 14th we arrived within two Miles of Venta Cruce,[61] which was the Landing place, where was a very narrow and dangerous passage, where the Enemy thought to put a stop to our further proceeding, but were presently routed by the forlorn,[62] Commanded by Captain Thomas Rogers; the rest of our men never firing shot and without any loss, saving three men slightly wounded; but the Enemies loss we could never learn. January the 15th we arrived at Venta Cruce, which is a very fine Village, and the place where they Land and Embarque all the Goods that comes and goes to Panama, where we though[t]

---

58 The vessels, heavily laden with supplies the buccaneers brought from Santa Catalina, struck the Laja Reef. "Fortunately there was time for the boats of the fleet to save much of the provisions and powder" (Pope, *Harry Morgan's Way*, 247).

59 Of the buccaneers who earlier gathered at Isla Vaca for the Panamá venture, "about one-third were French and the rest English." A nominally English buccaneer force could be diverse. In Morgan's 1668 expedition against Portobello, "not all the men were English by any means, even if they might describe Port Royal as their home port. There were forty Dutchmen, several Frenchmen, Italians, Portuguese, mulattoes and negroes, and according to Spanish sources, at least one Spaniard, a citizen of Cordoba. The invasion force was a mixed bunch socially as well as racially, ranging from gentlemen and impoverished planters and merchants to men whom even their best friends would have described as the scum of the earth." That said, in 1671 Morgan's prisoners included "many a respectable black citizen of Panamá [who] found himself reduced to the status of slave when he reached Jamaica" (Earle, *Sack of Panamá*, 53–54, 167, 228).

60 Don Juan Pérez de Guzmán wrote in his report that some Spanish commanders, "without having any Order of mine or Power to do it," abandoned fortifications at Barro Colorado and Barbacoa as the invaders approached (as translated in Ayres, *Voyages and Adventures*, 147–148).

61 Venta de Cruces, modern Las Cruces, "the last key outpost before Panamá; if the Spaniards were going to make a stand anywhere before the limits of their beloved city, it would be there" (Talty, *Empire of Blue Water*, 227). It "was described by an Englishman a few years later as 'a small village of inns and storehouses,' while the surrounding country was 'savannah and woodland intermixed, with thick short hills, especially towards Panama'" (Pope, *Harry Morgan's Way*, 241).

62 Akin to scouts or skirmishers. "Afoot, rovers sent an advance guard ahead, called the 'forlorn,' or 'forlorn hopes,' in French *les enfants perdues* – the lost children. Ranging from a few men to eighty or more, the purpose of the advance guard was to scout ahead, spring ambushes, engage advance parties of the enemy, and capture prisoners for intelligence, as well as to prevent an alarm. Obviously the task of the forlorn was more than usually hazardous, often leading to the selection of its members by lot" (Little, *Sea Rover's Practice*, 193).

we might be relieved, having marched three daies without Victuals, but found it as the rest, all on Fire, and they fled.

[The Attack on Panamá]

The 16th we began our March, the Enemy constantly galling us with Ambuscades and small Parties, and we still beating of them for a League[63] together, although they had all the advantage that could be of us, the way being so narrow that we could but march 4 abreast, and such a deep hollow, that the Enemy lay over our heads; about noon that day we got to the *Savanes*[64] safe, with the loss of three men killed outright, and six or seven wounded; and of the Enemy 20 killed, and one Captain, besides many wounded; we marched three Miles further, and then took up our Quarters to refresh our men, and thanked them for that daies service.[¶]

The 17th we began our March forward, but had no opposition, and about nine of the Clock in the Morning, saw that desired place the South Seas,[65] and likewise a good parcel of Cattle and horses, whereupon the G.[66] comanded a general halt to be made, and our men killed Horses and Beef enough to serve them all; about four of the Clock in the afternoon, our men having refreshed themselves, we marched again, and about five the same day we came in sight of the Enemy, where he lay in Batalia[67] with 2,100 Foot and 600 Horse, but finding the day far spent, we thought it not fit to engage, but took up our Quarters within three Miles of them, where we lay very quiet, not being so much as once alarm'd.[¶]

The next morning being the 18, betimes in the morning the Gen. gave order to draw our men in Batalia, and it was accordingly performed, and they were drawn in the form of a *Tertia*;[68] the Vant Guard was led by Lieutenant Col. Lawrence Prince, and Major John Morris, they being in number 300 men; the body containing 600; the Right wing was led by the Gen. and the left by Col. Ed. Collier; the rear-ward of the 300 was Commanded by Col. Bledry Morgan;[69] after having viewed our men, and a little encouraged them, the G. commanded the Officers every man should repair to his Charge; the enemy being drawn at such advantage, they still kept their Station;

---

63 Three miles.
64 Savannah, or grassland.
65 The Pacific Ocean.
66 The General, i.e. Morgan.
67 Organized into separate battalions (*Abridgment of the English Military Discipline*, 5).
68 A *tertia* was a "division of infantry," with a *tercio* being "a regiment" (*Oxford English Dictionary*, XVII:822). It appears to be used here to refer to the dividing of the buccaneer force into three segments – a vanguard, a main body, and a reserve – in a sense akin to *tertiation*, "a dividing into three" (Phillips, *The New World of English Words*, n.p.). A contemporary military manual contained drill instructions such as "Of Marching in Three Divisions" (*Abridgment of the English Military Discipline*, 118–138).
69 Bledry Morgan "had joined the buccaneers at Providence, bringing a message from Modyford for the admiral, to whom he does not seem to have been related" (Pope, *Harry Morgan's Way*, 261).

although often provoked, yet would not stir from their Ground, which we presently perceived, and [Henry Morgan also] gave order that our men should wheel their bodies to the left, and endeavour to gain a Hill that was hard by, which, if gained, we should have forc'd the Enemy to fight to their disadvantage, by reason he could not bring out of his great body more men to fight at a time, than we could out of our small body, and likewise that we should have the advantage both of Wind and Sun.[¶]

The Officers putting this Command in execution, and the Hill, and a dry Gut[70] accordingly gained, the Enemy was forced to fight upon their long March, having not room to wheel[71] his Battel, by reason of a Bogg that was drawn behind on purpose (as he thought) to entrap us, but we taking another ground, in the end proved a snare to himself;[72] whereupon one Francisco Detarro,[73] gave the Charge with his Horse upon the Vant Guard, and so furiously that he came upon the full speed; we having no Pikes[74] gave order that they should double their Ranks to the Right, and close their Files to the Right and Left inward to their close order; but his career[75] could not be stopt till he lost his life in the front Rank of our Vant-Guard, upon which the Horse wheel[ed] off to the Right, and their Foot advanced to try their Fortunes; but it proved like their fellows, for we being ready with the main Battel to receive them, gave them such a warm welcom, and pursued so close that every one thought it best to retreat, but they were so closely plyed by our left Wing, who could not come to Engage at first, by reason of the Hill, that the Enemies retreat came to plain running.[¶]

Although they did work such a Strategem that hath been seldom or never heard of, that is when the Foot Engaged in the Flank, he attempted to drive two Droves of Cattel of 1,500 apiece into the Right and Left Angles of the Reer; but all came to one

---

70 A creek or small riverbed.

71 "*To Wheel* … In a military sense, to move forward or backward in a circular manner, round some given point" (James, *Military Dictionary*, n.p.). It was an essential component of contemporary marching drill; see *Abridgment of the English Military Discipline*, 141–149.

72 In a version of this text later republished by Philip Ayres, which he "summarized and rephrased" (Baer, *British Piracy*, I:103), this passage was rendered as: "Our Officers streight put this command in execution, and in a small time we gained the Hill, together with a little dry Passage, of convenience for us. So the Enemy was constrained to fight us upon their hasty march, not having room enough to wheel their whole Body, by reason of a great Bogg, which was just at their Rear, and before which they had purposely drawn up, to entrap us: But we having thus changed our Ground, that proved in the upshot to be of prejudice to themselves" (From "The true Relation of Admiral Henry Morgan's Expedition against the Spaniards in the West-Indies, in the Year 1670," in Ayres, *Voyages and Adventures*, 138).

73 Don Francisco de Haro.

74 Unlike the spear, the pike was not for throwing but for close-quarter "shock" action, its use akin to that of the later bayonet. To dissuade enemy cavalry from attacking them, European pikemen formed up with the tips of their pikes positioned to meet any oncoming horses. Pikes were also used at sea to repel boarders. See the modern discussions in Eltis, *Military Revolution*; Bradbury, *The Medieval Archer*; and Willis, *Fighting at Sea*, 141, 150. Contemporary military manuals such as *Abridgment of the English Military Discipline* contained drills solely for pikemen (51–71) as well as for pikemen used in combination with troops armed with muskets (71–78).

75 Charge.

effect,[76] and helped nothing for their flight to the City, where they had 200 fresh men, and two Forts, one with six Brass[77] Guns, the other with eight, and the Streets Barricadoed, and great Guns in every Street, which in all amounted to 32 brass Guns, but instead of fighting he commanded the City to be fired, and his chief Forts to be blown up, the which was in such hast[e] that he blew up forty of his Souldiers in it; we followed into the Town, where, in the Market-place they made some resistance, and fired some great Guns, killed us four men, and wounded five. At three of the Clock in the afternoon we had quiet possession of the City, although on fire, with no more loss on our side in this daies work than five men killed, and ten wounded. And of the Enemy about 400, where we were all forced to put the fire out of the Enemies Houses; but it was in vain, for by 12 at night it was all consumed that might be called the City; but of the Suburbs, there was saved 2 Churches, and about 300 Houses;[78] thus was consumed that famous and antient City Panama, which is the greatest Mart for Silver and Gold in the whole World, for it receives all the Goods into it that comes from old Spain in the King's great Fleet, and likewise delivers to the Fleet all the Silver and Gold that comes from the Mines of Peru and Potazi.[79][¶]

[The Aftermath]

Here in this City we stayed 28 daies, making daily Incursions upon the Enemy by Land for 20 Miles round about, without having so much as one Gun shot at us in anger, although we took in this time near 3,000 Prisoners of all sorts, and kept likewise Barques[80] in the South Seas, crusing and fetching of Prisoners that had fled to the Islands with their Goods and Families.

---

76 According to Exquemelin, who gave the total number of bulls as 2,000: "The Spaniards had planned to drive the wild bulls into the rear of the invading army and thereby break their formation, but while the rest of the buccaneers carried on with the fight, the men on the exposed rear rank turned to confront the bulls, waving their flags and firing a few shots into the herd. The wild beasts turned about and stampeded – the drovers running for their lives, like the cattle" (*Buccaneers of America*, 194–195). On the Spanish side, Don Juan Pérez de Guzmán wrote that he had "two great Herds of Oxen and Bulls, drove thither by fifty Cow-keepers on purpose to disorder the Enemy." By his account, he led the "Squadron of the right Wing," and led a charge against the buccaneers, but "hardly did our Men see some fall Dead, and others Wounded, but they turned their backs, and fled" (as translated in Ayres, *Voyages and Adventures*, 152–155).

77 For a discussion of the use of brass in the ordnance of the era, see Ffoulkes, *Gun-Founders of England*, 20–39.

78 Contemporary sources disagree as to who started the fire. Exquemelin placed responsibility on Morgan himself (*Buccaneers of America*, 197). But Don Juan Pérez de Guzmán wrote that "the Slaves and Owners of the Houses had put fire" to the city (as translated in Ayres, *Voyages and Adventures*, 156). The later historian C.H. Haring cited archival sources supporting this (*The Buccaneers*, 186).

79 The inland Bolivian city Potosí housed Spain's colonial mint. "The discovery of silver at Potosí was made by a llama-driver about the middle of the 16th century. It was soon found that the mountain was traversed by veins of extremely rich ore. After the gold of the Incas had been gathered up and disposed of, Potosí became the most important part of all the Spanish possessions in America. At the beginning of the 17th century, when New York and Boston were still undreamed of, Potosí was already a large and very wealthy city" (Bingham, "Potosí," 4).

80 The term *bark* (or *barque*) was "a general name given to small ships: it is however peculiarly appropriated by seamen to those which carry three masts without a mizen top-sail" (Falconer, *Universal Dictionary*, n.p.).

"The Sacking of Panama" (Howard Pyle).

Feb. 14 we began our March towards our Ships, with all our Prisoners; and the next day came to Venta Cruce about 2 in the afternoon, which is from Panama five English Leagues, where we stayed refreshing ourselves till the 24th; the 26th we came to Changra, where the Plunder was divided amongst the Souldiers and Seamen, which amounted to about 30,000 £[81] The sixth of March we fired the Castle, spiked the Guns,[82] and began our Voyage for Jamaica, where some are arrived, and the rest daily expected. The reason that there was no more Wealth, was because they had two Months notice of us, and had Embarqued most of their Treasure into Ships, and sent them to Lima[83] in Peru; one Ship was laden with Gold, Silver and precious Stones, that contained 700 Tuns, and one of 300 Tuns.

Jan. 31, 1671.

By Command

John Peeke,[84] Secretary.

[**Editor's Note:** Exquemelin later wrote that not long after his return to Jamaica, Morgan planned another assault on Spanish territory but "was prevented from putting his ideas into action by the arrival of an English man-of-war, with orders from the King recalling the governor of Jamaica to England to account for all the injuries the buccaneers of Jamaica had done to the Spaniards. A new governor arrived on the same ship. Morgan himself also went back to England on the return voyage."[85] Though Morgan and Modyford would be conveyed as prisoners – Modyford would spend time in the Tower of London – both ultimately returned to Jamaica, Morgan with a knighthood and a commission as the island's lieutenant governor.]

---

81 According to Exquemelin, the share out was a source of discontent with the buccaneers, the writer noting that "each company received its share of the plunder – or as much at least as Morgan vouchsafed them. When it was dealt out individually, each man found his share came to no more than 200 pieces of eight. The wrought silver was reckoned at only ten pieces of eight the pound; the price offered in exchange for various jewels was dirt cheap, and many jewels were missing – for which Morgan was publicly accused by the buccaneers" (*Buccaneers of America*, 207).

82 To spike a cannon was to render it unusable by hammering a short iron nail or spike into the touch-hole. Using the cannon again required either carefully blowing the spike out using a gunpowder charge or else re-drilling the touch hole (Blackmore, *Armouries of the Tower of London*, I:244–245).

83 "Lima was founded in January 1535, by Francisco Pizarro, as the future capital of the Spanish conquests in the land of the Incas. Several situations [i.e. locations] had been fixed on and tried, during the two preceding years, particularly Jauja, where an university and several public institutions were founded; all, however, were abandoned; at last the valley of Rimac having been suggested, commissioners were despatched who having reported favourably, the buildings were commenced with great religious ceremony, and it was named 'Ciudad de los Reyes,' or 'City of the Kings,' but was more generally called, excepting in legal deeds, by its present name, from the valley and river Rimac, corrupted by Spanish pronunciation and orthography into Lima; it shortly became, and continued to be, for nearly three centuries, one of the richest and most populous of the cities of this celebrated country; indeed, so great was its wealth at one period, that on the arrival of the Duke de Palata as viceroy [in 1683], the streets through which he passed were paved with ingots of silver… " (Burford, *Lima*, 2).

84 Morgan's secretary John Peeke attained the rank of major and "later became a planter and speaker of the House of Assembly" (Pope, *Harry Morgan's Way*, 229, 232, 377).

85 Exquemelin, *Buccaneers of America*, 225.

2

"Through insuperable Difficulties" – Bartholomew Sharp's buccaneer campaign (1680–1682)

About a decade after Henry Morgan sacked Panamá with future author Alexandre Exquemelin in tow, another party of largely English buccaneers (with some Native American allies from the Kuna nation in the Darién region) launched a fresh series of assaults on Spanish possessions in the New World. Having first struck Portobello late in 1679, they regrouped in April 1680 to embark on a rambling, arduous trek that lasted until early 1682. They would at one point threaten Panamá, but bypassed it in favor of other Spanish targets, which the buccaneers attacked while ostensibly acting as mercenaries with commissions from the Kuna emperor.[1]

Buccaneer and explorer William Dampier (Thomas Murray).

It was an often-chaotic venture, marked by dissension and several changes in leadership. Even its final commander, Captain Bartholomew Sharp, was turned out of office at one point; when his replacement was killed, Sharp's reinstatement caused some to exit the campaign. The campaign was also, as Christopher Lloyd observed, "one of the most fully documented on record," with several participants keeping journals and publishing histories of it.[2] Among them was New England-born John Cox, a kinsman of Sharp (although the two would clash during the expedition) whose journal was published in 1684. Another version by Basil Ringrose appeared in London in 1685 as a second volume to Exquemelin's *Bucaniers of America*. Two others who quit the expedition when Sharp resumed command – William Dampier and Lionel Wafer – also left classic memoirs of their travels and experiences.

Presented here is Sharp's own command-level description of an operation that, despite its disorganization and the relatively small amount of plunder gained, has been

---

1 Haring, *The Buccaneers*, 223–229; Konstam, *Piracy*, 139–140; Cox, "Adventures of Capt. Barth. Sharp," 2–3; Little, *History's Greatest Pirates*, 126. For more on the Kuna and the buccaneers, see Preston and Preston, *A Pirate of Exquisite Mind*, 65–70, 72, 86, 90–93.
2 Lloyd, "Bartholomew Sharp, Buccaneer," 291.

"The Buccaneers" (Frank Brangwyn).

called "epic in scope and daring."[3] According to Lloyd, Sharp's report "is actually a heavily edited version of his manuscript journal now in the Admiralty library." One area subject to redaction was Sharp's mention of a *derrotero*, an invaluable set of Spanish nautical charts, the capture of which London apparently sought to keep quiet.[4]

Sharp was also among the earliest on record to speak of "going on the account." Details of this emerged during the legal proceedings for piracy the Spanish later brought against him, in an English court, for the campaign described in the following pages. In court, Sharp's teenaged servant (himself a prisoner taken from the captured Spanish vessel *Santo Rosario*, from which the *derrotero* was taken) quoted Sharp saying he "was endeavouring to get another ship to go to America upon the same account."[5] Like

3 Little, *History's Greatest Pirates*, 137.
4 Lloyd, "Bartholomew Sharp, Buccaneer," 291, 292, 297.
5 Quoted in Lloyd, "Bartholomew Sharp, Buccaneer," 295, citing High Court of Admiralty records 1/51. The phrase was still in maritime use in 1809, when a witness during a mutiny-and-piracy trial at Halifax made reference to going "on the runaway account" (*An Interesting Trial of Edward Jordan*, 12). An 1867 nautical dictionary also included the term (Smyth, *Lexicon*, 16).

Morgan, however, Sharp escaped punishment, the captured charts proving to be worth a pardon when presented to King Charles II.[6]

○○○○○

From "Captain Sharp's Journal of His Expedition; Written by Himself," in William Hacke, ed., *A Collection of Original Voyages: Containing I. Capt. Cowley's Voyage round the Globe. II. Captain Sharp's Journey over the Isthmus of Darien, and Expedition into the South Seas, Written by himself. III. Capt. Wood's Voyage thro' the Streights of Magellan. IV. Mr. Roberts's Adventures among the Corsairs of the Levant; his Account of their Way of Living; Description of the Archipelago Islands, Taking of Scio, &c.* (London: J. Knapton, 1699).[7]

Chap. I

The Buccaneers set forth for Sancta Maria, and their Entertainment and Adventures by the way; they take the Town, but little Booty, design to Plunder Panama, encounter many other Difficulties, and Fight and Beat Three Spanish Men of War: Divisions between 'em, and some return over-Land. Some Prizes taken by them.

On Monday the Fifth of April, in the Year 1680, I[8] Landed at Golden-Island[9] with my Company, to the Number of Three Hundred and Thirty Men, with a full Design to go and Attack the Town of Santa Maria,[10] a Place which the Indians inform'd us was very Rich, towards which we continu'd our March till towards two in the Afternoon of the same day, when we came to an Indian's House, about which we stay'd all night, having nothing but the cold Earth for our Beds; and somewhat also discouraged with the going back of some of our Men, being tired with the March, or at least-wise the apprehensions of it. Next Morning by Sun-rising we resumed our March and Design,

---

6 For more on the charts, see Howse and Thrower, eds., *Buccaneer's Atlas*.

7 © British Library Board (shelf mark G.15598). Used with permission.

8 Born about 1650, at the time of this expedition Sharp "had been a buccaneer for thirteen years, first taking up the profession of blood and plunder when he was sixteen, perhaps a legitimate buccaneer-privateer during the Second Anglo-Dutch War. Without doubt he served under Morgan in some capacity, and was almost certainly at Panama in 1671; at Segovia, Nicaragua, in 1675; and at the capture of Santa Marta in modern-day Colombia, in 1677" (Little, *History's Greatest Pirates*, 123). Sharp "first appears in the official documents as 'Batharpe,' i.e. Barth. Sharpe, when, on 18 October 1679, it is reported that he and [Captain John] Coxon have captured 500 chests of indigo, besides much cocoa and plate" (Lloyd, "Bartholomew Sharp, Buccaneer," 292).

9 This is "in the Bay of Darien, not very far distant from Porto Belo . . . " (Cox, "Adventures of Capt. Barth. Sharp," 2).

10 "There were two towns called Sancta Maria on the easternmost part of the Isthmus of Panamá. Sancta Maria del Darien . . . was on the coast of the Gulf of Darien in present-day Colombia. The second, Real de Sancta Maria (El Real), which is the town referred to here, was about 50 miles south-east of the mouth of the Gulf of San Miguel, the transshipment point for gold found in the nearby rivers and a frequent target of the buccaneers" (Baer, *British Piracy*, I:368).

being guided by several Indians, among whom was their Emperor himself,[11] as we called him, who the day before had sent some Men to advertise a Tributary[12] (so we were informed) of his, that he had join'd us; that therefore he should take care of Provision and Lodging for us against our Arrival. We Travelled all day up a steep Mountain, 'till about three in the Afternoon we got over it, and came to an hollow of Water, whereof we all greedily drank; from whence we Marched about six Miles farther to a River, where we took up our Lodging under the Canopy of Heaven.

On Wednesday early in the Morning we set out for King Golden-Cap's House, (for so the Buccaneers called him, from a Wreath of Gold he usually wore about his head) as they Dignified Don Andreas[13] with the Title of Emperor, and continued our Journey 'till about four in the Afternoon, when we were met by two Indians, with a quantity of Fruits which the King had sent us as a Present, and which we received exceeding kindly. We pursued our March for an hour longer, and then arrived at the King's House, near unto which stood several others, where we took up our Quarters, being Entertained by the King himself, and all his People, with whatever the Countrey could afford. The Inhabitants for the most part are very handsom, especially the Female Sex, who are also exceeding loving, and free to the Embraces of Strangers.[14] We found our Entertainment so good in this Place, that we tarried here all the next day; part of which however we spent in Consulting how we should get to Santa Maria undiscovered, and furnish our selves with a sufficient number of Canoes[15] to carry our Men and their Attendance down the River; For we were to have an hundred and fifty Indians in our Company to go to the Wars, for which end they were Armed with Bows, Arrows and Lances: Besides whom we were to be accompanied by the Emperor and King with their Sons in Person.

It was now the Ninth Day in the Morning, when after having taken our Breakfast, which consisted of such Fruits as the Countrey afforded, we set out and pursued our Journey along a very bad Path, which with our being necessitated to wade the River

---

11   Sharp later identified the Emperor as "Don Andreas," and his son as "King Golden-Cap." Ringrose refers to a sep-arate "Indian Captain Andræas" and affirmed that King Golden-cap was "the King's [i.e., the Emperor's] son" (*Dangerous Voyage*, 6, 8, 12–13).

12   *Tribune* (in the sense of being an officer or representative) was possibly intended.

13   See note above.

14   Cox wrote of their hosts that "These Inhabitants are very handsome people though Tawny, but clean limbed and well featured, and are very obliging and affable, as those of our men who afterwards marcht back again, over Land, experienced" ("Adventures of Capt. Barth. Sharp," 5). Ringrose observed that "These Indian women of the Province of Darien are generally very free, airy, and brisk; yet withal very modest, and cautious in their Husbands' presence, of whose jealousie they stand in fear" (*Dangerous* Voyage, 7). For more on the indigenous people the buccaneers encountered, see Wafer, *New Voyage, passim.*

15   "*Canoe*, a sort of Indian boat or vessel, formed of the trunk of a tree hollowed, and sometimes of several pieces of the bark fashioned together. Canoes are of various sizes, according to the uses for which they may be designed, or the countries wherein they are formed. . . . They are commonly rowed with paddles, which are pieces of light wood somewhat resembling a corn-shovel, and instead of rowing with it horizontally, like an oar, they manage it perpendicularly" (Falconer, *Universal Dictionary*, n.p.).

between fifty and sixty times, almost foundred our Men: However, we still kept on, 'till at length we came to three large Indian Houses that were of an extraordinary length; and here we thought fit to take up our Quarters that night, where we found all things provided for us, not only for the present, but also some store, and Canoes, by the fore-mentioned King's Direction, as we understood afterwards.

The following Day Light no sooner appear'd, but we prepar'd for our Departure; at what time Captain John Coxon,[16] one of our Commanders, happening to have some words with Captain Peter Harris,[17] another of the Commanders, the former fired his Gun upon him, which he [Harris] was ready to return, when I interposed, and brought him to be quiet; So that we proceeded on our Journey, but could not long continue so, for we were necessitated to part Company; the major part of whom was to March by Land, while the rest went down the River in the Canoes which the Indians had provided, but not in such a number as to supply us all. The Emperor, and the King, as we term'd them, assign'd those that went by Land a Place of Meeting, while themselves, I and Captain Coxon with the Canoes padled all day down the Falls and Currents of the River, and at Night took up our Quarters upon a Green Bank by the River-side, where we had Wild Fowl and Plantanes for Supper: But our Beds were made upon the cold Earth, and our Coverings were the Heavens and Green Trees we found there, while our Party that went by Land had no better Lodging than our selves, and a much worse Diet.

The next appearance of day-light made us step into our Canoes again, together with our Indian Consorts, when we put down the River with an intention to joyn our Party before Night: But we fell short of our Expectations, and our earnest Desires, for our passage proved very bad, and we were forced to haul our Canoes over Trees that unhappily lay cross the River; Tho' our Labour, I must say, was a Pleasure to us, because of that great unity there was then amongst us, all our hearts being fired with a general desire to proceed to the end of our Land Expedition, that we might have the opportunity to see the fair South-Sea, what Crosses or Troubles soever befel us. But always the longest Day has an end, and we thought fit before the closing in of the Night to take up our Lodging again upon a green Bank of the River, where our Supper-Entertainment was a very good sort of a Wild-Beast called a *Warre*,[18] which is much like unto our English Hog, and altogether as good. We found great store of

---

16 Captain John Coxon was "a fairly young yet veteran buccaneer, one of the new generation of captains that filled the places left by Henry Morgan and his captains who got rich and retired after the sack of Panama . . . in 1671" (Little, *History's Greatest Pirates*, 123).

17 Harris was later killed in a fight with Spanish vessels. He was "a brave and stout Souldier, and a valiant Englishman, born in the County of Kent; whose death we very much lamented" (Ringrose, *Dangerous* Voyage, 32).

18 Of this wild boar or *Warree*, Wafer observed: "It has little Ears, but very great Tusks; and the Hair or Bristles 'tis cover'd with are long, strong and thickset, like a course Furr all over its Body. The Warree is fierce, and fights with the Pecary, or any other Creature that comes in his way" (*New Voyage*, 111).

them in this part of the World: I observ'd that the Navels of these kinds of Animals grew upon their Backs. We reimbarked early the day following, pursued our Voyage without any difficulty at all, for we found a clear River, and a pleasant Day's passage of it, when about four in the Afternoon we reach'd the place appointed for our Rendezvous with the fore-mentioned Land-Party, and where we thought to have met with them; but failing hereof, we grew very suspicious of their safety. But the Emperor Commanded another Canoe to go up another Channel of the River in search of them, where they found them about an hour before Sun-set, [and] brought back some of their Number to us, who gave us an account that the rest of their Party was safe, and in good Health, and would joyn us next Morning, and that the Indians had been very Civil to them. Accordingly all our Party met on the 13th, and we were not a little joyous to see one another so well. We tarried in the said Place that whole day to refresh our selves, clear our Arms,[19] and to set all things in a good posture of defence, in case of any opposition from the Enemy; For now we were informed by the Indian King, that it was but a day and a night's Journey to the Place whether we were bound; whereat we were very joyful, and the Refreshment we also receiv'd here by the Emperor's Care, in Commanding his People to bring us several Canoes Laden with Warre, and Plantanes, did not a little contribute to exhilarate our Spirits.

Wednesday the 14th early, we Embark'd on Board our Canoes, which in the whole amounted to near the number of Sixty, as our whole Party, comprehending the number of the Indians made up six hundred Men, whereof there were no more than an hundred and sixty Christians, the rest being Indians, with the Emperor (as we Entituled him) to command them. His Habit consisted only of a Mantle, and another Cloath to hide his Nakedness, with an English Hat upon his Head; He was a very Old Man, and I could judge him to be no less than an hundred years of Age. As for the King, his Garb was a long white Cotten Coat, fringed at the bottom; about his Neck he wore a Belt of Tygers-Teeth; on his Head a Cap or Hat of beaten Gold; and in his Nose, by way of Ornament, he wore a golden Plate in form pretty much resembling a Cockle-shell.[¶]

Our Voyage was continued not only that day, but all the Night also, when about two hours before day-light we Landed our Men within two Miles of the supposed Town,[20] and lay still in the Woods till the light appear'd, when we heard the Spaniard discharge his Watch at his Fort by beat of Drum, and a volley of Shot: Upon this the

---

19 The buccaneers' main armament was the *fusil*, "a long-barreled, large-bored, club-butted flintlock musket. It was a reminder of their origins as hunters, reflecting a reliance on marksmanship . . . " (Little, *Sea Rover's Practice*, 57). The weapons were "four and a half feet long and manufactured in France" (Earle, *Sack of Panamá*, 55). Exquemelin described them as firing "a bullet of sixteen to a pound of lead"; each buccaneer regularly carried thirty prepared cartridges, paper or linen tubes containing a musket ball and a measured amount of gunpowder (*Buccaneers of America*, 75). Loading a muzzle-loading firearm was a complex, multi-step process; for a period text, see "Exercise of the Fire-Lock" in *Abridgment of the English Military Discipline*, 15–50.

20 Santa Maria.

forlorn of our Body began its March, the same being Commanded by Captain Richard Sawkins,[21] where my self was also in Person, gave the onset, and about seven in the Morning fell in with the Enemy. In about half an hour's time we stormed their Fortification, and had the success to take the Place before half of our Party came up with us. In this Brush we found we had killed and wounded about seventy Spaniards, whereas the damage on our side was no more than the wounding of two Men only. However we were very much baulk'd in our Expectations, in respect to the Town, for the same proved to be a little pitiful Place with Thatch'd Houses, and but one Church in it. And as for the Fort, it was only Stockadoes, being a Place built to fight the Indians in, tho' the same were very large, and at that time had three hundred and fifty Men therein. But what was worse to us than anything was, that we found neither Riches to speak of, nor yet as much Victuals as would satisfie our Hunger for three or four days, of which our wearied Carcasses at that time stood in no small need.[22]

Our Affairs standing in this difficult State, we thought it advisable on the 16th to hold a General Consultation of all our Commanders, in order to take a Resolution which way it were best for us to steer our Course: Some of the Company were for our pro-ceeding on to the South-Sea, but others were of Opinion it were better we return'd back to the Ships again; and of these Captain John Coxon was the Chief: Insomuch that upon such a Conjuncture (to perswade him to go with us) we were necessitated to make him our General, most of us being very unwilling to break our Party. Coxon seeming to be well satisfied hereupon, it was fully agreed on that we should now direct our Course towards the City of Panama,[23] and withal, that Captain Richard Sawkins should be dispatch'd away before in a Canoe to way-lay the River, that so no body might get thither before us to carry any Intelligence of our coming; While we in the mean time staid that night behind to prepare our selves to follow after as soon as possibly we could; and also sent twelve of our Men to our Ships to acquaint them with our Design.

---

21 Richard Sawkins, who would die in the forthcoming attack on Coiba, had earlier "eluded trial for piracy in 1679 by escaping from Port Royal jail" (Baer, *British Piracy*, I:368).

22 After taking Santa Maria, the buccaneers also "found and redeemed the eldest Daughter of the King of Darien," who had "been forced away from her Father's home by one of the Garison (which Rape had hugely incensed him against the Spaniards) and was with Child by him. After the Fight the Indians destroyed as many more of the Spaniards, as we had done in the assault, by taking them into the adjoining Woods, and there stabbing them to death with their Lances." The buccaneers saw that the young woman's abductor was spared after he promised to act as guide for them (Ringrose, *Dangerous Voyage*, 12–13).

23 This referred to "the new city built to the west of the city destroyed during Morgan's raid in 1671" (Baer, *British Piracy*, I:368). William Dampier described New Panama as "a very fair City, standing close by the Sea, about four Miles from the Ruines of the Old Town. . . . It is incompassed on the backside with a pleasant Country, which is full of small Hills and Valleys, beautified with many Groves and Spots of Trees, that appear in the Savannahs like so many little Islands. This City is all compassed with a high Stone Wall; the Houses are said to be of Brick. Their Roofs appear higher than the top of the City Wall. It is beautified with a great many fair Churches and Religious Houses, besides the President's House, and other eminent Buildings. . . . There are a great many Guns on her Walls, most of which look toward the Land. They had none at all against the Sea, when I first entered those Seas with Capt. Sawkins, Capt. Coxon, Capt. Sharp, and others; for till then they did not fear any Enemy by Sea: But since that they have planted Guns clear round" (*New Voyage*, 127).

Our Canoes being fitted up, and our selves stock'd with what Provision we could get, in order to [*sic* – for] the prosecution of our Enterprize, we Embark'd on the Seventeenth, and Row'd down the River with the Tide of Ebb,[24] which Ebbs and Flows here two Fathom up and down: It's very difficult to come into this River in the Night-time, because the same is full of Banks,[25] which at low-water are dry. However, having good Guides, we proceeded down the River 'till near twelve at night, with about thirty Prisoners with us, whom we took from the Spaniards, and put ashore in this Place, in order to get somewhat to drink, by reason the River is Salt a great way up: We came also up at this time with Captain Richard Sawkins, who told us of his misfortune, in not being able to overtake the Spanish Governour that had made his Escape: However, not to be discourag'd with any misadventure, we haul'd up all our Canoes, filled our Water, and lay here all night, by reason the Wind blew somewhat hard. The night was very dark, and our Canoes deep, for you must know this River is very wide below, and one great arm of it extends it self to the Gold Mines, as the Spanish Captain inform'd us. But we lost no time next Morning, but proceeded on our passage, and Rowed over the Laguna, having observ'd that there were two Places to go out at; whereof the one is not only somewhat narrower than the other, but also very deep, and runs with a very swift Current. About Eleven of the Clock we had a sight of the fair South-Sea, and about two in the Afternoon came to a small Island, whereon we found two Spanish Indian Women, whom the Spanish Governour had turn'd ashoar to lighten his Canoe, that he might make his Passage the better, as they informed us. Here it was that we refresh'd our selves till the Tide serv'd again, when we re-imbark'd in our Canoes, and passed over to another Island that lay about two Leagues distant from us, where we arrived a little before Night, and found here two Canoes with some Bows and Arrows, which we broke to pieces, but the People we could not reach, altho' we had sight of some of them. We lay this night upon this Island, which is a very pleasant green place, has excellent good water upon it, and ground fit for Anchorage near it; and because we would neglect nothing which we thought might tend to our advantage, we at the same time sent away Captain Richard Sawkins with one Canoe to see if possibly he could fetch up the Governour, and so to stay at Plantane Island for us, which last he did accordingly.

Monday the Nineteenth we put off from the Island, and had not been above half an hour on our way, when the Wind began to blow fresh out of the Sea, which occasioned a very great Sea, by reason of a strong tide of Ebb that runs out very swift, insomuch that we were in exceeding great danger, to lose both our Lives, and all our subsistence at one dash: For one of our Canoes with seven French-men in it was

---

24 *"Ebb-Tide*. The receding or running out of the sea, in contradistinction to *flood"* (Smyth, *Lexicon*, 272). *Flood* tide is "a rising tide. When it ceases rising it is *high tide"* (Patterson, *Illustrated Nautical Dictionary*, 66).

25 A *bank* is "an elevation of the ground, or bottom of the sea, which is often so high as to appear above the surface of the water, or at least so little beneath it, as to prevent a ship from floating over it. In this sense, bank amounts nearly to the same as shallows, flats, &c." (Falconer, *Universal Dictionary*, n.p.).

over-set, and they had certainly perish'd had not good Providence and our endeavours to save them prov'd very successful to them, so that we came off with the loss
of some Arms only: But this danger was no sooner over, than that there fell such a
terrible shower of Rain that forced us ashoar upon a long Sandy Bay, where we made
the best shift we could to build us some few Hutts, and haul up our Canoes, and to
take up our Quarters here for this night.

Next Morning we turn'd out betimes, and put forward on our passage with fair
weather 'till towards the Afternoon, when it began to blow westerly, yet not so hard,
but that we kept on our Course. About two we put ashoar to see for some water to
drink, and had the good luck for the present to find plenty of it lying in the holes of
the Rocks: This Island stands high, of a round form, Rocky, and full of Sea-Fowls: But
we made no long stay here, for about four we came to the Plantane-Island (for so it's
called) from whence, as we were now inform'd, the Spanish Governour before-men-
tion'd was gone but the day before for Panama; which made us once more this
Evening send Captain Sawkins away in a Canoe to see if he could overtake him, tho'
still in vain; so that he return'd to us again. However, just as it began to be duskish,
we had the Fortune to take a small Vessel of thirty Tuns, with several People in her of
different Nations, as Indians, Mullatoes, Negroes, &c. who upon our interrogating of
them concerning News, told us, They had heard none, for they had been out of
Panama fourteen Days.

We took up our Lodging here this Night, some on Board and others on Shoar, and on
Wednesday Morning I went on board the Bark,[26] our Prize, with an hundred and thirty
Men, our Canoes being so deep that we did not dare all to venture in them, while the
rest of our Party made use of their Canoes (the Gale proving fair) till about twelve a
Clock, when we were forced to part by reason of a Calm that was somewhat cross to
us; now we had but little Provision and no Water, and we continued becalm'd all
night: But our Canoes rowed away a-head with Captain John Coxon, Capt. Sawkins
and Captain Harris, to an Island called Chepillo,[27] standing about two Leagues distant
from the main Land. They found it to be an Island furnished with plenty of Provisions,
and so intended to tarry there for us; but all Things did not fall out as well as they
could have wished, for next Morning they had for their Breakfast a small Fight with a
Man of War's Bark, and that with the loss of one Man and five wounded, without
having the Satisfaction to know what Damage they had done the Spaniard: For the
Wind blew both fresh and fair for him, so that he got away into Panama. However

---

26 Ringrose wrote of "*Barcos de la Armadilla*, or little men of War; the word *Armadilla* signifying a Little Fleet"
    (*Dangerous* Voyage, 27).
27 Chepillo. Woodes Rogers wrote in 1712 that "From the City of Panama to the isle of Chepillo 'tis 7 leagues,
    E.S.E. and W.N.W. . . . The Island of Chepillo is about one league in compass, and low Land next the Water, but
    farther up is the Hill call'd Pacora" (*A Cruising Voyage Round the World*, appendix, 13).

they took one Peragua[28] which they found at Anchor before the Island, and presently put some Men on board her.

On the 22d in the Morning my Men complained grievously for want of Water, so that I was forced to bear up[29] and go to one of the Kings, alias Pearl-Islands, where I was informed by a Prisoner I had on board, That there was a new Brigantine[30] just launched fit for my purpose. About eleven I got to the place, and happily finding his Words to be true, I presently, with seven Men along with me,

A brigantine (artist unknown, late 17th century).

went on Shoar and took the Vessel. From thence I went up to an House I discovered, and finding no Body, searched the adjacent Wood, where I found a Woman and two Children, who were retired thither for fear of us: I brought the Woman, who was very young and handsome, to the House along with me, wherein I found a Case or two of Wines,[31] whereof I drank some, presenting my Service to the Woman of the House (for so she really was) who return'd me Thanks, in her Lingua, which I understood very well; but soon after I was yet a more pleasing Guest to her, when she understood what Country-man I was.[¶]

All our People by this time were come on Shoar, some of whom I imployed to dress Victuals for us, while others were to fit up the new Bark, that we might make a way to find out the rest of our Party. Our Bark was ready by Four in the Afternoon, our Water

---

28 The 1771 edition of William Falconer's nautical reference work described a *periagua* as "a sort of large canoe, used in the Leeward islands, South America, and the gulf of Mexico. It differs from the common vessels of that name, as being composed of the trunks of two trees, hollowed and united into one fabric; whereas those which are properly called canoes, are formed of the body of one tree" (Falconer, *Universal Dictionary*, n.p.).

29 To *bear up*, or *bear away*, is "in navigation, the act of changing the course of a ship, in order to make her run before the wind, after she had sailed some time with a side-wind, or close-hauled; it is generally performed to arrive at some port under the lee, or to avoid some imminent danger occasioned by a violent storm, leak, or enemy in sight" (Falconer, *Universal Dictionary*, n.p.).

30 "*Brig* or *Brigantine*, a merchant-ship with two masts. This term is not universally confined to vessels of a particular construction, or which are masted and rigged in a method different from all others. It is variously applied, by the mariners of different European nations, to a peculiar sort of vessel of their own marine" (Falconer, *Universal Dictionary*, n.p.). A modern source notes that generally a brig was "square-rigged on both masts," while a brigantine was "square rigged on the foremast and fore-and-aft rigged on the mainmast" (Dear and Kemp, *Oxford Companion*, 67–68).

filled, and Wood and Provision taken in, and so we took our leave of this Island (having first bor'd an hole in our old Bark) and steered for the Isle of Chepillo, in hopes to meet with our Friends there: But the Winds proving contrary, we were forced to anchor at another Island that lies about a League's distance from the first, and to stay here all that Night. Some of our Men went on Shoar in this place to see what they could find, but came all on board again before it was dark, and informed us they could meet with nothing good, nor anything in the Houses (for the Inhabitants were all fled into the Woods) saving a few Fowls about them, whereof they made me a Present, as also of some small pittances of Provision, wherewith was not very well satisfied, and so having taken our Supper we fell to our serious Repose.

Our Men went next Morning ashoar again to fill some Jars with Water, in order to proceed on our Voyage: It was Noon-tide before they had done and were all got on board, when we weigh'd Anchor, and set sail with the Wind at S.E. for Chepillo, which is not above five Leagues distance from the other Island: But it was dark before we could reach it, so that I was forced to send our Canoe with five Men ashoar, to see if our Party was there or no. She return'd about eight at night, and inform'd me that they had been there, and by all the Signs imaginable were but newly gone, for their Fire was not yet out, and all the Houses were burnt down to the Ground. Moreover, that there were dead People lying on the Ground, which made them conjecture our Men had had a Fight with the Spaniards: Upon this Information, and finding the Wind to be fair, I resolved to stand[32] for Panama; tho' all this while I could set no sight of our Party, I found all things to appearance very still and quiet in the Town, which made us judge it had been taken, tho' we were much mistaken: However, by the time we came within a League of the Harbour, we descryed six Vessels small and great, but seeing no Men, we began to be very doubtful of the welfare of our People; tho' after all we were resolved to clap the Ships on board: But as we were fitting our selves for the said adventure, we descryed a single Canoe come from them towards us, which proved to be one of our own (for that indeed was the Signal between us) and also when she came up informed us of the Engagement they had had the Day before with three sail of Ships manned with 280 Men, and whom through the Divine Assistance they overcame with the loss only of eleven Men killed and thirty four wounded (among whom was Captain Harris who died two Days after) out of two

---

31 Modern writer Benerson Little listed some popular wine choices for the region and the era: "'Madeira,' wrote Francis Rogers, 'is a racy strong-bodied noble wine, both red and white; 'tis chiefly drank in the West Indies and North America; it seems particularly adapted for the hot countries . . . 'tis the most wholesome and general liquor among our plantations in the West Indies.' According to John Atkins, Madeira, or 'Red Sack,' was 'limed' and would keep well in the West Indian climate when no other wines would. Sack in general was a popular wine although difficult to define exactly. Canary, Xerez (sherry, also called Sherry sack and Bristol milk), and Madeira were the most popular, although there were many others including claret and Rhenish. In the West Indies there were plantain, banana, and pineapple wines" (*Sea Rover's Practice*, 247).

32 "*Standing*, in navigation, the movement by which a ship advances towards a certain object, or departs from it: as the enemy stands in-shore: the English fleet are standing off: at day-break we discovered three sail standing to the northward, &c." (Falconer, *Universal Dictionary*, n.p.).

hundred or thereabouts; whereas on the Enemy's side there were not half a dozen that escaped whole, the rest being either killed or wounded, or else Sadly burnt with the Powder: Their General was killed in the first Fight, their Vice-Admiral run away manfully to the Town, only with the loss of almost all his Men; and the Rear-Admiral was taken by Captain Sawkins on board of whom there was not a Man left unhurt; the Commander, whose Name was Don Francisco Peralto, was indeed alive, but most sadly scalded. I had no sooner joined our Men, but they recounted to me all their Adventure at large, during our four Days Separation.[33]

I had also the Satisfaction to confer with Don Peralto concerning many Things, who among divers other remarkable Passages, as it came in by way of Discourse, told me of two strange Comets that had been seen the Year before, viz. 1679, at Quito, which is a great City in the Kingdom of Peru [. . .] .

I also recounted my small Adventures, while absent, to my Company, wherewith we were mutually satisfied; and having good store of Wine on board, we cheared up our Hearts for a while, and then having set our Centinels, betook our selves to our Repose for that Night.

But there was not so much Jollity and seeming Unanimity between us the Evening before, than that next day there arose as much Confusion and strong Contests among the Men, whether we should return back to our Ships, or continue any longer time in the South-Seas; however it did not last long, for all the Commanders except one, with the major part of the Men, were resolved to stay and try their Fortunes here for a time: But Captain Coxon with about Fifty more with him, which I think will not much redound to his Honour, left us this Night to go over-land homewards; and not only so, but left also about Twenty of his wounded Men behind, which was the greatest Cause of our staying here to get them well again; And had we been all of his Mind, not only these but fourteen more under the same Circumstances, who had so bravely demeaned[34] themselves in this Conflict, must have also perished.[35] Coxon not content with going off as aforesaid, and moreover to carry the best of our Doctors and Medicines with him, would have tempted others to do the like with him, and particularly my self who could not hear of so dirty and inhuman an Action, without Detestation.[¶]

---

33 Following the fight against the armed Spanish vessels the buccaneers took an additional prize, *La Santissima Trinidad*, a 400-ton vessel, the name of which the captors Anglicized and shortened to *Trinity* (Baer, *British Piracy*, I:368; Cox, "Adventures of Capt. Barth. Sharp," 14; and Ringrose, *Dangerous Voyage*, 31–32).

34 Conducted.

35 By John Cox's version, Coxon was "a little in disgrace amongst our Men, as something tainted with cowardize in the late action . . . " ("Adventures of Capt. Barth. Sharp," 14–15). William Dampier, who would join another breakaway group after the death of John Watling, in late May 1681 found "Capt. Coxen" at Springer's Key in the "Samballoes" or San Blas Islands off Panama's Caribbean coast; he was operating a ten-gun privateering vessel with 100 men (*New Voyage*, 27).

Coxon having thus relinquish'd his Charge and our Company, we made choice of Captain Richard Sawkins to succeed him as our Commander in Chief, on board of whom I went on Monday the 26th of April, to acquaint him I was minded to go with my Company to an Island that lay about three Leagues from us, in order to see what was become of some Men whom we had sent thither the day before; and so much the rather, that understanding there was a small Town upon the said Place, and they not returning according to Order, I had reason to doubt of their Safety. He readily agreed to my Motion, we sailed away, but happening to meet with our People half way on their return, I resolved to go back to the Ships; while the Wind in the mean time dying away, I was becalmed and forced to come to an Anchor until the Breeze came: My Canoe went on board the great Ship, and stayed there till it was almost Night, when the other descrying a Ship in the Offen,[36] she hoisted some Men on board the small Bark to go and look after her.[¶]

In the interim my Canoe made a Sign to me, and I presently weighed, stood to Sea, and got sight of the Bark, and sailing better than the other Ship, came up with him first and haled him. He answering from Lima, I bid him strike, so clapt them on board and entred some Men; but I had no occasion to put my self to that Trouble, for he had no Arms to defend himself with, save only Rapiers:[37] However I found him an useful Prize, having a matter of 1,400 Jars of Wine and Brandy on board, besides several more of Vinegar, a considerable quantity of Powder, and some Shot which came very luckily, for we had almost spent all our Ammunition. I am not to forget that there were also in the Vessel Fifty thousand pieces of Eight,[38] with Sweet Meats and other Things, that were very grateful to our dissatisfied Minds.[39] The Bark that came along to me, return'd the same Night to carry the good News to the rest of our Friends, but I was forced to anchor without[40] all Night, because the Wind did not serve to bring me in: However we weigh'd next Morning, and so joined our Ships that

---

36 An archaic form of the word *offing*, which in this setting is "the part of the visible sea distant from the shore or beyond the anchoring ground" (*Oxford English Dictionary*, X:724, 735).

37 A long, slender, sharply pointed weapon meant for thrusting attacks, impractical for use at sea in places such as belowdecks where the shorter cutlass prevailed. "From 1630 to 1660 or so, some rovers might have been armed with rapiers, and the Spanish and Portuguese of all social classes had an affinity for rapiers throughout the period. Primarily a thrusting weapon, the Spanish sort were often cup-hilted and usually quite long-bladed. Although much too long for practical work in a confined space, they were still dangerous. Their long blades gave them a pike-like reach, and their cup-hilts provided excellent protection to the hand. However, once an attacker was 'within the blade' they were a liability" (Little, *Sea Rover's Practice*, 69–70).

38 "The premier coin of the Atlantic world in the seventeenth and eighteenth centuries was the Spanish peso, or piastra – the piece of eight that in the seventeenth century came to be called the dollar and that later became the basic unit of the monetary system of the United States." Its approximate value in 1651 was £0.23; in 1702 it was £0.22 (McCusker, *Money and Exchange*, 7, 10).

39 Sharp's figure is roughly the same as that provided by Ringrose, who wrote that the ship contained 51,000 pieces of eight (*Dangerous Voyage*, 37). Cox wrote of a larger number being shared out: "60,000 pieces of eight, which we divided amongst us the next day, coming to 247 pieces of Eight per Man" ("Adventures of Capt. Barth. Sharp," 15).

40 I.e., outside the anchorage.

lay under two little Islands which form'd the Harbour, one whereof is called Perico,[41] but I never heard any Name for the other. Here we began to take in Provision of Flower, for as yet we could get no Meat, and when we had furnished our selves with about 1,200 Packs, we careen'd[42] four Sail, one of them being almost laden with Iron, another with Flower, the other two were small Barks. The biggest of our Ships was Three Hundred Tuns, we had two more of about One Hundred each, besides the two Barks, and one we gave the Prisoners to carry them ashore.

From this place we set Sail on the 29th of April, for the Isle of Tavoga,[43] where we intended fully to ecquip our Ships, fill our Water, cut our Wood, and provide our selves with such other Necessaries as might be convenient for so long a Voyage to undertake. During our stay here, the Spaniards came to Trade with us from the Town, to whom we sold [*] Wine and Brandy, to the Value of Three Thousand Pieces of Eight: But not to forget our main Business, while we lay in the Offen, we espy'd a Sail at Sea, bound in for the Town. Whereupon I in my small Bark, as also Captain Cook,[44] with his Sloop,[45] weighed to give him Chase; the same was done by the Admiral['s] Canoe; but we Sailing best, it was my good Fortune to come up with him first, and hailed him, who made answer he was from Paita,[46] and his lading Flower; whereupon I immediately clapt him on Board, entered some Men, and return'd with my Prize to our Ships again. There being got to an Anchor, I sold some Flower to the Spaniards, and fitted this Ship for my self, for I liked her very well, she being in Burden[47] about an Hundred Tuns. It was not past a Day or two after, that we discovered another Sail, to whom we gave Chase, and notwithstanding all our Diligence to come up with her, she was got almost into the Town, and had certainly Escaped, had not the Wind luckily died away, and she been becalmed; which was no sooner observed by us, but we sent out a small Bark with Eight Oars, that was in our Company, who quickly rowed in under her Guns, and fetch'd her out to us. There

---

41 Isla Perico. Ringrose located it "distant only two Leagues from Panama. On the aforesaid Island are to be seen several Store-houses which are built there, to receive the Goods delivered out of the Ships" (*Dangerous* Voyage, 27).

42 *Careening* was a necessary task but left a vessel and its crew vulnerable to attack. The process involved "heaving a ship down, by means of tackles [ropes and blocks] attached to its mastheads, so as to expose one side to bream, or repair, it, The vessel was laid ashore on a steeply sloping beach parallel to the shoreline. To control the angle of heel, and to bring the vessel back onto an even keel after it had been cleaned or repaired, relieving tackles were run under the keel and secured to convenient points on the exposed side. After one side had been cleaned, the ship was floated off on the tide, turned round to face the other way, and the operation repeated so that the opposite side could be cleaned" (Dear and Kemp, *Oxford Companion*, 88, 573).

43 Taboga, in the Gulf of Panamá.

44 Edward or Edmund Cook. On land he flew "red Colours striped with yellow, with a Hand and Sword for his devise" (Ringrose, *Dangerous* Voyage, 4).

45 A *sloop* is a small craft with one mast, rigged so that its sails – as with the schooner – run parallel to the keel (i.e., fore-and-aft-rigged). This is as opposed to sails being hung perpendicular to the keel (i.e., square-rigged) as with brigs, brigantines, ships, etc.

46 A Peruvian port on a bay of the same name.

47 *Burden*, or *burthen*, referred to "the weight or measure of any species of merchandize that a ship will carry when fit for sea" (Falconer, *Universal Dictionary*, n.p.).

were six Indians in her at first, five of whom leapt over-board and swam ashore, but the other stay'd: Her Lading consisted chiefly of Flower, to purchase which we adventured so near unto their Castle, that the Shot flew as far beyond us as it was to us, so that we came to an Anchor all Night without Gun-shot, and weighing next Morning joined our Ships again. Our stay here in fitting up and recruiting our Men was about fourteen or fifteen Days, within which time one of our Company, and a Frenchman born, ran away to the Spaniards, to whom he divulged all our Designs; and our stay to seek or him on this Island for a day or two proved all in vain. This Tavoga is an exceeding pleasant Island, abounding in all manner of Fruits, such as Pine-Apples, Oranges, Lemons, Albecatos,[48] Pears, Mammes,[49] Saportas,[50] Cocao-nuts, with a small but brave commodious fresh River running in it: The Harbour is also good, and the Anchorage clear.

Chap. II

They sail for Pueblo Nuebo, where Captain Sawkins their Commander is killed. To Quibo. Are left by many of their Company. Quibo described. Arrive at Gorgona; a description of it.

What with one and another thing it was Thursday Morning the 13th of May before we left Tavoga, when we weighed Anchor steering our Course for Pueblo Nuebo, or the New Town, with a design to get some Meat to victual our three Ships and two Barks, which had nine Men a-piece in them, for a Voyage; But one of the Barks after this Night we saw no more, the other the great Ship took into a tow at her Stern. We met with very bad Weather, much Rain and hard Gales, Cloudy and Dark; However we coasted up along the Shoar with the Wind westerly plying to the Westward, till we came to a point of Land called by the Spaniards Punta Mala,[51] where we intended to go ashoar to a Beef-Estancia[52] in order to supply our selves with Flesh; to which end we turned our Bark loose, thinking to go in this Night: But the Wind driving away all the while, attended with a strong Current which is common here, setting to the Westward, we were drove away and so lost our Bark: However we plied still to the West, as 'tis usual here, thereby endeavouring to get to an Island called Coyba or

---

48 Avocados.
49 The mamey apple. "On the Islands there are a great man Mammee-trees, which grow with a clear, streight Body, to 60 Foot high, or upwards. The Fruit is very wholesome and delicious; shap'd somewhat like a Pound-pear, but much larger, with a small Stone or two in the middle" (Wafer, *New Voyage*, 99).
50 "The Mammee-Sappota differs something from the other [i.e., the mamey apple, mentioned above], and is a smaller and firmer Fruit, of a fine beautiful Colour when ripe" (Wafer, *New Voyage*, 99). The word *sapota* itself originated with the Aztec language Nahuatl, and denoted "the tropical evergreen tree *Achras sapota* and its edible fruit. The earliest English form (from about 1560) is *sapote*, borrowed from Spanish or Portuguese *zapote*, itself a derivative from Nahuatl txapotl" (Watson, "Nahuatl Words in American English," 108).
51 On the Bay of Panamá (Wafer, *New Voyage*, 90–91).
52 *Estancia*, a ranch.

Quibo,[53] lying in 7 d. 30 m. N. Lat.[54] and distant from Panama about 60 Leagues; a little to Leeward[55] of which Place we had a hard Gale and so much Rain, that our main Sail[56] was split all to pieces in the Night-time: Yet on the Morrow I went on board the great Ship and got another, when some of the Men got to the Yard[57] and made up a Sail again.[¶]

But one Misfortune was hardly well over when another came on by the loss of our Consorts which hapned on the 21st at Night, to our no small Trouble on both sides: However we resolved still to go forward with our Design, had the good luck to join them again the next Day, and on the 24th we manned our Canoes with fifty Men, stood into the River of Pueblo Nuebo, rowed all Night till within an hour of Daylight, when we came up with two Vessels, on board of which we found no living Soul, and so we left them: But next Morning we landed at a Stockado built on purpose by the Spaniards, according to the advice of our Runagado-French[58] already mentioned, to oppose us, at which place we had a small Rencounter with the Enemy, who killed [of] us three Men, whereof the brave Captain Sawkins was one, and wounded four or five more, besides which we got nothing.[59] So that we found it our best way to retreat down the River again, to the two Ships above-noted, where we had somewhat better Fortune, for in the biggest of them we found the Sail in the great Cabbin, and that she was laden with Pitch, Tallow, some Indigo and Cotton, as the lesser Vessel was with Corn and Mantego:[60] Her we thought fit to burn, as I did also another small Bark I found in a Creek there, but the other we carried off.

The following Day I met with Captain Cook, and on the 27th late at Night, according to the Resolution we had taken, we were all got to Quibo; and going my self next

---

53 Coiba.
54 Sailors in this era could determine latitude (position north or south of the equator) using a quadrant, but measuring position by longitude (along an east-west axis) was a later development. Latitude herein is usually expressed in degrees, with 60 minutes in each; some writers seem to have omitted reference to "North" or "South" in relation to the equator (0° latitude), assuming reader familiarity with the region. See Dear and Kemp, *Oxford Companion*, 310, 324; Smyth, *Lexicon*, 433, 454; and Sobel, *Longitude*.
55 The *lee* is a term "used by seamen to distinguish that part of the hemisphere to which the wind is directed, from the other part whence it arises; which latter is accordingly called to windward. This expression is chiefly used when the wind crosses the line of a ship's course, so that all on one side of her is called *to-windward*, and all on the opposite side, *to-leeward* . . . " (Falconer, *Universal Dictionary*, n.p.).
56 The main sail is that which "on a square-rigger is bent to the main yard, but the sail that on a fore-and-after is spread by the main gaff and main boom" (Patterson, *Illustrated Nautical Dictionary*, 118). As noted above, a *square-rigger* was a vessel (such as a frigate or brig) with the sails hung perpendicular to the keel; a *fore-and-aft* rigged vessel (such as a sloop or schooner) had its sails hung parallel to the keel; hybrid types were also known.
57 A *yard* is a beam fixed either horizontally or diagonally to a mast, from which a sail is hung or "set" (Dear and Kemp, *Oxford Companion*, 649).
58 *Rinigado*, or renegade.
59 The settlement being attacked was Puebla Nova, described as "a Town upon the Main near the innermost of these Islands" (Dampier, *New Voyage* 151).
60 Montego Bay is a Jamaican port, but in this context the word refers to "a foodstuff, possibly yam, pumpkin or callaloo, that [the buccaneers] knew from Jamaica, especially Montego Bay; decidedly not the fare of lordly Spanish colonists" (Baer, *British Piracy*, I:369).

Morning on board the great Ship, I demanded of the whole Party what they intended to do: Hereupon some of them answered, they would go back over-Land, while others said they would follow me in my Adventures, of which number there were an hundred and forty-six; whereas the other were about seventy in all, to whom I gave them a Vessel for the[i]r Transportation.[61] This Island of Quibo (where we furnished our selves with Water and Wood, and fitted up our Ship) is a very fine Island, of about ten Leagues in Circumference, and five distant from the Main; here is good Anchoring in 20 Fathom-water, and clear Ground four or five Miles from the Shoar; It's full of fresh Rivers and of a temperate Air; abounds with wild Deer, and other wild Beasts, besides wild-Fowl and Fish in great plenty, with the largest Oysters and the best that ever I eat; whereof also there is another sort that have abundance of large Pearl in them, and which the Spaniards gather in great quantities: The Place is moreover plentifully stored with Green Turtle, but they do not eat so sweet as ours in the North-Seas.[62]

Having continued here for about ten Days, burnt the Ship I was in, and gone on board the great one, on Sunday the sixth of June we sailed away with a design to visit the Isles of Gallapallo,[63] that are a parcel of Islands lying under the Equator. We had variety of Winds and Weather, and nothing otherwise remarkable till the 17th at Six in the Morning we made Land, and the same Day anchored about 5, in the middle of the Isle of Gorgona,[64] against a small River of fresh Water wherewith it is very plentifully stored. The Island it self is about five Miles in length, at the South-west whereof stands another smaller one (where there is also good Water and without the same stands a small Rock, but the Anchoring is within Pistol-shot of the Shoar in 25, 20 or 15 Fathom-water, clear Ground, but you must be sure to come into no Shoal-water,[65] for then you have but eight or ten Fathom, because it ebbs and flows very much at N.E. and S.W. We found it also by Experience to be a good Road[66] for Careening. But the Place is much

---

61 From Cox's version: "When we came on board there hapned a great distraction amongst our Men, which was occasioned by the death of Captain Sawkins. In this mutiny seventy five more of our Men left us, and returned over Land as they came, delivering up their Commissions to our Emperour. Captain Cooke who was Commander of a Ship, not finding things answering to his desire and expectation, laid down his Commission and went on board Captain Sharp" ("Adventures of Capt. Barth. Sharp," 17).

62 "[I]n Port Royal, meat of a sea turtle's under shell, called the *calipee*, was cooked with spice, dry herbs, and forced meat, and was considered an excellent dish. It was also baked or roasted with salt and pepper. The upper shell was the *calipach*, and its meat was usually boiled to make a broth, often with turtle eggs added. . . . *Boucan de tortue*, or barbecued sea turtle – baked in the shell in the sand under coals – was also a common dish in Hispaniola at the seaside. South Sea privateers boiled, roasted, fried, baked, and stewed sea turtle" (Little, *Sea Rover's Practice*, 249).

63 The Galápagos Islands.

64 Gorgona Island. Dampier described it as "lying about 25 Leagues from the Island Gallo. . . . Gorgonia is an uninhabited Island, in lat. about three degrees North: It is a pretty high Island, and very remarkable, by reason of two Saddles, or risings and fallings on the top. It is about 2 Leagues long, and a League broad; and it is four Leagues from the Main" (*New Voyage*, 123).

65 A *shoal* is a "danger formed by sunken rocks, on which the sea does not break; but [the term is] generally applied to every place where the water is shallow, whatever be the ground" (Smyth, *Lexicon*, 619).

66 A *road* is "a bay, or place of anchorage, at some distance from the shore, on the sea-coast, whither ships or vessels occasionally repair to receive intelligence, orders, or necessary supplies, or to wait for a fair wind, &c. The excellence of a road consists chiefly in its being protected from the reigning winds, and the swell of the sea, in having a good anchoring ground, and being at a competent distance from the shore. Those which are not sufficiently enclosed are termed open roads" (Falconer, *Universal Dictionary*, n.p.).

incommoded with Rains from the Month of April to August, and we could meet with no other Refreshments but Conies, Oysters, a sort of Fowl which we call Carisoes, and some Turtle, wherewith it's pretty well stored. The Air is temperate, and the Island it self is very rich with Pearl, which the Spaniards get with little trouble out of their Oysters, and [with] this we experimented during our stay here: There are moreover a great number of Whales on this Coast. Before our departure among other Things, we fitted our selves with Bomkins (as we call them) to carry our Water in, for you are to know that from hence to Cape Pasado there is none to be had but where there are Inhabitants, to which Places we were very unwilling to go for fear of being discovered.

CHAP. III

They sail for Gorgona; have a fight off the Isle of Gallo. Of the Point of Mangroves. Cape Passao. Monte Christo. Arrive at the Isle of Plate, with some Account of it, They take a Spanish Bark. Then another Ship. Observations of the Magellanick Clouds.

On Sunday July 25th we set sail from the Isle of Gorgona with the Wind at West, to the Southward with our Star-board[a] Tacks on board;[67] we made the best of our way till Wednesday, when we had much Rain and but little Wind at W.S.W. and standing into the Shoar made the Island of Gallo,[68] which is about two or three Leagues long, and by Judgment two from the Main: It's not very high, but full of small Hills, at the South-west end whereof stands another small Island; but very low and rugged, where lives three Families of Spaniards. We continued our Course to the one and thirtieth, when in the afternoon we made Land again, which proved to be a Point of Mangroves, as the Spaniards call it, lying S.S.W. from the Isle of Gallo at about ten Leagues distance, low Land, and steep to the Shoar, for we stood very near and could find no Ground with about 20 Fathom of line, so that at 6 in the Evening we went about Ship[69] and stood off to Sea. By the fourth of August we made Land again which proved to be Cape St. Francisco,[70] and by Sunday the 8th having fair Weather and a fresh Gale, we fetcht close under Cape Passado or Pashao,[71] which is a bold Shoar and steep to the Cape, with all white Cliffs to the North-end, indifferent high and

---

67   "Sailing with the wind blowing on the starboard side" (Patterson, *Illustrated Nautical Dictionary*, 174).

68   "Isla del Gallo is located at the northernmost point of Tomaco harbour, south-west Colombia" (Baer, *British Piracy*, I:369).

69   "*About* . . . the situation of a ship immediately after she has tacked or changed her course by going about, and standing on the other tack. . . . *About-Ship!* . . . [T]he order to the ship's crew to prepare for tacking" (Falconer, *Universal Dictionary*, n.p.).

70   Cape St. Francisco "is in lat. 01 d. 00 North. It is a high bluff, or full point of Land, cloathed with tall great Trees. . . . The Land in the Country within this Cape is very high, and the Mountains commonly appear very black" (Dampier, *New Voyage*, 96).

71   Variant spellings for Cape Passaro. One mid-19th century navigation text observed that "Cape Passado is 13 miles North of Caracas Bay . . . " (Findlay, *Pacific Ocean*, I:203). The Cape "runs out into the Sea with a high round Point, which seems to be divided in the midst. It is bald against the Sea, but within Land, and on both sides, it is full of short Trees. The Land in the Country is very high and mountainous, and it appears to be very woody" (Dampier, *New Voyage*, 116).

craggy, but smooth; to the Southwards whereof stands a little Harbour, a matter of half a Mile broad. Next Day we reached to the Southards as far as Monte Christo,[72] which is about 10 Leagues. It's in form somewhat like unto a Sugarloaf, but a little squarer at the top, under which we had the sight of a small Village called by the Spaniards Manta, but settled by Indians, intermixt with some white People, and standing five Leagues North of the Cape. By the 13th we came to an Anchor at the Isle of Plate,[73] (which we had discovered the Day before) when we met with the Fellow that waited on us in a smaller Ship our Consort: Here we went ashoar and found great plenty of Goats, which we drove together and caught some alive, but others we killed and salted, and found them very refreshing to us, as were also the great store of Turtle we met with in this Place. The Island it self is pretty high and level at the top but barren, and there is no Water to be got there, save out of one very small Spring that issues from a Clift not worth mentioning, because we could not fill above 20 Gallons in a Day; the said Spring stands near the Anchoring-place at the N.E. side, where we dropt our Anchor within a Cable's length[74] of the Shoar in fourteen Fathom-water, for farther off you

"So the Treasure Was Divided" (Howard Pyle).

72 "Montecristi, a town a few miles south-east of Manta, Ecuador" (Baer, *British Piracy*, I:370).
73 "This island received its name from the fact that Sir Francis Drake had here made a division of his spoils, distributing to each man of his company sixteen bowlfuls of doubloons and pieces of eight. The buccaneers rechristened it Drake's Island" (Gosse, *Pirates' Who's Who*, 90). Dampier described it as "about four Mile long, and a Mile and a half broad, and of a good heighth. It is bounded with high steep Cliffs clear round, only at one Place on the East-side. The top of it is flat and even, the Soil sandy and dry: the Trees it produceth are but small-bodied, low, and grow thin; and there are only three or four sorts of Trees, all unknown to us. . . . There is good Grass, especially in the beginning of the Year. There is no Water on this Island but at one place on the East-side, close by the Sea; there it drills slowly down from the Rocks, where it may be received into Vessels. There was plenty of Goats, but they were now all destroyed" (*New Voyage*, 96–97).
74 In his entry for *cables*, Falconer noted that they should be 120 fathoms long (*Universal Dictionary*, n.p.). By the mid-1800s "cable's length" referred to a "measure of about 100 fathoms, by which the distances of ships in a fleet are frequently estimated." Additionally, in "all marine charts a cable is deemed 607.56 feet, or one-tenth of a sea mile" (Smyth, *Lexicon*, 151).

cannot do it, by reason that the Bank is steep, and your Anchors will not hold: This is that Island where Sir Francis Drake[75] shared his Mony.[76][¶]

From this Day forward to the 17th nothing memorable hapned to us, when some-what to our Surprize we saw the Isle of Plate again bearing N.E. at 10 Leagues dis-tance from us, and the Wind being at S.W. we stood along the Shoar, while the Coast with a strong Northern Current caused us to fall in with the Island beyond our expec-tation. We weather'd[77] Cape Helena[78] on the 25th in the Morning, but on the pre-ceding Evening took a Spanish Bark with forty odd Men in her: The Commander of the Vessel (which was fitted out on purpose to go see for us) was called Don Thomas Orgundonnuy, and had been formerly Governor of Guayaquill.[79] Upon the Examination of our Prisoners, they told us they had taken a Bark of ours with seven Men in her, and killed them all save one: We had three Men wounded in the Ingagement with them, whereof one whose Name was Robert Montgomery died on the 8th of September following: On the 26th we made Point Cambous, which is high Land with white Clifts; next Day stood in to the Shoar, and had the Misfortune in putting our Ship astays[80] to back aboard of our Consort, and stave[81] him in his upper Work: We bulg'd[82] the smaller Vessel the following Morning, when we had taken all

---

75 Elizabethan sea captain Sir Francis Drake (c. 1543–96) won fame for cruises against the Spanish in the New World and in the fight against the 1588 Spanish Armada. For a concise modern biography, see Dear and Kemp, *Oxford Companion*, 175–177.

76 While here, many of Sharp's buccaneers gambled away their loot; the company also "heilded [i.e. heeled – turned to one side] our Ship, and gave her a pair of Boot-hose-tops" (Cox, "Adventures of Capt. Barth. Sharp," 22). *Boot-topping* was "the act of cleaning the upper-part of a ship's bottom, or that part which lies immediately under the surface of the water, and daubing it over with tallow, or with a coat or mixture of tallow, sulphur, resin, &c. Boot-topping is chiefly performed where there is no dock, or other commodious situation for breaming or careening; or when the hurry of a voyage renders it inconvenient to have the whole bottom properly trimmed and cleaned of the filth which gathers to it in the course of a sea-voyage. It is executed by making the ship lean to one side, as much as they can with safety, and then scraping off the grass, slime, shells, or other material that adheres to the bottom, on the other side, which is elevated above the surface of the water for this purpose, and accordingly daubed with the coat of tallow and sulphur. Having thus finished one side, they make the ship lean to the other side, and perform the same operation, which not only preserves the bottom from the worm, but makes the ship slide smoothly through the water" (Falconer, *Universal Dictionary*, n.p.).

77 "*To weather*, is to sail to windward [the direction from which the wind comes] of some ship, bank, or head-land" (Falconer, *Universal Dictionary*, n.p.).

78 "Point St. Helena: at the northernmost reach of the Bay of Guayaquil, Ecuador" (Baer, *British Piracy*, I:369).

79 Guayaquil, or Santiago de Guayaquil, Ecuador. In writing of this episode, Cox described the Spanish vessel as "a small Man of War, fitted out of Guiaque or Wyake by a parcel of merry Blades, Gentlemen, who drinking in a Tavern, made a Vow to come to Sea with that Vessel and thirty Men, and take us; but we made them repent their undertaking. The Captain's name was Don Thomas d'Algondony, whom after we had severely School'd for his sawcy attempt we entertained on board our Admiral. In this conflict we had three of our Men Wounded; what they lost we knew not, because it was night; the next day we sunk the Vessel, and plied to the Southward" ("Adventures of Capt. Barth. Sharp," 23–24). The officer was Don Thomas de Argandona (Baer, *British Piracy*, I:369).

80 "*Stay*, to stay a ship, is to arrange the sails and move the rudder, so as to bring the ship's head to the direction of the wind, in order to get her on the other tack" (James, *Naval History of Great Britain*, I:xxiii).

81 To impact or collapse.

82 The *bilge* being "[t]hat part of the bottom of a vessel that is next to the keel," a vessel is said to have been *bilged* (sometimes *bulged*) "when the bilge is broken in by the bottom of the ship coming in contact with a rock, the shore, etc." (Patterson, *Illustrated Nautical Dictionary*, 18, 20; see also Smyth, *Lexicon*, 99–100).

that was valuable out of her, and weather'd Cape Blanco on the 29th: The same consists of high Clifts, white and barren Land, from whence there is no Water to be got within thirty Leagues, and the Spaniards themselves, when they travel by Land are forced to make use of Horses to carry some along with them.

By the first Day of September we fetcht[83] to Windward[84] of Paita bearing from us N.E. at 3 Leagues distance, the same being a craggy Ridge and marly Ground, but barren: On the second we saw a Ship to Windward of us, which we could not come up with till two Days after; we made bold with what he had for our purpose, and understanding by him he was come from Guayaquill, and bound for Lima, and that at the former Place there were some Men of War [that] lay ready to put out after us upon the first News of our being near, we put off from the Shoar as much as we could, and met with nothing worth our noting from hence to the one and twentieth, when being come to the Latitude of 19 d. 55 m. we saw the Magellaneck Clouds,[85] the Eastermost whereof, to our Judgment, was seemingly ten Foot long, and the Westermost round like a Hat.

CHAP. IV

Their Voyage continued. They descry Land. Observations of the Climate. They are in want of Water, and after several Attempts Land at Port Ely or Hilo, &c. Sail for Coquimbo.[86] Land, and take la Serena and burn it.

From this time forward to the 17th of October there was nothing occur'd but bare Sailing; but then about 7 in the Morning we made the Land, and kept plying[87] along the Coast Southwards the next Day: But this Clime is so much given to Fogs in the Morning, that a Man cannot see Land unless you be within two or three Leagues of it; neither does it ever Rain in these Parts; Yet a mighty Dew falls that makes the Vales very fruitful, for I found they produced all sorts of Fruits, and as good Corn as in England, besides [an] abundance of Wine which they make here also. However we made Port Ely[88] on the 22d, found the Land to be high, and a smooth Ridge with a Gap in the middle. There is moreover a small Hill just to the Southward of the River, besides which may be seen three or four little ones, under the smooth Land by the Water-side, but you must be near the Shoar before you can raise them.

---

83 "To reach, or arrive at; as, 'we shall fetch to windward of the light-house this tack" (Smyth, *Lexicon*, 292). ' .
84 *Windward* is the "point or direction from which the wind blows" (Patterson, *Illustrated Nautical Dictionary*, 195).
85 "A popular name for the two Nebiculae, or great cloudy-looking spots in the southern heavens, which are found to consist of a vast number of nebulae and clusters of stars" (Smyth, *Lexicon*, 462).
86 The Chilean city Coquimbo is on the Bay of Guayacán; "[D]uring colonial times it was often favored as a lair by pirates, from Sir Francis Drake onward" Bizzarro, *Historical Dictionary of Chile*, 191.
87 The "act of making, or endeavouring to make, a progress against the direction of the wind" (Falconer, *Universal Dictionary*, n.p.).
88 Ilo, Peru.

We attempted to land several times at different Places,[89] we labouring by this time under great want of Water,[90] but at last on Thursday-morning the 28th about six we got ashoar, leaving eight of our Men only to look after our Canoes till our return, or some Signal made by us for them to come up to us, which was agreed to be a Fire or Smoak. These Orders being given, and my self discerning a large Path, marched on with my Men, yet had not advanced above a Mile when I espyed an Horseman who was their Look-out standing upon an adjacent Hill; whereat being no whit discouraged we moved forward, but had not got in all above five Miles, when I espyed about sixty Horse and Foot drawn up in Battalia ready to give us Battle: But we minded them little, and jogged on, till we came up close with them, and then with little Resistance they yielded us the Priviledge of filling our Water and cutting our Wood; and not content with that, we made also bold to refresh our Men with the good Wine, Oyl and variety of other Provisions wherewith we found this Place to be plentifully stored, during a stay of about six Days. Next Morning our Ship came to an Anchor in fourteen Fathom Water and a very good Road, for the Bay lies two leagues deep within a Point of Land: However that we might not have the Jollity we exercised here go altogether uninterrupted, the Night before our departure we were in a manner surprized with the approach of a Body of three hundred of the Enemies Horse that came to fight us; But notwithstanding the inequality of the number, we having then but Eighty Men on Shoar, we gave them their Bellies full on't, and on the first of November got all aboard without any Damage.

However before our departure we thought fit to put them to the Ransom of a Sugar-work we had the disposal of, and agreed with them for eighty Head of Cattle: But instead of these they brought three or four hundred Men to give us Battle;[91] tho' in a short time they left us Masters of the Field; but in revenge of their Treachery, sent threescore Men up the Valley, who burnt both the House, Canes, and whatever else belonged to the said Work, in a very short time: With which the Spaniards seemed to be so provoked, that we were attacked next Day by a Body of three hundred Horse, who endeavouring to surround our Men, they retired to the adjacent Rocks, and made all the Resistance that was necessary till the Night approach'd, when being

---

89   The buccaneers at this time considered trying to attack Arica, but opted to bypass it then due to heavy seas and because the Spanish were aware of their presence (Ringrose, *Dangerous Voyage*, 92–93).

90   "At this time Water was worth 30 pieces of Eight per pint to those that could spare their allowance, and he that bought it thought he had a great peny-worth; ... " (Cox, "Adventures of Capt. Barth. Sharp," 33).

91   As Little observed, "these Spaniards knew well the ancient legal maxim, that it was no crime to break a promise made to a pirate" (*History's Greatest Pirates*, 129). Cicero had written that "an oath sworn with the clear understanding in one's own mind that it should be performed must be kept; but if there is no such understanding, it does not count as perjury if one does not perform the vow. For example, suppose that one does not deliver the amount agreed upon with pirates as the price of one's life, that would be accounted no deception – not even if one should fail to deliver the ransom after having sworn to do so; for a pirate is not included in the number of lawful enemies, but is the common foe of all the world; and with him there ought not to be any pledged word nor oath mutually binding" (*De Officiis* [III:29:107], 385, 387).

apprehensive of greater numbers of the Enemy, they silently retired in the Dark of the Night, and got safely off.[92]

On Wednesday the third of November we set Sail from Port Hilo bound to the Southwards, and pursued our Voyage for several Days without any remarkable Occurrence till Thursday December 2d, when having an hard Gale at S. and observing our selves to be in the Lat. of 30 d. 28 m. S. and our Course East, we made Land about five in the Morning that seemed to be high and barren, then stood in for the Harbour of Coquimbo,[93] which this proved to be, to get Wood and Water, whereof we had now but very little left on board.

Next Morning an Hour before Day-light, we landed five and thirty of our Men, who marched for the Town of la Serena; but we had not advanced above a League or some such Business, when we were attack'd by a Body of 250 of the Enemies Horse; whom we vigorously repulsed, and having cleared the Field of them, we thought convenient to make a Halt till the rest of our Party came up with us, which they did about an Hour after; and then moving on couragiously together we reach'd the Town about Eight, with an hundred Men. It's a large Place, being about three quarters of a Mile every way; and 'tis stored with all sorts of English Fruit, as also with Corn, Wine, Oyl and Copper, in great abundance, and 'tis very delightful living here.

Now the Inhabitants of the Town finding our small Arms a little too strong for them, entirely left it to us to refresh our selves, and next Morning held a Consultation with the Governor about the Redemption of it: There was a way made on purpose for each Party to advance, he coming on with three Men in his Company, and I met him with two. His Party also consisted of about five hundred Men, whereas mine did not amount to above an hundred and twenty. However we came to an Agreement for 100,000 pieces of Eight; but the treacherous Spaniard falsifying his Word, in revenge thereof we took care to set Fire to every House in the Town, that so it might be wholly reduced to Ashes, but first secured what Plunder we could; wherewith, as we were retiring to our Ships, we were way-laid by a Body of the Enemies Horse, which for all that we routed and got safe to our Ship, without the loss of a Man, only we had one wounded in the Body but not mortally. But we had like to have met with a very great Misfortune during our absence, or the Spaniards, by an unusual Strategem, had

---

92 According to Cox, "The Enemy came riding at full speed toward us, that we thought their Horse would have been in with our body and charged us home; but when they came within reach of our Fuzees, we dismounted most of their Front with a Volly of small Shot, which put a stop to their carreer and courages, and not finding it safe to come nearer, fairly wheeled off to the left, and took shelter Amongst the Hills. This confirmed us that we should get no other Beefs; so having filled our Water, we that night went on board our Ships . . . " ("Adventures of Capt. Barth. Sharp," 35–36).

93 The buccaneers' target was adjacent La Serena, "a town of seven churches and one chapel" which was "entirely unfortified" (Little, *History's Greatest Pirates*, 132–133). "Before the present city was built, 'Coquimbo' was often used to designate La Serena itself" (Bizzarro, *Historical Dictionary of Chile*, 191).

like to have burnt our Ship, which was actually set on Fire by them; however our Men by their Address and good Fortune soon espyed and extinguish'd it.[94]

CHAP. V

The Buccaneers sail from hence for Juan Fernandez. Their Arrival and Adventures there. Captain Sharp is turn'd out, and Watling made Commander. They Attack Arica, and are forced to retreat. Arrive at Masco. They land at Port Ely again.

I am to observe before I leave this Bay of Coquimbo, which I did on the 7th of December, that 'tis an excellent Harbour about a League deep, good Ground, and you may come to an Anchor in seven Fathom-water within three little Rocks that lie to the South-side thereof, which are bold; and within the Country is high Land. From hence I shall pass over the Particulars of the Journal till Saturday December 25th, being Christmas-day in the Morning, at Sun-rising we made the Eastermost Land of Juan Fernandez,[95] and found it to lie in the Lat. of 33 d. 40 m. S., a very high Land to the North-end, but Southward low with a small Island adjacent thereunto, where we anchored on the 26th in fourteen Fathom-water: We found it a very refreshing Place to us both in respect to the Goats we found here, whereof we salted about an hundred, and took as many onboard alive, as to the fresh Water wherewith we filled our Vessels.

On Tuesday Morning about Ten we were forced to weigh by reason of the Southerly Wind which blew right in and makes a very bad Road; but two of our Canoes being away from us in filling of Water, we came to an Anchor at the S.E. end to stay for them, which we had no sooner done and brought our Ship up, but our Cable gave way and we were forced to stand out to Sea, and could not get to an Anchor again till Four in the Afternoon, (and that with much difficulty) in the right harbour of this Island, which is a round deep Bay of half a Mile long, the same being Land-lockt upon the E.S.E. round to the Southwards, till you come to N. by W. We made a shift to get a Cable ashoar, which we made fast to the Trees there for fear of the great Flaws[96] that would blow us off: We met with great store of Fish, and particularly Lobsters, in this Place, as also three Springs of good Water.

---

94 Cox wrote that "there was an Indian with a couple of Seal Skins blown up like Bladers, of which he made a float, and in the dead of the night came under the Stern of our Ship, with a Ball of Pitch, Sulphur, Oakum, and such combustible matter, and stuck it between the Rudder and Stern-port, and set it on fire with a Brimstone match . . . " ("Adventures of Capt. Barth. Sharp," 43).

95 The volcanic Isla Robinson Crusoe in the Chilean Archipiélago Juan Fernández. Cox noted that the buccaneers named it for Queen Catherine, the Portuguese wife of Charles II ("Adventures of Capt. Barth. Sharp," 51). Dampier described the island as "about 12 Leagues round, full of high Hills, and small pleasant Valleys; which if manured, would probably produce any Thing proper for the Climate. The sides of the Mountains are part Savannahs, part Woodland" (*New Voyage*, 67).

96 A flaw is "a sudden breeze, or gust of wind" (Falconer, *Universal Dictionary*, n.p.).

Saturday the first of January we fell to caulking[97] our Ship, and fit her up to go to the Streights[98] with all the speed we could. Next Day died our Master Mr. John Hilliard, whom we buried in the best manner we could on Shoar, solemnizing his Obsequies with three Volleys of small Shot.[99] We were blown out of the Bay on the Fourth with an hard violent Wind, and having made a shift to get to an Anchor again in the North-Bay on the fifth, our unhappy Divisions which had been long on Foot began now to come to an Head to some purpose; some being resolved to return for England or the Foreign Plantations, and that round about the Streights of Magellan, while others would steer a quite contrary Course. However it were, the main of the Design seemed to have been leveled at [the] Deposing me from my Command; in pursuance whereof on Thursday the 6th of January my Company well knowing I was bound through this Year, some of them got privately ashoar together and held a Consult about turning me presently out and put another in my Room. The main Promoter of this Design, as I was afterwards cordially informed, was a true-hearted dissembling New England Man, John Cox by Name, whom meerly for old Acquaintance-sake I had taken from before the Mast, and made my Vice-Admiral; and not for any Valour or Knowledge he was possess'd of, for of that his Share was but small:[100] From Consultation they proceeded to Execution, took my Ship from me, clapt me up Prisoner, and advanced one John Watling to the Chief Command, who having been an old Buccaneer had gained the Reputation of being a stout Seaman, tho' I think it never appear'd much:[101] However, the first thing he had to exert his unjustly-gotten

97 "To drive oakum into the seams of a vessel to prevent leaking" (Patterson, *Illustrated Nautical Dictionary*, 38).
98 The Straits or Strait of Magellan link the Atlantic and Pacific Oceans and split the southernmost tip of South America off the continent's mainland. This long waterway was named for Portuguese navigator Ferdinand Magellan (c. 1480–1521), who discovered it in October 1520. For a concise modern biography, see Dear and Kemp, *Oxford Companion*, 331–332.
99 Used here to mean buckshot, small shot, also swan shot or grape shot, also refers to musket balls and other small munitions fired from cannon, meant specifically to wound or kill crew rather than inflict damage. "Grapeshot would carry further than musket shot, perhaps more than a mile..." (Willis, *Fighting at Sea*, 48). An account of a 1697 attack by a pirate ship captained by Robert Culliford recounted that: "Their small shott were most Tinn and Tuthenage (*tutenaga*, spelter). They fired pieces of glass-bottles, d[itto] teapots, chains, stones and what not, which were found on our decks" (quoted in Hill, "Episodes of Piracy," 6).
100 John Cox wrote of this episode that: "A party of the disaffected to Captain Sharp got ashoar and subscribed a Paper to make John Watling Commander, pretending liberty to a free election as they termed it, and that Watling had it by vote. The reason of this mutiny was, that Sharp had got about 3,000 pieces of Eight, and was willing to come home that year, but two thirds of the Company had none left, having lost it at play. And those would have Captain Sharp turned out, because they had no mind as yet to return home. This Fewd was carried on so fiercely, that it was very near coming to a civil War, had not some prudent men a little moderated the thing; . . . " ("Adventures of Capt. Barth. Sharp," 49). William Dampier wrote that "while we lay at the Isle of John Fernando, Captain Sharp was, by general Consent, displaced from being Commander; the Company being not satisfied either with his Courage or Behaviour" (*New Voyage*, 9). Dampier himself would be among those to exit the expedition when Sharp was voted back in as commander following Watling's death.
101 Like their outright pirate cousins, the buccaneers (who considered themselves privateers) were known for resisting authority. They elected officers who they could also turn out by vote, and were not generally held to be disciplined sailors. Dampier would advise a ship captain against a trek through the Straits of Magellan "because our Men being Privateers, and so more wilful, and less under Command, would not be so ready to give a watchful Attendance in a Passage so little known. For altho' these Men were more under Command than I had ever seen any Privateers, yet I could not expect to find them at a Minute's call in coming to an Anchor, or weighing Anchor" (*New Voyage*, 63).

Power upon, was in the putting of Edmund Cook into Irons, upon the Accusation of a Servant of his, of the same Name, that the former had several times acted the Sodomite with him.[102]

CHAP. VI

They escape three Spanish Men of War, and sail away for Iquequa,[103] and get some Intelligence. Arrive at Guasco with their Adventures there: At Mora de Sambo. Touch at several Places, and sail for Gulpho Dolce, and make Peace with the Indians. Golpho Dolce describ'd.

Just before our departure from Juan Fernandez, which was the 12th of January, we descry'd three Sail of Spaniards coming about the Island, which made us hasten all our Men on board but only one Indian, who at that time hapned to be in the Woods, and got under Sail, and next Morning had a sight of two of them again; but well knowing under our present Circumstances, how likely they were to overmatch us, we endeavoured to give them the slip, which succeeded accordingly; and from hence to Sunday the 23d, nothing of moment befel us, not then neither, only that we espyed a dead Whale floating upon the Water, and hoisted one of our Canoes to take it in, supposing the same had been a Sail; and about the same time we sent two of our Canoes to Land to see if we could get a Prisoner; one whereof return'd on the 25th, telling us, They could see no People at all: But the other, on the Day following, brought us four Prisoners, whereof two were white Men and the other Indians, who gave us Information of several Things, telling us of several Towns there, such as Arica,[104] Chamo and Peko.

In pursuance to the Intelligence we received from our Prisoners, we formed a Design to attack the Town of Arica; in consequence whereof on Friday the 28th pretty early in the Morning, we put from our Ship which we left lying off at Sea with an hundred Men, got next Day under the Shoar, from whence at Night we put away, and on the 30th at 6 in the Morning landed our Men about two Leagues to the Southwards of

---

102 For modern studies of this topic as it relates to pirates in this era, see Burg, *Sodomy and the Perception of Evil*; and Turley, *Rum, Sodomy, and the Lash*.

103 "Originally called Ayquique and founded in 1556, Iquique languished as a small fishing village until the 19th century discovery and development of the rich silver mines of Huantajaya" (Bizzarro, *Historical Dictionary of Chile*, 385).

104 Arica, Chile. It was "a strong Town advantageously situated in the hollow of the Elbow, or bending of the Peruvian Coast" (Dampier, *New Voyage*, 8). Ringrose observed, "The hill of Arica is very white, being occasioned by the dung of multitudes of Fowls that nest themselves in the hollow thereof" (*Dangerous* Voyage, 93). Cox wrote that "Arica is seated in a very pleasant Vally by a River side, and is the Barkador or place for Shipping off the Treasure which comes from the Mines of the Mountain of Potosy . . . " ("Adventures of Capt. Barth. Sharp," 60). "At the height of its development in the mid-17th century, its population may have been as high as 100,000. . . . Attracted by its early wealth, Sir Francis Drake took Arica in 1579 and made off with 370 kg (800 lbs.) of silver" (Bizzarro, *Historical Dictionary of Chile*, 52).

the Town. From thence we had not advanced quite to the Town, but we were assaulted vigorously by the Enemy, who came powring upon us in very great Numbers: However we stood stoutly to it, gave them several Repulses, and made a great Slaughter among them, insomuch that we possest our selves once of the greatest part of the Town, and took [an] abundance of Prisoners. But their Fort being strong and still holding out, and their Numbers increasing every moment, and we our selves by this time having lost 28 Men, whereof Watling our Captain was one, besides 17 wounded, we thought it our best way to retire to our Boats again, which we did almost through insuperable Difficulties.[105] And I hope it will not be esteemed a Vanity in me to say, that I was mighty helpful to facilitate this Retreat, which brought my Men to recollect a better Temper, and unanimously upon our getting to our Ship, to restore me to my Command again.

Our Entertainment in this Place was so very bad, that being no ways incouraged to make a longer stay, we sailed away on the 31st, and nothing for the whole next Month till the 13th of March that was memorable occurred in our Voyage, but then we arrived at the Port of Guasco[106] about 4 in the Afternoon, at the South-side whereof stands three or four Rocks of a good bigness: And that we might not lose time this very Night we landed threescore Men, and going up into the Country about 6 Miles, lay till the Morning in a Church-yard, when we went down into the River, filled us some Water, and got onboard about an hundred Sheep. We did the same also the succeeding Days, wherein we not only stocked our selves with Water but also found good store of Meat, Wine and Fruit fit for our turn, which you may be sure we made bold with; And indeed we found no Body to hinder us, for the People were all fled upon our approach.

Having stay'd here no longer than our Conveniency required, we steered off again on the 15th,[107] and continued our Course to the 27th, when we made Land, which proved

---

105 In Cox's version of the attack on Arica, he noted that Watling split his command "into two parties, of which 40 were designed for the Fort, and the rest for the City." The latter force exchanged fire with Spaniards outside their defenses near the city, until those buccaneers designated to attack the Fort attacked the Spaniards on their flank. This action "made them run in good Earnest, and with what haste they could, get into their Breast-works." Though under cannon fire, the buccaneers took the largest of the breastworks, then spent time rounding up prisoners, an action Cox blamed for delaying the subsequent attack on the fort itself by about an hour. Had the assault begun sooner, Cox asserted, "no doubt we had carried it in spight of all Opposition." The attack on the fort failed, and the eventual retreat was a desperate affair during which Watling was shot in the loins ("Adventures of Capt. Barth. Sharp," 55–60).

106 Huasco, Chile.

107 Another disaffected group of buccaneers left at about this point. In his entry for 17 April 1681, Cox related that: "This day about Noon, to our great trouble, 45 of our Men left us, quitting our Emperour's service, and went away with our Boat and two Canoes, with what necessary things they wanted for their journey over Land. They would have stayed if we would have chosen a new Commander, but would not serve longer under Captain Sharp" ("Adventures of Capt. Barth. Sharp," 74). See also Ringrose, *Dangerous Voyage*, 140–141; and Dampier, *New Voyage*, 9, 11.

to be Mara de Sambo,[108] situate[d] twelve Leagues to the Northward of the Town of Arica, and next Morning we landed our Men at Port Ely, that lies about five Miles distant from the Southern Point, and took the Village of Hilo, where we heard News of our Men that were taken at Arica, they satisfying of us that they were all very well. Next Morning we stood off to Sea, and made the best of our way till Monday the 25th of April, when in the Latitude of 8 d. 10 m. we came to an Island, called Isle de Cano,[109] where I went on Shoar to see if I could anchor there: It appears round to the sight, and level at top, but not very high: Here is a good Anchoring-place from the S.E. end to the Northward; where we made no long stay, but sailing on for several Days arrived at last May 7th, at a small Rocky Island on our Starboard-side, where my self next Day left the Ship and went with two Canoes with four and twenty Men in them, to see if I could find any People upon the Place, which was called Chira.[110] I had the Fortune to take three Indian Men and eight Women, and towards Evening our Ship came up, on board of which I sent for more Men to guard our Prisoners. From hence at 12 at night I went to a Place called Resto, in order to take two small Vessels we had discovered to be there, which I successfully performed before Morning, when I return'd on board: Two Days after I went with 24 Men to seize a parcel of Carpenters who I understood were a building of two great Ships at a Place called Dispensa; we took them in the Morning in their very beds, with what other Necessaries we could find there, and we were so much the more glad at this Adventure by how we had great need of such sort of Artificers, as also Tools and Iron-work. But we had the Mortification next Day to have one of our Canoes, that was a little too deeply laden with Iron-work, to sink, whereby one of our Men, whose Name was John Alexander, was drowned.

After a stay of several Days in this Place, we weigh'd on Thursday the 26th, and fell down[111] the Lagune with our Ship, which we had now taken down to one Deck,[112] having first turn'd our Prisoners ashoar: Next Day we drove down[113] as far as the isle of Cavallo,[114] where we had one of our Men, whose Name was Jacobus Markcos, a

---

108 Ringrose identifies this as Mora de Sama, observing that "Under the Hill of Mora de Sama are eighteen or nineteen white cliffs . . . " (*Dangerous* Voyage, 91–92).

109 The Costa Rican Isla del Caño.

110 This is "the largest of the islands in the Gulf of Nicoya" (Baer, *British Piracy*, I:370).

111 "To *Fall down*, in navigation, to sail, or be conducted from any part of a river, towards some other near to its mouth or opening" (Falconer, *Universal Dictionary*, n.p.).

112 Writing in his journal about the work the buccaneers did on this vessel, Cox wrote that they "Cut off her upper Deck, and sunk her quarter deck" ("Adventures of Capt. Barth. Sharp," 79). These efforts were apparently made to make the deck flush, a term which "implies a continued floor laid from stem to stern, upon one line, without any stops or intervals" (from *Deck* entry, Falconer, *Universal Dictionary*, n.p.). The benefits of doing this included lowering a vessel's profile, increasing its hull's stability, and increasing its speed (correspondence with John Frayler, 22 March 2013; and Chapelle, *American Sailing Navy*, 392–394).

113 *Driving* is "the state of being carried at random along the surface of the water, as impelled by a storm, or impetuous current. It is generally expressed of a ship when [it has] accidentally broke loose from her anchors or moorings" (Falconer, *Universal Dictionary*, n.p.).

114 "Isola del Cavallo, another of the Gulf of Nicoya islands" (Baer, *British Piracy*, I:370).

Dutch-man, run away to the Spaniards.[115] By the second of June we were got abreast of the Bay of Snakes, where we found a Beef-Estanza about a Mile from the Sea-side, whither it's a Day's March from the Town of Nicoya, and at what time we examined our Prisoners, who telling us we were descry'd to the Eastward, made us alter our Design and stand another Course.

On the Fifth we saw the Isle of Canes[116] bearing S.E. from us, where we lay by to the East thereof, being incommoded with much Rain, but next Morning we sailed for the Gulph of Dolce,[117] which is 19 Leagues distance to the Eastward: It's indifferent high Land, with several high Rocks lying off the Shoar a little way, from whence we anchored about a Mile, stood in on the 7th in the Morning, when we sent away our Canoe to see for a Place to lay our Ship on shoar, but without Success. However we weighed the Day following, and sailed about three or four Leagues farther into the Gulph, where our Canoe came on board with one Indian-man and two Boys whom she had taken Prisoners, who informed us of divers Things concerning the Spaniards, that very much manifested their Hatred of us. With the Indians we made a Peace, who thereupon came both Men, Women and Children, in great Clusters onboard, brought us Hony and Plantains, and promised not only their Harbour for our use at any time, but withal that we should always have their Assistance for our Security, for which we kindly thanked them.

We built us an House here on the Ninth to put our Provisions in, and at the same time got some Tallow on shoar, and cut Grass to heat our Graving.[118] Here we tarried till the 28th, by which time we had made an end of careening our Ship, and were ready to sail for the Equinoctial[119] from this Gulpho Dolce, which I dignified with the Name of King Charles's Harbour,[120] and whereof before my departure, take this short Account.

---

115 Cox wrote of this episode: "On Saturday Jacobus Marquess, our Truchman or Interpreter, and an Indian Boy ran away from us to the Spaniards; this person was a Dutchman, who was a good Linguist, and left behind him 2,200 ps. 8/8 [pieces of eight] besides Jewels and Goods: But we had one Mr. Ringrose with us, who was both an ingenious man, and spake very well several Languages" ("Adventures of Capt. Barth. Sharp," 80).

116 The aforementioned Isle of Cano, or Isla del Caño.

117 Costa Rica's Golfo Dulce.

118 A process similar to careening, *graving* was "the act of cleaning a ship's bottom when she is laid aground during the recess of the tide." The maintenance mentioned here seems to have involved *breaming*: burning "off the filth, such as grass, ooze, shells, or sea-weed, from a ship's bottom, that has gathered to it in a voyage, or by lying long in a harbour. This operation is performed by holding kindled furze, faggots, or such materials, to the bottom, so that the flame incorporating with the pitch, sulphur, &c. that had formerly covered it, immediately loosens and throws off whatever filth may have adhered to the planks. After this, the bottom is covered anew with a composition of sulphur, tallow, &c. which not only makes it smooth and slippery, so as to divide the fluid more readily, but also poisons and destroys those worms which eat through the planks in the course of a voyage" (Falconer, *Universal Dictionary*, n.p.).

119 Used here as a synonym for *equator*.

120 King Charles I (1600–1649) had been beheaded by Parliamentary forces; his death ushered in the Commonwealth, then the Protectorate, under Oliver Cromwell (d. 1658). The monarchy was restored in 1660 with Charles II ascending the throne. In his 30 January 1681 journal entry, which detailed the buccaneers' disastrous attack on Arica, John Cox observed "the Anniversary day in commemoration of the Martyrdom of King Charles the First, for which I believe the English both have and will suffer severely, and Seas of our Blood be shed for Sacrifices to expiate the Murther of the best of Princes . . ." ("Adventures of Capt. Barth. Sharp," 55).

It's a most excellent Harbour and most secure from all the Winds that blow, the Water is deep and a bold Place, there being no Danger but what you can see: Here we found very good Water, and great plenty of Fish, Oysters and Muscles, with very good Plantains: On the North-side there is a good anchoring Place from 25, 20 to 14 Fathom-water close to the Shoar, and low Land; and on the S.E. end stands a pretty Island about two Miles long, and of an indifferent height, whose entrance is on the N.W. side thereof. About six Miles off stands a Point of land which I called Point Borrica, off of which lies an indifferent big Island and high. The Harbour it self [is] lying in North and South about four Leagues, and the W.N.W. and E.S.E. part, in about six.

CHAP. VII

They sail away. Their Passage and Arrival at the Isle of Plate, &c. Attempt to land at Paita in vain. Arrival at the Duke of York's Harbour, with some Account of it. Two Islands of Ice. Their other Adventures till their Arrival at Nevis.

We departed June 29th from Golpho Dolce, designing for the Isle of Plate, or Sir Francis Drake's Island, and on the 8th of July about six in the Afternoon fetcht in with Cape St. Francisco, plied still next Day to the Southwards, and on the 10th, the Wind being at S.W. espyed a Sail at 6 in the Morning which we chased all Day, and about 8 at Night took her. She came from Guayaquill and was bound for Panama, being loaden with Cocoa-Nuts, with which (they being much for our turn) we made bold, then turn'd our Prize loose with all the People. We tarried some Days at the River of

Period dress and period drama as depicted in "Capture of the Galleon" (Howard Pyle).

San Tiago to take in Water, during which time we thought fit to share our Booty, which amounted to 234 Pieces of Eight a Man; then continued our Voyage, and by Tuesday the 16th fell in 6 Leagues to leeward of Cape Passao, and next Morning espying a Sail to the E.S.E. we gave her Chase, came up with her about Ten and took her, the same proving to be an Advice-boat from Panama, wherein was no Booty, and whose Company told us many Things as News which we our selves mostly knew to be false. However two Days after, we lighted on a Ship[121] whose Cargo made us amends for the Deficiency of the other, the same being come from Lima, and laden with the very useful Commodities of Wine, Brandy, &c out of which we took about five hundred and fifty Jars: In this Vessel we took also a Prize of the lady call'd Donna Joanna Constanta, about 18 Years of Age, Wife to Don John _____, and the beauti-fullest Creature that my Eyes ever beheld in the South Seas.[122]

On Wednesday Aug. 3d we weighed and stood to Sea, weather'd Cape Passao next Day, made Monte Christo and the Town of Manta on the 6th, weathered Cape St. Laurence[123] on the 11th, and anchored next Morning at the Isle of Plate, where we sent about ten Hands ashoar to see and get us some Goats; but they found them so very shy that they could not take above half a score. We left this Place next Day plying to the Southwards, weather'd Cape Blanco on the 24th about four Leagues to the S.E. where there is a small Hill of Land that makes like an Island; but whether it be so or no, I know not. We arrived at Paita on the 28th, and attempted to Land there with our Men, but durst not, the whole Place being in Arms, and ready to receive us.

The remainder of this, and the whole Month of September, with part of October, being spent purely in Sailing, without any other Occurrences than Storms, Calms, and the like, which we do not think worth while the mentioning; We at last, on October the 12th, being Wednesday Morning by break of Day, fell in with a parcel of Islands, that were very high and craggy, the tops whereof were barren, and full of Snow; whereat we were somewhat concern'd, by reason we made the Place so unexpect-edly: But the reason hereof was the Current which deceiv'd us, no less than 120

---

121 The ship was the richly laden *El Santo Rosario*; Cox dated this episode to 29 July 1681, noting that the bucca-neers refused to take more than one of 670 cast metal ingots found aboard, believing them to be tin. The one taken turned out to be silver, later sold at Bristol for £75 ("Adventures of Capt. Barth. Sharp," 88–89). Baer described *El Santo Rosario* as the expedition's "great prize, from which the pirates took silver, gems and a *derrotero*, a secret book of Spanish charts of South America's west coast" (*British Piracy*, I:370). The *derrotero* later "bought Sharp his pardon . . ." (Lloyd, "Bartholomew Sharp, Buccaneer," 294).

122 According to Lloyd, Sharp's original manuscript of this campaign expanded on the taking of *El Santo Rosario*, including mention of the *derrotero*: "In this prize I took a Spanish manuscript of a prodigious value – it describes all the ports, roads, harbours, bayes, Sands, rocks and riseing of the land and instructions how to work the ship into any port or harbour between the latt. of 17 d.15" N to 57. S Latt.– they are going to throw it overboard but by good luck I Saved it – the Spaniards cryed out when I gott the book (farewell South Seas now) – allso I took in this prize another Jewell viz. a young lady about 18 years of age – her name was Dona Jowna Constantz – a very comely creature – her husbands name was Don Juan etc. The ship was called the *Rosario*" (Quoted in Lloyd, "Bartholomew Sharp, Buccaneer," 292).

123 "Cabo Lorenzo forms the southern boundary of the Bay of Manta, Ecuador" (Baer, *British Piracy*, I:369).

Leagues in our Meridional[124] distance: We being Strangers, and having no opportunity to try the Currents but by our Land-fall, we judged the same to set from the Lat. of 30 d. S. to the Streights of Magellan S. E. in the Lat. of 52 d. 15 m. S. About Eleven we came to a Commodious Harbour that was Land-lock'd, where we Anchored in 45 Fathom-water; but here we lost our Anchor at a flat Rock, and in our coming in, had the Misfortune to have a Man drop out of our Sprit-sail-top,[125] whom we took up again, but Dead, where we bury'd him ashoar, his Name being Henry Sherrall.

But tho' this Harbour is so secure from all Winds, yet it is subject to great flaws of the Mountains, so that good Cables and Anchors are requisite here, where we thought fit to ground our Ship, and unhang our Rudder, by reason of our Cables breaking: We met with good fresh Water, and store of wild Fowl here, to say nothing of the quantity of Mussels, Limpids, &c. which our Canoe brought us, as she did also an Indian Boy, who we took (while several others escaped) and brought on Board, but we could not understand a Word he said, only by Signs we could apprehend so much as that there was more People in the Lagune.

All that I could do, could not induce these People to come and Traffick with us; so that we bare away[126] on the 5th of November, and nothing memorable fell out to the 12th, when we struck two Fowls with our Fish-gigg[127] that were half Fish, half Fowl, for they had two fore Fins like a Turtle, and were belly'd like a Shark.[128] Five Days after we descry'd two Islands of Ice, which were near two Leagues in Circumference, and of a great height, for we were close to the side of one of them to see if they were Ice or no, and found it really so, as it was also exceeding Cold, and very Snowy Weather.

We were by this time come to a short Allowance, and you may be sure it was not like to mend with us, as long as we were out at Sea, which lasted for many Days; for tho' we saw some Land-fowl upon the 21st, yet we did not come up with any for many Days after; and nothing occurred in our Passage, besides the Death of a Negro-Boy

124 "Meridians, better known as lines of longitude, cross the equator and all parallels of latitude at right angles" (Dear and Kemp, *Oxford Companion*, 365).

125 Falconer described a *spritsail* as "a sail attached to a yard which hangs under the bowsprit. . . . It is furnished with a large hole in each of its lower corners, to evacuate the water with which the cavity, or belly of it is frequently filled, by the surge of the sea when the ship pitches" (*Universal Dictionary*, n.p.).

126 "*To bear up*, to put the helm up, and keep a vessel off her course, letting her recede from the wind and move to leeward; this is synonymous with *to bear away*, but is applied to the ship instead of the helm" (Smyth, *Lexicon*, 90).

127 "[A]n instrument used to strike fish at sea, particularly dolphins. It consists of a staff, three or four barbed prongs, and a line fastened to the end, on which the prongs are fixed: to the other end is fited a piece of lead, which serves to give additional force to the stroke when the weapon flies, and to turn the points upward after the fish is penetrated" (Falconer, *Universal Dictionary*, n.p.).

128 Of the creature seen on 12 November 1681, Ringrose wrote: "The Spaniard calleth these Fowles *Paxaros Ninos*. They weigh most commonly about six or seven pound, being about one foot, a little more of less in length" (*Dangerous* Voyage, 191).

we had on Board, who had both his Legs bitten off with Cold, till Christmas-Day; When to Solemnize that Festival as well as we could, we eat the only Hog we had left, drank some Jars of Wine, and made our selves as merry as we were able, which I did the rather that my Men might not mutiny.[129] I shall say nothing of the variable Winds, Tornadoes, and other inconveniences we laboured under from time to time, nor yet of the Porpoises, Grampusses, Dolphins, and huge Whales we met with, of which I am not able to give a particular Description, as I would, no more than of the vast Albicores we saw, whereof one that we caught weighed 140 Pounds. Neither do I know anything of an Enchanted Island some of our Company have talked of[i] to have seen in this Voyage.[130] However, I cannot pass over remarking the Death of one of our Men, whose Name was William Stephens, a Cornish Man, January the 15th, and who was observed, after his eating of three Manchaneel Apples[131] at King Charles's Harbour, to waste away strangely, till at length he was become a perfect Skeleton. To conclude therefore the whole, I shall only tell you, That after I had Sailed near 60 d. S. Lat. and as far, if not farther, than any before me,[132] I arrived on the 30th of January at Nevis,[133] from whence in some time I got passage for England.

[**Editor's Note:** John Cox, in his journal, provided the following brief summary of the end of the voyage.[134]]

[28 January] . . . When we were about the North end of Barbados, we stood in for Spike's Bay, and there coming a Boat off to us, who told us, they belonged to the *Richmond* Frigat,[135] we invited them on Board, being desirous to know how affairs stood since our Maritime pilgrimage; but they refusing, and standing in to the Shoar,

---

129 The Christmas Day feast included both a suckling pig originally taken from a bark at Nicoya and fattened up, and a spaniel the quartermaster sold for 40 pieces of eight (Cox, "Adventures of Capt. Barth. Sharp," 108–109).

130 In his entry for 9 January 1682, Ringrose wrote: "There was now a great ripling sea, rising very high; and it is reported, that sometimes and somewhere hereabouts, is to be seen an enchanted Island; which others say, and dare assert, that they have sailed over" (*Dangerous* Voyage, 205).

131 In Spanish, the *manzanilla de la muerte*, or little apple of death. Other buccaneer accounts remarked on its poisonousness, and that contact with its sap could cause intense blisters. See Exquemelin, *Buccaneers of America*, 42; Wafer, *New Voyage*, 100–101; and Ringrose, *Dangerous Voyage*, 44, 206.

132 At this point, Sharp's journal (according to the copy his editor William Hacke made for the Admiralty) added the words: "therefore do find by experience that there is no such a tract of land as the dutch call Terra Australis incognito." Glyndwr Williams observed, "The reference is to the supposed great southern continent of these latitudes, and there is some reason to think that Hacke, like many others, was a believer in the existence of this supposed land-mass. Not only does he seem to have edited out this skeptical reference, but Herman Moll's world map in the 1699 *Collection* marks the coastline of 'Davis Land.' This was a buccaneer 'discovery' of 1687 which added strength to the arguments for a southern continent" (From Williams' introduction to the 1993 facsimile edition of Hacke, *Collection of Original Voyages* [Delmar, NY: Scholars Facsimiles & Reprints], 14).

133 Sharp would later stand trial for piracy at Nevis, part of the Leeward Islands, being acquitted of separate charges in late 1686 and early 1687.

134 Cox, "Adventures of Capt. Barth. Sharp," 113–114.

135 HMS *Richmond* originated as the 89–foot long *Wakefield* in the Portsmouth Dockyard in 1656; it was renamed at the time of the 1660 restoration of the monarchy. Captain James Dunbar took it to Barbados in 1680–81. It was converted to a fireship in 1688 but was never used in this capacity. Recommissioned, it served for ten more years, being sold in New York in 1698 (Winfield, *British Warships 1603–1714*, 157).

made us suspect That the Frigat might make Prize of us; so we bore up the Helm for Antego,[136] where we arrived the 31 instant.

Our Commander sent a Letter to the Governour, and a Present of Jewels to his Lady: But the Governour refusing to let us come publickly on Shoar for common refreshment, the Lady returned the Present;[137] so we gave the Ship to 7 Men which had played away all their Money, and every Man shifted for himself. Some came into England, others went to Jamaica, New England, &c. And those who came to London were committed by his Majesties Order, and tryed and acquitted at a Court of Admiralty, where the Spanish Ambassador was Prosecutor.

[**Editor's Note**: Sharp's luck continued to hold for a while; he was twice acquitted of piracy at Nevis in 1686–7. A year later "he 'commanded' the tiny island of Anguilla, or Snake Island, the northernmost of the Leeward Islands, the haunt of Captain Kidd the pirate, and the home of a sparse population living 'without Government or Religion.'"[138] In 1699, when aged 49, he was at St. Thomas "under arrest for various 'misdemeanors.'"[139]]

---

136 The Caribbean island of Antigua.
137 William Kidd would try a similar tactic in 1699, when negotiating with colonial governor Lord Bellomont for his safe return to Boston. "As a sign of his good intentions he sent Lady Bellomont an enameled box with four jewels in it. By not sending it to his lordship, Kidd helped him keep his promise not to have anything to do with the treasure." He later sent her "another present, this time a gold bar; but on the advice of her husband she returned it." Kidd was later arrested, convicted of piracy, and hung in chains (Ritchie, *Captain Kidd*, 178, 180).
138 Lloyd, "Bartholomew Sharp, Buccaneer," 298–301.
139 Little, *History's Greatest Pirates*, 137.

3

"Those vile Remains of that abominable Crew" – Samuel Bellamy and the wreck of the *Whydah* (1717)

Samuel Bellamy is among the best-known of American "Golden Age" pirates, due in part to the 1984 discovery of his three-masted ship, the former slave transport *Whydah*, artifacts from which today grace a museum in Provincetown, Massachusetts.[1] He was born in Devon, England, circa 1689, just as the *boucanier* era was passing into that of a new breed of Anglo-American pirates. While the buccaneers at least paid lip service to the idea of legitimate privateering, the newcomers (in the words of one historian) "pretended neither lawful commission nor nationalistic justification and preyed on the vessels of all nations at their whim. They were 'a declared enemy to Mankind.'" Among their first incarnation were figures like the "arch pirate" Henry Every, privateer-turned-pirate Thomas Tew, and pirate-hunter-gone-wrong William Kidd, each of whom became known mainly for deeds in African and Asian waters.[2]

Many in the next generation of pirates active in the Americas gained experience as privateers during the long War of the Spanish Succession that opened the 1700s. Bellamy may have been among them. At some point after the 1713 Treaty of Utrecht ended that war, he joined up with ex-privateers such as Edward Teach drifting into piracy under Captain Benjamin Hornigold. Bellamy would, in fact, replace Hornigold when the latter's crew ousted him in May 1716 for refusing to attack English shipping. Bellamy then sailed for a while with the French pirate known as "La Buse" (The Buzzard), taking a few prizes near the Virgin Islands before separating at La Blanquilla. By early 1717, while cruising with pirate Captain Paulsgrave Williams as consort, Bellamy took the slaver *Whydah* near the Bahamas. Named for the West African slave port Ouidah, the *Whydah* was on its way from Jamaica to London carrying a cargo that included (according to testimony later introduced in court) about £20,000 worth of silver and gold coin. After a chase that lasted several days, its captain surrendered his vessel, which Bellamy put to use as his flagship.

Bellamy's flotilla was off South Carolina in early April, when Williams took a vessel commanded by a captain named Beer. The latter was taken into the presence of

---

1 See Clifford, *Expedition Whydah*.
2 Little, *Sea Rover's Practice*, 14–15.

Bellamy, who (according to Captain Charles Johnson in his *General History of the Robberies and Murders of the most Notorious Pyrates*) condemned his law-abiding prisoner as "a sneaking Puppy, and so are all those who will submit to be governed by Laws which rich Men have made for their own Security, for the cowardly Whelps have not the Courage otherwise to defend what they get by their Knavery. . . . " Bellamy then set forth his professional viewpoint: " . . . I am a free Prince, and I have as much Authority to make War on the whole World, as he who has a hundred Sail of Ships at Sea, and an Army of 100,000 Men in the Field. . . . "[3]

Captain Charles Johnson remains mysterious to historians – Daniel Defoe has been among those suggested as the real author of the *General History*[4] – and his quotation of Bellamy has likewise raised questions.[5] A short account of the episode (sans quotes) appeared in the *Boston News-Letter*.

[*Boston News-Letter*, 29 April–6 May 1717, 2]

Rhode Island, May 3. On Monday last arrived here one Capt. Beer from Block-Island, who belongs to this Place, and sail'd from hence about the beginning of April last, for South Carolina; who in that Latitude, about 40 Leagues from Land, was taken by a Pyrate Sloop and 40 Men, commanded by one Paul Williams, Captain, and Richard Cavily,[6] Master, both of this Island. This Capt. Williams has a Consort, a very fine London built Gally,[7] of 30 Guns, 200 brisk Men of several Nations; she is call'd the *Whido*, Samuel Bellame Commander, said to be born in the West of England: Capt. Beer was carry'd aboard the said Gally, where he was kept two Hours: Capt. Williams was for giving Beer his Sloop again after they had took out her Loading, but the Ship's[8] Crew ordered her to be sunk; so Williams put him on shore at Block-Island;

---

3   Schonhorn, ed., *General History*, 587.

4   For a recent work on the disputed authorship of the *General History*, see Bialuschewski, "Daniel Defoe, Nathaniel Mist, and the *General History of the Pyrates*."

5   "Some writers have questioned whether this conversation . . . actually took place, asking who would have transcribed the conversation," observed modern author Colin Woodard. He suggested that its source was Captain Beer, who later arrived in Newport. "Details of the conversation were almost certainly recorded by Rhode Island authorities and forwarded to London, where they were made available to the author of the *General History*" (*Republic of Pirates*, 174). Scholar Manuel Schonhorn, who identified a number of the evident published sources used in the *General History*, noted that its author sometimes applied a writer's license to them to help develop more interesting narratives. See Schonhorn, ed., *General History*, xxxi–xl, and endnotes.

6   Richard Caverley, who had been "seized from an English sloop on account of his navigational skills" (Woodard, *Republic of Pirates*, 145).

7   Describing the rigged galley prior to its capture by Bellamy, Woodard wrote: "The *Whydah* had everything a pirate might want. She was powerful, with eighteen six-pounders mounted and room for ten more in time of war. She was fast: a galley-built three-master capable of speeds of up to thirteen knots, perfect for transporting slaves across the Atlantic. Her 300–ton hull was capable of carrying between 500 and 700 slaves or a large cache of plundered treasure. It represented one of the most advanced weapons systems of its time, the sort of technology that could be extremely dangerous if it fell into the wrong hands" (*Republic of Pirates*, 156). A *galley-built* ship was one "whose decks are on a continued line for the whole length of the ship," as opposed to *frigate-built* ones which "have a descent of four or five steps from the quarter-deck and fore castle into the waist" (from *Frigate* entry, Falconer, *Universal Dictionary*, n.p.)

8   Note that in this era the term *ship* was usually reserved for large vessels with three masts, all of them square-rigged, i.e. with four-sided sails, hung in line with the bow-to-stern axis.

and we are told that the said Ship is cast away at Cape Cod, and 30 of her Crew drown'd.

Bellamy was dead by the time that article appeared; the ship mentioned as being lost at Cape Cod was the *Whydah*, though the figure given for loss of life was too small.

Bellamy on 26 April had made his last capture, a vessel named the *Mary Anne*. With a prize crew aboard the *Mary Anne*, Bellamy's flotilla continued along the coast, but a ferocious storm blew up that night. Both the *Mary Anne* and the *Whydah* ran aground. All on the former survived, but the storm's fury broke apart the *Whydah*, and only two of those aboard it came ashore alive. The authorities would soon round them up along with several survivors from the *Mary Anne*. Meanwhile, local residents spent several days gathering items from the wreck, from which over a hundred bodies were washed ashore (Bellamy's was never identified). Some showed signs of wounds, allegedly because when their vessels struck the pirates slaughtered their prisoners and those they had "forced" into their crew so they could not be witnesses against them.[9] On 4 May Governor Samuel Shute issued a proclamation which marked an effort to gather valuables and material evidence that had been recovered, as well as to track down any other survivors.[10] A month later, with eight alleged pirates in jail awaiting trial, a public auction was announced of "The Goods saved out of the Ship *Whido*, Capt. Samuel Bellame Commander, a reputed Pirate, Lately Cast away at the Back side of Cape Codd . . . "[11]

The eight suspects were eventually brought to trial. Two would be acquitted; the other six were sentenced to hang. The trial itself was documented in a 25-page report published in 1718, excerpts from which appear below. Among its contents are a wealth of material about Bellamy's operations, including to his time spent with Hornigold and La Buse; the forcing of crew aboard pirate craft; and Bellamy's use of what has become the classic Jolly Roger, a black flag "with a Death's Head and Bones a-cross."

ooooo

From *The Trials of Eight Persons Indited for Piracy, &c. Of whom Two were acquitted, and the rest found Guilty. At a Judiciary Court of Admiralty Assembled and Held in Boston within His Majesty's Province of the Massachusetts-Bay in New-England, on the 18th of October 1717, and by several Adjournments continued to the 30th. Pursuant to His Majesty's Commission and Instructions, found on the Act of Parliament Made in the 11th & 12th of King William IIId. Intituled An Act for the more effectual Suppression of Piracy. With an Appendix, Containing the Substance of their Confessions*

---

9   Konstam, *Piracy*, 210–211; Woodard, *Republic of Pirates*, 182–193; Cahill, *Shipwrecks and Treasures*, 15–17; Schonhorn, ed., *General History*, 592.
10 "A Proclamation," *Boston News-Letter*, 6–13 May 1717, 1.
11 "Advertisements," *Boston News-Letter*, 10–17 June 1717, 2.

given before His Excellency the Governour, when they were first brought to
Boston, and committed to Goal[12] *(Boston: John Edwards, 1718)*[13]

[**Editor's Note:** The trial opened on 18 October 1717, at Boston's Town House.[14] The court was headed by a commission including Governor Samuel Shute, Lieutenant Governor William Dummer (who will figure in other trials discussed in this volume), and HMS *Squirrel* Capt. Thomas Smart. After appointing a register for the proceedings, the court then directed the Suffolk County sheriff to "bring into Court the Bodies of Simon Van Vorst, John Brown, Thomas South, Thomas Baker, Hendrick Quintor, Peter Cornelius Hoof, and John Shuan, from His Majesty's Goal in Boston, they being Accused of and Imprisoned for Piracy, Robbery and Felony committed on the high Sea."

James Smith, the attorney presenting the case against the accused, read out the indictment, which involved charges stemming from the 26 April boarding and robbing of the Dublin-based vessel *Mary Anne*, then traveling from Boston to New York. That incident had also seen the prize's master and five crewmen forced aboard the *Whydah*, and their former vessel kept as consort to it. The document concluded that if found guilty of the said crimes, "all and each of them ought to be punished by Sentence of the said Court with the pains of Death, and loss of Lands, Goods and Chattels, according to the direction of the Law, and for an Example and Terror to all others."[15]

With former English barrister Robert Auchmuty appointed as their counsel, and local merchant Peter Lucy appointed as translator to assist French-speaking Shuan, the accused eventually entered Not Guilty pleas.[16] The court then adjourned to 9 a.m. on Tuesday, 22 October when, the indictment being read again, Smith began the case against the defendants:]

["]May it please Your Excellency, The Prisoners at the Bar stand Arraigned for sundry Acts of Piracy, Robbery and Felony by them committed at the time and place and in manner set forth in the Articles of their Indictment, to which they have severally pleaded Not Guilty. It is therefore my duty, in order to convict them of the heinous crimes they are charged with, to shew first, that the facts laid in the Indictment amount to Piracy, Robbery and Felony; and secondly, that they are all and each of them guilty of these facts; And if it shall plainly appear to your Excellency & the

---

12   An archaic rendering of *gaol* (jail).
13   Margin notes in the original text have generally either been eliminated or incorporated into footnotes in this transcription, which includes some corrections specified in the document's errata section.
14   The pirates were kept at Boston Prison, on the site of present-day 26 Court Street, about a hundred yards from the Town House, known today as the Old State House (Woodard, *Republic of Pirates*, 227).
15   "Convicted pirates, as traitors, were stripped of land and goods, a terrible punishment for their families," (Baer, *British Piracy*, II:397).
16   "Robert Auchmuty, a recent émigré from Scotland, became a prominent lawyer and jurist in Boston, rising to Advocate-General of the colony and, in September 1728, judge of the Vice-Admiralty court" (Baer, *British Piracy*, II:396). He would become one of the early associate judges of the Massachusetts Superior Court (Warren, *Harvard Law School*, 47–48).

Honourable, His Majesty's Commissioners now in Court Assembled, that both these points are proved by the strongest and most convincing Evidence, that a case of this Nature can admit of, I doubt not, but from a deep and awful sense of Your duty to God and the King, and a zealous just concern for the common rights and interest of Mankind, the safety of His Majesty's good Subjects in these remote parts, the Preservation and Security of their Trade, the Reputation of this Colony, and the honour of your Excellency's wise and happy Administration, You will Unanimously concur in Attainting & Condemning them to suffer the Punishment, which the Law requires, and their crimes most justly deserve.

["]Though the word, *Pirate*, in its proper & genuine Signification, implies no more than a Seafaring Person, it having been first invented and used by a People, I mean the Greeks, who in early and barbarous Ages, long before Solon and Lycurgus[17] had contrived their Laws, or Athens had become the Seat of Learning, thought it not only lawful, but honourable to practice Piracies and Depredations within their Seas, yet the Laws of all Nations, that have setled into regular Governments, define & declare a Pirate to be an Enemy of Mankind.

["]And therefore he can claim the Protection of no Prince, the privilege of no Country, the benefit of no Law; He is denied common humanity, and the very rights of Nature, with whom no Faith, Promise nor Oath is to be observed, nor is he to be otherwise dealt with, than as a wild & savage Beast, which every Man may lawfully destroy. *Quippe adversus Latronem*, &c. i.e. All persons by the right they have to preserve Mankind in general may and ought to draw the Sword against Robbers, with whom Men can have no Society nor Security.[18] Every one, that findeth me, shall slay me,[19] is the voice of Nature, that the sense of guilt must needs force from such impious Wretches, who have renounced the rights of Nature and Society, and declared themselves to live in opposition to the rules of Equity and Reason, which is the measure set to the Actions of Men for their Mutual Support and Preservation. And to finish the hateful character of this Monster, He is perhaps the only Criminal on Earth, whose crime cannot be absolutely pardoned, nor his punishment remitted by any prince or State whatever. For as a Pirate is equally an Enemy and dangerous to all Societies, the bonds, which are to secure them from violence and injury, being by him slighted & broken, every Power has equally a right to Insist upon Reparation and his being Punished. [. . .]

["]Now as Piracy is in its self a complication of Treason, Oppression, Murder, Assassination, Robbery and Theft, so it denotes the Crime to be perpetrated on the High Sea, or some part thereof, whereby it becomes more Atrocious,

---

17 Ancient lawmakers from Athens and Sparta, respectively.

18 *Quippe adversus latronem, si nequeant pro salute, pro ultione tamen sue omnes ferrum stringere* (Justinus, *Justini Historiae Philippicae* [38:4], 426). It can be translated as: "Since everyone draws his sword against a robber, if not for his own safety, at least for revenge" (Adler, *Valorizing the Barbarians*, 180, 182).

19 Genesis 4:14.

["]First, Because it is done in remote and Solitary Places, where the weak and Defenceless can expect no Assistance nor Relief; and where these ravenous Beasts of Prey may ravage undisturb'd, hardned in their Wickedness with hopes of Impunity, and of being Concealed for ever from the Eyes and Hands of avenging Justice. One of the most aggravating Circumstances, that attend a Crime, is the facility of its being committed, that is, where the Malefactor cannot easily be prevented nor discovered. Thus by the Law of God Theft in the Field was more grievously Punished, than Theft in a House.[20] And he that lay in wait for his Neighbour and slew him, was to be forced from the Sanctuary & put to Death without Pity.[21] By the Roman Law every Secret attempt on a man's Life by Assassination, Poison or other ways is Punished Capitally. So is Stealing Cloaths in places for Bathing. And both by that and the Divine Law a Night Thief may lawfully be Kill'd. *Ea sunt animadvertenda peccata Maxime, quae difficillime praecaventur,*[22] i.e. Those Crimes ought to be Punished with the utmost Severity, which cannot without the greatest difficulty be prevented.

["]Another Aggravation of this Crime is, That the unhappy Persons on whom it is acted, are the most Innocent in themselves, and the most Useful and Beneficial to the Publick; whose indefatigable Industry conveys amidst innumerable Dangers, besides that of falling into the hands of Pirates, Blood into the Veins of the Body Politick, and nourishes every Member. Ships are under the Publick Care, *Interest Reip. Us naves exerceantur,* i.e., It is the Interest of the State, that Shipping be improved. And to this Improvement our Nation owes its Greatness, Safety and Riches. Masters of Ships are Publick Officers, and therefore every Act of Violence and Spoliation committed on them or their Ships, may justly be accounted Treason, and so it was before the Statute of the 25th of Edward III.[23]

["]The Third Circumstance, which blackens exceedingly and augments a Pirate's Guilt, is the Danger, wherewith every State or Government is threatned from the Combinations, Conspiracies and Confederacies of Profligate and Desperate Wretches, united by no other tie (for what other can there be among such?) than a mutual Consent to extinguish first Humanity in themselves, and to Prey promiscuously on all others. [. . .]

["]But I need not go far to find out instances of this kind. It was but the other day we saw and felt with horrour the formidable power of such confederated Villains, who increasing in Strength in proportion to the number of their Crimes, & by every repeated act of cruelty being inabled to commit a greater, dared at last not only to

---

20 Exodus 22.
21 Deuteronomy 19.
22 The prosecutor is citing Marcus Tullius Cicero in *Pro Sexto Roscio Amerino*, 40:116 (Cicero, *Pro Publio Quinctio* . . . , 224).
23 The 1352 statute 25 Edward III defined treason; the legal connection between attacks on shipping and treason originated with jurist Sir Edward Coke (Stephen, *Constitution of Great Britain*, 58–59; Rediker, *Villains of All Nations*, 128).

infest our Coasts, seize our Ships, & put a full stop to our Commerce, but to enter our Harbours, and if Providence had not raised the Winds & Waves for our deliverance, who can say, but these vile Remains of that abominable Crew, reserved in a wonderful manner for Publick Justice, that others may be amended and deter'd by their example, might have been now giving Laws to those, from whom they expect to receive their doom.

["]Having offered to your Excellency this short and imperfect view of the Nature and Effects of Piracy in General, I beg leave in the next Place to observe briefly from the Principles of the Civil Law, which is appointed to rule and direct the proceedings of this Honourable Court, what Acts do necessarily infer the guilt and penalty of that Crime.

["]The first Act consists in the mind, *animus depradandi,*[24] and if it rests there only, it cannot fall under the censure of any humane Judicature; for as no Person can receive prejudice by Acts merely internal, it cannot reasonably be supposed to be the interest or concern of any to have one punished for them. But when these inward motions come to discover themselves by undoubted tokens, and break out in some open Act, tho' that proceeds no farther, than an endeavour or bare attempt, yet the Guilt and Punishment are the same, as if the intended mischief had been fully executed. [. . .]

["]It is otherwise at Common Law, and I wish the nature of the Prisoners' Guilt were such, as to leave the least room for considering the difference of the Laws in this point. How many Innocent lives had been saved, how many Families preserved from extream Misery and Ruin? Heaven has suffered them to prevail in their Attempts, and to pursue their execrable designs to the last degree of Wickedness. Their own Confessions, emitted before your Excellency, open a dreadful scene of Depredations, Robberies and barbarous Cruelties, exercised by them before they came on this Coast, where, to fill up the measure of their Guilt, they committed the Crimes, for which they are now Indicted, Namely, That on the 26th of April last they surprized and with Force and Arms entered a Vessel belonging to His Majesty's Subjects in Ireland, and having subdued the Master and his Crew and made themselves Masters of the Vessel and Cargo, they forced the Master with five of his hands (there being in all eight on Board) to abandon his Vessel and to go on board the Piratical Ship *Whido*, where soon after they perished in the Shipwreck. And in this respect, tho' the Prisoners are not charged with Murder in the Articles of their Indictment, yet I may justly affirm on the best Authorities in Law that they are truly Murtherers. *Nihil interest, Occidat quis, an cansam Mortis prabeat.*[25] They Robb'd the Cargo and Goods on board, and Navigated the Vessel in company with their Accomplices, who

---

24 Intent to commit depredation.

25 A Latin phrase that might be translated as "It makes no difference whether the man commits the homicide himself, or supplies the means of effecting it." See Allen, *Inquiry into the Rise and Growth of the Royal Prerogative in England,* 178–179.

were then possessed of several Ships and Vessels under the Command of their Capital Ship the *Whido*, in order to carry Destruction to the utmost parts of our Territories. The bare naming of these Facts is enough to prove the first point, viz. That the Facts laid in the Indictment amount to Piracy, &c. That the Prisoners are all and each of them Guilty of these Facts will evidently appear to your Excellency from the Testimonies of three Persons, who belonged to the Vessel, and were detained on Board after the Master and five more were turned away. And albeit the law presumes every Act of Piracy to be habitual, yet that in Fact they have long ago given themselves up to such a Flagitious course of Life, several worthy and credible persons will testify and declare. The Witnesses are here in Court, and I humbly move that they may be examined and interrogated on the several Articles of the Indictment.["]

[Prosecution Witnesses]

Then the Witnesses for the King were called into Court, and the Prisoners were asked if they had any just Challenge or Objection to make against them; but none being offered, the Witnesses were severally Sworn in order following, Viz.

An assortment of pistols and cutlasses figures in this illustration by N.C. Wyeth ("Preparing for the Mutiny," for an edition of Robert Louis Stevenson's *Treasure Island*).

Thomas Fitzgerald, late Mate of the Pink[26] *Mary Anne* of Dublin in Ireland, Testifyeth and saith, That on or about the Twenty-fourth day of April last past, the said Pink left Nantasket[27] in New-England, bound for New York, under Command of Capt. Andrew Crumpsley; and on Friday the 26th day of the said Month, between the Hours of Four & Six of the Clock in the Morning, they discovered two Sail a-Stern, viz. a large Ship and a Snow,[28] between Nantucket Shoals & St. George's Banks, which came up with the Pink in the Morning, with the King's Ensign and Pendant flying; the large Ship was found to be the *Whido*, whereof Samuel Bellamy, a Pirate, was Commander, Who ordered the Pink to strike[29] her Colours, and then hoisted out their Boat, and sent the Seven Prisoners, now at the Bar, on board the said Pink, all Armed with Musquets, Pistols and Cutlashes,[30] except Thomas South and John Shuan.[31] And further the Deponent, Declares & saith, That the said Thomas South, soon after he came on board, Declared to him the Deponent his Intention to make his escape from the *Whido*, as soon as he could, but Shuan was very forward & active on board the Pink, altho' he had no Weapon with him.

That Thomas Baker[32] went to the said Capt. Crumpsley with his Sword drawn, and ordered him to go on board the said Ship with all his Papers, and five of his hands, who were forced to obey, and accordingly Rowed on board the said Ship *Whido* in the Boat, while the Seven Pirates now at the Bar tarryed on board the Pink with the Deponent, and Alexander Mackconachy & James Dunavan. And in a little time after several more Men came from the Ship on board the Pink for some Wine, but finding it difficult to be come at, returned to their own Ship, with a small quantity of Wine and some Cloaths which belonged to the Ship's Company. And soon after the Boat

---

26 A *pink* was "a ship with a very narrow stern; whence all vessels however small, whose sterns are fashioned in this manner, are called pink-sterned" (Falconer, *Universal Dictionary*, n.p.). From a modern source: "a small, square-rigged ship with a narrow and overhanging stern, often used for the carriage of masts" (Dear and Kemp, *Oxford Companion*, 428).

27 An early English settlement in Massachusetts.

28 "A two-masted merchant vessel of the 16th-19th centuries, the largest two-masted ship of its period with a tonnage of up to 1,000 tons or so. It was rigged as a brig, with square sails on both masts" (Dear and Kemp, *Oxford Companion*, 541).

29 To *strike* in this context "implies to lower or let down anything, as an ensign, or topsail, in saluting, or, as the yards and topmasts in tempestuous weather. It is, however, more particularly used to express the lowering of the colours, in token of surrender, to a victorious enemy" (Falconer, *Universal Dictionary*, n.p.).

30 In fighting at sea at "close quarters, the usual tactic was to close aggressively with cutlasses and pistols. The cutlass, its blade ranging from two to two and a half feet (61 to 76 cm), was the close-quarters weapon used to clear the decks and deliver the coup de grace after other weapons had been used. Firearms and grenades were the weapons of choice – grenades to help clear the decks, muskets to kill men at longer range, pistols to kill men within a few feet, and seldom beyond six or seven yards (5.5 or 6.4 m). But once grenades had been thrown and pirates had boarded and discharged their pistols, the cutlass by default was the primary weapon at hand" (Little, *History's Greatest Pirates*, 154).

31 South, about 30, was from Boston in Lincolnshire; Shuan was 24 and had been born in Nantes, France. These and other details about the defendants cited in footnotes in this chapter emerged in the interrogation reports contained in this document's appendix.

32 Thomas Baker, 29, was born in Vlissingen (Flushing) in the Netherlands, and worked sometimes as a tailor ashore.

was again hoisted into the Ship, from whence he hail'd the Pink and gave orders to the Prisoners now at the Bar (who had forcibly taken Command of her) to Steer North-West and by North; Who answered, They would, and accordingly followed that Course, till about Four of the Clock in the afternoon, when the Ship and the Snow, which last was also taken and made a Prize of by Capt. Bellamy, and the Pink lay too,[33] it being very thick, foggy Weather. And presently after the Snow came under the Ship's Stern, and told Capt. Bellamy, They had made discovery of Land. Wherefore he ordered the Pink to Steer away North, which the prisoners did; And when Night came on the Ship put out a Light a-Stern, as well as the Snow and the Pink: And also a Sloop from Virginia surprized and taken by Capt. Bellamy the same day; and then all of them made Sail again.

The Deponent further saith, That Capt. Bellamy Commanded the said Simon Van Vorst[34] and Company on board the Pink to make more haste: Whereupon John Brown[35] Swore, That he would carry Sail till she carried her Masts away. That when the Deponent & Mackconachy were Prisoners, Simon Van Vorst told Mackonachy, That if he would not find Liquor he would break his Neck. Thomas Baker said they had got a Commission from King George, and Simon Van Vorst answered, ["]We will stretch it to the World's end.["][36] The Prisoners at the Bar Drank plentifully of the Wine on board the Pink that day they took her; went to the Helm[37] by turns and had the government of the Pink; and some of them ordered the Deponent to help to reef[38] the Topsail,[39] and do other services; She proved Leaky, so all hands were forced to Pump hard, and therefore they Damn'd the Vessel and wished they had never seen her.

The Prisoners Van Vorst, Baker and Brown with the Deponent, were divided into two Watches,[40] and about Ten a Clock at Night the Weather grew so thick, it Lightned and Rained hard, and was so very dark that the Pink's Company could not see the Shoar

---

33 The nautical term *lie to* (like *bring to* or *heave to*) means "to check the course of a ship by arranging the sails in such a manner that they shall counteract each other, and keep her nearly stationary; when she is said to *lie by* or *lie to*, having, according to the sea-phrase, some of her sails aback, to oppose the force of those which are full" (James, *Naval History of Great Britain*, I:xx–xxi).

34 Van Vorst was 24, and had been born in New York.

35 Jamaica-born Brown was 25 and unmarried.

36 Baer (*British Piracy*, II:397) noted that this remark invoked a line in the broadside *Verses Composed by Captain Henry Every, Lately Gone to Sea to seek his Fortune* (London, 1694). It ran in part: "My Commission is large, and I made it my self, / And the Capston shall stretch it full larger by half; / It was dated in Corona, believe it my Friend, / From the Year Ninety three, unto the World's end."

37 "Properly the word *helm* should relate only to the tiller," but the term was often used to include "the rudder, tiller, wheel and power applied" (Patterson, *Nautical Dictionary*, 90).

38 To shorten.

39 "The second sail above the deck. Men-o'-war carry a large single topsail, but merchantmen carry double topsails, as they are much easier to handle with a limited crew. A ship carries fore, main and mizzen topsails. The topsails are named respectively *upper* and *lower topsails*" (Patterson, *Illustrated Nautical Dictionary*, 187–188).

40 A *watch* is "the space of time wherein one division of a ship's crew remains upon deck, to perform the necessary services, whilst the rest are relieved from duty, either when the vessel is under sail or at anchor" (Falconer, *Universal Dictionary*, n.p.).

till they were among the Breakers: When the Deponent was at Helm, and had lost sight of the Pirate Ship, Snow and Sloop, and discerning that they were among the Breakers; they were about to trim the Head-sail,[41] but before they could do it the Pink run a-shore, opposite to Slutts-bush,[42] so called, to the South-ward of Cape Cod, between Ten and Eleven a Clock at Night, about which time the Prisoners at the Bar or some of them (being fearful as the Deponent supposed lest they should be Apprehended on Shoar) Cryed out saying, ["]For God's sake let us go down in to the Hould[43] & Die together.["] And the whole Pink's Company tarry'd on Board her all that Night: And in their Distress the Prisoners ask'd the Deponent to Read to them the Common-Prayer Book,[44] which he did about an Hour; And at break of Day they found the shoar-side of the Pink dry, so all of them jumpt out upon an Island, where they tarryed till about Ten a Clock, and eat Sweetmeats and other things taken out of a Chest, which Quinter[45] and Shuan broke open, and drank of the Wines which came out of the Pink: About which time two Men, viz. John Cole and William Smith, came over to the Island in a Cannoe, and carry'd the Pink's Company to the Main Land; and then Mackconachy discovered the Pirates, so that they were Apprehended by Warrant from Mr. Justice Doan at Eastham, from whence they were brought to Boston Goal. The Deponent further saith, That while they were on the Island, Brown and others would have him call himself Captain of the Pink, and give out that the Pirates on Board were his Men: and after the Prisoners had got on the Main Land they talked in divers Languages, and were in a great hurry to go to Rhode-Island the better to make their Escape, as the Deponent imagines.

James Dunavan, Mariner, late belonging to the Pink *Mary Anne*, and Brother-in-Law to Captain Crumpsley, late Master thereof, saith, That the said Pink belonged to Ireland, was Owned by the Subjects of the King of Great-Britain, and was Taken on the 26th Day of April last past, under English Colours by Samuel Bellamy, Commander of the Pirate Ship *Whido*, That Simon Van Vorst and the rest of the Prisoners at the Bar came on Board the Pink Armed, and had their Pistols Charged

---

41 *Head-sail* is a "general name for all those sails which may be set on the foremast and bowsprit, jib, and flying jib-boom, and employed to influence the fore-part of the ship" (Smyth, *Lexicon*, 376).

42 "The *Mary Anne* had been driven ashore on Pochet Island in the Southern Parish of Eastham, across from Slut's Bush, which was an overgrown piece of swampland in the middle of what was then the Isle of Nauset, and which had been given this intriguing name in 1626. That year, the *Sparrow Hawk* had been wrecked in this same area. One of the passengers, a Mr. Fells, had brought with him to the New World a woman he described as his maid and housekeeper, but who was suspected of being his mistress. When it became obvious that she was pregnant, the couple was ostracized by the rest of the ship's company and forced to camp out alone on this section of the Isle of Nauset, forever after called Slut's Bush" (Vanderbilt, *Treasure Wreck*, 52).

43 The *hold* is "the whole interior cavity or belly of a ship, or all that part of her inside, which is comprehended between the floor and the lower-deck, throughout her whole length. This capacious apartment usually contains the ballast, provisions, and stores of a ship of war, and the principal part of the cargo in a merchantman" (Falconer, *Universal Dictionary*, n.p.).

44 The Church of England's *Book of Common Prayer* originated during the reign of Henry VIII, who "conceived the idea of an English Litany (service book), and commanded Archbishop [Thomas] Cranmer to prepare it" (Weir, *Henry VIII*, 470).

45 Amsterdam-born Quinter (or Quintor) was 25.

with Powder and Ball, except Thomas South and John Shuan, and Ordered the Captain, with Five Hands more to go on Board the Ship with his Papers: And that the Prisoners at the Bar steer'd the Pink after Bellamy's Ship, as he gave Orders. That they drank plentifully of the Wines on Board; That Thomas South's Behaviour in the Pink was civil and peaceable. The Deponent further saith, That he heard John Baker threaten to shoot Mackconachy, Cook of the Pink, thro' the head, because he steer'd to the windward of his Course; and said moreover, That he would make no more to shoot him, than he would a Dog; and that he should never go on shoar to tell his Story. That one of the Prisoners asked the Deponent what he thought they were? To which Baker, who stood by, said, That the King had given them a Commission to make their Fortune, and they were sworn to do it. After the Pink was cast on shoar, they said, they were in as bad a condition then as before.

Alexander Mackconachy, late Cook of the Pink *Mary Anne* of Dublin, saith, That on the 26th day of April last past, in the course of their Voyage from Nantasket to New-York, they were taken by a Pirate Ship called the *Whido*, Commanded by Capt. Samuel Bellamy, That all the Prisoners at the Bar came on board the said Pink armed, except Thomas South and John Shuan, and made themselves Masters of the Pink; and that Simon Van Vorst ordered the Captain to go on board the Ship *Whido*, with his Papers and five of his hands. The Deponent further said, That the Pink was cast away opposite to an Island, called Slutts-bush; and after the Prisoners were carryed to the Main Land they looked very sorrowful, and made all imaginable speed in order to escape from the hands of Justice. That Thomas South behaved himself Civilly. That Thomas Baker cut down the Fore-mast & Mizen-masts[46] of the Pink when she run on shoar.

John Brett, Mariner, Testifyeth and saith, That in the Month of June 1716, he was taken by two Pirate Sloops, one Commanded by Capt. Samuel Bellamy, and the other by Capt. Labous;[47] They Damn'd the Deponent, and bid him bring his Liquor on board; they carryed him to the Island of Pynes,[48] and he was detained a Prisoner by them there Eighteen days; During which time John Brown was as active on board the Pirate Sloop as the rest of the Company: He told a Prisoner then on board, that he would hide him in the Hold, and hinder him from complaining against him, or telling his Story.

Thomas Checkley, Mariner saith, That he knows John Shuan the Prisoner at the Bar, That he belonged to the *Tanner* Frigot, one John Stoner, Master, and sometime in

---

46 The *foremast* is the "forward lower mast in all vessels," the *mizen* or *mizzen* is "the aftermost mast of a ship" (Smyth, *Lexicon*, 316, 481).

47 This French pirate's name has been given across different sources by variants such as Louis de Boure, Olivier le Vasseur or Levasseur, Oliver La Bouse or La Buse or De La Bouche. After evading Royal Navy pursuers at La Blanquilla in 1718, La Buse "eventually made his way to West Africa, meeting up with a number of Bahamian colleagues, including Edward England and Paulsgrave Williams. He had a long and generally prosperous career in Africa and the Indian Ocean until 1730, when he was apprehended by French authorities and executed on the island of Réunion. His grave is a popular tourist site there" (Woodard, *Republic of Pirates*, 321).

48 The Island of Pines, off Cuba.

March last the said Ship or Frigot was taken in the prosecution of her Voyage from Pettyguavue[49] to Old France, by Capt. Samuel Bellamy and Monsieur Labous, they pretended to be Robbin Hood's Men.[50] That Shuan declared himself to be now a Pirate, and went up and unrigged the Main top-mast by order of the Pirates, who at that time forced no Body to go with them; and said they would take no Body against their Wills.

Moses Norman says, That he knows Thomas [Brown] [Baker], and saw him in company with the Pirates belonging to Capt. Bellamy, & Monsieur Labous when the Deponent was taken with Capt. Brett in the Month of June, 1716. That he was carryed to the Isle of Pynes, and kept Prisoner Seventeen or Eighteen days, during all which time the said Thomas [Brown] [Baker] was very active on board of Capt. Labous.

John Cole saith, That on the Twenty-seventh day of April last he saw the Prisoners now at the Bar, in Eastham soon after they were cast on shore, That they tarryed a short time at his house, and look'd very much dejected and cast down; they enquired the way to Rhode-Island, and made great haste from his house, tho' he asked them to tarry and refresh themselves.

John Done, Esq., saith, That hearing there were some pirates journeying towards Rhode-Island, he pursued them with a Deputy Sheriff and other Assistants, and seized the Prisoners now at the Bar at Eastham Tavern about the 27th of April last; When they confessed that they belonged to Capt. Bellamy, Commander of the Ship *Whido*, and had taken the Pink *Mary Anne* in which they run on shoar.

[Defense Statements]

After the afore-named Witnesses were examined, the Court in favour of the Prisoners by giving them time to make their Defence, Adjourned till three a Clock Post Meridiem.

The Court met about that time, and the Prisoners were sent for & brought again to the Bar. When the President observed to them, That this Court had given them time, till now, to make their own Defence; Then demanded what they had to say for themselves.

Simon Van Vorst alledged, That he was forced by Capt. Bellamy's Company to do what he did, and would have made known his intentions to make his escape from the Pirates unto the Mate of the said Pink, but that he understood by the Mate's discourse that he inclined to be a Pirate himself; and therefore he did not discover his Mind to the Mate.

---

49   Petit Goâve, on Hispaniola.
50   For a recent study of this outlaw figure of medieval English ballads and folktales, see Knight, *Robin Hood*.

[~~Thomas~~] *[John] Brown* pretended himself also to be a forced Man, but produced no Evidence to make it appear to the Court.

Thomas South alledged, That he belonged to a Bristol Ship, whereof one James Williams was Master; That he was taken by Capt. Bellamy, and forced to tarry with him, otherwise was threatned to be put upon a desolate Island, where there was nothing to support him.[51]

A pirate marooned on a desert island (Howard Pyle).

Thomas Baker saith, That he and Simon Van Vorst were both taken out of one Vessel; That he attempted to make his escape at Spanish Town,[52] and the Governour of that Place seemed to favour his design, till Capt. Bellamy and his Company sent the Governour word that they would burn & destroy the Town, if that the said Baker, and those that concealed themselves with him were not delivered up. And afterwards he would have made his escape at Crab Island, but was hindred by four of Capt. Bellamy's Company.

Hendrick Quintor saith, That he was taken by Capt. Bellamy and Monsieur Labous, and they had agreed to let him go to the Coast of Crocus[53] in the French Vessel which they took him in, but the Commander thereof soon after dyed, and so Capt. Bellamy would not permit him to proceed the said Voyage, and he was unavoidably forced to continue among the Pirates.

---

51 This punishment was known as marooning. It was, the author of the *General History* wrote, "a barbarous Custom of putting the Offender on Shore, on some desolate or uninhabited Cape or Island, with a Gun, a few Shot, a Bottle of Water, and a Bottle of Powder, to subsist with, or starve" (Schonhorn, ed., 211).

52 Spanish Town, Jamaica.

53 Anguilla's Crocus Bay (Baer, *British Piracy*, II:397).

Peter Cornelius Hoof[54] declares and saith, That he was taken by Capt. Bellamy in a Vessel whereof John Cornelius was Master, That the said Bellamy's Company Swore they would kill him unless he would joyn with them in their Unlawful Designs.

John Shuan by his Interpreter saith, That he was sick at the time when Capt. Bellamy took him, and went on board the Pirate Vessel at the Instance[55] of Capt. Bellamy's Doctor, who advised him to stay with him till his Cure. And that when he went on board the Pink *Mary Anne* he did not carry any Arms with him; and that he hoped by going on board the Pink he should the sooner make his escape from the Pirates, for that he had a better way of getting his living than by Pirating.

[Prosecution Summary]

The Evidences[56] for the King being fully heard, and also the Pleas & Allegations made by the Prisoners at the Bar; His Majesty's Attorney General in a very handsome and learned Speech summed up the Evidence, and made his Remarks upon the whole; and after him the Advocate General having resumed the Articles of Indictment, the Depositions of Witnesses, and the Prisoners' defences, observed to the Court, That their pretence of being forced out of the respective Ships and Vessels they belonged to, by Bellamy and Labous, if it was true, can never excuse their Guilt, Since no case of Necessity can justify a direct violation of the Divine and Moral Law, and give one the liberty of Sinning, whatever exceptions may be allowed from Laws purely Possitive, and humane establishments: But on the contrary, that they acted freely and by their own choice, is most plain and obvious, for when they had the fairest opportunity, that could have happen'd, to make their escape, if they had intended it, by means of the Weather, Wind and nearness of the Shoar, they were obstinately resolved rather to hazard the Vessel and their Lives, than lose company with the *Whido*. That Shuan and South's going on board the Pink unarmed, is not material, nor does that circumstance extenuate the Crime in the least; if the rest had gone without Arms, as they might with security enough, considering their Number, and the weak condition of those, they had to deal with, and that the Pink then lay under Bellamy's command, Can any Person imagine they would have been less criminal? Suppose one or two Ruffians having no Arms meet a Man in the High way, and instead of threatnings and force, give him good Words, and at the same time put their hands in his Pockets and rob him of his Money, Are they not to be accounted Robbers because they did not draw a Sword or Pistol? The guilt is incurred by possessing the Innocent Person's mind with such just apprehensions and dread of extream danger, as to determine him to avoid a greater evil by exposing himself to a less one, that is to save his Life by delivering up his goods. That it appears evidently by the Deposition of Checkley, that Shuan at the time they both belonged to one Vessel voluntarily

---

54 Swedish and 34 at the time of his trial, Hoof had earlier served on Dutch vessels.
55 Insistence.
56 Witnesses.

joined the Pirates, and the three first Witnesses declare, That he acted his part on board the Pink with as much forwardness as the rest. That as to South's inoffensive behaviour on board, and his inclination to make his escape, it shews the presure of his guilt, but does not take off the weight in the eye of the Law. He was a part of the Crew, marked in the Watch Roll, intituled to a share of the booty, and imployed in such interprizes, as none but experienced and accomplished Villains could have been trusted with, and tho' at last perhaps he might not seem so active as the rest, yet his very presence on board the Pink involved him in the same crime, and *Facinus, quos inquinat, Æquat.*[57] Besides, it being proved by the Oaths of some of the Witnesses, That Bellamy and Labous did not press any body (nor indeed is it credible they would) and there being no reason to doubt of his listing himself amongst those, with whom we found him, his Repentance may save his Soul, but cannot except him from the punishment due to his crime: It being a Maxim both in Law and Morality, That an involuntary act taking its rise from an act that is voluntary, is likewise accounted voluntary. And as it hath ever been the glory of our August Monarchs to suppress Piracies by force & wholesome Laws, whilst other Nations have to their perpetual disgrace called Pirates to their assistance, and admitted them to a share of the Plunder.[58] As the English Trade is in the utmost danger at present in America from the prodigious Number of Ships exercised in Piracies, and as Providence hath wonderfully preserved us by destroying their Capital Ship with her Numerous Crew, and hath no less wonderfully delivered into the hands of Publick Justice, the Prisoners at the Bar, to teach others by their Exemplary Punishment to abhor the barbarous and inhumane practices, which have been fully proved against them, and whereof they stand convicted. He humbly moved His Excellency and the Honourable the Commissioners to proceed to pass Sentence of Death upon all and each of them, they being all equally Guilty; and concluded with saying, That to shew the least Pity in matters of this kind, where the Proofs are so full and Pregnant, and not the least presumption in favour of the Prisoners, would be the greatest cruelty. *Unnum Pietatis genus, in hac re esse crudelem.*[59]

[Conviction of Van Vorst, Brown, Baker, Quintor, Hoof, and Shuan; and the Acquittal of South]

The Court was Cleared, and the Evidences and Pleadings there upon against the Prisoners, with their Defences, having been duly considered, and the Question put with respect to each of the Prisoners severally, Guilty or not Guilty. The Court Voted Simon Van Vorst, John Brown, Thomas Baker, Hendrick Quintor, Peter Cornelius Hoof,

---

57 This might be rendered as: "Guilt makes equal those whom it stains."
58 "Smith was no fool and no doubt knew the stories of Drake, Hawkins, Raleigh and Morgan as well as anyone, so that this piece of historical revisionism may be a way of shaming the jurors into supporting the guilty verdicts to come, despite their community's fondness for pirate gold" (Baer, *British Piracy*, II:292).
59 *Pietatis genus est in hac re esse crudelem*: "In these matters to be cruel is a son's duty." See Garrison, *Pietas From Vergil To Dryden*, 35.

and John Shuan, Guilty of Piracy, Robbery, and Felony, according to the Indictment. But forasmuch as Thomas South at the time when the Pink *Mary Anne* was taken, went on board her without Arms in a Peaceable manner; and manifested and declared unto Fitz Gyrald the Mate of the Pink when she was in sight of the Ship *Whido*, and there was no sufficient grounds to hope for his escape, That he was taken from on board of a Jamaica Vessel and compelled utterly against his Will to joyn with the Pirates; And that he was fully resolved to leave them the first opportunity that should afterwards present, and his Behaviour and Carriage towards the Mate being always Civil and Kind; The Court were of opinion, and accordingly Voted, That Thomas South is Not Guilty.

[Sentencing of Van Vorst, Brown, Baker, Quintor, Hoof, and Shuan]

Then the Prisoners were brought again to the Bar, and severally asked (except Thomas South), Whether they had any thing further to say why Sentence of Death should not be Pronounced against them according to Law. And nothing being offered, more than what was said upon their Trial, by any of them, except John Brown; who pleaded the benefit of Clergy, which was denied him, being contrary to Law; The President Pronounced the Decree of the Court against the said Simon Van Vorst, John Brown, Thomas Baker, Hendrick Quintor, Peter Cornelius Hoof, and John Shuan in the words following. Viz.

["]This Court having duly considered the Indictment & the Proofs of the several Articles contained therein, together with your Defences, Have found you Simon Van Vorst, John Brown, Thomas Baker, Hendrick Quintor, Peter Cornelius Hoof, and John Shuan, Guilty, of the Crimes of Piracy, Robbery and Felony, as is set forth in the Indictment, And do therefore Adjudge and Decree, That you Simon Van Vorst, John Brown, Thomas Baker, Hendrick Quintor, Peter Cornelius Hoof, and John Shuan, shall go hence to the Place from whence you came, and from thence you shall be carryed to the Place of Execution, and there you and each of you, shall be hanged up by the Neck until you & each of you are Dead; And the Lord have Mercy on your Souls.

["]And the Court do also ordain, That all your Lands, Tenements, Goods and Chattles be forfeited to the King, and brought into His Majesty's use.["}

President. ["]Thomas South, The Court have found you not Guilty["]: Whereupon he put himself upon his Knees and Thanked the Court, &c. And after he was duly Admonished and had Promised Amendment of Life, &c. he was Dismist, and taken out of the Bar.

Then Charge was given to the Sheriffs to take special Care of the Condemned Prisoners, and the Court was Adjourned till Monday the 28th of October Currant at Nine a Clock in the Forenoon.

The Sentence was accordingly executed by Mr. Vincent, Marshal of the Court of Admiralty, the Sheriffs assisting, on the 15th day of November following at Charlestown[60] Ferry within flux and reflux of the Sea.

[Trial of Thomas Davis]

[Editor's Note: The session of 28 October began with the arraignment of Thomas Davis, on charges that included being involved in the original pursuit of the *Whydah*; its subsequent capture and the theft of both the ship and its cargo; the use of the *Whydah* as a pirate vessel; the late March or early April taking of a Scottish vessel traveling from Barbados to Britain; the stealing of its cargo; and its ultimate sinking. Attorney John Valentine was assigned him, and Davis pleaded Not Guilty to all charges. At this point the case was adjourned until 9 a.m. on 30 October, when prosecutor James Smith made his opening statement.]

The Prisoner[61] by order of Court being brought to the Bar, the King's Advocate[62] moved, That if the Prisoner's Council had any just Objections against the Indictment, that it would be proper to make them before the Witnesses on His Majesty's behalf were examined; but no Objections being offered, he spoke in the manner following.

["]May it please Your Excellency, The Prisoner at the Bar is arraigned before You, for Crimes of Piracy, Robbery and Felony by him committed on the High Sea, in Confederacy, combination and conspiracy with others like himself, i.e. Profligate and Felonious Persons; And has pleaded Not Guilty.

["]Tho' the Nature of the Proof, that is now offered to be made, is cumulative, yet your Excellence will easily observe, That the Facts to be proved are not so joyned and connected, as to make up and Accumulate the Crime, for take them singly and apart, every one is a direct and compleat act of Piracy, but are laid down as so many aggravated Circumstances,[63] whereby the Crime becomes more heinous, and the Prisoner's guilt proportionably more black and odious.

["]To attack a Free trading Ship is unquestionably an act of Piracy, and the subsequent Facts, viz. Entering on board, seizing and imprisoning the Master and his Crew, carrying away one Ship & her Cargoe, and robbing the Cargoe of another, and sinking the Vessel, are so many distinct Superveening Crimes, which differ only according to the several degrees of the wrongs and oppressions, which necessarily flow from

---

60 Charlestown, then a port adjacent to the north of Boston, Massachusetts; now incorporated within that city.
61 Shipwright Thomas Davis was 22 and was from Carmarthenshire, Wales.
62 James Smith.
63 "Aggravating circumstances are circumstances suggesting that a convicted defendant deserves a more severe sentence" (Nolfi, *Legal Terminology Explained*, 346).

thence. The Evidence, which I shall lay before Your Excellency is of three kinds. 1st. By the Prisoner's Confession. 2. By Witnesses. 3. By Presumptions called in the Civil Law *Argumenta et Indicia*.[64] [. . .]

[Prosecution Witnesses]

Then the King's Evidences were called into Court, and no objections against them being made by the Prisoner.

Owen Morris, Mariner, was first Examined upon Oath, Who Solemnly Testifyed & Declared, That he knew the Prisoner at the Bar, That he belonged to the Ship *St. Michael* whereof James Williams was Master; And in the Month of Sept. 1716 they left Bristol bound to Jamaica, & in Decemb. following the said Ship was taken by two Pirate Sloops, one commanded by Capt. Sam Bellamy, & the other by Loues Lebous, about Twenty Leagues off Sabria.[65] That they gave the said Williams his Ship and detained the Prisoner because he was a Carpenter & a Single Man, together with Three others of the Ship's Company. And further the Deponent saith, That the Prisoner was very unwilling to go with Bellamy, and prevailed with him by reason of his Intreaties to promise that he should be discharged in the next Vessel that was taken: And afterwards the Deponent was again taken in the Ship *Whido*, commanded by Capt. Prince[66] by the said Capt. Bellamy, who was then commander of the Ship *Sultania*,[67] taken from Capt. Richards, as the Deponent understood, and then he saw the Prisoner aboard the said Ship; at which time the Prisoner reminded the said Bellamy of his promise: when he asked him, If he was willing to go, He answered, ["]Yes["]; and then the said Capt. Bellamy replied, If the company would consent he should go: And thereupon he asked his company, If they were willing to let Davis the Carpenter go? Who expressed themselves in a Violent manner, saying ["]No, Damn him,["] they would first shoot him or whip him to Death at the Mast.

Thomas South, Mariner, lately taken by Capt. Samuel Bellamy in the Pirate Ship *Whido* cast away upon this Coast, and discharged upon his Trial, was admitted an Evidence, and being accordingly Sworn, saith, That the said Bellamy while he was in command of the said Ship *Whido*, took a Scotch Vessel off the Capes of Virginia last

---

64   Arguments and indications. For discussion and analysis of the evidence presented in this and other piracy trials, see Baer, *British Piracy*, II:xiii–xvii, and II:289–292;

65   Saba, an island near St. Eustatis.

66   Slave ship Captain Lawrence Prince fared well among Bellamy's men after they took the *Whydah* from him. "A number of them probably knew Prince, at least by reputation. He had been to Jamaica several times and been stranded there for months after his previous command was sunk in the great hurricane of 1712. . . . They could vouch that Prince, unlike many other captains, treated his crews fairly" (Woodard, *Republic of Pirates*, 169).

67   Late in 1716, Bellamy, operating off Saba with La Buse, captured the British *Sultana*, a ship-rigged galley similar to the *Whydah*, for which they would later exchange it. At the time of the encounter "*Sultana*'s captain, John Richards, was in his cabin, suffering from wounds he'd received earlier in the voyage and entirely unable to organize her defense" (Woodard, *Republic of Pirates*, 149).

Spring, Cut down her Masts & sunk her; That he heard the said Thomas Davis went on board her; but did not see him. That this Deponent thought it not prudent to be too familiar with the Prisoner, because it might tend to create a jealously in the pirates; that the Deponent and the Prisoner (whom they suspected, because he was a forced Man) would run away together. The Deponent saith further, That Capt. James Williams, commander of the Ship *St. Michael* (whose Carpenter the Prisoner was), Intreated the said Capt. Bellamy when he took him to let the Prisoner go. But the Ship's company would by no means consent thereto by reason he was a Carpenter; and Swore that they would shoot him before they would let him go from them.

Capt. John Brett, Mariner, Sworn, saith, That he was taken by Capt. Samuel Bellamy, before the Ship *Sultana* was taken from Capt. Richards, and then it was the Custom among the Pirates to force no Persons, but those that remained with them were Volunteers.

Capt. Thomas Fox, Sworn, saith, That he was taken by the Pirates in July last, and robbed, and they Questioned him, Whether any thing was done to the Pirates in Boston Goal: The Deponent answered, He knew nothing about them. And in particular a Dutch-man belonging to the Pirates, asked him about his consort a Dutch man in Boston Prison;[68] and said, That if the Prisoners suffered they would Kill every body they took belonging to New-England.[69]

Seth Smith, Prison-keeper in Boston, Sworn, saith, That when the Prisoner at the Bar was first brought to Goal, his illness hindred their talking together; but sometime after as they were discoursing, the Deponent observed to the Prisoner, That if he would be ingenuous & make a confession, he might save his Life, and be a good Evidence against the other Pirates in Prison. To which the Prisoner made answer, That he was abused by several of the Pirates that were Drowned, and was glad he had got from them, but knew nothing against the rest of the Pirates in Prison.

Then the King's Council[70] moved the Court that Capt. Thomas Glyn, a Prisoner for Debt upon Execution, might be brought into Court to give Evidence on His Majesty's behalf in this Trial: Whereupon the Court directed the Sheriffs, who have the keeping of His Majesty's Goal, to bring the said Glyn into Court.

Capt. Isaac Morris, Sworn, saith, That on the 14th of Sept. 1716 he was taken by the Pirates, but knows nothing of Capt. Bellamy or his Accomplices.

---

68   Presumably a reference to Thomas Baker, born in the Netherlands.
69   It is unclear what pirate outfit captured Fox/Fawkes, but no less a figure than Edward Teach later threatened to "burn all Vessels belonging to New England for Executing the six Pirates at Boston" (*Boston News-Letter*, 9–16 June 1718, 2).
70   Counsel.

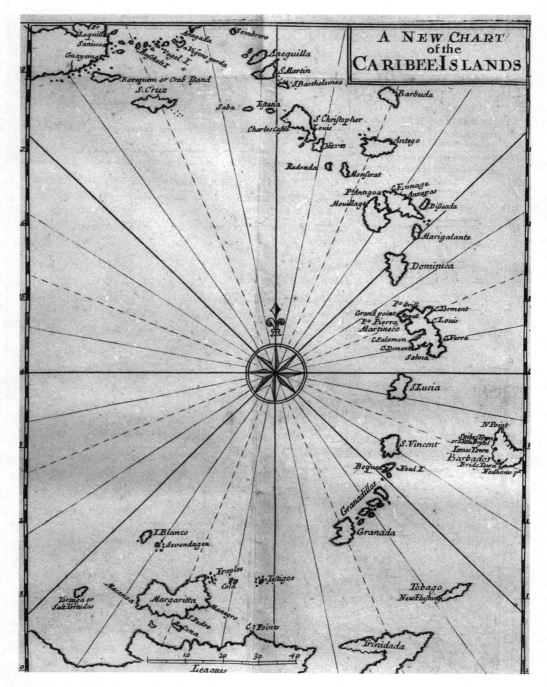

Blanco, or La Blanquilla, is visible at lower left in this map of the Caribbean Islands from Sir Hans Sloane, *A Voyage to the Islands Madera, Barbados, Nieves, S. Christophers and Jamaica . . .* (London: B. M., 1707 and 1725). Courtesy of the LuEsther T. Mertz Library of The New York Botanical Garden, Bronx, New York.

Capt. Thomas Glyn being brought into Court by the Sheriffs, and Interrogated upon Oath, saith, That he never knew the Prisoner till he was committed to Goal for Piracy, that he frequently afterwards conversed with him, but knew nothing against him.

[Defense Statements]

After which the Prisoner was desired by the President to speak for himself, Who said, That he was Carpenter of the Ship *St. Michael*, whereof James Williams was Capt., and Sailed out of Bristol in Great Britain in the Month of Sept. 1716 bound for Jamaica; and in Decemb. following the Ship was taken about Twenty Leagues off Sabria by two Pirate Sloops commanded by Capt. Samuel Bellamy, and Monsieur Lebous, who carryed the Ship's company to the Island of Blanco[71] where they were detained till the Ninth day of January last, when he and fourteen other Prisoners were put on board the *Sultan Galley*, then under the said Bellamy's command who had taken her from Capt. John Richards: And afterwards took another Ship called the *Whido*, in which Ship to his great grief & sorrow, he was forced to come upon this Coast, where she was cast-away: And he with one John Julian[72] only escaped Drowning. He further saith, That he was no way active among the Pirates, only as he was compelled by them.

Then Mr. John Valentine, the Procurator in Defence of the Prisoner, observed to the Court, That if he believed the Prisoner to be guilty of the crimes, for which he was Indicted, he should not appear on his behalf: That he hoped this Honourable Court upon consideration that there was little or nothing said, much less proved, against the Prisoner, they would acquit him as being Innocent, for that in all Capital crimes[73] there must be down-right Proofs and plentiful Evidence to take away a Man's Life, and then he made the following remarks on the Evidences. Viz.

["]That Owen Morris Testifyed, That the Prisoner at the Bar was forced and con-strained against his Will to continue with the said Capt. Bellamy and his company. And it appears by the Oath of Thomas South as well as by Morris, That the Prisoner desired Capt. Bellamy to release him upon his Caption[74] of another Vessel according

---

71 Dampier described La Blanquilla or Blanco as "a pretty large Island almost North of Margarita. . . . It is a flat, even, low, uninhabited Island, dry and healthy: most Savannah of long Grass, and hath some Trees of Lignum Vitae growing in Spots, with shrubby Bushes of other Wood about them" (*New Voyage*, 48).

72 Identified in testimony as a vessel pilot, John Julian was a "Cape Cod Indian, [who] was brought to Boston with the others but never was tried. He disappears from the records and may have died" (Dow and Edmonds, *Pirates of the New England Coast*, 130). According to Woodard, "Julian was separated from the rest, destined, by dint of his dark skin, for the slave market." He added: "It's possible that John Julian became a slave to the family of a future president. Around this time, a man named John the Indian was sold to John Quincy of Braintree, great-grandfather of president (and abolitionist) John Quincy Adams, and grandfather of President John Adams's wife, Abigail" (*Republic of Pirates*, 193).

73 A "*capital crime* or *capital offense* is a serious crime punishable by death. A case involving a capital crime or capital offense is a *capital case* or *capital criminal case*" (Nolfi, *Legal Terminology Explained*, 299).

74 Capturing.

to his Promise, but his company would not consent thereto; And altho' South says, that he believes the Prisoner was on board the Scotch Vessel when her Masts were cut down, yet the Prisoner utterly denies it, and South's belief was grounded upon hear-say.

["]Capt. Brett's Evidence serves only to inform the Court that the Pirates did not Press Men before the Prisoner was taken, but it is well proved, That when they took the Prisoner they compelled him to be among them, to his great sorrow and grief.

["]The Evidence of Thomas Glyn avails nothing, and if the Prisoner had been never so Guilty, his confession made in Prison, shall not be taken as Evidence against him on the Trial. And whereas the Prisoner stands charged in the Indictment with Accumulative crimes; the Procurator in Defence was pleased to say, That in the Trial of my Lord Strafford his Attainder was reversed because he was Indicted upon Accumulative Crimes, which is contrary to Act of Parliament.[75]

Then *Oliver Noyes*, Esq; was Sworn, and Declared, That he heard Capt. Richards say, That when he was taken by Capt. Bellamy, the Prisoner at the Bar was very desirous to be released & cryed, giving out that he was undone by being detained among them. And one of the Pirates hearing him lament his sad condition, said, ["]Damn him, He was a Presbyterian Dog, and should fight for King James,["] &c.[76]

Peter Osgood, Mariner, Sworn, saith, That he well knew the Prisoner, That he was a Sober, Honest Man, of good Conversation &c.

John French, Sworn, saith, That he has known the Prisoner above a Year & an half being frequently with him at Bristol, and in Antegoa,[77] that he had a good Character, and was reputed an Honest Man, &c.

Capt. John Corney, Sworn, saith, That he knew the Prisoner at Antegoa, when he was Carpenter to Capt. Moor, and never heard any harm of him.

Capt. Samuel Shrimpton, lately Arrived here from Jamaica, Sworn, saith, That he heard one of Davis's company say, That Davis the Prisoner was a forced Man, and he would Swear it.

---

75 Lord Strafford (Sir Thomas Wentworth) was tried and executed for treason in 1641. His accusers had "invented a kind of accumulative or constructive evidence, by which many actions, either totally innocent in themselves, or criminal in a much inferior degree, shall, when united, amount to treason, and subject the person to the highest penalties inflicted by the law" (Hume, *History of England*, 570). Baer noted that "Valentine's observations constitute a closing argument by defence counsel not allowed in English courts of the golden age but tolerated sometimes in the colonies. Its effect was to permit the accused to forego a full statement at trial's end" (*British Piracy*, II:397).

76 A reference to the Jacobite Rebellion of 1715.

77 Antigua.

Mr. Valentine moved, That an Affidavit[78] under the firm [and][79] Seal of a Notary Publick[80] in Great Britain, and in favour of the Prisoner should be read in open Court, but his Motion was rejected, being contrary to Act of Parliament, which directs that all Evidences respecting Pirates shall be given into Court *Viva Voce*.[81]

The President asked the Prisoner, What he had to say for himself: The Prisoner answered, He was not on board of the Scotch Ship that was sunk as was reported; and that he humbly conceived the Evidence produced in order to his condemnation sufficiently proved his Innocence: That his Attorney had fully spoke his Mind & Sentiments, and therefore he should not trouble this Honourable Court any longer in his Defence, or to that purpose.

[Prosecution Summary]

The Evidence on both sides being closed, the Advocate General reduced the whole under the following Heads. That the Indictment consisted chiefly of two parts. The first charges the Prisoner with Piracy committed by him sometime in February or March last, in the Windward passage on an English Ship named the *Whido*; the second with another Piracy about a Month after on a Scotch Vessel off the Capes of Virginia.

As to the first, Morris Depones, that when he was taken with Capt. Prince in the *Whido* he saw the Prisoner on Board the Piratical Ship *Sultana*, and heard Belamy ask him, if he was willing to go, which necessarily proves that the Prisoner at that time was under no confi[n]ement nor restraint, but one of the Crew, otherwise no such question could have been put to him. This he himself acknowledges and in his Confession[82] further declares, that tho' at first the old Pirates were a little shy of the new ones, and it seems not without good reason, they being only 80 in number to 130, yet in a short time the New Men being sworn to be faithful, and not to cheat the Company to the Value of a Piece of Eight, they all consulted and acted together with great unanimity, and no distinction was made between Old and New. Capt. Brett, who was likewise taken by Belamy, expressly says, that it was not the Pirates' custom to Force any Person, and that such as were amongst them were Volunteers. And whatever Sentiments the Prisoner might entertain of his Companions, it is plain from Capt. Fawke's Evidence that they had a very tender concern for him. Had he been really

---

78 An *affidavit*, "a sworn statement, is a written statement made under oath before an appropriate government official (usually a notary public) or a written statement sworn or affirmed by the maker to be true" (Nolfi, *Legal Terminology Explained*, 28).
79 Added as per the errata.
80 A "government official whose sole functions are to administer oaths and to be an official government witness to statements made under oath" (Nolfi, *Legal Terminology Explained*, 28).
81 By word of mouth.
82 See the report on the interrogation of Thomas Davis below.

affected with so much grief and sorrow as he pretends, it was not impossible for him to have made his Escape at some of the Places where he touched before he came on this Coast, viz. Blanco, the Spanish Main, Testages and Long Island; but it is not so much as suggested, that ever he attempted it, nor is it to be presumed as matters stood; the spoil was not yet divided, and it is obvious he expected to receive his share.

To the second, South declares, that Bellamy took the Vessel, cut down her Masts and afterwards sunk her, that the Deponent being Sick at that time was told by Bellamy's Crew, and does believe, that the Prisoner went on Board the Vessel: And further saith, that the Pirates could not be prevail'd with to discharge the Prisoner because he was a Carpenter. The truth is, Bellamy sent the Prisoner and another Carpenter on Board, who by his Order cut away the Masts and bored a hole in the bottom of the Vessel, and so destroyed her. This was a piece of work properly belonging to Carpenters, and it was for performing such Services the Prisoner made himself so acceptable and necessary to his Accomplices. To take off the weight of this Evidence it is said, that is it only Hear say,[83] but the Court will consider that the Deponent's belief, as it is grounded on the constant Reports of 120 Persons, to whom the Fact must needs have been notoriously known, is no less certain, than if he had seen the Fact committed. But admiting the Prisoner not to be directly concerned in sinking the Vessel, yet it is clear beyond contradiction, that he was on board the *Whido*, and one of the Crew, that surprized and took her, and consequently Guilty of Piracy; the other Facts laid in the Indictment being only circumstances, which help to give light to the discovery of his Crimes.

For the manner of proof required in capital Crimes, especially such as are Atrocious, as in the present case, He referred the Court (in answer to what was alledged on that point in behalf of the Prisoner) to the Authorities produced already, adding, that if the Crimes did appear by the Qualifications and Circumstances as they were libelled, to be made out by undoubted presumptions, altho' every circumstance be not proved by two direct Witnesses, the same ought to be held for Clear & Plain Evidence. And as to the Exception touching Accumulative Crimes, no reply seem'd needful, it being founded on a palpable Mistake, as if Accumulative probation and Accumulative Crimes were the same.

He observed in the last place, that the only plausible Argument offered in defence of the Prisoner was his being taken and detained by Force, which he could not possibly withstand, and since Necessity has no Law, and every Man is carried on with an irresistible Ardour to any means of preserving himself, some perhaps might believe him innocent, as not being answerable for the Crimes, which for his own safety he was

---

83 *Hearsay* is "[u]nfair evidence in the nature of rumor, technically an out-of-this-court statement offered to prove the truth of the matter asserted. . . . For the purposes of hearsay, a statement may be oral or written or nonverbal conduct intended to substitute for an oral or written statement. As a general rule, such secondhand testimony is not admissible" (Nolfi, *Legal Terminology*, 284).

obliged to commit; therefore to prevent any mistake that might happen concerning this important point, he Pray'd His Excellency and the Honourable Bench to consider, That Force can never justify nor excuse an Action, that is contrary to the Divine and Moral Law, for as it cannot be committed without expressing indirectly at least some contempt for the supreme Legislator, it would be the heighth of impiety to think that these Laws can admit any exception of Cases of Necessity. [...]

To conclude, The Crimes charged upon the Prisoner being direct Violations of the Laws of Nature as well as His Majesty's, and the proofs adduced being sufficient to convict him, He ought to suffer the pains of death, &c.

[Acquittal of Thomas Davis]

Where-upon the Court was cleared, and after a short debate, were of Opinion that there was good proof of the Prisoner's being forced on board the Pirate Ship *Whido* (in which he was cast on shoar) which excused his being with the Pirates; and that there was no Evidence to prove that he was Accessory with them, but on the contrary that he was forced to stay with them against his Will. And this Question being put, Whether Thomas Davis is Guilty of Piracy, Robbery and Felony according to the Indictment, or not? The Court Voted, That the said Thomas Davis is Not Guilty. And in less than half an Hour the Prisoner was brought again to the Bar, And the President declared, That the Court found him Not Guilty of the crimes for which he was Indicted; So he put himself on his Knees, Thanked the Court, &c. and was dismissed with a suitable Admonition. And then the Court Adjourned to Monday the Thirtieth day of December next at Nine a Clock Ante Meridiem.

APPENDIX
[Statement of John Brown]

The Substance of the Examinations of John Brown, &c. Taken by Order of His Excellency the Governour, on Monday the 6th of May, 1717.
John Brown being interrogated saith, That he was born in the Island of Jamaica, is 25 Years old, and Unmarried. About a Year ago he belonged to a Ship Commanded by Capt. Kingston, which in her Voyage with Logwood[84] to Holland was taken to the Leeward of the Havana by two Piratical Sloops, one Commanded by Hornygold[85] and

---

84 Since the mid-1600s "communities of logwood cutters had been scattered along the Caribbean shoreline of Central America. . . . Logwood was the boom crop of its day, producing a vivid red dye that transformed the clothing industry in Europe" (Konstam, *Blackbeard*, 28).

85 Benjamin Hornigold (often rendered Hornygold in period texts) began his pirate career at Nassau in late 1713, not long after the Treaty of Utrecht ended the War of the Spanish Succession. He was operating with Edward Teach by early 1715 near the Bahamas, where he ran what author Colin Woodard termed a "pirate republic." Hornigold would later accept the King's pardon and serve the governor of Nassau, Woodes Rogers, as a pirate-hunter. He died, either in battle or in prison, after a fight with Spanish ships in 1719 (Woodard, *Republic of Pirates*, 88–89, 97–100, 112–113, 131, 284–286, 314; and Konstam, *Blackbeard*, 62–67).

the other by a Frenchman called Labous, each having 70 Men on Board. The Pirates kept the Ship about 8 or 10 Days and then, having taken out of her what they thought proper, delivered her back to some of the Men who belonged to her. Labous kept the Examinate on board his Sloop about 4 Months, the English Sloop under Hornygold's command keeping company with them all that time. Off Cape Corante[86] they took two Spanish Briganteens without any resistance laden with Cocoa from Maraca.[87] The Spaniards not coming up to the Pirates' demand about the ransom were put a-shore and their Briganteens burn'd.[¶]

They Sailed next to the Isle of Pines, where meeting with 3 or 4 English Sloops empty, they made use of them in cleaning their own, and gave them back. From thence they Sailed to Hispaniola in the latter end of May, where they tarryed about 3 Months. The Examinate then left Labous and went on board the Sloop Commanded formerly by Hornygold, at that time by one Bellamy, who upon a difference arising amongst the English Pirates because Hornygold refused to take and plunder English Vessels, was chosen by a great Majority their Captain & Hornygold departed with 26 hands in a prize Sloop, Bellamy having then on Board about [90?] Men, most of them English. Bellamy and Lebous sailed to the Virgin Islands, and took several small Fishing Boats, and off St. Croix a French Ship laden with Flower and Fish from Canada, and having taken out some of the Flower gave back the Ship. Plying to the Windward the Morning they made Saba they spy'd 2 Ships, which they chased and came up with, one was Commanded by Capt. Richards, the other by Capt. Tosor, both bound to the Bay.[¶]

Having plundered the Ships and taken out some Young Men they dismist the rest & likewise Tosor's Ship, and made a Man of War of Richards's, which they put under the Command of Bellamy, and appointed Paul Williams Captain of their Sloop. Next Day they took a Bristol Ship, Commanded by James Williams from Ireland laden with Provisions, and having taken out what Provisions they wanted and 2 or 3 of the Crew, let her go. They parted with their French consort at the Island of Blanco and stood away with their Ship and Sloop to the Windward passage, where in the latter end of February last they met with Capt. Lawrence Prince in a Ship of 300 Ton called the *Whido* with 18 Guns mounted, and 50 Men bound from Jamaica to London laden with Sugar, Indigo, Jesuits Bark[88] and some Silver and Gold, and having given chase 3 Days took him without any other resistance than his firing two chase Guns at their Sloop, & came to an Anchor at Long Island.[89] Bellamy's crew and Williams's consisted then of 120 Men. They gave the Ship taken from Capt. Richards to Capt. Prince, and loaded her with as much of the best and finest goods as She could carry, and gave

---

86 "Cabo Corrientes, western Cuba" (Baer, *British Piracy*, II:397).
87 An "island off the north-west coast of Brazil" (Baer, *British Piracy*, II:397).
88 From which quinine was made.
89 In the Bahamas.

Capt. Prince above Twenty Pounds in Silver and Gold to bear his charges. They took 8 or 10 Men belonging to Capt. Prince, the Boatswain and two more were forced, the rest being Volunteers.[¶]

Off Pettiguavis[90] they took an English Ship hired by the French laden with Sugar and Indigo, and having taken out what they had occasion for, and some of the Men, dismist her. Then they stood away for the Capes of Virginia, being 130 Men in company, and having lost sight of their Sloop the Day before they made the Land, they cruised ten Days according to agreement between Bellamy and Williams, in which time they seized 3 Ships and one Snow, two of them from Scotland, one from Bristol, and the fourth a Scotch Ship from Barbadoes with a little Rum and Sugar on Board, so leaky that the Men refused to proceed farther. The Pirates sunk her. Having lost the Sloop they kept the Snow, which was taken from one Montgomery, being about 100 Ton, and manned her with 18 hands, which with her own Crew made up the number of 28 Men; the other 2 Ships were discharged being first plundered.[¶]

They made the best of their way for Cape Cod intending to clean their Ship at Green Island (having one Lambeth & an Indian[91] born at Cape Cod for Pilots), and on Friday the 26th of April last to the Eastward of Cape Cod took a Pink laden with Wine from Madera, last from Boston, bound to New York. They sent seven Men on Board called out on the Watch Bill, of whom the Examinate was one. He further saith, that there were about 50 Men forced, over whom the Pirates kept a watchful eye, and no Man was suffered to write a word, but what was Nailed up to the Mast. The names of the forc'd Men were put in the watch Bill and fared as others; they might have had what Money they wanted from the Quarter Master,[92] who kept a Book for that purpose, but this Examinate took only Cloaths. It was the common report in their Ship, that they had about 20,000 Pounds in Gold and Silver. That Peter Hooff was once whip'd for attempting to Run-away, and that he and every one of the other Prisoners were forced to Join the Pirates.

[Statement of Thomas Baker]

Thomas Baker being Examined saith, That he was Born in Flushing,[93] Aged 29 Years, by Trade a Taylor, and sometimes went to Sea, and sometimes followed his Trade ashore. That he was taken with 9 more in a little Boat coming from Cape Francois,[94]

---

90 Petit Goâve, on Hispaniola.
91 John Julian.
92 The quartermaster on a navy vessel was "an inferior officer appointed by the master of a ship of war to assist the mates in their several duties; [such] as stowing the ballast and provisions in the hold, coiling the cables on their platforms, overlooking the steerage of the ship, and keeping the time by the watch-glasses" (Falconer, *Universal Dictionary*, n.p.). A pirate ship's quartermaster, on the other hand, effectively commanded the crew until a pursuit or battle began, at which time the captain had total authority. See Schonhorn, ed., *General History*, 213–214.
93 The Dutch port of Vlissingen.
94 Cap-Haïtien, Haiti.

by Bellamy and Lebous, but they were sent away being Married Men.[95] This Examinate was never sworn as the rest were. Being on Board of Lebous he asked leave to go on Board of Bellamy, that he might have an opportunity of getting away, and accordingly he went, but found that Bellamy would not discharge him, on the contrary threatned to set him ashore on a Moroon Island if he would not be easy.[¶]

Samuel Bellamy's use of a "a large black Flag, with a Death's Head and Bones a-cross" provided the basis for depictions of the Jolly Roger such as this one (Richard H. Rodgers).

When they took Richards, Tosor and Williams they spread a large black Flag, with a Death's Head and Bones a-cross, and gave chase to Captain Prince under the same Colours.[96] They had on Board 20,000 or 30,000 Pounds, and the Quarter Master declared to the Company, that if any Man wanted Money he might have it. The Examinate came on Board the Pink which was taken off Cape Cod, Armed. The reason why he and the other Prisoners did not discover themselves to the Government when

95   As noted in a later chapter, pirate Edward Low would also refuse to force married men.
96   Pirates of this era often used red or black flags, usually incorporating symbols of threat, such as weapons; limited time, such as an hourglass; and mortality, such as the skull and crossed bones mentioned here, which commonly appeared on gravestones. If a chase began under a black flag, a red or "bloody" flag might be raised if prey showed fight or refused to slow down, to signal that quarter would not be given (Cordingly, *Under the Black Flag*, 116–117). By the early 1800s, pirates in the Caribbean and Gulf of Mexico tended to use only red flags.

they first came ashore was because they expected to get to Boston and there Ship themselves as Sailors. In all other particulars he agrees with what is above.

[Statement of Thomas Davis]

Thomas Davis Examined saith, He was born in Carmarthenshire[97] in Wales, Aged Two & twenty Years, is by Trade a Ship wright, and has used the Sea these five Years. He Sail'd from Bristol with Capt. Williams, and was taken on the 19th of December last, by Lebous 9 leagues to the Leeward of Blanco, and in January he joyned Bellamy's company. When the company was called together to Consuls,[98] and each Man to give his Vote, they would not allow the forced Men to have a Vote. There were One hundred and thirty forced Men in all, and Eighty of the Old company; and this Examinate being a forced Man had no opportunity to discover his Mind. From Blanco they Sail'd to the Spanish Main and water'd there, and from thence to a Maroon Island[99] called Testegos,[100] where they fitted up a Ship and Sloop of their own. All the New Men were Sworn to be true and not to cheat the company to the value of a piece of Eight. That when they chased the *Whido* they thought they had lost her, but came up with her the third day. Capt. Prince was treated civily. What Money they got in the *Whido* was not shared. Seven or eight of the *Whido*'s Crew joyned them. That their design in coming on this Coast was to get Provisions: That three of the Vessels, they took off the Capes of Virginia, belonged to Scotland, and the fourth to Bredhampston,[101] and when a Prize was taken the Watch-bill was called over, and Men put on board as they stood named in the Bill, and no more imposed on the forced Men than the Volunteers, they being all alike. The same day the *Whido* was lost, they took a Sloop coming from Virginia. The Ship being at an Anchor, they cut their Cables and ran a shoar; in a quarter of an hour after the Ship struck, the Main-mast was carried by the board, and in the Morning She was beat to pieces. About Sixteen Prisoners drown'd, Crumpsley Master of the Pink being one, and One hundred and forty-four in all. The riches on board were laid together in one heap.

[Statement of Peter Hoof]

Peter Hoof declares, That he was born in Sweden, is about 34 Years old, and left his Country 18 Years ago. He Sail'd for the most part with the Dutch on the Coast of Portobello, and has been with the Pirates fourteen Months. When he was taken by Bellamy in a Periaga, he belong'd to a Ship whereof one Cornelison was Master:

---

97   In the south-west of Wales, on the Atlantic coast.
98   Councils.
99   While *maroon* could refer to an escaped slave (and maroon communities emerged in the Caribbean and else-where), the term here may mean a remote place, as to maroon was to abandon a sailor on a desolate island. See *Trials of Major Stede Bonnet and Thirty-three Others*, in Cobbett, Howell, and Howell, *State Trials*, XV:1261–1262.
100 Venezuela's *Islas Los Testigos* are in the Caribbean to the northeast of Margarita.
101 Possibly a reference to Bedhampton, near Portsmouth on the south coast of England.

Three Weeks after he was taken they went to Portobello in a French Sloop with 60 Men on board; then stood for the Havana, and from thence to Cuba, where they met with a Pink, an English-man Master, and took out some Powder and Shot, and some Men. A difference arising amongst them about taking Prisoners; Some being for one Nation and some for another; and having at that time Two Sloops and about 100 Men, Hornygold parted from them in One of the Sloops, and Bellamy and Lebous kept company together. They turned to the Windward from the Isle of Pines to look out for a Ship of Force. The Money taken in the *Whido*, which was reported to Amount to 20,000 or 30,000 Pounds, was counted over in the Cabin, and put up in bags, Fifty Pounds to every Man's share, there being 180 Men on Board. No Married Men were forced. Their Money was kept in Chests between Decks without any guard, but none was to take any without the Quarter Master's leave.

[Statement of John Shuan]

John Shuan declares, That he was born in Nants,[102] 24 Years old, a Mariner. That Two Months and an half ago he was taken by Bellamy in an English Ship coming from Jamaica, commanded by an English-man, and a French-man, bound from Pettiguavis to Rochel,[103] with Sugar. This Examinate knows nothing of the Scotch Vessel's being sunk. When Crumpsley's Pink was taken on this Coast, He desired Bellamy to give him leave to go on board her, but could not obtain it, by reason he had not taken up Arms, yet afterwards Bellamy let him go. He further declares, That he never was upon the List as the rest were: That in the Ship he belong'd to the Pirates found 5,000 Livres,[104] and on board of Bellamy's there was a great quantity of Silver and Gold.

[Statement of Simon Van Vorst]

Simon Van Vorst declares, That he was born in the City of New-York, aged 24 Years. That he went from New-York to St. Thomas's, and from thence to Cape Francois, where he staid three Months, and came from thence in October last in a Boat with Captain Simson's Men, who were Prisoners there, and standing over to Cape Nicholas they spy'd two Sail, which came pretty near them, and firing a Gun brought them on board, three were dismist, being Married. The Examinate desired Labous to let him goe on board of Bellamy, and accordingly he went, Bellamy told him he must be easy until they could find Volunteers, or he would put him a-shoar on some Maroon Island. Next day they took a Sloop coming from Cape Francois, and soon after a French Ship, out of which they took Claret and Provisions. They cleaned at St. Croix,[105] where 3 of their Men Ran away, and one of them being brought back was severely whipped.

---

102 Nantes, France.
103 "La Rochelle, an Atlantic port in central France" (Baer, *British Piracy*, II:397).
104 Versions of the *livre* in France's colonies had different exchange values. For a comprehensive discussion, see McCusker, *Money and Exchange*, 280–290.
105 In the Virgin Islands.

Plying to Windward for what they could get they took Richards, Tosor and a Bristol Ship laden with Beef. He further declares, That he saw many of William's, Tosor's and Richard's Men Cry & express their Grief upon their being compelled to go with Bellamy. After the *Whido* was taken they gave Richard's Ship to Capt. Prince and put as great a quantity of Goods on Board, as he desired. They took 10 or 12 of Prince's Men of whom the Boatswain[106] and 2 or 3 more were forced. The Examinate went on Board Crumpsly's Pink Armed with a Gun and Pistol, and he and the other 6, who were with him were all equal as to the commanding part, being in course according to the list or Watch Bill.

[Statement of Hendrick Quintor]

Hendrick Quintor declares, He was born in Amsterdam, Aged 25 Years, a Mariner. That he was taken in a Spanish Briganteen by Lebous, Commander of the Sloop *Postillon*, and Bellamy, Commander of the Sloop *Mary Anne*,[107] and being bound to [L–?] the Pirates told him he should go the Coast of Crocus,[108] but afterwards they compelled him to stay, and during the time he was with them they took 3 French Ships and then clean'd at the Main Land of Hispaniola. After that they took 3 English Ships, viz. Richards's, Tosor's and Williams's, and went to the Main to Water, from thence to Testegos, the Wind blowing very hard they went to St. Croix; where a French Pirate was blown up. That this Examinate and the other six, who were sent on Board the Pink, were Forced men.

[Statement of Thomas South]

Thomas South saith, He was born in Boston in Lincolnshire, about 30 Years of Age, a Mariner. That he came from Cork in Ireland in a Ship Commanded by Capt. Williams bound to Jamaica, and was taken by the Pirate Bellamy about four Months ago. The Pirates forced such as were Unmarried, being four in number, two of them were drown'd in the *Whido*, a Dutchman and a Welshman. This Examinate further saith, That the Pirates brought Arms to him, but he told them, He would not use any, for which he was much threatned; they staid sometime at Spanish Town; when Captain Richards's Ship was taken this Examinate did not take up Arms, he only stood by the Rigging. That they came on this Coast to meet their consort Paul Williams, whom they expected to find at Block Island. That he was One of Seven, who were sent on board the Pink. He told the Mate that he was a forced Man, and if he could get a-shoar he would run-away. And further declares, That he has heard the other Prisoners say, They were compelled to joyn the Pirates.

---

106 *Boatswain* (usually pronounced "bosun") was defined in the era as a specialist "officer who has the boats, sails, rigging, colours, anchors, and cables committed to his charge" (Falconer, *Universal Dictionary*, n.p.).
107 Not to be confused with the pink *Mary Anne* taken just before the wreck of the *Whydah*, this was a captured sloop that Benjamin Hornigold gave Bellamy to command in 1716 (Konstam, *Piracy*, 208).
108 Caracas, on Venezuela's north coast.

[Editor's Note: Puritan Clergyman Cotton Mather (1663–1728) ministered to several of the condemned men, and later published a treatise on the *Whydah* episode.[109] While much of the pamphlet is a moralizing work, the convicted pirates themselves are sometimes quoted, and the contents occasionally shed light on life in Bellamy's company. The pamphlet also includes a brief description of the execution.]

> From *Instructions to the Living from the Condition of the Dead: A Brief Relation of Remarkables in the Shipwreck of above One Hundred Pirates, Who were Cast Away in the Ship Whido, on the Coast of New-England, April 26, 1717. And in the Death of Six, who after a Fair Trial at Boston, were Convicted & Condemned, Octob. 22. And Executed, Novemb. 15, 1717. With some Account of the Discourse had with them on the way to their Execution. And a Sermon preached on their Occasion* (Boston: John Allen, 1717).

[...]

About the latter end of April, there came upon the Coast a Ship called The *Whido*, whereof one Bellamy was Commander: A Pirate Ship, of about 130 Men, and 23 Guns. These Pirates, after many other Deprædations, took a Vessel which had Wines aboard; and put Seven of their Crew on Board, with Orders to Steer after the *Whido*. The seven Pirates being pretty free with the Liquor, got so Drunk, that the Captive who had the Steering of the Vessel, took the opportunity of the Night, now to run her ashore, on the backside of Eastham.

A Storm was now raised and raging, and the *Whido* ignorantly following the Light of her Stranded Prize, perished in a Shipwreck, and the whole Crew were every one of them drowned, except only one Englishman, and one Indian, that were cast on Shore alive.

It is credibly affirmed, That when these Barbarous Wretches, perceived that their Ship was breaking under them, and that they must Swim for their Lives, they horribly Murdered all their Prisoners (whereof they had a great Number) aboard, lest they should appear as Witnesses against them. The doleful Cries heard unto the Shore, a little before they Sank, and the Bloody Wounds found in the Bodies afterwards thrown ashore; were two great Confirmations of this Report.[110]

Alas! How far the Wickedness of Men may carry them!

The Good People of the Cape, saw a Marvelous Deliverance, in the Time of Tide, when these Monsters perished. Had it not been [such?] as it was, they had reach'd

---

109 For a modern biography, see Silverman, *Life and Times of Cotton Mather*.
110 At least one author has dismissed this, remarking that Mather "had observed storms not at sea but from the study of his manse in Boston" (Vanderbilt, *Treasure Wreck*, 50).

the Shore alive; and have made their way thro' the Blood of the Inhabitants, which Lived between Eastham and the Hook of the Cape, where they would there have met with Vessels to have served them, in a Return to the Trade, which they had hitherto been upon. The Delivered People said, Blessed be the Lord, who hath not given us as a Prey to their Teeth!

After some waiting for Direction, His Excellency, Colonel Shute, the Governour of New-England,[111] received such Orders, that the Trial of the Pirates, who had not been drowned, might be proceeded in.

Accordingly on Tuesday, October 22, 1717, there was held at Boston, a Special Court of Admiralty (according to the Act of Parliament) for the Trial of:

Simon Vanvoorst, who was Born at New-York.

John Brown, Born in Jamaica.

Thomas Baker, Born at Flushing in Holland.

Henrick Quinter, Born in Amsterdam.

Peter Cornelius Hoof, Born in Sweden.

John Shuan, Born at Nants in France.

And T.S.[112] Born at Boston in England.

The Last was Cleared;[113] But the other Six, after a very fair Trial, were found Guilty, and received Sentence of Death.

The Ministers of Boston, improved the Time, which the Clemency of the Governour allowed for that purpose, to bestow all possible Instructions upon the Condemned Criminals; Often Pray'd with them; Often Preached to them; Often Examined them, and Exhorted them; and presented them with Books of Piety, suitable to their Condition. And perhaps, there is not that Place upon the face of the Earth, where more pains are taken for the Spiritual and Eternal Good of Condemned Prisoners. On Friday, P.M. Novemb. 15 Came on the Execution of these Miserables.

What may now be offer'd is A Recollection of several Passages, which occurred in Discourse with the Prisoners, while they walked from the Prison to the Place of Execution.

---

111 Samuel Shute (1662–1742), governor since 1716.
112 Thomas South. Mather presumably referred to South by his initials as he had been acquitted.
113 As was Thomas Davis.

[Interview with Thomas Baker]

I. [Minister] Your determined Hour is now arrived. You Cry in the Destruction which God this Afternoon brings upon you. I am come to help you what I can, that your Cry may turn to some Good Account. How do your find your Heart now disposed.

[Baker] Oh! I am in a dreadful Condition! Lord Jesus, Dear Jesus, Look upon me!

[Minister] You are sensible That you have been a very Great Sinner, and that you are by your Sins Exposed unto the dreadful Displeasure of the Glorious and Holy God; Hands, which it is a fearful Thing to fall into!

[Baker] Oh! Yes; I am! And is it possible that such a Sinner should ever find mercy with God! O God, wilt thou pardon such a Sinner!

[Minister] My Friend, This is the very First Thing that I am to advise you of. There is a Pardon to be had! The Blessed God has made this Gracious Proclamation; That His Name is, A God Gracious and Merciful, Forgiving Iniquity, and Transgression and Sin. He is a God Ready to pardon. 'Tis your Duty to Lay hold on the Proclamation. The Pardoning Mercy of God is an Infinite Mercy. You have not Sinned beyond the Bounds of a Mercy that has no Bounds. Poor man, Try to Believe, Embrace, Admire this Wonderful Mercy. You have Sinned enough already: Don't add the Sin of Despair to all the rest. Our Good God is One who takes pleasure in them that hope in His Mercy.

[Baker] Oh! I wish I could! I wish I could!

[Minister] God help thee! I say this to you, As Great as your Sins have been, there are now Comforted in the Paradise of God, the Spirits of some who once committed the very same Sins that you are now guilty of.

[Baker] Lord! I have been guilty of all the Sins in the World!

[Minister] But now, O Give all the Attention of a Dying Man! I am to shew you, how the Pardoning Mercy of God may come to reach you. The infinite Merit in the Blood of your Saviour: 'Tis in this, that a Pardon swims down unto you. Mark attentively, Every word that I speak unto you. Our Lord Jesus Christ is God and Man in one Person. This Glorious Person has Died for us; has undergone the Punishment that is due to us for our Sins; has had His Blood shed, as a Sacrifice for us. This Blood obtains a full Pardon, for all that come and humbly plead it, with the Dispositions of a Repenting Soul. To Believe in the Blood of your Saviour [for it] is the way to obtain a Pardon. And, I have a Commission to make you now an offer of that Blood. O Take it, O Prize it, O Plead it! Beg of the Glorious God, that He would be Gracious to you for the sake of it! Friend, Here is a Ransom for thee!

[Baker] Oh! That I could do it.

[Minister] This Blood, I tell you, is what the Chief of Sinners are Welcome to. 'Tis a Fountain set open for them!

At the same time I am to tell you; That if the Blood of your Saviour be indeed applied unto you for your Pardon, it will, as I may say, Run warm in the Veins of your Soul. My meaning is, You will feel a Quickening Efficacy of it, It will Quicken such Wishes in your Soul as these: Oh! That the Sins which my Saviour hates, may be hateful to me! Oh! That the Lusts of my Heart may dy such a Death as my Saviour died! Oh! That my Mind may be filled with the Love of God, and have the Image of my Saviour produced in it. These Wishes will flame in you wonderfully, if the Blood of your Saviour be Sprinkled on you, for a Pardon.

[Baker] Oh! I can't come! I can do nothing! Pity me, O God! Sweet Jesus, Pity me!

[Minister] I'll mention to you a sweet word of your Great Saviour; A word worth a Thousand Worlds! Have you not a mighty Load Lying on you?

[Baker] Oh! A Load, A Load, that is too heavy for me!

[Minister] Now hear the Word of your Saviour: Come to me, All ye that Labour, and art heavy Laden, & I will give you Rest. Answer to it; But first Look to Him, for Help to give the Answer; my Saviour, I come unto thee!

[Baker] O Almighty God, Look upon me!

[Minister] I perceive you are in a very Great Agony. But, The Strait Gate must be Entred with such an Agony.[114]

[Interview with Simon Van Vorst]

II. [Minister] Poor Vanvoorst, What shall be done for thee? How do you find your Heart, in the dreadful Hour, that is now come upon you!

[Van Vorst] I hope, a Little Better than it has been.

[Minister] You will give all possible Attention, unto the Admonition of Piety, which are now to be given you.

Tho' you have so wickedly Chosen Other Gods; Yet the Glorious God, is Willing to be Your God. The God [whom you?] have denyed so many thousands of times; the God whose Baptism you have Sinned against; the God against whom you have Rebelled,

---

114 A reference to the "strait" or "narrow" gate mentioned in Luke 13:24.

after you had been by Religious Parents dedicated unto Him; This God is yet Willing to be Your God; then you are Happy to all Eternity! You will have a Place in His Holy City assign'd unto you.

[Van Vorst] What shall I do to be so Happy?

[Minister] Nothing in your own Strength. But having begg'd of God, that He would Strengthen you. You must first Bewail it Bitterly, that you have Served Other Gods. You have set up your Self in the Throne of God. You have placed on the Riches of this World, the Dependence you should have had only on God. You have hearkened unto Satan more than unto God. Are you sorry for this?

[Van Vorst] I hope I am.

[Minister] Well; What remains is this. Our Great Saviour is the Head of His People in the Covenant of God. You come into the Covenant of God, and He becomes Your God, when you heartily Consent, that your Saviour do for you those two Grand Things which in His Covenant with God for His People, He Engaged the doing of. God help you to understand this important Matter. Attend unto the Two Proposals.

In the first place, Do you Consent unto this; That the Sacrifice of your Great Saviour, should be your Atonement; and that God should be favourable to you for the sake of that alone?

[Van Vorst] I hope I do.

[Minister] But then, at the same time, Do you heartily Consent unto this; That your Saviour should by His Good Spirit quicken you to Live unto God; and render every Sin Loathsome unto you; and incline you to every thing that is Holy and Just and Good; and give you a New Heart; and make you a New Creature; and set up His Kingdom in your Soul, and Dwell and Rule there for ever.

[Van Vorst] I hope I do.

[Minister] In thus Returning to God, it is most necessary, that you should have a Heart full of Contrition, from the Sense of your horrid Sins against Him.

[Van Vorst] I have been a very Great Sinner.

[Minister] Of all your past Sins, which are they, that now Ly most heavy upon you?

[Van Vorst] My Undutifulness unto my Parents; And my Profanation of the Sabbath.

[Minister] Your Sinning against a Religious Education, is a fearful Aggravation of all your Sins. I pray you, to count it so.

[Van Vorst] I do, Syr.

[Minister] But I wish, that you, and all your miserable Companions here, were more sensible of the Crime, for which you are presently to be chased from among the Living.

Robbery, and Piracy! You felt the Light of God in your own Soul, condemning you for it, while you were committing of it. All Nations agree, to treat your Tribe, as the Common Enemies of Mankind, and Extirpate them out of the World. Besides all this, and the Miseries you brought on many good people, in their Disappointed Voyages, I am told, that some were Kill'd in your subduing of them. You are Murderers! Their Blood cries to Heaven against you. And so does the Blood of the poor Captives; (Fourscore, I hear,) that were drown'd when the *Whidau* was Lost in the Storm, which cast you on Shore.

[Van Vorst] We were Forced Men.

[Minister] Forced! No; There is no man who can say, He is Forced unto any Sin against the Glorious God! Forced! No; You had better have Suffered any thing, than to have Sinn'd as you have done. Better have died a Martyr by the cruel Hands of your Brethren, than have become one of their Brethren.

Or, If I should allow that you were at first a Forced Man, what were you Anon, when you came upon the Coast of Cape-Cod? Were not you one of those, who came Armed Aboard the Prize, wherein you were Lost? When the Mate so managed the Tack, that you Lost the Sight of the *Whidau*, and you might have Escaped easily from your Masters into our Arms, did not you Curse the Mate, and Compel him with a thousand Menaces, to Recover the Sight of your Ship? After your Shipwreck, did you fly into our Arms like men Escaped out of Prison? Or, did not you Endeavour still such a Flight from us, as might Enable you to Return unto the Trade you were now used unto? Is this the Conduct of a Forced Man?

We are Blessed with one of the Best Governours and a Person of uncommon Goodness, and Candour, and Clemency. He was as full of Desire to have shown Mercy, unto you, and your Friend Baker here, as was possible. Instances were made unto him on your behalf, by Friends; whom he set all possible value upon: I my self bore my part in the pressing Instances. But, when he Remonstrated unto us, the strong and full Proofs which there were of your being Active Pirates; and of your having the Cry of so much Innocent Blood against you; and we saw, his Apprehension, that he could not answer it unto God, no more than unto the King (whose Commands for all Severity upon you were very positive), we could say no more; but I must Approve and Applaud the Inflexible Justice that we see joined with a Temper full of Mercy in him.

Say now; What think you of the Bad Life, wherein you have Wandred from God? Can you say nothing, that your Worthy Parents (whom you have so kill'd!) may take a little Comfort from! [and] have some Light in their Darkness!

[Van Vorst] I am heartily sorry for my very bad life. I dy with hope that God Almighty will be Merciful to me. And I had rather Dy this Afternoon, I would chuse Death, rather than return to such a Life as I have Lived; rather than Repeat my Crimes.

[Minister] 'Tis a Good and a Great Speech; But such as I have heard uttered by some, who after a Reprieve (which you cannot have), have returned unto their Crimes. I must, now Leave you, in the Hands of Him who Searches the Heart; and beg of Him, Oh! May there be such an Heart in you!

[Interview with John Brown]

III. [Minister] Brown, In what State, in what Frame, does thy Death, now within a few Minutes of thee, find thee?

[Brown] Very Bad! Very Bad!

[Minister] You see your self then a most miserable Sinner.

[Brown] Oh! most Miserable!

[Minister] You have had an Heart Wonderfully hardened.

[Brown] Ay, and it grows harder. I don't know what is the matter with me. I can't but wonder at my self!

[Minister] There is no Help to be had, any where, but in the admirable Saviour, whom I am now to point you to. Behold, an Admirable Saviour so calling on you, Look to me and be Saved. O Wonderful Call! Salvation to be had for a Look!

[Brown] Ay, But I can't Look!

[Minister] Ah, poor, sad, lost Creature. Look for Help to Look! But mind What I say unto you. Set your Heart unto these Things, They are your Life. You are to Look unto your Saviour in all his Offices, for all His Benefits, [as?] you would hope to be received by a Saviour, who Receiveth Sinners.

First, You must Consider your Saviour, as a Priest; and you must say to Him, O my Saviour, I Rely upon thy Blood, that I may be cleansed from all my Sin! Is this the Language of your Soul?

[Brown] Yes, Syr.

[Minister] You must Consider your Saviour then also as your Prophet; and you must say unto Him; O my Saviour, Teach me thy Ways; and let not a Deceived Heart be my Ruine at the last! Is this also the Language of your Soul!

[Brown] Yes, Syr.

[Minister] You must now Consider your Saviour as your King; and you must say unto Him; O my Saviour, Enter into my Heart; Set up thy Throne there; Let thy Love be written there. Subdue all the Enmity of my Carnal Mind Against God. Cause me to Love Him! Is this the Language of your Soul?

[Brown] Yes, Syr.

[Minister] Oh! I wish it may be so. I take notice, you have your Prayer-Book with you; *Forms of Prayer*[115] may be of use to those who need the Assistances. You have had such put into your Hands; and you have also had the Bible bestow'd on you, with Leafs folded unto Psalms, proper for you to turn unto Prayers. But after all, A Soul touched with a sense of your Condition, and fired with the Sight of what [illegible], and what you want, and what your Saviour is willing to do for you, will cause you to Pray, beyond what any Forms in the World can do. I am jealous, that what you read sometimes, is rather for an Amusement, than from any real and lively Sentiment raised in you: For some of the Prayers you Read, are not pertinent unto your Condition. Friend, Make that Prayer, O Lord, I beseech thee, deliver my Soul! Make that Prayer, O Lord, Gather not my Soul with Sinners! Make that Prayer, God be merciful to me a Sinner. These are Great Prayers, though Short ones Great Prayers, when they proceed from an Heart broken before the Lord.

[Brown] Oh! God be merciful to me a Sinner!

[Minister] A Sinner. Alas. What cause to say so! But, I pray, What more Special Sins, Ly now as a more heavy Burden on you?

---

115 Prayer books employing this title in the era included *Forms of Prayer Proper to be Used before, at, and after the Receiving of the Holy Sacrament*, 2nd ed. (London: Benjamin Barker, c.1706); John Jeffery, *Forms of Prayer for the Morning and Evening of Every Day in the Week* (Norwich: F. Burges. 1706); John Worthington, *Forms of Prayer for a Family* (Gloucester: Luke Meredith, 1693); and *Forms of Prayer Collected for the Private Use of a Soldier* (London: H. Bonwicke, 1687).

[Brown] Special Sins! Why, I have been guilty of all the Sins in the World! I know not where to begin. I may begin with Gaming! No, Whoring, That Led on to Gaming; and Gaming Led on to Drinking; and Drinking to Lying, and Swearing, and Cursing, & all that is bad; and so to Thieving; And so to This!

[Minister] You ought now to Dy Warning [of] all People against those Paths of the Destroyer.

I will say to you, but this one thing more. God has distinguished you from your Drowned Brethren, by giving you a Space to Repent, which was denied unto them. I am Sorry you have made no Better use of it. It may be, the Space has been given, because God may have some of His Chosen, among the Six Children of Death.[116] God forbid, that the Space must be of no use to you, but only to aggravate your Condemnation, when you appear before Him.

[Interview with Peter Cornelius Hoof]

IV. [Minister] Hoof, A melted Heart would now be a comfortable Symptom upon thee. Do you find any thing of it?

[Hoof] Something of it; I wish it were more!

[Minister] To pursue this Good Intention, I will now give a Blow with an Hammer, that breaks the Rocks to pieces. I will bring you the most Heart-melting Word, as ever was heard in the World. We find in the Sacred Scripture such a word as this; Christ, who is God, does beseech you, Be ye Reconciled unto God. That ever the Son of God, should come to us, with such a Message from His Eternal Father! What? After we have so Offended His Infinite Majesty! After we have been so Vile, so Vile! – and He stands in so little Need of us! – To beseech such Criminals, to be Reconciled unto the Holy God, and be willing to be Happy in His Favour! O Wonderful! Wonderful! Methinks, it cannot be heard without flowing Tears of Joy!

[Hoof] Ah! But what shall I do to be Reconciled unto God?

[Minister] Make an Answer, make an Echo, unto this Wonderful Word of your Saviour. And, what can you make but this? – And for this also, you must have the Help of His Grace to make it; O my dear Saviour, I beseech thee to Reconcile me unto God.

[Hoof] Oh! That it might be so!

[Minister] A Reconciliation to God is the Only thing that you have now to be concern'd about. If this be not accomplished, before a few minutes more are Expired,

---

116 A reference to those sentenced to be hanged.

you go into the Savage Punishment reserved for the Workers of Iniquity. You go where He that made you, will not have Mercy on you; He that formed you will shew you no favour. But it is not yet altogether Too Late. An Hearty Consent unto the Motions of the Reconciler, will prepare you to pass from an Ignominious Death, unto an Inconceivable Glory.

[Hoof] Oh! Let me hear them!

[Minister] First, You must Consent unto This; O my Saviour, I fly to thy Sacrifice; I beg, I beg, that for the sake of That, thy Wrath may be turned away from me; I cannot bear to have thy Wrath Lying on me! Can you say so!

[Hoof] I say it, I say it!

[Minister] But then, You must Consent unto This also; O my Saviour, I Cry unto thee, to take away all that is contrary to God in my Soul; and cause me to Love God with all my Soul; and Conquer my depraved Will; and bring to Rights all that is Wrong in my Affections; and let my Will become entirely subject unto the Will of God in all things. Can you say so.

[Hoof] I say it, I say it!

[Minister] If it be heartily said, The Reconciliation is accomplished. But if you were to Live your Life over again, how would you Live it?

[Hoof] Not as I have done!

[Minister] How then?

[Hoof] In Serving of God, and in doing of Good unto Men.

[Minister] God accept you. Oh! That your Saviour might now say to you, as He said in a Dying Hour, unto One who died as a Thief, This Day thou shalt be with me in Paradise. I do with some Encouragement leave you in His Glorious Hands.

[Hoof] O my dear Jesus! I Lay hold on thee; and I resolve, never, never, to let thee go!

[Minister] May He help you to keep your Hold of the Hope set before you.

[Hoof] My Death this Afternoon 'tis nothing, 'tis nothing; 'Tis the wrath of a terrible God after Death abiding on me which is all that I am afraid of.

[Minister] There is a Jesus, who delivers from the Wrath to come; With Him I Leave you.

[Interview with Hendrick Quintor]

V. [Minister] Quinter, Thou are come into a Dark Time.

[Quintor] 'Tis a Dark Time with me.

[Minister] But will you receive it, if I bring you Light in this Darkness?

[Quintor] God be merciful to me!

[Minister] One who had been a Great Sinner, had this Experiment [*sic* – Experience?]; I said, I will confess my Transgressions unto the Lord, and thou forgavest the Iniquity of my Sins.[117] May not this be your Experience too?

[Quintor] I wish it may!

[Minister] When you have Sinned, you have swallowed a Deadly Poyson. With a Vomit of Repentance, and Confession, you must cast up this Deadly Poyson. If your Soul go away with it, you are Banished from God, and fixed in Eternal Miseries.

[Quintor] What shall I do?

[Minister] Do you Confess, That you are a very Great Sinner.

[Quintor] Yes, I confess, I have committed all manner of Sins.

[Minister] Are you Sorry for what you have done?

[Quintor] Heartily Troubled.

[Minister] But are you sensible, That you have an Heart full of Sin; An Heart that is desperately wicked? All the Sin in your Life, came out of your Heart. Are you Troubled, that you have such an Heart?

[Quintor] Heartily Troubled.

[Minister] Do you Look up to God for a New Heart?

[Quintor] With all my Heart.

[Minister] Do you own that God is Righteous in all the Evil that is come upon you?

[Quintor] Yes, I do.

---

117 Psalms 32:5.

[Minister] But now, Your Confession must be made, with a Faith Leaning on the Great Sacrifice. On every Stroke in your Confession of your Sin, you must add; Lord, Pardon my Sin, for the sake of the Blood of my Saviour.

[Quintor] I desire to do so.

[Minister] But, we are taught, He that confesseth and forsaketh shall find mercy. You will have no Opportunity now, for the Experiment of a Reformed Life; You cannot now Live to see whether you don't Return unto Folly. But however, your Heart must be so set against all Sin, that your Choice must be, Rather to Dy than to Sin.

Tho' Man cannot show you Mercy; your Life is forfeited, beyond the Reach of Mercy from the Government; yet upon a True Repentance, you will find Mercy with God. This Repentance is also the Gift. Oh! Keep Looking up unto Him; Lord, Give me a Repenting Heart! O my Saviour, Thou givest Repentance and Remission of Sins!

Man, Thy Immortal Soul is presently to Return unto God. A soul doing so, can look for nothing but His Fiery Indignation, and a dreadful Banishment from Him; Except it be a Soul with another Biass upon it, than what men have in their Depraved Nature. It must be, A Soul to which a Christ is Precious; to which a Christ is the Prince of Life, the Living Spring of all that is Good: A soul to which all Sin is odious, and more Bitter than Death: A Soul groaning under all its Evil Inclinations, as the most heavy Burdens; A Soul sick of attempts to find Satisfaction in Creatures: A Soul desirous above all things to Serve and please the Glorious God.

My Friend, May thy Soul now be found so disposed!

[Interview with John Shuan]

VI. The Last among the Sons of Death, was a poor Frenchman (called John Shuan), to whom, inasmuch as he understood not English, and had been a Roman Catholick, the Minister thus applied himself. [. . .][118]

Translated into English, at the Desire of the Bookseller.

[Minister] Most Miserable Sinner; You are a Prisoner of Justice, but, you are yet a Prisoner of Hope.

Our Lord and Saviour Jesus Christ is the Hope of Sinners; and indeed there is not Salvation in any other.

---

118 The French version of the interview has been omitted here.

This is a Saying most certain, and worthy to be of all Entirely received; That Jesus Christ is Come into the World, for to save Sinners.

But it is most Necessary, that you call upon your Saviour.

You make this Lamentable Outcry; O wretched man that I am; who shall deliver me?

Jesus Christ, the Great Saviour of the World, gives this Answer, Look unto me, and be Saved.

Understand you what I say?

[Shuan] Yes, Syr; I understand you very well.

[Minister] Ah, My Brother; The Cords of Death compass you, the Anguishes of Hell come upon you. But now, Call on the Name of the Lord, and say, O Lord, I beseech thee, Deliver my Soul.

Sinful Man, Return to the Lord, and He will have pity on you; and He will abundantly pardon you.

Do you understand me?

[Shuan] Yes Syr; and I thank you.

[Minister] But you must then take up with the Only Sacrifice and Intercession of Jesus Christ. No one comes at the Pardon of his Sins, on the account of his own Deserts, or thro' the Mediation of any Creature. Your Prayer must be this; O my God, The Obedience of Jesus Christ unto thy Law is my only Righteousness. For the sake of that Righteousness only grant that I may find pardon and mercy with thee! I Renounce, I Renounce all other Mediators.

What do you say to This? Do you Renounce all other Mediators?

[Shuan] I can't well tell, what to say to it?

[Minister] I commit your Spirit into the Hand of Jesus Christ, your Redeemer.

[The Execution]

At the Place of Execution, a Prayer was made by a Minister of the City; The Chief Heads whereof were;

An Adoration of the Divine Justice in the Evil pursuing Sinners;

– Whereof here was now a dismal Spectacle;

– And of the Divine Mercy in the Forgiveness offered unto the Chief of Sinners.

A Confession of what we have Committed, when we have Sinned;

– And of what we have Deserved;

– And of the Wicked Heart, which does Expose to all.

An Admiration of the Grace, which is Ready to Pardon;

And of the Blood which does purchase the Pardon;

With an Essay to Lay hold on it.

And Aspirations after the Token and Effect of a Pardon, in an Heart hating of, and mourning for, all Sin, and filled with the Love of God.

An Application of these things more particularly unto the Case of the Miserables now standing on the Scaffold;

With ardent Cries to Heaven, that Free Grace might yet have Triumphs and Wonders in them; and all Heaven be filled with Praises.

– Pleading, That nothing Less than an Almighty Arm, could change such Vicious and Obstinate Hearts as theirs; but that the Holy Spirit, who is the Arm of the Lord, is nothing Less than the Almighty God.

A Supplication, that God would Sanctifie the horrible Spectacle unto the vast Croud of Spectators now assembled; and Effectually Caution them to Shun the Paths of the Destroyer.

Especially, the Young People; That they might Betimes give themselves up to the Conduct of their Saviour; Lest their Disobedience provoke Him to Leave them in the Hands of the Destroyer.

And a Supplication for our Sea-faring People; That they may more generally Turn and Live unto God; That they may not fall into the Hands of Pirates; That such as are fallen into their Hands, may not fall into their Wayes; That the poor Captives may with Cries to God that shall pierce the Heavens, procure His Good Providence to work for their Deliverance; And, That the Pirates now infesting the Seas, may have a Remarkable Blast from Heaven following of them; the Sea-monsters, of all the most cruel, be Extinguished; and that the Methods now taking [sic – being taken] by the British Crown for the Suppression of these Mischiefs may be prospered.

On the Scaffold, as the Last Minute came on, several of the Malefactors discovered a great Consternation.

Baker and Hoof appeared very distinguishingly Penitent.

But Brown behaved himself at such a rate as one would hardly imagine that any *Compos Mentis*[119] could have done so. He broke out into furious Expressions, which had in them too much of the Language he had been used unto. Then he fell to Reading of Prayers, not very pertinently chosen. At length he made a Short Speech, which every body trembled at; Advising Sailors, to beware of all wicked Living, such as his own had been; especially to beware of falling into the Hands of the Pirates: But if they did, and were forced to join with them, then, to have a care whom they kept, and whom they let go, and what Countries they come into.

In such amazing Terms did he make his Exit! With such Madness, Go to the Dead!

The rest said Little, only Vanvoorst, having (with Baker) Sung a Dutch Psalm, Exhorted Young Persons to Lead a Life of Religion, and keep the Sabbath, and carry it well to their Parents.

Behold, Reader, The End of Piracy!

---

119 Sound mind.

4

"A sort of People, who may be truly called Enemies to Mankind" – The *Boston News-Letter* covers the era of Blackbeard (1717–1719)

The first issue of the *Boston News-Letter* appeared late in April, 1704. For fourteen years (until the *Jamaica Courant* began publication) it was the only newspaper in the British colonies in America. In the words of the modern writer Colin Woodard, "[t]he existence of the *News-Letter* made Boston the hub of eighteenth-century America's information infrastructure. . . . Were there news of relevance to the inhabitants of Boston – a pirate attack for instance – the *News-Letter* was where most of them would first hear of it."[1]

Some of its most vivid piracy coverage involved the doings of one Edward Teach or Thatch (or other variant spellings), whose remarkable facial hair earned him the nickname "Blackbeard."[2] Possibly born in or near Bristol, England circa 1680, he was presumably among the many privateers active in the War of the Spanish Succession. After the Treaty of Utrecht ended that conflict, Teach (like Samuel Bellamy) began his piracy career in the crew of Benjamin Hornigold, eventually going off on his own in a prize vessel Hornigold gave him late in 1716. Word of Bellamy's death in 1717 and the trial and hanging of several of his crew in Boston enraged Teach, who (in Woodard's words) "appears to have declared war on the British Empire."[3] He certainly succeeded in terrorizing parts of the Atlantic coast, causing what historian Angus Konstam called a "pirate crisis that swept North America in the summer of 1718. . . . "[4]

Teach was not the only pirate operating at the time, as can be seen in this chapter's selection of 1717–1719 articles from the *Boston News Letter*. He was, however, the most colorful. In describing the long black beard that gave Teach his nickname, Captain Charles Johnson wrote in the *General History* how the pirate "was accustomed to twist it with Ribbons, in small Tails, after the Manner of our Ramilies Wiggs,[5] and

---

1 Woodard, *Republic of Pirates*, 93; and http://republicofpirates.net/blog/2007/12/post.html.
2 For a modern biography, see Konstam, *Blackbeard*.
3 Woodard, *Republic of Pirates*, 206.
4 Konstam, *Blackbeard*, 293.
5 "A single queue, braided but not bound, with a large bow at the top and a small bow at the bottom, was known as a 'Ramillies wig' after the battle at that place (1706). The wearer of a Ramillies often doubled the end of the queue back up to the wig and held it with a comb or ribbon" (*The Wigmaker in Eighteenth-Century Williamsburg*, 17).

"Blackbeard in Smoke and Flame" (Frank Schoonover).

turn them about his Ears: In Time of Action, he wore a Sling over his Shoulders, with three Brace of Pistols, hanging in Holsters like Bandaliers; and stuck lighted Matches under his Hat, which appearing on each Side of his Face, his Eyes naturally looking fierce and wild, made him altogether such a Figure, that Imagination cannot form an Idea of a Fury, from Hell, to look more frightful."[6]

6   Schonhorn, ed., General History, 84–85.

Such tactics were effective enough to permit Blackbeard to use force selectively, for his activities mostly constituted robbery without violence.[7] One historian who classed him as "not a very successful pirate, nor a very daring one," allowed that the pirate was "a brilliant showman."[8] While he emerges from Johnson's *General History* as a hell-raising bigamist, Konstam noted: "Many contemporaries mention Blackbeard's charm and social ease. . . . He was described as intelligent, and seems to have had a modicum of social grace."[9]

He was also operating in an environment where pirate crews could theoretically turn leaders out by a show of hands. Much has been written about rudimentary democracy on pirate ships, but Teach was unlikely to meekly allow it to be applied to him.[10] He once shot and crippled one of his own men because "if he did not now and then kill one of them, they would forget who he was."[11] He could set aside other pirate captains (his arrangement with Stede Bonnet was a strange alliance at best) and be treacherous to his own followers, as indicated by his apparently deliberate grounding of his flagship, the *Queen Anne's Revenge*.

Following that incident Teach obtained a pardon from the governor of North Carolina. While he kept a low profile for a while, the fear he had generated continued along American coasts; in one case (as noted in an article that appears in this chapter) the sight of a dark sail triggered an alarm. Under any circumstances, his retirement from piracy was short-lived.[12] Blackbeard's apparent return to cruising prompted the governor of Virginia to organize an expedition against him using Royal Navy sailors. Teach subsequently met his death at the hands of a force led by Lieutenant Robert Maynard, who would bring the pirate's head back swinging from his vessel's bowsprit.[13]

ooooo

[**Editor's Note:** For a time after striking out on his own, Teach operated in consort with Stede Bonnet – the "Major Bennet" referred to in the first article below – a Barbados

---

7   Woodard, *Republic of Pirates*, 205–206.
8   Williams, *Captains Outrageous*, 153.
9   Schonhorn, ed., *General History*, 76, 77, 85; Konstam, *Blackbeard*, 284.
10 According to Peter Leeson, egalitarianism and democratic tendencies among pirates stemmed from pragmatic issues of survival and economics (*Invisible Hook*, 23–81). As the *General History* included details about democracy among pirates, its author's fictional story of a pirate Utopia called Libertalia has been analyzed as part of the case then being made for social change. See for example Schonhorn, ed., *General History*, xxxviii, 683; Hill, "Radical Pirates?," 163–165; and Turley, *Rum, Sodomy and the Lash*, 73–91, 101–108.
11 Schonhorn, ed., *General History*, 84.
12 John Rose Archer probably spoke for many recidivists when, while awaiting hanging for piracy in 1724, he admitted to Puritan clergyman Cotton Mather that "I was one of Teaches Crue; But came in upon the Act of Grace. And yet falling again into the Hands of the Pirates, I was easily drawn into the old Trade again; and spent one half Year more in Piracy, till God would bear no longer with me" (Mather, *The Converted Sinner*, 39). Archer had been quartermaster to pirate Captain John Phillips (Schonhorn, *General History*, 343). Angus Konstam observed that any pirate receiving a pardon still "would be marked as a troublemaker by any future employer" (*Blackbeard*, 47).
13 Schonhorn, ed., *General History*, 76–77, 80–83.

"Blackbeard told Bonnet that he was not fit to be a pirate captain, and that he would send somebody to take charge of the *Revenge*" (George Varian).

planter who had taken to piracy. Bonnet was born into wealth on Barbados in 1688, evidently losing both parents in his childhood. Receiving a formal education and earning a major's commission in the Barbados militia, he married a planter's daughter in 1709. They had four children together, but the death of his firstborn seems to have triggered a lasting depression and ultimately severe mental disorder. A lifelong landsman, circa 1716 he commissioned the building of what would become the *Revenge*, a 60-ton sloop in which he stocked a full library before adopting the alias Edwards and setting off on a pirating cruise. The only pirate on record to buy his ship and pay his crew a wage, Bonnet joined forces with Teach – the timeline is indistinct – in a move that produced an awkward alliance. Although they took 28 vessels during their time together, at some point Teach removed the inexperienced Bonnet from command of the *Revenge*.[14]]

---

14 Konstam, *Blackbeard*, 70–80; Konstam, *Piracy*, 201; Woodard, *Republic of Pirates*, 197–199; *Trials of Major Stede Bonnet and Thirty-three Others*, in Cobbett, Howell, and Howell, *State Trials*, XV:1245, 1246.

[*Boston News-Letter*, 4–11 November 1717, 2]

Philadelphia, October 24th. Arrived Linsey from Antigua, Codd from Liverpool and Dublin with 150 Passengers, many whereof are Servants.[15] He was taken about 12 days since off our Capes by a Pirate Sloop called the *Revenge*, of 12 Guns 150 Men, Commanded by one Teach, who formerly Sail'd Mate out of this Port: They have Arms to fire five rounds before they load again. They threw all Codd's Cargo over board, excepting some small matters they fancied. One Merchant had a thousand Pounds Cargo on board, of which the greatest part went overboard, he begg'd for Cloth to make him but one Suit of Cloths, which they refus'd to grant him. The Pirate took Two Snows outward bound, Spofford loaden with Staves for Ireland and Budger of Bristol in the *Sea Nymph* loaden with Wheat for Oporto,[16] which they threw over-board, and made a Pirate of the said Snow; And put all the Prisoners on board of Spofford, out of which they threw overboard about a Thousand Staves, and they very barbarously used Mr. Joseph Richardson, Merchant, of the *Sea Nymph*. They also took a Sloop Inwards Bound from Madera, Peter Peters Master, out of which they took 27 Pipes[17] of Wine, cut his Masts by the Board, after which She drove ashore and Stranded. They also took an other Sloop, one Grigg Master, bound hither from London, with above 30 Servants, they took all out of her, cut away her Mast and left her at Anchor on the Sea. They also took another Sloop from Madera, bound to Virginia, out of which they took two Pipes of Wine, then Sunk her. It's also said they took a Sloop from Antigua, belonging to New-York, and put some of the London Servants and other things on board her. The Pirates told the Prisoners that they expected a Consort Ship of 30 Guns, and then they would go up into Philadelphia, others of them said they were bound to the Capes of Virginia in hopes to meet with a good Ship there, which they much wanted. On board the Pirate Sloop is Major Bennet, but has no Command, he walks about in his Morning Gown, and then to his Books, of which he has a good Library on Board; he was not well of his wounds that he received by attacking of a Spanish Man of War, who kill'd and wounded him 30 or 40 Men.[18] After which putting into Providence, the place of Rendevouze for the Pirates, they put the aforesaid Capt. Teach on board for this Cruise. [. . .]

---

15 Indentured servants. Some pirates "had been indentured servants, especially the fourteen-year variety, which meant that they had been transported to the colonies in punishment for crimes committed in England." Yet not all indentured servants would have been recruitment material for a pirate crew. "Piracy emphatically was not an option for most landlubbers, since sea robbers 'entertain'd so contemptible a Notion of Landmen'" (Rediker, *Villains of All Nations*, 46).

16 Porto, Portugal.

17 A pipe contained 126 gallons.

18 "Regrettably, we have to assume that the Philadelphia correspondent for the *Boston News Letter* muddled his story, one he presumably heard third-hand from a prisoner on board the *Revenge* who landed in Philadelphia two weeks later. While it is not impossible, we have to assume that Stede Bonnet fabricated the story about the encounter with the Spanish man-of-war, which after all sounded far more heroic than saying he meekly threw up his hands when Blackbeard overhauled his sloop" (Konstam, *Blackbeard*, 78–79).

New-York, October 28th. Bloodworth is arrived from Curacoa, Demilt from Virginia, Capt. Farmer from Jamaica, who was twice taken by the Pirates on his passage, the last off the Capes of Delaware by Capt. Teach, who took out his Mast, Anchors, Cables, what money was on board, and put some Servants on board him and then turned him a-drift; he made a Shift to get into Sandy-hook,[19] where he run his Sloop ashore, having no Anchors and came up for help to get her [her] off. One Sipkins in a great Sloop of this Place is taken by the Pirates, which Sloop they have mounted with 12 Guns and made a Pirate. It's also said that Capt. Rolland of this place in a large Sloop from Jamaica is taken by the Pirates. On Wednesday last a Sloop was seen standing off and on in sight of Sandy-hook, and since 'tis reported a Sloop and a Snow stood along Long-Island to the Eastward, and 'tis thought to be the Pirates gone to Gardeners[20] or Block-Island.[21] [. . .]

Philadelphia, October 31. Arthur in a Sloop is arriv'd from Barbadoes, who met Sandford going in. One of our Pilotes that was on board Teach the Pirate says that they very much threaten New-England Men, in case any of their fellow Pirates suffer there, that they will revenge it on them. [. . .]

New York, Novemb. 4. [. . .] On the 30th past arrived Capt. Goelet, who was lately taken by Teach the Pirate, coming hither in a Sloop from Curacoa, half loaden with Cocoa, which the Pirates threw overboard, and man'd the Sloop for a Pirate, and gave Goelet and his Crew the *Sea Nymph* Snow to bring them in; Goelet saw the Pirate take a Ship & a Briganteen or Snow after parting with them. [. . .]

[Editor's Note: Late in 1717 near the Windward Islands Teach seized the 250–ton French slaver *La Concorde*, which he took as his flagship and renamed the *Queen Anne's Revenge*.[22] The title "suggests Jacobite political leanings among Blackbeard's crew, evoking the name of the last Stuart monarch and promising vengeance in her name against King George and his Hanoverian line."[23] By the following March Teach's flotilla was active in or near the Bay of Honduras. There, late that month, one of his consort sloops on its own tried but failed to capture a well-armed ship, the *Protestant Caesar*,

---

19 A peninsula on the New Jersey coastline, with an adjacent bay named for it.
20 Gardiners Island, off New York, where William Kidd left some of his treasure prior to his arrest (Ritchie, *Captain Kidd*, 230–231).
21 Off the Rhode Island coast.
22 Woodard, *Republic of Pirates*, 210–214.
23 Woodard, *Republic of Pirates*, 214. From another modern source: Queen Anne "was the last of the Stuart dynasty, and on her death without an heir she was succeeded by George I, a Hanoverian whose succession owed more to his Protestantism than to his lineage. Anne was the daughter of the King James who was overthrown and exiled in the Glorious Revolution of 1688. Many pirates expressed their support for the exiled James, so creating the 'Jacobite' cause that remained a nascent threat to the Hanoverians for another three decades. By including the term 'revenge' after 'Queen Anne,' Blackbeard might have been suggesting he supported the last of the Stuarts and saw his actions as a form of revenge against the usurping Germans on behalf of the Jacobite cause. He would not be the only pirate of the era to claim some form of legitimacy by linking himself with the deposed British monarch" (Konstam, *Blackbeard*, 87).

captained by William Wyer. After the pirate vessels reunited, Teach took them in search of Wyer's ship.[24]]

[*Boston News-Letter*, 9–16 June 1718, 2]

Boston. On the 31st of May last, arrived here the Sloop *Land of Promise*, Thomas Newton, Master, who says that about the 5th of April last at the Island Turneff[25] he was taken by Capt. Edward Teach, Commander of a Pirate Ship of 40 Guns, and about 300 Men, and a Sloop of 10 guns. Capt. Teach told Capt. Newton after he had took him, that he was bound to the Bay of Hundoras to Burn the Ship *Protestant Caesar*, Commanded by Capt. Wyer who had lately fought the abovesaid Sloop, that Wyer might not brag when he went to New-England that he had beat a Pirate. In the said Sloop came also Capt. William Wyer, late Commander of the Ship *Protestant Caesar*, burthen about 400 Tuns, 26 Guns, Navigated with 50 Men, who on the 28th of March last about 120 Leagues to the Westward of Jamaica, near the Latitude 16 off the Island Rattan,[26] espyed a large Sloop which he supposed to be a Pirate, and put his Ship in order to Fight her, which said Sloop had 10 Guns and upwards of 50 Men, and about nine a Clock at Night came under Capt. Wyer's Stern, and fired several Cannon in upon the said Ship and a Volley of small Shot, unto which he returned two of his Stern Chase Guns,[27] and a like Volley of small Shot, upon which the Sloop's Company hail'd him in English, telling him that if he fired another Gun they would give him no Quarter, but Capt. Wyer continued Fighting them till twelve a Clock at Night, when she left the Ship, and so he continued his Course to the Bay of Hundoras where he arrived the first of April last, and the eighth Day he had got on Board about 50 Tuns of Logwood, and the remaining part of the Ship's loaden lay ready cut to be taken on Board, when on the Morning of the said Day, a large Ship and a Sloop with Black Flags and Death's Heads in them and three more Sloops with Bloody Flags all bore down upon the said Ship *Protestant Caesar*, and Capt. Wyer judging them to be Pirates, call'd his Officers and Men upon Deck asking them if they would stand by him and defend the Ship, they answered, if they were Spaniards they would stand by him as long as they had Life, but if they were Pirates they would not Fight, and thereupon Capt. Wyer sent out his second Mate with his Pinnace[28] to discover who they were, and finding the Ship had 40 Guns, 300 Men, called the *Queen Ann's Revenge*, Commanded by Edward Teach, a Pirate, and they found the Sloop was the same that they Fought the 28th of March last, Capt. Wyer's Men all declared they would not Fight and quitted the Ship believing they would be Murthered by the Sloop's Company, and so all went on Shore.[¶]

---

24 Konstam, *Blackbeard*, 128–129; Schonhorn, ed., *General History*, 72; Woodard, *Republic of Pirates*, 241–242.

25 The Turneffe islands are off the coast of Belize.

26 Roatán, in the Bay of Honduras.

27 Chase guns were cannon positioned in the bow or stern, respectively meant to be fired while in pursuit or to deter a pursuer.

28 A "small vessel, navigated with oars and sails, and having generally two masts," rigged with sails running parallel to the keel (Falconer, *Universal Dictionary*, n.p.).

And on the 11th of April, three Days after Capt. Wyer's Ship *Protestant Caesar* was taken, Capt. Teach the Pirate sent word on shore to Capt. Wyer, that if he came on Board he would do him no hurt, accordingly he went on Board Teach's Ship, who told him he was glad that he left his Ship, else his Men on Board his Sloop would have done him Damage for Fighting with them; and said he would burn his Ship because he belonged to Boston, adding he would burn all Vessels belonging to New England for Executing the six Pirates at Boston.[29] And on the 12th of the said April Capt. Wyer saw the Pirates go on Board of his Ship, who set her on Fire and Burnt her with her Wood, and Capt. Wyer took his passage hither in Capt. Thomas Newton's Sloop, taken from him by Capt. Teach the Pirate unto whom he gave back his sloop again, because she belonged to Rhode-Island. Capt. Wyer, Capt. Newton and three others have attested upon Oath to the Truth of the above Account.

[**Editor's Note**: Subsequently Teach sailed north and, with three or four vessels in his flotilla, brazenly cruised off Charleston harbor. After taking and keeping several prizes, along with their crews and passengers, he sent several captives ashore to demand from the governor £400 of medicines in exchange for the hostages and their ships. Besides the man named Mark or Marks mentioned below, Teach's captives included Samuel Wragg, a wealthy landowner and local official, whose four-year-old son was taken with him off the London-bound ship *Crowley*.[30]]

[*Boston News-Letter*, 30 June–7 July 1718, 2]

South-Carolina, June 6. Capt. Teach in a Ship of 40 Guns with two Sloops and about 300 Men, came to our Barr[31] and took two Outward Bound Ships for London, one Clark and Craig, with two Inward Bound Ships from England: Clark had several Gentlemen Passengers, as Mr. Mark and Mr. Wragg, &c. the former they sent up with two of the Pirates to demand a Chest of Medicines (which was sent them down) on Penalty of Burning all the Vessels and Men, which they afterwards plundred, and took all their Provisions, and some Rice, and about 4,000 Pieces of Eight, and stript them of all their Cloaths and dismist the Ships and Men, which were forced to come in to refit;[32] they staid here about ten dayes, & we are afraid they are not far off this Coast. We hear that they are bound to the Northward and Sware Revenge upon New-England Men & Vessels.

---

29 Those who had convicted of being part of Samuel Bellamy's company.

30 Schonhorn, ed., *General History*, 74–75, 87–92; Konstam, *Blackbeard*, 141–146; Woodard, *Republic of Pirates*, 250–253; *Trials of Major Stede Bonnet and Thirty-three Others*, in Cobbett, Howell, and Howell, State Trials, XV:1244–1245.

31 "*Bar* of a port or haven, a shoal or bank of sand, gravel. &c. thrown up by the surge of the sea, to the mouth of a river or Harbour, so as to endanger, and sometimes totally prevent the navigation" (Falconer, *Universal Dictionary*, n.p.).

32 "Blackbeard had paralyzed an entire colony for over a week but, for reasons unknown, was willing to settle for plunder worth less than £2,000" (Woodard, *Republic of Pirates*, 253).

[**Editor's Note**: The same page of the same issue also contained a short report of how Teach ran the *Queen Anne's Revenge* aground, apparently deliberately, at Beaufort, North Carolina.[33]]

[*Boston News-Letter*, 30 June–7 July 1718, 2]

Philadelphia, June 26th. Last Night Hurst in a Sloop arrived here from South Carolina, who on Sunday last was two Weeks [was] in company with Capt. Teach, &c., tells us, That Teach has lost his Ship at Top-Sail Inlet at North Carolina. That he had two Sloops in company, on board one of which is Major Bonnet who has no command.[34] [. . .]

[**Editor's Note**: After the loss of the *Queen Anne's Revenge*, Teach moved its crew and loot aboard Bonnet's old *Revenge*. He then returned command of the latter to Bonnet, who immediately left in a boat to apply to the governor for a royal pardon to pirates then being offered by King George. In his absence, Teach, with about a hundred of his own men, moved the company's accumulated loot to another sloop and sailed away, leaving some of Bonnet's crew marooned. When Bonnet returned and discovered this act of treachery, he rescued the castaways and then, with revenge in mind, set off in an unsuccessful pursuit of Teach, who had gone to secure his own pardon.[35] Teach lay low for a while after receiving it, and other pirates took his place in the newspaper. Among them was La Buse, the French pirate with whom Samuel Bellamy once operated.]

[*Boston News-Letter*, 21–28 July 1718, 2]

New-York, July 21st. Capt. Bedlow is Arrived from St. Christopher's,[36] who says that the *Scarborough* Man of War[37] brought in there a Pirate Ship of 18 Guns with 17 French Men on Board, upwards of 50 English Men on Board her finding they were like to be taken got on Board a Sloop and made their Escape; The Pirate Ship is thought to be a Portuguise Ship, having a quantity of Brazil Sugar and Tobacco on board. [. . .]

---

33 *Trials of Major Stede Bonnet and Thirty-three Others*, in Cobbett, Howell, and Howell, *State Trials*, XV:1249.

34 According to a report from Captain Ellis Brand of HMS *Lyme*, on station in Virginia, "on the 10th of June or thereabouts a large pyrate Ship of forty Guns with three Sloops in her company came upon the coast of North carolina ware they endeavour'd To goe in to a harbor, call'd Topsail Inlett, the Ship Stuck upon the barr att the entrance of the harbor and is lost; as is one of the sloops" (quoted in Konstam, *Blackbeard*, 286).

35 Schonhorn, ed., *General History*, 75, 97; Woodard, *Republic of Pirates*, 255–257, 274; *Trials of Major Stede Bonnet and Thirty-three Others*, in Cobbett, Howell, and Howell, *State Trials*, XV:1249, 1254–1255.

36 One of the Leeward Islands, also known as St. Kitts, situated near Eustatis and Nevis.

37 The frigate HMS *Scarborough* was a 108–foot long, 32–gun fifth-rate English warship, launched at Sheerness in 1711. Captain Francis Hume brought it to Barbados in 1716. The fight with the 18–gun pirate vessel mentioned here took place near the island of St. Vincent; while some sources have suggested this fight was with Teach this has not been proven (Winfield, *British Warships 1603–1714*, 182).

"New York as it appeared in about 1690" (Howard Pyle)

Boston. By Capt. Macdowell from St. Christopher's we are informed that on the 29th of June past His Majesty's Ship the *Scarborough*, Capt. Hume Commander, had taken a Pirate Ship off the Island of Blanko, Commanded by one Labouss, who had been on the Coast of Brazil, where he took several Prizes, which Pirate seeing the Man of War gave him Chase, Labouss their Capt. with 70 or 80 of his Men betook themselves to a Sloop they had taken two Days before and run for it, having on Board abundance of Chests both of Gold and Silver. Capt. Hume could not come up with the Sloop, having only taken the Pirate Ship with 19 of his Crew he left on Board, which he brought in to St. Christopher's, where she is condemned and said to be worth four Thousand Pounds Sterling, and the Pirates put in Prison.

And by Capt. Brooker from Cowes[38] who arrived on Friday last we are informed, that the Day before about ten Leagues East off Cape Codd he was chased by a Sloop with a black Flag till he made the Shore, and then he stood off again, which Sloop he Judges to be a Pirate.

ooooo

[*Boston News-Letter*, 28 July–4 August 1718, 2]

Philadelphia, July 24. On Monday last arrived here a Pirate Sloop of 8 Guns, 10 Men, 2 Boys and 6 Negros, who surrendered themselves to our Governour not as Pirates,

---

38 Port on the Isle of Wight.

but Persons who had unfortunately been taken by them out of Merchants Service, and rescued themselves, the Account whereof being long we must defer till our next. [. . .]

Boston [. . .] Our last gave you an Account of a Sloop with a Black Flag, supposed to be a Pirate upon our Coast, which was only a Black Sail of a Sloop Inward Bound which is since come in.

ooooo

[*Boston News-Letter*, 4–11 August 1718, 2]

The following Paragraph we promised you in our last.

Philadelphia, July 24. Our last acquainted you of a Pirate Sloop of 8 Guns, 10 Men, 2 Boys and 6 Negros, who surrender'd themselves to our Governour not as Pirates, but those who had been in Merchants Service and taken by them, they delivered themselves and their Vessel into the Governour's Hands claiming only his Protection, upon which the Governour secured the Sloop, and they being Examined it appeared that the Sloop sailed out of Jamaica about 5 Months ago, under the Command of Capt. Pinkersman[39] with several of these Men on a Lawful Voyage, so that they were dismist and treated as Persons who had done acceptable Service to their King and Country, in rescuing themselves from the Pirates.

The above Sloop was Built at Rhode-Island, belong'd to Capt. Pinkersman, who took in the Negroes at Barbadoes and Jamaica for Divers at the Wreck:[40] But since that she has been a Pirate Sloop Commanded by Capt. Grinnaway, a Bermudian, who in the Lat. of 29 about [60?] Leagues East of Bermuda, (having in Company a Bermuda Sloop which he had taken) took a Ship belonging to Liverpool homeward bound from St. Christopher's, on board of which Grinnaway and the greatest part of his Hands went, and having been scant of Liquors for some time, they fell to drinking and carousing on Board the Ship, the Sloop standing after them, and the Hands on Board the Sloop being mostly Pinkerman's Men that had been forced among the Pirates, the Sloop being an extraordinary Sailer having left the Ship above a League they resolved to rescue themselves and make the best of their way and Leave the Pirates,

---

39 "Pinkentham, a sea captain with ties to Jamaica and Rhode Island, had been a privateer during the War of Spanish Succession, commanding a swift vessel with a crew of 160 men; Blackbeard would certainly have known him, and may have even served on his crew . . . " (Woodard, *Republic of Pirates*, 224).

40 A Spanish treasure fleet sank on the Florida coast in July 1715, sparking a long-running Spanish salvage effort, which also attracted independent mariners, including those such as Henry Jennings who raided the Spanish operations (Konstam, *Piracy*, 155; and Konstam, *Blackbeard*, 95–98). Captain Pinkentham (see note above) had at one time "planned to sail to Jamaica and then on to Florida to dive the Spanish wrecks and already had official British permission to do so"; the capture of his vessel by pirate Captain Grinnaway ended that plan (Woodard, *Republic of Pirates*, 224–225).

which 8 of the Pirate's Crew perceiving they designed to oppose by riseing upon them; whereupon one of the Pirates snapt a Pistol twice at the Man at the Helm, which mist firing, upon which one of the Negroes shot the Pirate down, after which they soon Mastered and bound the rest, and put them into a Periyanger,[41] but loosened the last Man to untie the rest, and Judge they saw the Ship take them up. [. . .]

[Editor's Note: The same issue of the *Boston News-Letter* gave an update on Stede Bonnet. Failing to track down Blackbeard after the affair at Topsail Inlet, Bonnet eventually convinced his followers to head to St. Thomas and apply for a Danish privateering commission. But he proved unable to control his crew, who seem to have dragged him with them back into piracy. Bonnet may have retained some nominal command, trying to hide his identity by having his company call him Edwards or Thomas; genuine authority was in the hands of quartermaster Robert Tucker.[42]]

[*Boston News-Letter*, 4–11 August 1718, 2]

Rhode-Island, August 8. On Saturday last arrived here a Sloop with 7 [?] Pirates, one Englishman and a Molatto, the Sloop was taken from one Thomas Downing, off the Capes of Virginia by Capt. Edward,[43] a Pirate, she belonged to Bermuda, and the abovesaid Men Edward put on Board the Sloop (excepting the English Man and Molatto that belonged to her when taken) to take charge of her, but next Day after they parted with the Pirate Edwards, they made the best of their way for this Port, in order to lay hold on the Act of Grace[44] as they said, being forced out of Merchants Service by Capt. Teach, and desired from the Governour the benefit of the said Act: Whereupon our Governour ordered them into the Custody of an Officer till he examined the English Man and Molatto, who gave an Account that the Sloop was taken from the said Downing the 20th of July last, off the Cape of Virginia, by Edward, a Pirate, who gave them charge of the Sloop, that they left the Pirate next Day, and that since that time this Company has taken three Sloops, one from Virginia, one from North Carolina to New-York and one from Barbadoes to Philadelphia. The Pirates gave Downing the Carolina Man's Sloop, the Carolina Man a Boat to go on Shore: They took a Cable and Anchor and 4 Hogsheads[45] of Rum[46] and other things out of the

---

41 Periagua.
42 Schonhorn, ed., *General History*, 97–99; Woodard, *Republic of Pirates*, 274–277; *Trials of Major Stede Bonnet and Thirty-three Others*, in Cobbett, Howell, and Howell, *State Trials*, XV:1254–1255, 1261–1265, 1267–1269, 1293–1297.
43 An alias for Stede Bonnet.
44 On 5 September 1717, King George I of Great Britain offered to pardon pirates for crimes committed before 5 January 1718, the later date allowing for the slow pace of getting word of the proclamation to the colonies. Pirates seeking pardon were to surrender to a British governor by 5 September 1718; that deadline was later extended into 1719 (Woodard, *Republic of Pirates*, 226, 315).
45 A hogshead was a large barrel; its weight/volume standards varied by contents, those containing wine and rum usually holding 63 gallons.

Philadelphia Sloop, and some other things from the Carolina Man. The Pirates being examined, deny the taking [of] any Vessels since they came on Board this Sloop, and are all Committed to close Goal: The Sloop and Goods are seized by the Deputy Collector. [. . .]

Piscataqua,[47] Aug. 8. Benj. Gatchel in a Pink from Virginia Arrived here the 4th Currant, the 19th of July he Sail'd from thence, and next day 8 Leagues off the Capes he was Attack'd by a Pirate Sloop of 14 Ports, 8 Guns Mounted, had on board about 70 Men, but knew not the Commander's Name, tho' several of his Men were known to Gatchel's men. It is thought they were a New Crew, lately cut out and run from some Harbour, being scant of everything, they took from him two Anchors, one Cable, 19 Barrels of Flower, a thousand of Bread, a hundred pound worth of English Goods, Chests, Cloaths and Instruments, and forced John Oliver their Carpenter to go with them, their Sloop being Leaky. In ravaging the Vessel they met with two or three Bibles, at the sight whereof some started and said, They had nothing to do with them, nor with God, nor anything Above. Three days after he was chased by another Sloop with 20 men who hal'd him, fired a Musket and commanded him to strike, which he did, but another Vessel coming near them the Pirate gave chase to her and left Gatchel.

ooooo

[*Boston News-Letter*, 11–18 August 1718, 2]

Philadelphia, August 7. On the first Instant arrived Combs from Barbadoes, who on the 27th past off the Capes of Virginia Spoke with the *Pearl* and *Lime* Men of War,[48] who were conveying off the Coast the Homeward bound Virginia Merchant Men: They were advised to keep a good Look-out for there were Pirates on the Coast; and on the 29th Capt. Combs was taken by a Pirate Sloop of ten Men and two Boys, one

---

46 The tradition of keeping and issuing rum aboard ships began in the Royal Navy at Jamaica in 1655, when it was noted that the liquor stayed potable longer than beer and water. Rum itself "derives its name from the Latin *saccharum* meaning sugar, but it was also known in an early form as 'rumbustion' – a seventeenth-century word believed to have originated in the sugar cane plantations. After the bulk of the sugar had been extracted from the cane the residue made a 'wash' which was fermented and distilled. During fermentation the spirit developed the characteristic flavor which distinguished it from other liquors, and the longer it was kept the better it became" (Pack, *Nelson's Blood*, 14–16).

47 Portsmouth, New Hampshire, through which the Piscataqua River runs.

48 HMS *Pearl* was a 117-foot long English frigate (or fifth rate) of 42 guns, built at Rotherhithe in 1708. Under Captain Henry Lawson it took a pair of French privateers off Portugal in September 1711. Captain George Gordon took command of the *Pearl* in 1716 on cruises in the Baltic and North Sea prior to bringing it to Virginia, where it was stationed from 1717–19. HMS *Lyme* was also a frigate, a Plymouth-built, 109-foot fifth rate of 32 guns, launched in 1695. It also took a pair of French privateers in separate actions in 1702 and 1703. A year later, its Captain Edmund Lechmere died commanding it in a fight off Dodman Head with a better-armed French privateer of 46 guns. Rebuilt as a 24-gun sixth rate warship, HMS *Lyme* (like HMS *Pearl*) arrived in Virginia in 1717 and stayed two years (Winfield, *British Warships 1603–1714*, 170, 177).

Jones, a Young Man, Commander, from whom they took 6 Hogsheads of Rum, and about 500 £ in Cash, four hundred of it belonged to a Young Man on board, whom they stript of all. They have two Consorts; the chief is Major Bonnet[49] with 40 or 50 hands; they took a Pilot Boat in our Bay that they kept several Days. They put on board Combs a Carpenter they took out of a London Ship off the Capes, to whom they offered 40 £ to stay with them but he refused it, and was kept Eleven days by force.

Last Night Arrived a Scooner bound from North Carolina to Boston, he was taken by one of the above Pirates, who took from him Pitch and Tarr, and most of his Sailes; he came in to refit.

The said Pirate on the 28th past took Capt. Mac Glenan & Mairee, two outward bound Snows for Bristol, and took from them some hundreds of Pounds in Cash, and what else they liked, and barbarously used Mac Glenan for hiding his Money.

They also took Brown and Read in two outward bound Sloops for Barbadoes, out of the first they took 50 Barrels of Flower. They also took Manwaring from Antigua, and out of him 14 Hogsheads of Molasses; on the Lord's day they went off our Coast and carryed Read and Manwaring with them, their Sloop Sails extraordinarily well. [. . .]

Rhode-Island, August 15. [. . .] On Monday Night last five of the Pirates broke out of our Goal, two remain in Irons; the Governour has issued forth a Proclamation for all Persons to sieze them, and that none presume to harbour and conceal them.[50]

[Editor's Note: Bonnet and his crew were captured at Cape Fear at the end of September 1718; Bonnet escaped before his trial but was retaken after about two weeks. He was convicted and, while his fragile state evoked pity from some, the unlikely pirate was hanged on 10 December.[51] Teach meanwhile had, in spite of his pardon, been returning to his old ways with the alleged connivance of North Carolina officials, prompting some victims to take their complaints to the neighboring colony of Virginia.[52] The lieutenant governor there, Alexander Spotswood, deemed Blackbeard enough of a threat to single him out, with a special bounty on his head, in a proclamation offering rewards for the "Apprehending or Killing of Pirates." Spotswood subsequently organized an expedition, using Royal Navy personnel on station in Virginia, which ended Teach's career and life.]

---

49 "Bonnet tried to keep the company from invalidating his pardon. To conceal his identity, he insisted that he be called Captain Edwards or Captain Thomas, a ruse that didn't fool all their captives" (Woodard, *Republic of Pirates*, 275).

50 See the Rhode Island entry above from the issue of 4–11 August 1718.

51 Schonhorn, ed., *General History*, 100–113; Woodard, *Republic of Pirates*, 298–301. See also *The Trials of Major Stede Bonnet and Thirty-three Others*.

52 Schonhorn, ed., *General History*, 76–77; Konstam, *Blackbeard*, 198–205.

[*Boston News-Letter*, 9–16 February 1719, 1]

Virginia, ss.[53] By His Majesty's Lieutenant Governour and Commander in Chief of the Colony and Dominion of Virginia.

A Proclamation, Publishing the Rewards given for Apprehending or Killing of Pirates.

Whereas by an Act of Assembly made at a Session of Assembly begun at the Capitol in Williamsburgh the Eleventh Day of November in the fifth Year of His Majesty's Reign, Entituled, an Act to encourage the Apprehending and destroying of Pirates; It is amongst other things Enacted, That all & every Person or Persons who from and after the fourteenth Day of November in the Year of our Lord one Thousand Seven Hundred and Eighteen, and before the Fourteenth Day of November, which shall be in the Year of our Lord one Thousand Seven Hundred and Nineteen, shall take any Pirate or Pirates, on Sea or Land, or in case of Resistance, shall Kill any such Pirate or Pirates, between the Degrees of Thirty four and Thirty nine of Northern Latitude, and within one Hundred Leagues of the Continent of Virginia, or within the Provinces of Virginia or North Carolina, upon the Conviction or making due proof of the killing of all and every such Pirate and Pirates, before the Governour and Council, shall be Entituled to have and receive, out of the Publick Money, in the Hands of the Treasurer of this Colony, the several Rewards following; That is to say, for Edward Tach, commonly called Capt. Tach or Black-beard,[54] one Hundred Pounds; for every other Commander of a Pirate Ship, Sloop or Vessel, Forty Pounds; for every Lieutenant, Master, Quarter Master, Boatswain or Carpenter, Twenty Pounds; for every other Inferiour Officer, Fifteen Pounds; and for every Private Man taken on Board such Ship, Sloop or Vessel, Ten Pounds; and that for every Pirate which shall be taken by any Ship, Sloop or Vessel belonging to this Colony, or North Carolina, within the time aforesaid, in any place whatsoever, the like Rewards shall be paid, according to the quality and condition of such Pirate: Wherefore for the Encouragement of all such Persons, as shall be willing to serve His Majesty and their Country, in so just and Honourable an undertaking, as the suppressing a sort of People, who may be truly called Enemies to Mankind; I have thought fit, with the Advice and Consent of His Majesty's Council, to issue this Proclamation, hereby declaring the said Rewards shall be punctually and justly paid, in Current Money of Virginia, according to the Directions of the said Act. And I do order and appoint this Proclamation to be publish'd by the Sheriffs, at the respective Court-houses, and by all Ministers and Readers, in the several Churches and Chappels throughout this Colony.

---

53 The initials s.s. represent "an abbreviation for a traditional part of the venue section of a notary certificate. The letters stand for the Latin word *scilicet* which means 'in particular' or 'namely'" (*Notary Notes*, II:5 (Oct. 2001), published by the Licensing Division, North Dakota Secretary of State's Office, 2)

54 A modern author has called Spotswood's subsequent expedition against Teach "entirely illegal, as neither the governor nor the officers had the authority to invade another colony. Blackbeard was, legally speaking, a citizen in good standing; he had been pardoned for his previous crimes . . . and had yet to be indicted for any crime" (Woodard, *Republic of Pirates*, 289).

Given at the Council Chamber at Williamsburgh this 25th Day of November 1718. In the fifth Year of His Majesty's Reign.

A. SPOTSWOOD[55]

GOD Save the King

ooooo

Edward Teach's last battle, as depicted in "The Combatants Cut and Slashed with Savage Fury" (Howard Pyle).

---

55 Alexander Spotswood (1676–1740) had been named lieutenant governor of Virginia in 1710; the nominal title of governor had been given to the Earl of Orkney.

[*Boston News-Letter*, 16–23 February 1719, 4]

Boston, By Letters of the 17th of December last from North Carolina, we are informed, That Lieutenant Robert Maynard[56] of His Majesty's Ship *Pearl* (Commanded by Capt. Gordon)[57] being fitted out at Virginia, with two Sloops, mann'd with Fifty Men and small Arms, but no great Guns, in quest of Capt. Teach the Pirate, called Blackbeard, who made his Escape from thence, was overtaken at North Carolina, and had ten great Guns and Twenty one Men on board his Sloop.[58] Teach when he began the Dispute Drank Damnation to Lieutenant Maynard if he gave Quarters.[59] Maynard replyed he would neither give nor take Quarters, whereupon he boarded the Pirate and fought it out, hand to hand, with Pistol and Sword; the Engagement was very desperate and bloody on both sides, wherein Lieutenant Maynard had Thirty five of his Men killed and wounded in the Action, himself slightly wounded. Teach and most of his Men were killed, the rest carryed Prisoners to Virginia, by Lieut. Maynard to be tried there; who also carrys with him Teach's Head which he cut off, in order to get the Reward granted by the said Colony.[60]

[*Boston News-Letter*, 23 February–2 March 1719, 2]

Rhode Island, February 20. On the 12th Currant arrived here John Jackson from Piscataqua for Connecticut, and Humphry Johnson in a Sloop from North Carolina, bound to Amboy[61] who sailed the next Day, and informs that Governour Spotswood of Virginia fitted out two Sloops, well mann'd with Fifty pickt Men of his Majesty's Men of War lying there, and small Arms, but no great Guns, under the Command of Lieutenant Robert Maynard of his Majesty's Ship *Pearl*, in pursuit of that Notorious and Arch Pirate Capt. Teach, who made his Escape from Virginia, when some of his

---

56   The lieutenant of HMS *Pearl* would find his bravery unrewarded. "Shortly after killing Blackbeard, Lieutenant Robert Maynard was found to have kept a number of valuables taken from the *Adventure* [Blackbeard's sloop], having disobeyed a direct order from Captain Gordon to return them to the inventory of seized plunder. His self-aggrandizing accounts of the battle at Ocracoke further discredited him with his superiors and Governor Spotswood, in whose letters praise for the lieutenant is conspicuously absent. Maynard was not promoted to commander for another twenty-one years. He eventually made captain and was given command of the sixth rate *Sheerness* in September 1740, when he must have been a old man. He died in England in 1750" (Woodard, *Republic of Pirates*, 323–324).

57   George Gordon became a Royal Navy captain on 9 April 1709, being posted to HMS *Lowestoffe*; he died 12 July 1732 in England (Hardy, *Chronological List*, 30).

58   Called the *Adventure*.

59   Maynard's own report stated: "At our first salutation, he drank Damnation to me and my Men, whom he stil'd Cowardly Puppies, saying, He would neither give nor take Quarter" (Cordingly, *Under the Black Flag*, 196).

60   In his logbook entry for 3 January 1719, Maynard wrote: "Little wind & fair weather this day I anchored here [Williamsburg, Virginia] from N Carolina in the *Adventure* Sloop Edward Thache formerly Master (a Pyrat) whose head I hung Under the Bowsprete of the said Sloop in order to present it to ye Colony of Virginia & ye goods & Effects of the Said Pyrat I Deliver'd to my Commanders Disposal" (quoted in Cordingly, *Under the Black Flag*, 200).

61   On Raritan Bay in New Jersey.

Men were taken there,[62] which Pirate Lieutenant Maynard came up with at North Carolina, and when they came in hearing of each other, Teach called to Lieutenant Maynard and told him he was for King George, desiring him to hoist out his Boat and come aboard. Maynard replyed that he delighted to come aboard with his Sloop as soon as he could, and Teach understanding his design, told him that if he would let him alone, he would not meddle with him; Maynard answered that it was him he wanted, and that he would have him dead or alive, else it should cost him his life; whereupon Teach called for a Glass of Wine, and swore Damnation to himself, if he

Blackbeard's death (George Varian).

---

62   Teach's quartermaster William Howard had been arrested in Virginia on piracy charges. Howard's lawyer later filed a suit seeking compensation on Howard's behalf. The civil action faded after Howard was found guilty (Konstam, *Blackbeard*, 205–207; Woodard, *Republic of Pirates*, 288).

either took or gave Quarters: Then Lieut. Maynard told his Men, that now they knew what they had to trust to, and could not escape the Pirates' hands if they had a mind; but must either fight and kill or be killed: Teach begun and fired several Great Guns at Maynard's Sloop, which did but little damage, but Maynard rowing nearer Teach's Sloop of Ten Guns, Teach fired some small Guns, loaded with Swan shot, spick [*sic* – spike] Nails and pieces of old Iron, in upon Maynard, which killed six of his Men, and wounded ten; upon which Lieutenant Maynard, ordered all the rest of his Men to go down in the Hould, himself, Abraham Demelt of New York, and a third at the Helm stayed above Deck. Teach seeing so few on the Deck, said to his Men, the Rogues were all killed except two or three, and he would go on board and kill them himself, so drawing nearer, went on board, took hold of the fore sheet and made fast the Sloops; Maynard and Teach themselves two begun the Fight with their Swords, Maynard making a thrust, the point of his Sword went against Teach's Cartridge Box, and bended it to the Hilt. Teach broke the Guard of it, and wounded Maynard's Fingers but did not disable him, whereupon he [Maynard] Jumpt back, threw away his Sword, and fired his Pistol, which wounded Teach. Demelt struck in between them with his Sword and cut Teach's Face pretty much; in the Interim both Companies ingaged in Maynard's Sloop; one of Maynard's Men being a Highlander, ingaged Teach with his broad Sword, who gave Teach a cut on the Neck, Teach saying, ["W]ell done Lad,["] the Highlander reply'd, ["I]f it be not well done, I'll do it better,["] with that he gave him a second stroke, which cut off his Head, laying it flat on his Shoulder. Teach's Men being about 20 and three or four Blacks were all killed in the Ingagement, excepting two carried to Virginia:[63] Teach's body was thrown overboard, and his Head put on the top of the Bowsprit.

(How many of Lieut. Maynard's Men were killed in the Action besides the first six, we know not, only his Letter to his Sister in Boston, mentions 35 killed and wounded.)[64]
[. . .]

---

63 According to historian W. Jeffrey Bolster: "No accurate numbers of black buccaneers exist, although the impression is that they were more numerous than the proportion of black sailors in commercial or naval service at that time." He added: "As welcoming as most white pirates were to skilled black sailors, . . . sea robbers were not race-blind. None of the renowned pirate captains at the turn of the eighteenth century was a black man, and pirates generally sold captured slaves with the rest of their plunder" (*Black Jacks*, 13–15). Kenneth Kinkor, who compiled some approximate figures on black pirates based on accounts of the day, wrote that pirate "multiculturalism sprang not from idealistic sentiments of the 'brotherhood of man,' but from a pragmatic spirit of revolt against common oppressors" ("Black Men under the Black Flag," 197, 200–201). From another perspective, Peter Leeson observed that "[e]conomic concerns, not lofty ideals, drove pirates to enroll black sailors as paid, full-fledged crew members. Simple self-interest in the unique context in which pirates operated explains some pirates' progressive racial practices" (*Invisible Hook*, 157). See also Rediker, *Villains of All Nations*, 54–56; and Linebaugh and Rediker, "The Many-Headed Hydra."

64 "There are differing accounts of the final casualty list. Captain [Ellis] Brand [of HMS *Lyme*] reported to the Admiralty that eleven seamen were killed (two from the *Lyme* and nine from the *Pearl*) and more than twenty were wounded. Some of the pirates jumped overboard and were killed in the water. One body was only discovered several days later because of the number of birds hovering overhead. The final death toll of the pirates varies between nine and twelve, with nine badly wounded men taken prisoner" (Cordingly, *Under the Black Flag*, 198–199).

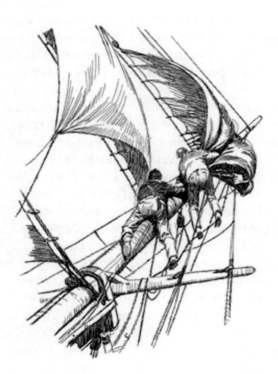

Stowing the outer jib (19th century, artist unknown).

Boston [. . .] By Capt. Thomas from Bilboa,[65] who was beat[66] off the Coast to Antigua, we are informed, that there are still a great many Pirates in the West Indies; he met on this Coast Capt. Bull bound hither from Surranam,[67] who was riffled by them of some Rhum and Molasses:

Besides what we gave you in our Last and this, of the taking and killing of Teach the Pirate by Lieut. Maynard, we have this further account of it by a Letter from North Carolina of December 17th to New York, viz. That on the 17th of November last, Lieut. Maynard of the *Pearl* Man of War Sail'd from Virginia with two Sloops, and 54 Men under his Command, no Guns, only small Arms, Sword and Pistols. Mr. Hyde Commanded the Little Sloop with 22 Men, and Maynard had 32 in his Sloop, and on the 22d Maynard Engaged Teach at Obercock[68] in North Carolina, he had 21 Men, Nine Guns Mounted. Mr. Hyde was killed, and one more, and Five wounded in the Little Sloop, and having nobody aboard to Command them they fell a Stern and did not come up to Assist Lieut. Maynard till the Action was almost over. Maynard shot

---

65 The Spanish province of Bilbao on the Bay of Biscay.
66 *Beating* in this setting may refer to the "operation of making progress by alternate tacks at sea against the wind, in a zig-zag line, or transverse courses; beating, however, is generally understood to be turning to windward in a storm or fresh wind" (Smyth, *Lexicon*, 91).
67 Suriname.
68 Ocracoke.

away Teach's Gibb[69] and Fore-halliards,[70] and put him ashore, then run him aboard, and had 20 Men killed and wounded. Teach Entered Maynard's Sloop with Ten Men, and he [Maynard] had [10?] stout Men Left, so that they fought it out Sword in hand. Maynard's Men behaved like Heros, and kill'd all Teach's Men that Entered without any of Maynard's dropping, but most of them Cut and Mangled; in the whole he had Eight killed and Eighteen wounded. Teach fell with Five Shot, and 20 dismal Cuts, and 12 of his Men kill'd, and Nine made Prisoners, most of them Negros, all wounded. Teach would never be taken had he not been in such a hole that he could not get away.

---

69 The *jib* is "the foremost sail of a ship, being a large stay-sail extended from the outer end of the bowsprit, pro-longed by the jib-boom, towards the fore-top-mast-head. . . . The jib is a sail of great command with any side-wind, but especially when the ship is close-hauled, or has the wind upon her beam, and its effort in casting the ship, or turning her head to leeward, is very powerful, and of great utility, particularly when the ship is working through a narrow channel" (Falconer, *Universal Dictionary*, n.p.).

70 "The ropes or tackles usually employed to hoist or lower any sail upon its respective masts or stay" (Falconer, *Universal Dictionary*, n.p.).

5

"Like a parcel of Furies . . . " – Bartholomew Roberts captures the *Samuel* (1720)

Born in Wales circa 1682, the prolific Bartholomew Roberts took some 400 vessels during a short but far-ranging pirate career, one that he apparently entered unwillingly. With more than two decades' worth of experience at sea, in early 1719 he was serving aboard a slaver that Welsh pirate Howell Davis took at the Ghanian port of Anomabu. Forced into Davis' flotilla, Roberts' abilities were soon noted; eventually he formally joined the pirates to improve his situation among his captors. Such were his talents that when Davis died in an ambush on the Portuguese island of Príncipe that June, the company voted Roberts in as his replacement.[1]

Under Roberts' command, the pirates then cruised off West Africa, robbing a series of slave ships along the way, forcing much of the crew of an English slaver into their service. Crossing the Atlantic and operating off Brazil, they took a Portuguese treasure ship carrying a small fortune. This success turned sour when, while Roberts was busy chasing another potential prize, a vessel in his flotilla captained by Irish pirate Walter Kennedy sailed off, taking the Portuguese ship with him.[2] Roberts and company displayed a subsequent aversion to Irish sailors, something that kept one of the crew of the *Samuel* (the mid-1720 capture of which is detailed below) from being forced.

Roberts would go on to cut several swathes through merchant shipping off the Americas and Africa. He was also, according to one historian, "in many ways an untypical pirate. He was a strict teetotaler, refused to allow his men to play at dice or cards for money, and insisted that all disputes between members of the crew should be settled on shore by duels. He took pains to ensure that no female prisoner was molested and was something of a Sabbatarian: 'The musicians to have a rest on the Sabbath day,' ran one of his articles."[3] He was undoubtedly a skilled seaman and accomplished leader, but also had experience in the dehumanizing slave trade and was perfectly capable of routine violence. Moreover, his crew, like any pirate outfit, was hard to control. Nor was Walter Kennedy the only member of it with whom Roberts had problems. He killed one man

---

1   Schonhorn, ed., *General History*, 175, 193, 194–195; Konstam, *Piracy*, 234; Baer, *British Piracy*, III:67. For modern biographies, see Richards, *Black Bart*, and Sanders, *If a Pirate I Must Be. . . .*
2   Schonhorn, ed., *General History*, 195–196, 205–206; Konstam, *Piracy*, 234–236.
3   Williams, *Captains Outrageous*, 185–186.

Bartholomew Roberts (artist unknown, from the *General History*).

who insulted him while drunk; when one of the dead man's friends, named Jones, cursed Roberts, the latter ran him through with a sword. Jones (according to Captain Charles Johnson) "notwithstanding his Wound, seized the Captain, threw him over a Gun, and beat him handsomely." Roberts' reputation among his men was such that the act earned Jones two lashes from every member of the crew.[4]

His career and life would end in February 1722, off the African coast, when HMS *Swallow* bested Roberts' flagship the *Royal Fortune*. Roberts died in battle, his throat torn open by a piece of grape shot; his men threw his body overboard still dressed in the distinctive finery he wore in battle.[5]

The following 1720 newspaper account of the capture of the *Samuel* off Newfoundland offers a dramatic glimpse of Roberts and his crew in action, as well as background on the arch-pirate himself. It also reveals something of the terror a pirate attack could convey.

[*Boston News-Letter*, 15–22 August 1720, 2–3]

Boston, On Monday last the 15th Currant arrived here the Ship *Samuel*, about eleven Weeks from London, and ten from Land's end,[6] Capt. Samuel Carry Commander, who in his Voyage hither on the 13th of July past, in the Latitude of 44 about 30 or 40 Leagues to the Eastward of the Banks of Newfoundland,[7] was accosted and taken by two Pirates, viz. A Ship of 26 Guns, and a Sloop of ten, both Commanded by Capt. Thomas[8] Roberts, having on board about a hundred Men, all English: The dismal Account whereof follows:

The first thing the Pirates did, was to strip both Passengers and Seamen of all their Money and Cloths which they had on board, with a loaded Pistol held to every one's breast ready to shoot him down, who did not immediately give an account of both, and resign them up.[9] The next thing they did was, with madness and rage to tare up

---

4   Schonhorn, ed., *General History*, 224–225.

5   Schonhorn, ed., *General History*, 243–244. For the subsequent trial of the men captured in Roberts' flotilla, see *A Full and Exact Account of the Tryal Of all the Pyrates, Lately taken by Captain Ogle*.

6   In Cornwall, the south-westernmost point of England.

7   The author of the *General History* wrote that "Newfoundland is an Island on the North Continent of America, contained between the 46° and 53 of N. Latitude. . . . The Island is deserted by the Natives and neglected by us, being desolate and woody, and the Coast and harbor only held for the Conveniency of the Cod Fishery, for this alone they were settled. The Bays and harbours about it, are very numerous and convenient, and being deeply indented, makes it easy for any Intelligence quickly to pass from one Harbour to another over Land . . . when the Appearance of an Enemy makes them apprehend Danger." The *General History* also noted that the fishing industry there "accidentally contributes to raise, or support the Pyrates already rais'd" by importing workers from England who later found themselves unable to pay debts or support themselves. As a result, many turned to piracy or were recruited by visiting pirate craft (Schonhorn, ed., 346–348; see also Rediker, *Villains*, 44–45).

8   Bartholomew.

9   "Men and women who were attacked by pirates found it a terrifying and shocking experience. There was the violence and the noise of the approach as the pirate ship fired warning shots and swung alongside with her heavy

the Hatches, enter the Hould like a parcel of Furies, where with Axes, Cutlashes, &c. they cut, tore and broke open Trunks, Boxes, Cases and Bales, and when any of the Goods came upon Deck which they did not like to carry with them aboard their Ship, instead of Tossing them into the Hould again they threw them over-board into the Sea; The usual method they had to open Chests was by shooting a brace of Bullets with a Pistol into the Key-hole to force them open: The Pirates carryed away from Capt. Carry's Ship aboard their own 40 barrels of Powder, two great Guns, his Cables, &c. and to the value of about nine or ten Thousand Pounds Sterling worth of the Choicest Goods he had on board. There was nothing heard among the Pirates all the while, but Cursing, Swearing, Dam'ing and Blaspheming to the greatest degree imaginable, and often saying they would not go to Hope point in the River of Thames to be hung up in Gibbets a Sundrying as Kidd & Bradish's Company did,[10] for if it should chance that they should be Attacked by any Superiour power or force, which they could not master, they would immediately put fire with one of their Pistols to their Powder, and go all merrily to Hell together![11] They often ridicul'd and made a mock at King George's Acts of Grace with an Oath, that they had not got Money enough, but when they had, if he then did grant them one, after they sent him word, they would thank him for it. They forced and took away with them Capt. Carry's Mate, and his Seamen, viz. Henry Gilespy, Mate, Hugh Minnens, both North Britains,[12] Michael Le Couter, a Jersey Man,[13] and Abraham, a Kentish Man,[14] could not learn his Sir-name, the Captain's Book[15] being carryed away (except one Row born in Dublin which they

sails flapping thunderously. There was the confrontation with tough and brutal young men armed with knives, cutlasses, and boarding axes who deliberately knocked down or slashed at anyone who showed resistance. There was a confused and frightening phase during which the pirates ransacked the ship, interrogated the captain and crew, and frequently employed torture to extract information. And all too often the attack ended with some of the victims lying dead on the deck or with their bleeding bodies being thrown over the side to the sharks" (Cordingly, *Under the Black Flag*, 241).

10 Joseph Bradish (b. 1672 in Cambridge, Massachusetts) was a contemporary of the better-known William Kidd. In 1698, when the vessel *Adventure* (on which Bradish was mate) stopped in the Spice Islands, Bradish and followers ran off with it, dividing up its cargo of coins (individuals received £1,600 plus other goods aboard) and sailing their prize to Long Island. From there, Bradish returned to Massachusetts where he was arrested. He escaped but was recaptured, and sent to England for trial, where he was found guilty and hanged in 1700. As with Kidd, his corpse was displayed in chains as a warning (Ritchie, *Captain Kidd*, 174–175, 179; and Baer, *British Piracy*, I:373).

11 After HMS *Swallow* captured Roberts' ship in early 1722, the warship kept well away from the pirate vessel, fearing such an effort to blow it up; prisoners were collected via the *Swallow*'s longboat (Schonhorn, ed., *General History*, 244–245). As noted elsewhere in this volume, similar plans existed aboard the ships of Edward Teach and Charles Harris. Some merchant sailors, fearing sadism at the hands of pirates, also discussed blowing up their vessel if captured (Bradlee, *Piracy in the West Indies*, 141).

12 I.e., from Scotland.

13 Jersey being one of the Channel Islands off the English coast.

14 The county of Kent, situated between London and the English Channel.

15 Sailing vessels kept several types of records. Data on course, wind direction, and other occurrences were first entered onto the *log-board*, the more important entries later transcribed into the *log-book*. This material also informed the captain's *journal*, which was "a sort of diary, or daily register of the ship's course, winds, and weather, together with a general account of whatever is material to be remarked in the period of a sea voyage" (Falconer, *Universal Dictionary*, n.p.). Ship captains drew a death's head in the margin of their records to mark a sailor's passing, something that likely influenced the use of that symbol on the Jolly Roger (Rediker, *Between the Devil and the Deep Blue Sea*, 279).

would not take because [he had been] born in Ireland):[16] holding a pistol with a brace of Bullets to each of their breasts to go with them, or be presently shot down, telling them that at present they wanted none of their Service; but when they came to any Action, they should have liberty to Fight and Defend the Ship as they did, or else immediately to be shot, that they should not tell tales.[17] They had on board the Pirate near 20 Tuns of Brandy, However the Pirates made themselves very merry aboard of Capt. Carry's Ship with some Hampers of fine Wines that were either presents, or sent to some Gentlemen in Boston; it seems they would not wait to unty them and pull out the Corks with Skrews, but each man took his bottle and with his Cutlash cut off the Neck and put it to their Mouths and drank it out. Whilst the Pirates were disputing whither to sink or burn Capt. Carry's Ship they spy'd a Sail that same evening, and so let him go free.

And at Midnight they came up with the same, which was a Snow from Bristol,[18] Capt. Bowls Master, bound for Boston, of whom they made a Prize, and serv'd him, as they did Capt. Carry, unloaded his Vessel & forced all his Men, designing to carry the Snow with them to make her a Hulk to Carreen their Ship with.

The abovesaid Capt. Roberts in Novemb. 1718 was third Mate of a Guinea Man[19] out of London for Guinea,[20] Capt. Plummer Commander, who was taken by a Pirate, and by that means Roberts himself became a Pirate, and being an active, brisk Man, they voted him their Captain, which he readily embraced.

The said Roberts in the abovesaid Sloop, Rhode Island built, with a Briganteen Consort Pirate, was some time in January last in the Latitude of Barbadoes, near the Island, where they took and endeavoured to take several Vessels; but the Governour hearing of it, fitted out one Capt. Rogers of Bristol,[21] in a fine Gally;[22] a Ship of about

---

16 Roberts and his followers had "an implacable Aversion" to the Irish because of their experience with Walter Kennedy. That Irish pirate, a member of Roberts' company, made off with a vessel from the flotilla and brought a treasure-laden prize with him. He took several prizes on his own but was eventually captured, and in a bid to save his own life gave evidence against his comrades. The effort failed, and Kennedy was hanged in July 1721 (Schonhorn, ed., *General History*, 206–210).

17 In his discussion of the 1722 trial of members of Roberts' company, Joel H. Baer remarked that "There were five ways used aboard Roberts's ships to demonstrate innocence: getting a letter from your former captain before he was let go attesting to your being forced, having notice of your situation placed in a newspaper, attempting to escape, frequently expressing your rejection of piracy to other forced men, and never volunteering to board a target during battle. Those willing to join would sometimes hint broadly to Roberts, who obliged by making a show of forcing them" (*British Piracy*, III:69).

18 Port in south-west England.

19 A slaveship operating from West African ports (Smyth, *Lexicon*, 354). For recent works on the slave trade, see Rediker, *The Slave Ship*, and Thomas, *The Slave Trade*.

20 On the west coast of Africa.

21 Perhaps a reference to Speightstown on the northwest coast of Barbados. Speightstown "was once a whaling station and the colony's major port, commercial and slaving center until the development of Bridgetown, picking up the nickname 'Little Bristol' because of the regular ships calling here on the triangular route between Bristol, in England, the Gold Coast in West Africa (picking up slaves), and the West Indies (dropping off slaves and picking up sugar)" (Shales, *Barbados*, 81).

22 The *Summersett* (Konstam, *Piracy*, 237).

Bartholomew Roberts' ships *Royal Fortune* and *Ranger* in the Whydah (Ouidah) Road in early 1722 (artist unknown, from the *General History*).

20 Guns, and a Sloop,[23] Capt. Graves Commander; Capt. Rogers killed and wounded several of Roberts's Men, and made a great hole in his Sloop, which his Carpenter with very great Difficulty (hundreds of Bullets flying round him) stopt, and finding Capt. Rogers too strong for him, tho' Graves did nothing, which if [he] had, he must of necessity been taken, he therefore run for it, as also did his Consort Briganteen, which he never saw nor heard of since.

---

23   The "six-gun sloop *Philippa*, which had just limped into port from Tobago" (Konstam, *Piracy*, 237).

From Barbadoes, Roberts went to an Island called Granaad[24] to the Leeward of Barbadoes, where he carreen'd his Sloop, and from thence this Spring with 45 Men he came to Newfoundland, into the Harbour of Trepassi,[25] towards the latter end of June last, with Drums beating, Trumpets sounding, and other Instruments of Musick, English Colours flying, their Pirate Flagg at the Topmast-Head,[26] with Death's Head

"Captain Roberts' crew carousing at Old Calabar River (artist unknown, from *The Pirates Own Book*).

---

24 Grenada, a Caribbean island, then a French colony.
25 Trepassey Bay off Newfoundland. According to a later (1819) description, "Trepassey-Bay, formerly Abram Trepassé, about seven leagues north-west of Cape-Race, is a wide bay with a harbor large, well secured, and having excellent anchorage, Biscay-Bay lying to the north-east, and Sailing-Bay to the north-west" (Anspach, *History of the Island of Newfoundland*, 309).
26 Over time Roberts' company would employ several black flag designs, one of which conveyed a direct threat to officials of Barbados and Martinique: "The Jack had a Man pourtray'd in it, with a flaming Sword in his Hand, and standing on two Skulls, subscribed A.B.H. and A.M.H., i.e. a Barbadian's and a Martinican's Head . . . " (Schonhorn, ed., *General History*, 234).

and Cutlash, and there being 22 sail in that Harbour; upon sight of the Pirate, the Men all fled on Shore and left their Vessels, which they possess'd themselves of, burnt, sunk, and destroyed all of them, excepting one Bristol Gally, which they designed to be their best Pirate Ship, if a better did not present: After they did all the mischief they could in that Harbour, they came on upon the Banks,[27] where they met nine or ten sail of Frenchmen, one of whom is the Pirate Ship of 26 Guns abovesaid, taken from a Frenchman, unto whom Roberts the Pirate gave the Bristol Gally, but sunk and destroyed all the other French Vessels, taking first out what Guns were fit for his own Ship and all other valuable Goods.

Roberts the Pirate designed from Newfoundland to range thro' the Western and Canary Islands, and so to the Southward, to the Island of New Providence,[28] possest by Negroes, in South Latitude 17 which they say is the place of the Pirates' General Rendezvous, where they have a Fortification and a great Magazine of Powder, &c. where they intend to spend their Money with the Portuguize Negro Women. Roberts the Pirate says, that there is a French Pirate on the North Coast of America, who gives no Quarter to any Nation, and if he met him, he would give him none.[29] The Pirates seem[s] much enraged at Bristol Men, for Capt. Rogers' sake, whom they hate as they do the Spaniards.

---

27 "The Great Bank is almost constantly covered with . . . fogs, extremely thick and cold. A great swell marks the place where it lies; the waves are always in a state of agitation, and the winds high about this bank. The cause of this is said to be, that the sea being irregularly driven forward by currents bearing sometimes on one side, sometimes on the other, strikes with impetuosity against the borders of this bank, and is repelled from them with equal violence: whilst, on the bank itself, at a little distance from the borders, the situation is as tranquil as in a harbour, except in cases of heavy gales coming from a greater distance" (Anspach, *History of Newfoundland*, 292–293).

28 The Bahamian island of New Providence then "was more than a pirate haven. . . . [I]t was a place where the flotsam and jetsam of the Caribbean washed up, an island that attracted some of the most unsavory people in the Americas. It also served as a finishing school for pirates. . . . Plunder and slaves could be bought and sold there, captured ships could be refitted and re-crewed, and successful voyages could be celebrated in an orgy of riotous indulgence. Above all, it was a place where pirate captains could meet, exchange, swap intelligence, and plan even darker deeds for the future" (Konstam, *Blackbeard*, 93).

29 Possibly the French pirate Montigny de Palisse, who cruised in the sloop *Sea King* for a while with Roberts off Barbados early in 1720. De Palisse fled at the approach of Rogers' galley and another pirate-hunting craft, and Roberts may have perceived De Palisse as having abandoned him in an act of cowardice. They later rejoined and De Palisse apologized "for fleeing the fight off Barbados" (Konstam, *Piracy*, 237–239).

6

"Profligate, cursing and swearing much, and very ready and willing to do any Thing on Board" – The trial of Ann Bonny and Mary Read (1720)

Ann Bonny and Mary Read are not the only, nor are they the earliest, female sea rovers on record.[1] That they are so well known is largely because Captain Charles Johnson's *General History* included a fascinating, highly detailed account of their lives before and during their pirate career in Jack Rackam's crew. Unfortunately very little of it can be verified today, and many long-accepted elements of the Bonny-Read tale may be open to question.

In 1718 Rackam (or Rackum or Rackham), with whom their story is forever linked, was serving in Captain Charles Vane's crew as quartermaster. On a pirate ship this position effectively put him in charge at all times except in battle, when the captain's word became law. That November, Vane's small flotilla clashed with a better-armed French warship. Vane – against the wishes of most of his men, but probably sensibly – gave the order to turn away. Although his men obeyed, once in the clear Rackam spoke up for the majority who had wanted to try boarding the French vessel. Questioning Vane's courage, Rackam called for a vote to replace him. The result was that Rackam took over as captain; Vane and a few loyalists were sent away in a captured sloop. For his part, Rackam – known as "Calico Jack" from his colorful shirts – went on to further cruises until, after losing a prize ship filled with loot to pirate hunters, he decided to take advantage of King George's offer of a pardon, which he obtained through Woodes Rogers, the new governor at Nassau.[2]

It was there that Rackam met and began a romance with one Ann Bonny. The principal source about this is Captain Johnson, who described Bonny as a "Libertine" then married to a pirate named James Bonny. Ann suggested Rackam pay her husband to divorce her, but when the governor learned of this he threatened Ann with jail and a flogging. Ann then ran off with Rackam, who was returning to piracy.[3]

---

1 Examples of modern scholarship on this topic include works such as Murray, "One Woman's Rise to Power: Cheng I's Wife and the Pirates"; Appleby, "Women and Piracy in Ireland: From Gráinne O'Malley to Anne Bonny"; Bracewell, "Women among the Uskoks: Literary Images and Reality"; and Stanley, ed., *Bold in Her Breeches*.
2 Schonhorn, ed., *General History*, 138–141, 148–150, 620–623; Woodard, *Republic of Pirates*, 237, 315–316.
3 Schonhorn, ed., *General History*, 623–624.

Mary Read kills another pirate in a duel; a story related in the *General History*, depicted here in *The Pirates Own Book* (artist unknown).

It is an enduring story, although a Jamaica court would later classify Bonny as a spinster, which was "the proper legal designation of one still unmarried" in the era.[4] The court would apply the same term to Read, who at some point joined the pair at sea. According to Captain Johnson, Read had spent a good part of her life passing herself off as male, her adventures including service aboard a warship and in an army regiment.[5] She, like Bonny, adopted male dress among the pirates when in battle.

With Bonny and Read aboard, Rackam's small crew spent several weeks making a nuisance of themselves around the Bahamas, as the following newspaper article attests.

[*Boston Gazette*, 10–17 October 1720, 2]

New-Providence, Sept. 4th.

Several Pirates are on the Coast of the Bahamas,[6] among which is one Rackum who Run away with a Sloop of 6 Guns, and took with him 12 Men, and Two Women. The Governour of this Place sent a Sloop of 45 Men after him. And on the 2d Instant

---

4   *Tryals of Captain John Rackam*, 16; *Oxford English Dictionary*, XVI:244. From a 1662 dictionary: "*Spinster*, a Law term, being appropriated to unmarried women in all deeds, bonds, and evidences" (Phillips, *The New World of English Words*, n.p.).

5   Schonhorn, ed., *General History*, 153–159.

6   Their location made the Bahamas a popular cruising spot for pirates. "The islands sat on the edge of the relatively narrow Bahamas Channel and the Florida Straits, each less than a hundred miles wide. Given a radius of visibility of twenty miles on a clear day, two or three pirate ships working in concert just within sight of each other could cover most of the channel, ensuring that they stood a good chance of encountering any ships that fell into their net" (Konstam, *Blackbeard*, 36). For more on the connections between Bahamas-based pirates, see the diagram in Rediker, *Between the Devil and the Deep Blue Sea*, 268.

Doctor Rowan with his Sloop, and 54 Hands, 12 Guns, went out in order to suppress them; as did Capt. Roach who arriv'd here from Barbadoes. The Pirates Swear Destruction to all those who belong to this island.

The same issue contained a proclamation by Woodes Rogers identifying the female pirates by name.

[*Boston Gazette*, 10–17 October 1720, 3]

By his Excellency
Woodes Rogers, Esq;
Governour of New-Providence, &c.
A Proclamation.

Whereas John Rackum, George Featherstone, John Davis, Andrew Gibson, John Howell, Noah Patrick _____ &c. and two Women, by Name, Ann Fulford alias Bonny, & Mary Read, did on the 22d of August last combine together to enter on board, take, steal and run-away with out of this Road of Providence, a Certain Sloop call'd the *William*, Burthen about 12 Tons, mounted with 4 great Guns and 2 Swivel ones,[7] also Ammunition, Sails, Rigging, Anchor, Cables, and a Canoe, owned by and belonging to Capt. John Ham, and with the said Sloop did proceed to commit Robery and Piracy upon the Boat and Effects of James Cohier Esq; on the South Side of this Island, also upon Capt. Isaacs, Master of a Sloop riding at Berry-Islands in his Way from South-Carolina to this Port:

Wherefore these are to Publish and make Known to all Persons Whatsoever, that the said John Rackum and his said Company are hereby proclaimed Pirates and Enemies to the Crown of Great Britain, and are to be so treated and Deem'd by all his Majesty's Subjects.

Given at Nassau, this 5th of
September, 1720
Sign'd WOODES ROGERS.

The pursuit of Rackam and his gang ended in late October, 1720 when they were captured on Jamaica's west coast. They were soon sharing a Spanish Town jail with Rackam's former commander Charles Vane, who after several adventures had been recognized as a pirate and taken in irons to Jamaica, where he would eventually be tried and hanged.[8]

---

7 Mounted on "a pivot working freely round in a socket," swivel guns were "small cannon of ½ lb. or 1 lb. caliber . . . " (Smyth, *Lexicon*, 670).
8 Woodard, *Republic of Pirates*, 309–310, 318–319.

While the legend of Bonny and Read was born at this time, sources independent of Captain Charles Johnson's work have been hard to trace. In 1972, Manuel Schonhorn observed that outside of the brief official report of their trial, he had "been unable to find published material on the Rackam-Bonny-Read liaisons, though contemporary accounts seem to have been readily available" to the author of the *General History*.[9] In a later analysis of the Bonny-Read story, Julie Wheelwright commented on the "relative vacuum of factual evidence."[10] Still later, Joel H. Baer observed that "[l]engthy eighteenth- and late twentieth-century accounts to the contrary notwithstanding, *The Tryals of Captain John Rackam* is the only source for the few facts we have about the two women pirates."[11]

This 1721 document contains, besides the portion related to the trial of Bonny and Read excerpted here, the report of the trial of Rackam and the male pirates in his crew, as well as that of Vane. All were convicted and sentenced to death, Baer remarking on the "striking . . . contrast between process and substance" in the trials, in which the court "was exemplary as regards form, [but] repeatedly over-indicted and based its lethal verdicts on weak evidence."[12] Rackam and his men died in a spate of hangings in November 1720 at Port Royal and Kingston, some "hung on Gibbets in Chains, for a publick Example, and to terrify others from such-like evil Practices."[13] The court stayed the executions of their female companions, both found to be pregnant; Angus Konstam noted that "exactly who the fathers were has never been explained."[14] Read would die of fever in prison, and be buried, according to the burial records of the Jamaican parish of St. Catherine, on 28 April 1721.[15] Most accounts agree that Bonny somehow escaped the gallows, but a widely accepted version of her fate does not exist.

Part of the fascination of the female pirates' story, as Konstam noted, is that they "had broken all the rules, and had escaped from the restrictions imposed on the lives of women of the time. If this was not shocking enough, they had also turned to a life of crime, and had used their bodies to avoid sharing the fate of Rackam and his men."[16] While the court report affirms this, there are few other details in it. The trial itself lasted just one day; the summaries of testimony and proceedings occupy only two pages.[17] Nothing in them appears to support the detailed account Captain Charles Johnson gave of the two female pirates' backgrounds, nor, for that matter, many of Johnson's other assertions about the duo.[18]

---

9   Schonhorn, ed., *General History*, 674.
10   Wheelwright, "Tars, Tars, and Swashbucklers," in Stanley, *Bold in Her Breeches*, 178.
11   Baer, *British Piracy*, III:2.
12   Baer, *British Piracy*, III:2.
13   *Tryals of Captain John Rackam*, 15.
14   Konstam, *Piracy*, 166.
15   Black, *Pirates of the West Indies*, 117.
16   Konstam, *Piracy*, 166.
17   *Tryals of Captain John Rackam*, 18–19.
18   See also Wheelwright, "Tars, Tars, and Swashbucklers," in Stanley, *Bold in Her Breeches*, 178–190.

That said, trial reports did not usually include such background data, Baer noting that "their limitations as historical sources stem from the nature of trials and of reporting in the period from 1660 to 1730." He continued:

> Criminal trials usually lasted no more than an hour because the prosecution quickly elicited the necessary inculpatory evidence from two or three witnesses, the defence cross-examined them superficially and rarely called its own, there were no defence lawyers to object to or probe the state's case, and the jury returned a verdict in less time than the trial. Important, "state" trials or those with many defendants might last more than one day, but the information generated even from these was far less than from the average, non-capital case today.[19]

A result, Jo Stanley observed in *Bold in Her Breeches*, is that "the pirates (female and male) in these admiralty court reports are written up as voiceless dogs. By comparison, Johnson tried to provide biographical information that made pirates into understandable characters – perhaps not least because of his antipathy to the elite ashore."[20] However, Johnson's account has proved hard to accept in its entirety. Julie Wheelwright, in a chapter Stanley included in *Bold in Her Breeches*, noted that "[t]he first published accounts of Read and Bonny's adventures coincided with the popularity of a particular heroic archetype in eighteenth-century Anglo-American balladry," that of the "the fictional 'female warrior' [who] masquerades as a man and sets off to war to follow a lover, escape a husband or defend her country. She usually makes an excellent warrior but inevitably gives up her Amazonian skills for love and retires from battle covered in glory." Johnson's handling of the Read-Bonny tale "suggests that the fictional "female warrior" overshadowed the facts."[21]

The trial report does, however, speak to the female pirates' activity among Rackam's men. It also shows Bonny and Read urging their male counterparts on to violence against a female captive, Dorothy Thomas, taken prisoner during an episode off the north coast of Jamaica. She told the court how the women pirates urged Rackam's men to kill her to prevent her from bearing witness against them someday. Thomas would be the first person called to give testimony at their trial.[22]

ooooo

---

19   Baer, *British Piracy*, II:vii.
20   Stanley, *Bold in Her Breeches*, 57.
21   Wheelwright, "Tars, Tars, and Swashbucklers," in Stanley, *Bold in her Breeches*, 178.
22   *Tryals of Captain John Rackam*, 18.

From *The Tryals of Captain John Rackam, and Other Pirates* (Jamaica: Robert Baldwin, 1721), 15–19.[23]

[**Editors Note:** The High Court of Admiralty's proceedings "against Mary Read and Ann Bonny, alias Bonn, late of the Island of [New] Providence, Spinsters, for Piracies, Felonies, and Robberies committed by them, on the High Sea," began in St. Jago de la Vega, or Spanish Town, Jamaica on Monday, 28 November, 1720. The prisoners were brought into the court, where Register William Norris read out the charges against them. The first article charged that on the previous 1 September Read and Bonny, as part of a crew including John Rackam, George Featherston, Richard Corner, John Davies, John Howell, Patrick Carty, Thomas Earl, and Noah Harwood,[24] began a piratical cruise "upon the high Sea, in a certain Sloop of an unknown Name," and that two days later they robbed seven fishing boats off Harbor Island in the Bahamas, netting their crews' belongings along with ten Jamaican pounds' worth of fish and tackle. More substantial prizes had followed. The second article charged Read and Bonny with involvement in the 1 October capture, off Hispaniola, of two merchant sloops; the third article with the 19 October taking, off Port Maria on Jamaica's north coast, of a schooner captained by Thomas Spenlow; and the fourth with the 20 October seizure of the merchant sloop *Mary and Sarah*, captained by Thomas Dillon, off Jamaica's Discovery or "Dry Harbour" Bay. Both Read and Bonny pleaded Not Guilty to the charges, and Norris began calling witnesses for the prosecution.]

> *Dorothy Thomas* deposed, That she, being in a Canoa at Sea, with some Stock and Provisions, at the North-side of Jamaica, was taken by a Sloop, commanded by one Captain Rackam (as she afterwards heard), who took out of the Canoa most of the Things that were in her: And further said, That the Two Women, Prisoners at the Bar, were then on Board the said Sloop, and wore Men's Jackets, and long Trouzers, and Handkerchiefs tied about their Heads; and that each of them had a Machet[25] and Pistol in their Hands, and cursed and swore at the Men, to murther the Deponent; and that they should kill her, to prevent her coming against them; and the Deponent further said, That the Reason of her knowing and believing them to be Women then was, by the largeness of their Breasts.
>
> *Thomas Spenlow*, being sworn, deposed, That when he was taken by Rackam, the two Women, Prisoners at the Bar, were then on Board Rackam's Sloop.
>
> *John Besneck*, and *Peter Cornelian*, two Frenchmen, were produced as Witnesses against the Prisoners at the Bar, and were sworn.

---

23   Courtesy of the UK National Archives (CO137/134).

24   The trial report earlier (15) listed all these men as having been hanged at Port Royal or Kingston on 18–19 and 21 November; Fetherston was identified as sailing master of Rackam's vessel, Corner as quartermaster.

25   "The machete was a common tool and weapon among the Spanish in the New World, as well as among the Native Americans in contact with them. Its weakness was its lack of hilt" (Little, *Sea Rover's Practice*, 70).

Mr. Simon Clarke was sworn Interpreter;

Then the said Two Witnesses declared, That the Two Women, Prisoners at the Bar, were on Board Rackam's Sloop, at the Time that Spenlow's Scooner,[26] and Dillon's Sloop, were taken by Rackam; That they were very active on Board, and willing to do any Thing; That Ann Bonny, one of the Prisoners at the Bar, handed Gun-powder to the Men, That when they saw any Vessel, gave Chase, or Attacked, they wore Men's Cloaths; and, at other Times, they wore Women's Cloaths; That they did not seem to be kept, or detain'd by Force, but of their own Free-Will and Consent.[27]

Thomas Dillon, being sworn, declared, That on or about the Twentieth Day of October last, he was lying at Anchor, with the Sloop *Mary and Sarah*, whereof he was Master, in Dry-Harbour, in Jamaica; and that a strange Sloop came into the said Harbour, which fired a Gun at the Deponent's Sloop; whereupon the Deponent and his Men went ashoar, in order to defend themselves, and Sloop; And after that several Shot had been fired at them, by the said Sloop, the Deponent hailed them, and one Fetherston (as the Deponent believ'd) answer'd, That they were English Pirates, and that they need not be afraid, and desired the Deponent to come on Board; where-upon the Deponent went on Board, and found that the said Sloop was commanded by one John Rackam; afterwards the said Rackam, and his Crew, took the Deponent's Sloop, and her Lading, and carried her with them to Sea; and further said, That the two Women, Prisoners at the Bar, were then on Board Rackam's Sloop; and that Ann Bonny, one of the Prisoners at the Bar, had a Gun in her Hand, That they were both very profligate, cursing and swearing much, and very ready and willing to do any Thing on Board.[28]

After the aforesaid Witnesses had severally been examined, His Excellency the President,[29] asked both the Prisoners at the Bar, if they, or either of them, had any Defence to make, or any Witnesses to be sworn on their behalf; or if they would have any of the Witnesses, who had been already sworn, cross-examined; that if they would, they should propose and declare to the Court what Questions they, or either of them, would have asked, and if they had any, the Court, or himself, would interro-

---

26 "*Schooner*, a small vessel with two masts, whose main-sail and fore-sail are suspended from gaffs reaching from the mast towards the stern; and stretched out below by booms, whose foremost ends are hooked to an iron, which clasps the mast so as to turn therein as upon an axis, when the after-ends are swung from one side of the vessel to the other" (Falconer, *Universal Dictionary*, n.p.).

27 "This testimony suggests that the women were not disguised on the ship but simply wore male clothes for con-venience during raids. The masquerade would have made them relatively anonymous, signaled their role as active crew members, and possibly even afforded them a degree of protection from sexual assault had they been cap-tured" (Wheelwright, "Tars, Tarts and Swashbucklers," 180).

28 "In this and other descriptions, no exception seems to have been made for the women's presence by the pirate crew or by their captives. They were not marginalised but played a central role in Rackham's raids, as integral members of a tightly knit group" (Wheelwright, "Tars, Tarts, and Swashbucklers," 180).

29 Sir Nicholas Lawes served as president of the court.

gate them. Whereto they both of them answer'd, That they had no Witnesses, nor any Questions to ask.

Then the Prisoners were taken away from the Bar, and put into safe Custody, and all the Standers by withdrew from the Court, except the Register.

Afterwards His Excellency the President, and Commissioners, then sitting, took the Evidence which had been given against the Prisoners into Consideration; and having maturely, and deliberately, considered thereof, and of the Circumstances of the Prisoners' Case, all the Commissioners then sitting, and his Excellency the President, unanimously agreed, That Mary Read, and Ann Bonny, alias Bonn, were both of them Guilty, of the Piracies, Robberies, and Felonies, charged against them, in the Third and Fourth Articles, of the Articles aforesaid.[30]

Then the Prisoners before-named were brought back to the Bar, and His Excellency the President, acquainted them, That the Court had unanimously found them both Guilty of the Piracies, Robberies, and Felonies, charged against them, in the Third and Fourth Articles, of the Articles which had been Exhibited against them.

And being severally asked, Whether they, or either of them, had any Thing to say, or offer, Why Sentence of Death should not pass upon them, for their said Offences? And they, nor either of them, offering any Thing material, His Excellency the President pronounced Sentence of Death upon them in the Words following, viz.

["]You Mary Read, and Ann Bonny, alias Bonn, are to go from hence to the Place from whence you came, and from thence to the Place of Execution; where you shall be severally hang'd by the Neck, 'till you are severally Dead.["]

["]And GOD of His infinite mercy be merciful to both of your Souls.["]

After Judgment was pronounced, as aforesaid, both the Prisoners inform'd the Court, that they were both quick with Child, and prayed that Execution of the Sentence might be stayed.

Whereupon the Court ordered, that Execution of the said Sentence should be respited, and that an Inspection should be made.[31] [. . .]

---

30 "Dorothy Thomas was the sole witness against the accused on the first article, for which reason the court did not convict. There were no witnesses to carry the second article" (Baer, *British Piracy*, III:443).

31 "While there is no record of whether the inspection was undertaken or what its results revealed, it is certain that neither woman was hanged" (Wheelwright, "Tars, Tarts, and Swashbucklers," 181).

7

"All the Barbarity imaginable" – Edward Low, George Lowther, and associates (1722–1725)

The psychopathically violent Edward or Ned Low emerges from contemporary accounts like a terrible ghost from a very dark age, committing acts of sadism to rival the worst of those Exquemelin attributed to the *boucaniers*. Born in Westminster, he is said to have started his criminal life by shaking down other boys, and to have moved on to gambling in crooked games. One of his brothers ended up on a Tyburn gallows, but another brother brought Edward to sea with him. After a few years Edward took a job in a Boston rigging house, married, and fathered at least one child. Being "too apt to disagree with his Masters" in the rigging business, when his wife died Low left the child behind and signed aboard a sloop bound for the Bay of Honduras, where the crew were to gather the Central American logwood valued for its dye-making qualities. After arriving and starting work, a disagreement between Low and the sloop's captain turned violent; Low fired a musket at him but missed, hitting another man by mistake. The end result was that Low and a dozen companions left in the sloop's boat, and headed off on the account.[1]

They soon after joined forces with pirate George Lowther, Low serving as his lieutenant on operations in the Caribbean, though Low's ambition and attitude reportedly strained the partnership.[2] Whatever the case, the two parted late in May 1722, Low sailing off in command of a captured brigantine, along with about forty others. The newspaper accounts appearing in this chapter begin not long after the Low–Lowther partnership dissolved; note that reports would occasionally continue to link the two.

Lowther (as noted herein) would eventually come to grief on the island of La Blanquilla, shooting himself while being pursued by pirate hunters. For his part, after their separation Low veered north onto the first of several far-ranging pirate cruises, establishing a reputation for brutality along the way. His quartermaster for a time was Francis (or Farrington) Spriggs, who will be seen more closely in the next chapter, and who would also eventually go off on his own. Another confederate was London-born Charles Harris, who commanded Low's consort vessel, the sloop *Ranger*.

---

1 Schonhorn, ed., *General History*, 318–319; Ashton's recollections about his time as Low's prisoner (in the next chapter) mention Low's wife and child.
2 Schonhorn, ed., *General History*, 312, 314.

Edward Low (artist unknown, from the *General History*).

George Lowther (artist unknown, from the *General History*); note the process of careening taking place in the background.

Low's small flotilla was operating off New York in mid-1723 when its activities brought a response from HMS *Greyhound*, which on 10 June confronted both Harris's *Ranger* and Low's sloop *Fortune*. During the engagement the *Ranger* was captured, its captain and crew subsequently taken to Rhode Island for trial. A few prisoners were able to support their claims to having been forced and were acquitted; most were found guilty and hanged, the executions taking place on a gallows to which their dark blue version of the Jolly Roger was affixed. The record of the trial, excerpted in this chapter, provides a comprehensive source on a Golden Age pirate outfit, yielding information not only on Harris and his men, but on all of Low's company, including a copy of their articles.

Low continued with a series of long-ranging cruises, frequently leaving horror stories in his wake. The last newspaper articles cited herein show him active around Martinique in 1724 when his crew turned him out of office, setting him and two loyalists loose in a captured sloop. He seems to have met his ultimate fate at the hands of the French.

ooooo

[**Editor's Note:** One early public notice of Edward Low's pirate career came in the form of an advertisement. In this case, it was a reprinted deposition regarding the forcing of several men from the brigantine *Rebecca*, the text adding some details about the breakup of the Low-Lowther partnership. Printing such "ads of force" was a formality of the day to help exonerate those impressed to serve aboard pirate craft. Forced men Joseph Swetser and Joseph Libbey, when later tried in Newport as part of Charles Harris' crew, would both cite the ads reprinted below. In Libbey's case it would fail to counteract testimony that he had become an active member of the pirate company.]

[*Boston News-Letter*, 11–18 June 1722, 2]

Advertisements

John Smith of Boston in New-England, late Mate of the Briganteen *Rebecca* of Charlstown, burthen about Ninety Tons, whereof James Flucker was late Commander, and Charles Messon of Boston aforesaid Mariner, late belonging to the said Briganteen, Severally Declare and say, That the said Briganteen in her Voyage from St. Christopher's of [*sic* – to] Boston, on the Twenty-eighth day of May last past, being in the Latitude of Thirty-eight degrees and odd Minutes North, the said Briganteen was taken by a Pirate Sloop Commanded by one Lowder,[3] having near One Hundred Men and Eight Guns Mounted, and the day after the said Briganteen was taken, the said Pirate[s] parted their Company, Forty of them went on board the said Briganteen Commanded by Edward Loe of Boston aforesaid, Mariner, and the rest of the said Pirates went on board the Sloop Commanded by the said Lowder; and the Declarants further say, That

---

3   George Lowther (whose name frequently appears as "Lowder" in these texts) began his piracy career by joining renegade British soldiers in seizing the armed merchant ship *Gambia Castle*, on which Lowther was second mate. For a short biography, see Schonhorn, ed., *General History*, 304–317.

Joseph Sweetser[4] of Charlestown aforesaid and Richard Rich, and Robert Willis of London, mariners, all belonging to the said Briganteen, were forc'd and Compelled against their Wills to go with the said Pirates, viz. Joseph Sweetser and Richard Rich on board the Briganteen, and Robert Willis on board the Sloop; The said Willis having broke his Arm by a fall from the Mast, Desired that considering his Condition they would let him go, but they utterly refused and forced him away with them.

Signum
John Smith
Charles Cl. Messon

Suffolk ss   Boston, June 15, 1722

The above named John Smith and Charles Messon personally appearing made Oath to the Truth of the above-written Declaration.

Coram me[5] J. Willard Secr. & Just. Peace[6]

ooooo

[*Boston News-Letter*, 25 June-2 July 1722, 2]

Boston. The Pirate Lowe upon our Coast, has taken to the Eastward upwards of a Dozen of Fishermen, whom he plunder'd, and robb'd of all their Cloaths and Provisions, and used them very Barbarously; two Nantucket Indians after cruel Usage the Pirates hang'd;[7] he also took a Scooner of about 50 Tuns, and relinquish'd the Briganteen he was in, belonging to Charlstown, whereof Mr. Flucker was Commander from St. Kitts, when he was taken by a Pirate Sloop, one Lowder Commander. Mr. Flucker being still kept on Board this Vessel, with some of the Captivated[8] Fishermen, are at last come in here. [. . .]

Advertisements

These are to give Notice, That on the fifteenth and sixteenth Days of June 1722, the following Persons were taken at Port Roseway[9] in Nova Scotia by a Pirate Briganteen, one Lowe Commander, viz. Nicholas Merit *tertius*,[10] Joseph Libby, Philip Ashton,[11] and

---

4   Bostonian Joseph Swetser was 24 a year later at the time of the trial of Charles Harris' company (*Boston News-Letter*, 27 June–4 July 1723, 2).

5   Before me.

6   The same page of the same issue of the *Boston News-Letter* included a short item about Lowther: "Capt. King from Barbadoes was Accosted by a Pirate Sloop Commanded by Lowder, who robb'd him of about 14 Hogsheads of Rhum, five or six barrels of Sugar, Five Trunks of Goods, &c." Another item reported a ship "well fitted & man'd with upwards of a hundred Men" being dispatched from Boston in response to reports of pirate activity.

7   Thomas Mumford would testify at the trial of Captain Charles Harris and his men that he was one of six Nantucket Indians Low forcibly took off a fishing sloop. Of these, Low hanged the two mentioned here, and evidently assigned Mumford to Charles Harris' vessel; the others presumably remained aboard Low's own craft.

8   Captured.

9   Shelburne, Nova Scotia.

10   The third, although Merritt will refer to himself as "Jun." (junior) in the closing of his recollection of captivity, transcribed in the next chapter.

11   An excerpt from Ashton's memoir of time spent as Low's captive appears in the next chapter.

Lawrence Fabens, all Fishermen of Marblehead[12] in New-England, whom the said Low Forced and compelled against their Wills from on board their respective Fishing Vessels to serve on board his said Briganteen.

ooooo

[*Boston News-Letter*, 2–9 July 1722, 2]

Advertisements [. . .]

The Depositions of Thomas Trefry, late Master of the Scooner *Mary*; Robert Gilford, Master of the Shallop[13] *Elizabeth*; and John Collyer, one of the Crew belonging to the Scooner *Samuel*, William Nichols Master, all of Marblehead in the County of Essex, Fisher men, Testify and say, That as they were upon their Lawfull Imployment nigh Cape Sables[14] on or about the 14th, 15th and 16th Days of June last past, they were taken Prisoners by Capt. Edward Low, a Pirate then Commander of the Brigantine ————— but since removed himself into the before named Scooner *Mary*, which they took from the Deponent Trefry; and besides these Deponents they took several other Fishing Vessels, viz. Nicholas Merritt, Master of the Shallop *Jane*, Philip Ashton, Master of the Scooner *Milton*, Joseph Libbey, one of the said Ashton's Crew, Lawrence Phabens, one of the Crew belonging to the Scooner *Rebeckah*, Thomas Salter Commander; all these four Men to wit, Nicholas Merrit, Philip Ashton, Joseph Libbey, and Lawrence Phabens, being Young Nimble Men of about Twenty Years of Age, the Pirates kept them by force and would not let them go tho' they pleaded as much as they dare to, yet nothing would avail, so as they wept like Children; yet notwithstanding they forceably Carried them away to the great Grief and Sorrow of the afore named four Young Men, as well as these Deponants; and when any of the Deponants mentioned any thing in favour of the said four Young Men, the Quarter Master of the Pirate Publickly Declared, They would carry them, and let them send to New-England and Publish it if they pleased. These Deponants further say, That the said Pirates Constrained four more Fisher men belonging to Piscataqua and the Isle of Sholas[15] to go with them against their wills also.

Salem, July the 3d 1722

Thomas Trefry

John Collyer

Robert Gilford

Essex Ss Salem, July the 3d, 1722

---

12 Then a fishing settlement north of Boston.
13 The 1771 edition of Falconer's nautical reference work defined a *shallop* as "a sort of large boat with two masts, and usually riged like a schooner" (*Universal Dictionary*, n.p.).
14 Island off Nova Scotia.
15 The Islands of Shoals, off the New Hampshire/Maine coast.

Then Thomas Trefry, John Collyer, and Robert Gilford, the Three Deponents above named personally Appearing made Oath to the Truth of the foregoing Deposition taken *ad Perpetuam rei memoriam*.[16]

Coram nobis[17]

Joseph Wolcot

Stephen Sewall

Justices of the Peace [. . .]

○○○○○

Court of Admiralty

Sundry Goods left on Board the Briganteen *Rebecka*, James Flacker Master (by the Pirates) which by Decree of Court are Ordered to be Sold by Publick Vendue on Wednesday the 11th Currant at the House of Capt. Long in Charlstown. The Sale to begin about Five a Clock P.M. Viz 1 Turtle Net, 1 Scarlet Jacket, 1 Small Still, 2 pair of Steelyards,[18] 1 Jack and Pendant,[19] 2 Doz. of Plates, 2 Papers of Pins, 5 Horn books, 2 pieces of Cantaloons,[20] 1 main sail, Boom and Small Cable belonging to a Scooner, a small Boat and 20 Yards of old Canvas. The above Particulars are to be seen in Charlstown aforesaid. *Per Curium*,[21] John Boydel, Regist.

[**Editor's Note:** Low followed these activities off Nova Scotia and New England by heading back toward the Caribbean, sailing for the Leeward Islands, surviving a hurricane along the way. After a stop to rest and refit, the company voted to head for the Azores, in part because of stepped-up naval activity in the West Indies. After cruising off the Azores and the Cape de Verde Islands, Low's company returned to Central American waters by early 1723.[22]]

[*British Journal* (London), 11 May 1723, 5][23]

By Letters Yesterday, there is Advice, That a Spanish Pyrate of 10 Guns and 60 Men, had on the 10th of March last visited the Bay of Anderos,[24] and took nine Ships out

---

16 For perpetual remembrance.
17 Before us.
18 Weighing scales.
19 Falconer defined a jack as "a sort of flag or colours, displayed from a mast erected on the outer end of a ship's bowsprit." The same source described a pendant (or pennant) as "a sort of long narrow banner, displayed from the mast-head of a ship of war, and usually terminating in two ends or points . . . " (*Universal Dictionary*, n.p.).
20 Cantaloon was a type of British-made woolen cloth (Dow, *Every Day Life in the Massachusetts Bay Colony*, 72).
21 By the court.
22 Schonhorn, ed., *General History*, 321–326.
23 © British Library Board (*The British Journal*, London 11 May 1723, 5). Used with permission.
24 The Bay of Honduras, although English writers sometimes referred to the northern Spanish coastal city of Santander, with an adjacent bay, as St. Andero or St. Anderos.

of eleven that lay in the Bay; none escaping, but the Captains Lloyd and Young. About three Hours after came in two English Pyrates, viz. Capt. Low, of six Guns and 100 Men, with his Companion Lowther,[25] who retook all the Ships, and put the Spanish Pyrates to the Sword.[26]

[Editor's Note: Operating in the sloop *Fortune*, and with the sloop *Ranger* captained by Charles Harris as consort, in early May 1723 Low took the *Amsterdam Merchant* off the west Cuban coast – an action that would figure prominently in the later trial of Harris and his men. He continued his vicious cruise north, and by early June was operating off the coasts of the mid-Atlantic colonies. Word of pirate activities reached the warship HMS *Greyhound*, under Captain Peter Solgard, which caught up with Low and Harris off Long Island. "Mistaking the *Greyhound* for a merchant vessel, the pirates attacked her. They soon discovered their error and tuned to flee. Solgard overtook and captured Harris and brought him and his crew in to Newport."[27]

Harris had been second mate aboard a merchant ship Lowther captured in January 1722, and though initially a forced man, evidently came to serve with the pirates willingly.[28] It is unclear when he parted company with Lowther; he may have been among those who left with Low in May 1722. At the Newport piracy trial in July 1723, he would be among 26 men convicted of piracy and sentenced to hang. Meanwhile, Low's company's brush with the Royal Navy did nothing to soften their subsequent treatment of captives.]

[*Boston News-Letter*, 13–20 June 1723, 1–2]

Rhode Island, June 14. On the 11th Instant arrived here His Majesty's Ship *Grayhound*,[29] Capt. Peter Solgard Commander,[30] from his Cruize at Sea, and brought in a Pirate Sloop of 8 Guns, Barmudas built, 43 White Men and 6 Blacks; of which number eight were wounded in the Engagement and four killed; the Sloop was com-

---

25 As noted earlier, the Low-Lowther partnership dissolved late in May, 1722. This may have been a reference to Charles Harris, operating in consort with Low in this period. However, one Nicholas Lewis, captured with Lowther's company and executed, would refer to what was possibly this episode (see below entry for *London Daily Courant*, 12 June 1724), suggesting that some interchange between Low's and Lowther's companies continued.

26 According to Captain Charles Johnson's version, the Spanish pirates, operating in a six-gun sloop, robbed "five English Sloops and a Pink" inside the Bay, and took their captains aboard their craft for ransom. When Low's men took the Spanish pirate craft, and found English captives and English goods aboard, "the Resolution pass'd to kill all the Company" (Schonhorn, ed., *General History*, 326).

27 Hawes, *Off Soundings*, 61.

28 Schonhorn, ed., *General History*, 312–313, 321.

29 HMS *Greyhound* was a 105–foot long sixth rate warship built in Deptford and launched and commissioned in 1720. The Spanish captured it off Cuba on 19 April 1721, Captain John Waldron and the ship's surgeon losing their lives in the battle, but it was retaken that night. It was based in New York under Peter Solgard in 1723–24; the ship later served in the West Indies, off the Barbary Coast, and in the Mediterranean. It was broken up at Deptford in 1741 (Winfield, *British Warships 1714–1792*, 246–247).

30 Solgard attained captain's rank on 2 July 1722, when he was posted to the *Greyhound*. He would die in the service, commanding HMS *Berwick*, in the Mediterranean in 1740 (Hardy, *Chronological List*, 36).

manded by one Harris, very well fitted; and loaded with all sorts of Provisions: one of the wounded Pirates died on board the Man of War, with an Oath at his Departure; thirty lusty bold young Fellows, were brought on shore, and received by one of the Town Companys under Arms guarding them to Goal, and are all now in Irons under a strong Guard: The Man of War had but two Men wounded, who are in a brave way of Recovery.

Here follows an Account (from on board the Man of War) of the Engagement between Capt. Solgard and the two Pirates Sloops:

Capt. Solgard being informed by a Vessel, that Low the Pirate in a Sloop of 10 Guns & 70 Men, with his Consort of 8 Guns and 48 Men, had sailed off of the East End of Long-Island; the Capt. thereupon steered his Course after them; and on the 10th Currant, half an hour past 4 in the Morning we saw two Sloops N. 2 Leagues distance, the Wind W.N.W.; at 5 we tack'd and stood Southward and clear'd the Ship, the Sloops giving us Chase; at half an hour past 7 we tack'd to the Northward, with little Wind, and stood down to them; at 8 a Clock they fired each a Gun, and hoisted a Black Flag; at half an hour past 8 on the near approach of the Man of War, they haul'd it down, (fearing a Tartar) and put up a Bloody Flag, stemming[31] with us distant 3 quarters of a Mile. We hoisted up our Main-sail and made easy Sail to the Windward, received their Fire several times; but when a breast we gave them ours with round & grape Shot, upon which the head Sloop edg'd away, as did the other soon after, and we with them; the Fire continued on both sides for about an hour; but when they gail'd [sic] from us, with the help of their Oars, we left off Firing, and turn'd to Rowing with 86 Hands, and half an Hour past two in the Afternoon we came up with them; when they clapt on a Wind to receive us; we again kept close to Windward; and ply'd them warmly with small and grape shot; during the Action we fell between them, and having shot down one of their Main Sails we kept close to him, and at 4 a Clock he called for Quarters; at 5 having got the Prisoners on board, we continued to Chase the other Sloop, when at 9 a Clock in the Evening he bore from us N.W.b.W. two Leagues, when we lost sight of him near Block Island. One Desperado was for blowing up this Sloop rather than surrendering, and being hindered, he went forward, and with his Pistol shot out his own Brains.

Capt. Solgard designing to make sure of one of the Pirate Sloops, if not both, took this, seeming to be the Chief, but proved otherwise, and if we had had more Daylight, the other of Low's had also been taken, she being very much batter'd; and 'tis tho't he was slain, with his Cutlas in his hand, encouraging his Men in the Engagement to Fight, and that a great many more Men were kill'd and wounded in her, than the other we took.

The Two Pirate Sloops Commanded by the said Low and Harris intended to have boarded the Man of War, but he plying them so successfully they were discouraged,

---

31 "*To stem*, to make way against any obstacle. 'She does not stem the tide,' that is, she cannot make head against it for want of wind" (Smyth, *Lexicon*, 655).

and endeavoured all they could to escape, notwithstanding they had sworn Damnation to themselves, If they should give over Fighting, tho' the Ship should even prove to be a Man of War. They also intended to have hoisted their Standard upon Block-Island, but we suppose now, there will be a more su[i]table Standard hoisted for those that are taken, according to their Desarts.

On the 12th Currant Capt. Solgard was fitting out again to go in Quest of the said Low the other Pirate Sloop (having the Master of this with him, he knowing what Course they intended by Agreement to Steer, in order to meet with a third Consort), which we hope he'll overtake and bring in. [. . .]

Boston. Since we receiv'd the above account about the Pirates, we are Informed by a Letter from Nantucket, That on the 12th Instant, Capt. Low in a Sloop of 12 Guns, and about 100 Men, very well fitted, has taken a Sloop belonging to that Island, Nathan Skiff Master, who they barbarously kill'd, and kept 2 Indians; the rest of the Men they sent ashore in their Whale Boats without any other sustenance than Water.

ooooo

[*Boston News-Letter*, 20–27 June 1723, 2]

Rhode Island, June 21. We are informed from Nantucket That the Pirate Low, in a few Days after he [parted?] with his Majesty's Ship the *Greyhound*, took a Nantucket Sloop that was Whale fishing about Eighty Miles out of sight of Land which had two Whale Boats; one of them and her Crew was fortunately at some considerable distance from their Vessel, when she was taken; as soon as they perceived it, they rowed with all speed to another Sloop that was at some distance to acquaint them of their Misfortune, and to save Themselves from being taken, who all got safe away. The Master of the Sloop that was taken was very barbarously Murder'd by the Pirates, his name was Nathan Skiff, a Young Man and Unmarried; first of all they cruelly whipt him about the Deck, then they cut off his Ears, and after they had wearied themselves with making a game and sport of the poor Man, they told him that because he was a good Master, he should have an easy death and then shot him thro' the Head: They kept with them an English Boy and two Indian Men that belonged to the Sloop; three more that belonged to the same Company they ordered to sink their Sloop, which they did; then they told them they might take their Whale boat and go about their Business, which they accordingly did, and having a Compass, some Water, and a few Bisket, by the Providence of God it being good Weather, they got to Nantucket, beyond all Expectation.

Last Night arrived here a Scooner belonging to this Port from the Vineyard,[32] whose Company informs, that there was a Vessel arrived there, that brought Advice, that the

---

32   Martha's Vineyard, an island south of Cape Cod, Massachusetts.

Pirates had taken two Plymouth Vessels, and had Killed the Masters very Barbarously, viz. By riping the one alive and taking out his heart and roasting it and then made his Mate eat it, the other by slashing and mauling him, and then cutting off his Ears, they roasted them and made him eat them, who afterwards dyed of his Wounds.

ooooo

From *Tryals of Thirty-Six Persons for Piracy, Twenty-Eight of them upon full Evidence were found Guilty, and the Rest Acquitted. At a Court of Admiralty for Tryal of Pirates, Held at Newport within His Majesties Colony of Rhode-Island and Providence-Plantations in America, on the Tenth, Eleventh and Twelfth Days of July, Anno Dom. 1723. Pursuant to His Majesties Commission, Founded on an Act of Parliament, made in the Eleventh & Twelfth Years of King William the Third Entituled An Act for the more Effectual Suppression of Piracy and made Perpetual by an Act of the Sixth of King George* (Boston: Printed and Sold by Samuel Kneeland, in Queen-Street, below the Prison, 1723).

[**Editor's Note:** The trial of the alleged pirates captured by HMS *Greyhound* began on 10 July, 1723, in the Town House of Newport, Rhode Island, with the swearing-in of William Dummer, lieutenant governor of Massachusetts, as president of the court. Its other commissioners included Rhode Island Governor Samuel Cranston; Rhode Island notary Richard Ward was named register. Its only other business that day was to issue a warrant to bring prisoners to the bar on the following day at 8 a.m. to hear the indictment read against them for felony, piracy, and robbery.

When the proceedings began again, Ward read out the document, which had been prepared by advocate general John Valentine, who had in 1717 defended Bellamy's men in their trial in Boston.[33] The indictment charged that on or about 8 May the accused had captured the 100–ton *Amsterdam Merchant*, captained by John Welland, and that before sinking it they took £7 worth of beef, £150 worth of gold and silver, and a slave worth £50. In the episode, they also cut off Welland's right ear. They were also charged with attacking HMS *Greyhound* on 10 June, seven British sailors being wounded in the episode. All of the prisoners pleaded Not Guilty to the charges.

Those to be tried immediately were Charles Harris, Thomas Linnicar, Daniel Hyde, Stephen Mundon, Abraham Lacy, Edward Lawson, John Tomkins, Francis Laughton, John Fitz-Gerrald, William Studfield, Owen Rice, William Read, John Wilson and Henry Barns. Fourteen others were returned to prison for later trial. (A few others would also eventually be arraigned and enter pleas.) Valentine then opened the proceedings for the prosecution.]

---

33   The commission would also include John Menzies or Meinzies, who had served as defence counsel at the 1704 piracy trial of Captain John Quelch, and as part of the court at the 1717 trial of Bellamy's men; he would also sit on the court at the 1726 trial of William Fly. Valentine, by now Advocate-General of Massachusetts, had been defence counsel at the 1717 trial of Bellamy's company; he would hang himself in 1724 (Baer, *British Piracy*, II:258, III:168–170, 446).

Then the Advocate-General proceeded,

["]May it please Your Honour, and the rest of the Honourable Judges of this Court.

["]The Prisoners at the Bar stand Articled against, and are Prosecuted for, several Felonies, Piracies, and Robberies by them committed upon the High Sea. To which they have severally pleaded Not Guilty.

["]The Crime of Pyracy is a Robbery (for Pyracy is a Sea Term for Robbery) Committed within the Jurisdiction of the Admiralty.

["]And a Pirate is describ'd to be, One who to enrich himself either by surprize or open force, sets upon Merchants, and others, Trading by Sea, to spoil them of their Goods and Treasure, often times by Sinking their Vessels, as the Case will come out before You.

["]This sort of Criminals are engag'd in a perpetual War with every Individual, with every State, Christian or Infidel; they have no Country, but by the nature of their Guilt, separate themselves, renouncing the benefit of all lawful Society, to commit these heinous Offences: The Romans therefore justly held 'em, *Hostis humani Generis*, Enemies of Mankind,[34] and indeed they are Enemies, and Arm'd, against themselves, a kind of *Felons de Se* – Imparting something more, than a natural Death.[35]

["]These unhappy Men, satiated with the Number and Notoriety of their Crimes, had filled up the measure of their Guilt, when, by the Providence of Almighty God, and thro' the Valour and Conduct of Capt. Solgard, they were delivered up to the Sword of Justice. [. . .]

["]And 'twill doubtless be said for the Honour and Reputation of this Colony (tho' of late Scandalously reprov'd to have favour'd, or combin'd with Pirates)[36] and be evinced by the Process and Event of this Affair, that such Flagitious Persons, find as little Countenance and Shelter, and as much Justice at Rhode-Island, as in any other Port of His Majesties Dominions.

["]But your Time is more precious than my Words. I will not mispend it in attempting to set forth the Aggravations of this Complex Crime big with every Enormity, nor in declaring the Mischief, and evil Tendencies of it; for you better know these Things before I mention them; and I consider to Whom I speak, and that the Judgment is Your Honours'.

---

34 For more on this legal definition of pirates, see Goodwin, "Universal Jurisdiction and the Pirate," 989–990.
35 The prosecutor is likening pirates to self-murderers, or suicides. "Self-murderers were tried posthumously by a coroner's jury, and if they were found to have been responsible for their actions savage penalties were enforced against them and their families. They were declared to have been *felones de se*, felons of themselves: their chattels, like those of other felons, were forfeited to the crown and placed at the disposal of the king's almoner or the holder of a royal patent" (MacDonald, "The Secularization of Suicide in England," 53).
36 Rhode Island officials in the era were seen as soft on piracy. Baer found it significant that the "nine-man piracy commission that investigated, indicted and judged the prisoners had only two members from Rhode Island, the governor and the collector of customs. The other seven were from Massachusetts, the colony with the best record of using the new [1700] law to destroy the pirates" (*British Piracy*, III:169).

["]I shall therefore call the King's Evidences[37] to prove the several Facts, as so many distinct Acts of piracy charged on the Prisoners Not by light Circumstances and Presumptions, Not by strained and unfounded Conjectures, but by clear and positive Evidence: And then I doubt not, since 'tis for the interest of Mankind, that these crimes should be punished; Your Honours will do justice to the prisoners, this Colony, and the rest of the world in pronouncing them Guilty, and in passing sentence upon them according to Law.["]

[Prosecution Witnesses]

The King's Evidences being Sworn and Examined, deposed as follows,

John Welland of Boston, Mariner, to the first Article charged, deposed, That upon the Eighth Day of May 1723, being in the aforesaid Ship the *Amsterdam Merchant*, and Master of her off of Cape Antonio,[38] he was Chased by two Sloops, whereof one of them came up with him, and hoisted a Blew Flag, and took him. And was called the *Ranger*, a Pirate under the Command of Edward Low, who was in the other Sloop that chased him; and that the Deponant was ordered aboard the *Ranger*, where he went aboard with Four of his Men; and the Quarter Master Examined him how much Money he had aboard, and he told him about 150 £ in Gold and Silver, which they took out of the Vessel: and after he had been aboard the *Ranger* Sloop three Hours, he was carried on Board the Sloop *Fortune* where Low was, where he was very much abused, having several Wounds with a Cutlass, and at last they cut off his right Ear; and the next Day following, after they had taken out of his Ship one Negro, some Beef, and other things they Sunk the Ship. And the Day after he was taken the said Pirate took one Capt. Eastwick of Piscataqua,[39] on board of whom they afterwards put this Deponent & dismissed him; the Pirates were all harnessed with Weapons, except Thomas Jones.

And also further deposed, that Henry Barns, now one of the Prisoners at the Bar, was forced out of his Ship at the said Time; and was very low and weak, and that the said Barns being ordered by the Pirates to go from Vessel to Vessel with them (that is, their Prizes), when he got on board of Capt. Eastwick, he endeavoured to get away and hid himself, and the Pirates threatned to burn the Ship unless they discovered the said Barns, whereupon the said Barns was compelled to go on Board the Pirate Sloop.

John Ackin, Mariner, and late Mate of the Ship *Amsterdam Merchant*, deposed, that he was Mate of the abovesaid Ship taken as aforesaid by Low the Pirate and his Crew in the two Sloops *Fortune* & *Ranger*; and that the said Pirate forced from out of the said Ship *Amsterdam Merchant*, one Henry Barns now a Prisoner at the Bar, who cryed and

---

37 Witnesses.
38 Cabo de San Antonio, on Cuba's western coast.
39 Portsmouth, N.H., on the Piscataqua river.

took on very much: and desired this Deponant to acquaint his three Sisters living in Barbadoes that he was a forc'd Man, and also very sick and weak at the said time.

John Mudd, Ship Carpenter, and late Carpenter on board the aforesaid Ship *Amsterdam Merchant*, being Sworn and Examined, deposeth, that he was Carpenter on board the said Ship when she was taken by Low's Company in the Sloops *Fortune* and *Ranger* off of Cape Antonio, and that he was carried on board the Sloop *Ranger*; and most of the Pirates were harnessed, that is, Armed with Guns, &c.

Capt. Peter Solgard, Commander of His Majesties Ship the *Grey-hound*, deposeth, that being Cruizing in the said Ship *Grey hound*, in or near the Lat. 39 D. N. on the seventh Day of June last, he spoke with the Master of a Virginia Ship, who informed him, that the day before he had been taken by two Pirate Sloops, that rifled his Ship, in the Evening they left him and steered to the Northward as he believed for Block Island; whereupon Capt. Solgard immediately pursued them, and on the Tenth being about Fourteen Leagues to the Southward of the East End of Long-Island, saw two Sloops which he concluded to be the Pirates, and seemed for some time to stand from them to encourage them to give him Chase, which they did with Sails and Oars; when they came near they hoisted black Flags, and fired each a Shot, and soon afterwards they haul'd down their Black and hoisted Red Flags; then he hoisted His Majesties Colours, and they began the Engagement; the Fire continued on both sides near an Hour, when they perceiving themselves over-powered put away before the Wind, and endeavoured by rowing to make their escape, and there being but little Wind, he got out his Oars and pursued them; about Three of the Clock in the Afternoon he came near them again, when they renewed the Engagement; about Four he got between them, and shot down their Mainsails, which obliged them soon after to call for Quarter; he then immediately sent on board the Lieut. and took out the Prisoners now at the Bar, several of which were wounded. The exact number of their slain is yet unknown; and that during the whole Action they seemed to use their utmost endeavours to annoy His Majesties Ship, and wounded seven of his people, and did much damage in her Rigging and Sails.

Edward Smith,[40] Lieut. of His Majesty's Ship *Grey-hound*, deposed the same that Capt. Solgard did.

Archibald Fisher, Chirurgeon[41] of the *Grey-hound* Man of War deposed, that there were Seven of the *Grey-hound*'s Men wounded in the Fight by the two Pirate Sloops' Companies in the Engagement between the *Grey-hound* Man of War and them, but none Mortal.

---

40   Edward Smith attained captain's rank 16 November 1739, being posted to command HMS *Eltham*. He died in Antigua on 18 April 1743 on HMS *Burford* (Hardy, *Chronological List*, 43).
41   Surgeon.

William Marsh, Mariner, being duly Sworn, deposed and said, that sometime last January, he was taken in the West-Indies by Low's Company in a Schooner & Sloop near Bonaire,[42] and that he saw on board of the Schooner Francis Laughton and William Read, and on board of the Sloop he saw Charles Harris, Edward Lawson, Daniel Hyde, and John Fitz-Gerrald, all Prisoners at the Bar, and that Gerrald asked him whether he would seek his Fortune with him.

[Prisoners' Statements; Prosecution Summary]

After the Witnesses had been severally Examin'd, the Prisoners at the Bar were asked, whether they had anything to say in their own defence? whereto they answered and said, they were forced Men on board of Low, and did nothing voluntarily, but as they were compelled.

Advocate General: ["]Your Honours, I doubt not have observ'd the weakness, and vanity of the defence which has been made by the Prisoners at the Bar, and that the Articles (containing indisputable flagrant Acts of Piracy) are surpassed against each of them. Their Impudence and unfortunate Mistake, in Attacking His Majesty's Ship, tho' to us fortunate, and of great Service to the Neighbouring Governments: Their malicious & cruel Assault upon Capt. Welland, not only in the spoiling of his Goods, but what is much more, the cutting off his Right Ear, a Crime of that nature and barbarity which can ever be repaired: Their Plea of constraint, or force (in the mouth of every Pirate), can be of no avail to them, for if that could Justify or Excuse No Pirate would ever be Convicted, nor even any profligate Person in his own account offend against the Moral law; if it were asked, it would be hard to answer: Who offer'd the Violence? It's apparent they forced or perswaded one another, or rather the Compulsion proceeded of their own corrupt and avaricious Inclinations: But if there was the least semblance of truth in the Plea, it might come out in Proof, That the Prisoners or some of them did manifest their uneasiness and sorrow, to some of the Persons whom they had surpriz'd and Robb'd; But the contrary of that is plain from Mr. Marsh's Evidence, That the Prisoners were so far from a dislike, or regretting their wicked Course of Life, that they were for increasing their Number by inviting him to join with them, and so seem'd resolv'd to live and dye by their Calling, or for it, as their fate is like to be. And now seeing that the Facts are as evident as Proof by Testimony can make 'em, I doubt not Your Honours will declare the Prisoners to be Guilty.["]

Then the Prisoners were taken away from the Bar, and the Court was Cleared, and in Private.

[Verdict and Sentencing]

Then the Court having duly and maturely weighed and considered the Evidences against the Prisoners, unanimously agreed and Voted, That Charles Harris, Thomas

---

42 Dutch island off the Venezuelan coast.

Linnicar, Daniel Hyde, Stephen Mundon, Abraham Lacy, Edward Lawson, John Tomkins, Francis Laughton, John Fitz-Gerrald, William Studfield, Owen Rice, and William Read were Guilty of the Piracies, Robberies and Felonies Exhibited against them at this Court, and that John Wilson and Henry Barns were not Guilty.

And then the Court Adjourned to two of the Clock in the afternoon of said Day.

The Court Met and Opened by Proclamation, according to Adjournment, and the aforesaid Prisoners that were Tried the Forenoon, were brought to the Bar again.

And the President acquainted them that the Court by Unanimous Voice had found the aforesaid Charles Harris, Thomas Linnicar, Daniel Hyde, Stephen Mundon, Abraham Lacy, Edward Lawson, John Tomkins, Francis Laughton, John Fitz-Gerrald, William Studfield, Owen Rice, & William Read Guilty of Piracies, Robberies and Felonies, according to the Articles Exhibited against them. And asked them, whether any of them had any thing to say, why Sentence of Death should not pass upon them for their said Offences.

And the Prisoners offering nothing Material, the President pronounced Sentence against them in the following Words,

["]You, Charles Harris, Thomas Linnicar, Daniel Hyde, Stephen Mundon, Abraham Lacy, Edward Lawson, John Tomkins, Francis Laughton, John Fitz-Gerrald, William Studfield, Owen Rice, and William Read, are to go from hence to the place from whence you came, and from thence to the place of Execution, and there you and each of you are to be hanged by the Neck until you are Dead, And the Lord have Mercy upon your Souls.["]

And the President then Pronounced the said John Wilson, and Henry Barns, not Guilty.

[Trial of Thomas Hugget, Peter Cues, Thomas Jones, William Jones, Edward Eaton, John Brown, James Sprinkly, John Brown, Joseph Sound, Charles Church, John Waters, Thomas Mumford, and William Blades]

Then the Court ordered Thomas Hugget, Peter Cues, Thomas Jones, William Jones, Edward Eaton, John Brown, James Sprinkly, John Brown, Joseph Sound, Charles Church, John Waters, and Thomas Mumford, Indian, who was Arraigned in the Morning, and had severally pleaded not Guilty, to be brought to the Bar, and they were brought accordingly, and William Blades was also brought, and Articles of Piracies, Robberies and Felonies exhibited against him read to him in the same Words as before mentioned, whereunto he pleaded, Not Guilty.

Advocate General: ["]May it please Your Honours, The Prisoners before the Court are a part of that Miserable Crew of Men already under Sentence of Death.

["]The Articles, the Crimes, and Evidences being the same with those of their Brethren, and their Guilt Equal, I doubt not they will meet with the like Condemnation.["]

The King's Evidences being called and Sworn, deposed as followeth,

John Welland deposeth, That he was Master of the Ship *Amsterdam Merchant*, in the Month of May last past, and that on the Eighth of May he was taken by Low and Company, Pirates, in two Sloops off of Cape Antonio, who used him as aforesworn, and that he saw Charles Church, John Waters, Edward Eaton, William Blades, Thomas Mumford, Indian, and Thomas Jones, a Lad, on board the *Ranger*; that the Day after he was taken, the said Pirate took one Capt. Eastwick of Piscataqua. The Pirates were all harness'd (as they call'd it, viz. Armed,) except Thomas Jones, who was a Lad on board.

John Ackin, late Mate of the Ship *Amsterdam Merchant*, deposed, that he was taken in the Ship *Amsterdam Merchant* by Low and Crew as aforesaid, and that John Waters and Thomas Jones, a Lad, Prisoners at the Bar, were then on Board one of the Pirate Sloops called the *Ranger*, That Waters demanded what Rum they had, and that Thomas Jones was not Armed as he knows of.

John Mudd, late Carpenter of the Ship *Amsterdam Merchant*, deposed, That the Ship aforesaid was taken in manner as aforesaid by the aforesaid Low and Crew of Pirates, and that he well remembers Joseph Sound, Thomas Jones and Thomas Mumford, Indian, on board the *Ranger* where the said Joseph Sound and most of the Company were harness'd, viz. Arm'd; and said Sound took his Buttons out of his Sleeves, but that Thomas Jones was not in Arms as he knew of.

Benjamin Weekham of Newport, Mariner, deposed, That on the Tenth of March last he was in the Bay of Honduras on Board of a Sloop, Jeremiah Clark Master. Low and Lowder's Companies being Pirates, took the aforesaid Sloop, and that this Deponent then having the Small Pox[43] was by John Waters, one of the Prisoners at the Bar, carried on board another Vessel; and that he begg'd of some of the Company two Shirts to shirt himself, the said Waters said ["]Damn him, he would beg the Vessel too,["] but at other times he was very civil; and the Deponent further saith, he saw William Blades now Prisoner at the Bar amongst them.

---

43 Now largely eradicated, in its most dangerous form the smallpox virus killed 10 to 30 percent of those infected. "After a two-week incubation period, smallpox racked the body with high fever, headache, backache, and nausea, and then peppered the face, trunk, limbs, mouth, and throat with hideous, pus-filled boils. Patients with the infection were in agony – their skin felt as it it was being consumed by fire, and although they were tormented by thirst, lesions in the mouth and throat made it excruciating to swallow. The odor of a smallpox ward was oppressive: The rash gave off a sweetish, pungent smell reminiscent of rotting flesh. For those who survived, the disease ran its course in a few weeks. Pustule formation concluded on days eight to ten of the illness, after which the boils scabbed over and were gradually reabsorbed. On days fifteen to twenty, the crusty dry scabs separated and fell off, leaving depigmented areas of skin that later turned into ugly, pitted scars" (Tucker, *Scourge*, 2).

William Marsh deposed, That he was taken in manner as aforesaid, and that John Brown the Tallest was on board the Schooner, and the said Brown told him he had rather be in a tight Vessel than a leaky one, and that he was not forced.

Capt. Solgard and *Lieut. Smith* deposed, that they took the Sloop *Ranger* at Time, Place and Manner as aforesaid; and that the Prisoners at the Bar were taken from on board her.

Henry Barns, Mariner, being duly Sworn, deposed, that he being on Board the Sloop *Ranger* during her Engagement with the *Grey-hound* Man of War, saw all the Prisoners at the Bar on board the said Sloop *Ranger*, and that he saw John Brown the shortest in Arms, that Thomas Mumford, Indian, was only as a servant on board.

John Wilson being duly Sworn and Interrogated, deposed, that the major part of the Prisoners now at the Bar were active on board the Sloop *Ranger* in Attacking and Engaging the *Grey-hound* Man of War, and that Edward Eaton was Hurt in the Knee by a Great Gun, and that he saw John Brown the shortest in Arms, that Thomas Mumford, Indian, was only as a servant on Board.

[Defense Statements]

After the Witnesses had been severally Examined, the Prisoners at the Bar were asked, whether they had any thing to say in their own Defence.

William Blades said he was forced on board of Low about Eleven Months ago, and never agreed to their Articles, and that he had when taken about Ten or Twelve Pounds, and that he never shared with them, but only took what they gave him.

Thomas Hugget said he was one of Capt. Mercy's Men on the Coast of Guinea, and in the West Indies was put on board Low, but never shared with them, and they gave him about 21 Pounds.

Peter Cues says, that on the Twenty Third or Twenty Fourth of January last he belonged to one Layal in a Sloop of Antigua, and was then taken by Low and detained ever since, but never shared with them, and had about Ten or Twelve Pounds when taken, which they gave him.

Thomas Jones says, he is a Lad of about Seventeen Years of Age, and was by Low & Company taken out of Capt. Edwards at Newfoundland, and kept by Low ever since.

William Jones saith, he was taken out of Capt. Eger at the Bay of Honduras the beginning of April last by Low and Lowder, and that he had been forced by Low to be with him ever since; that he never shared with them, nor signed the Articles till compelled three Weeks after he was taken, and the said Jones owned he had Eleven Pounds of the Quarter-Master at one time, and Eight Pounds at another.

Edward Eaton says, that he was taken by Low in the Bay of Honduras, about the beginning of March, and kept with him by force ever since.

John Brown the tallest says, that on the Ninth of October last he was taken out of the *Liverpool Merchant* at the Cape De Verde by Capt. Low who beat him black and blue to make him sign the Articles, and from Cape De Verde they Cruiz'd upon the Coast of Brazil about seven Weeks, and from thence to the West Indies, and he was on board of the *Ranger* at the [taking?] of Welland.

James Sprinkly says, he was forced out of a Ship at the Cape de Verds by Low in October last, and by him compelled to sign the Articles, but never shared with them.

John Brown the shortest says, he is about Seventeen Years old, and was in October last at the Cape De Verdes taken out of a ship by Low, and kept there ever since, and that the Quarter-Master gave him about Forty Shillings, and the People aboard Three Pounds.

Joseph Sound says, he was taken from Providence, about three Months ago, by Low & Company and detained by force ever since

Charles Church says, he was taken out of the *Sycamore Galley* at the Cape de Verds, Capt. Scot Commander, about seven or eight Months ago, by Capt. Low, never shared, but the Quarter-Master gave him about Fourteen Pounds.

John Waters says, he was taken by Low on the Twenty-ninth of June last, out of —————, and they compelled him to take charge of a Watch, and that he had Thirteen Pistoles[44] when taken, which was given him, and that he said in the time of the Engagement with His Majesties Ship they had better strike, for they would have the better Quarter.

Thomas Mumford, Indian, says, he was a Servant a Fishing the last Year, and was taken out of a Fishing Sloop with Five other Indians off of Nantucket by Low and Company, and that they hanged two of the Indians at Cape Sables, and that he was kept by Low ever since, and had about six Bitts[45] when taken.

And then the Prisoners were taken from the Bar, and secured, and the Court in Private.

[Verdicts and Sentencing]

Then the Court maturely weighed and considered the Evidence and the Prisoners' Case, and Unanimously found William Blades, Thomas Hugget, Peter Cues, William Jones, Edward Eaton, John Brown, James Sprinkly, John Brown, Joseph Sound, Charles Church, and John Waters, all Guilty of Piracy, Robbery and Felony, according to the Articles Exhibited against them.

---

44 Another word for the Spanish gold coin known as the *doublon, doblon,* or *doubloon.* Among the most common in the New World, it was worth approximately £0.86 in 1702 (McCusker, *Money and Exchange,* 5, 6, 11).

45 *Reals* – portions of a Spanish *peso* (see McCusker, *Money and Exchange,* 99).

And by an Unanimous Voice found Thomas Jones and Thomas Mumford, Indian, Not Guilty.

The aforesaid Prisoners were brought to the Bar, and the President acquainted them that the Court by an Unanimous Voice had found the aforesaid Wm. Blades, Thomas Hugget, Peter Cues, William Jones, Edward Eaton, John Brown, James Sprinkly, John Brown, Joseph Sound, Charles Church, and John Waters, all Guilty of the Piracies, Robberies & Felonies according to the Articles Exhibited against them; and asked them whether any of them had any thing to say, why Sentence of Death should not pass upon them for their Offences.

And the Prisoners offering nothing material, the President pronounced Sentence of Death against them in the following Words.

["Y]ou William Blades, Thomas Hugget, Peter Cues, William Jones, Edward Eaton, John Brown, James Sprinkly, John Brown, Joseph Sound, Charles Church, and John Waters, are to go from hence to the Place from whence you came, and from thence to the Place of Execution, and there you and each of you shall be hanged by the Neck until you are Dead, And the Lord have Mercy upon your Souls.["]

Then the President pronounced the said Thomas Jones, and Thomas Mumford, Indian, Not Guilty.

Then the Court Adjourned until to Morrow Morning, at Eight of the Clock in the Forenoon.

[Trial of John Kencate]

July the Twelfth Day 1723.

The Court Met according to Adjournment and was Opened by Proclamation. [. . .] [It was] Ordered that John Kencate, Doctor, who was arraigned yesterday, be brought to the Bar, and he was brought to the Bar accordingly.

Advocate General: ["]May it please Your Honours, The next Person brought in Judgment before this Honourable Court is the Doctor of the Piratical Crew, and altho' it may be said, he used no Arms, was not Harness'd (as they term it) but was a forc'd Man; yet if he received part of their Plunder, was not under a constant durance, did at any time approve, or join'd in their Villanies, his Guilt is at least Equal to the rest; The Doctor being ador'd among 'em as the Pirates' God for whom they chiefly confide for their Care and Life, and in this Trust and Dependance it is that they Enterprize these Horrid depredations not to be heightened by aggravation, or lessened by any Excuse.["]

The King's Evidences being called, Sworn and Interrogated, deposed as follows,

John Welland desposeth, he was taken as aforesaid, and that he saw the Doctor aboard the *Ranger*; he seem'd not to rejoice when he was taken but solitary, and he was inform'd on board he was a forc'd Man; and that he never signed the Articles as he heard of, and was not on board the Deponant's Ship.

John Ackin, Mate, and *John Mudd*, Carpenter, Swear, they saw the Prisoner at the Bar walking forwards and backwards disconsolately on board the *Ranger*.

Benjamin Wickham deposed, that he doth not know the Prisoner at the Bar by sight, but that while he was at the Bay under Confinement with said Crew of Pirates, there came a Man on board the Vessel whom they called Doctor, who drank and was merry with some of the Pyrates then there, and told him the Deponent he would send him something to take, but sent it not.

Capt. Peter Solgard, Commander of His Majesties Ship *Grey-hound*, and *Edward Smith*, Lieut. on Board said Ship, deposed, that the Prisoner at the Bar was on board the Sloop *Ranger* when taken by them in manner and Time as aforesaid.

Archibald Fisher, Physician and Chirurgion on board the said *Grey-hound* Man of War, deposed, that when the Prisoner at the Bar was taken and brought aboard the King's Ship he searched his Medicaments, and the Instruments, and found but very few Medicaments, and the Instruments very mean and bad.

John Wilson, *Henry Barns* and *Thomas Jones*, severally deposed, that the Prisoner at the Bar was forced on Board by Low, and that he never signed Articles as they knew or heard, but used to spend [a] great part of his Time in reading, and was very courteous to the Prisoners taken by Low and Company, and that he never shared with them, as they knew or heard of.

After the Witnesses were duly Interrogated, the Court asked the Prisoner whether he had anything to say in his own defence, and if he had he might speak.

John Kencate, Doctor, saith, he was Chirurgeon of the *Sycamore Galley*, Andrew Scot Master, and was taken out of the said Ship in September last at Bonavista, one of the Cape De Verde Islands, by Low and Company, who detained him ever since, and that he never shared with them, nor sign'd their Articles.

The Prisoner was taken from the Bar, and the Court Cleared.

Then the Court Examined and Considered the Evidences and Pleas for the King, and the Prisoner's Case, with great Care, and by an Unanimous Voice found the said John Kencate, Doctor, Not Guilty.

Then the Court was again opened, and the said Prisoner John Kencate was brought to the Bar, and the President pronounced him, Not Guilty.

[Trial of Thomas Powell, Joseph Swetser, and Joseph Libbey]

[It was then] Ordered, that Thomas Powell, who was Arraigned and Pleaded not Guilty yesterday, and Joseph Swetser, who was Articled against yesterday in the aforesaid Articles but not Arraigned, and Joseph Libbey, Articled against since with others for

Piracies, Robberies and Felonies, be brought to the Bar, and they were brought to the Bar accordingly.

Where the Register read the aforesaid Articles exhibited against Joseph Swetser, in the Words aforesaid, to which he pleaded, Not Guilty.

Then the Register read the Articles exhibited against Joseph Libbey for Piracies, Roberies, and Felonies.

Then the Register asked the said Joseph Libbey whether he was Guilty of the articles exhibited against him or not Guilty, and the Prisoner Joseph Libbey pleaded not guilty. Whereupon the Register bid the said Thomas Powell, Joseph Swetser, and Joseph Libbey attend to their Tryal.

Advocate General: ["]May it please Your Honours, The Three Prisoners at the Bar charg'd for the same Crimes, and tried together in their desire, in hopes to distinguish themselves by their innocency from [those?] under condemnation, will I doubt not find their mistake in their Conviction and in the sentence they may justly expect to hear from this Honorable Court.["]

Then the King's Evidences being called, Sworn and Interrogated, deposed as follows.

John Welland, late Master of the Ship *Amsterdam Merchant*, deposed, that when he was taken as aforesaid by Low and Company he saw Joseph Swetser and Thomas Powell aboard the Sloop *Ranger*, and that they were harnessed on board the Sloop.

John Ackin, late Mate of the said Ship, deposed, that he saw Joseph Swetser harnessed on board the Sloop *Ranger* at the taking of Capt. Welland by Low, and he saw Thomas Powell on board, but not harnessed.

John Mudd, late Carpenter of the Ship *Amsterdam Merchant*, deposed the same as Ackin.

William Marsh deposed that Thomas Powell, a Prisoner at the Bar, was on board Low the Pirate some time in January last, when this Deponent was taken by Low, and that Powell seemed to be a brisk, stirring, active Man amongst them, and told the Deponent they always kept a Barrel of Powder ready to blow up the Sloop rather than be taken,[46] and that the said Powell searched the Deponant's Pockets for Gold and Silver, in the great Cabbin on board of Low.

John Kencate deposed, that during his being on board of Low the Pirate, he well knew Thomas Powell, Joseph Swetser, and Joseph Libbey, now Prisoners at the Bar, and that Thomas Powell acted as Gunner[47] on board the *Ranger*, and that he went

---

46 As noted earlier, similar plans for self-immolation in case of capture existed aboard the ships of Edward Teach and Bartholomew Roberts.

47 The *gunner* on a warship or privateer was a petty officer responsible for artillery and ammunition, as well as teaching "the sailors the exercise of the cannon" (Falconer, *Universal Dictionary*, n.p.).

on board several Vessels taken by Low and Company, and Plundered, and that Joseph Libbey was an Active Man on board the *Ranger*, and used to go on board Vessels they took, and Plundered, and that he saw him fire several Times; and the Deponent further deposed, that Joseph Swetser, now Prisoner at the Bar, was on board the Pirate Low, and that he has seen him armed, but never see[n] him use them, and that the said Swetser used often to get alone by himself from amongst the rest of the Crew, he was melancholly and refused to go on board any Vessels by them taken, and got out of their Way. And the Deponent further saith, That on that Day, as they engaged the Man of War, Low proposed to attack the Man of War, first by firing his great Guns, then a Volley of Small Arms, heave in their Powder Flasks, and board her in his Sloop, and the *Ranger* to board over the *Fortune*, and that no one on board the *Ranger* disagreed to it as he knows of, for most approved of it by Words, and the others were silent.

Thomas Jones deposed that he well knows the Prisoners at the Bar, and that Thomas Powell acted as Gunner on board the *Ranger*, and Joseph Libbey was a stirring active Man among them, and used to go aboard Vessels to Plunder, and that Joseph Swetser was very dull aboard, and at Cape Antonio he cryed to Danwell to let him go ashore, who refused, and asked him to drink a Dram, but Swetser went down into the Hold and cryed [a] good part of the Day, and that Low refused to let him go, but brought him and tied him to the Mast and threatned to Whip him; And he saw him Armed, but never use his Arms as he knows of: And that Swetser was Sick when they engaged the Man of War, tho' he assisted in rowing the Vessel.

John Wilson deposed, he knows the Prisoners at the Bar to be all on Board the *Ranger*, and Thomas Powell was Gunner of her; and the Sabbath Day before they were taken the said Powell told the Deponent he wished he was ashore at Long Island, and they two went to the Head of the Mast, and Powell said to him, ["]I wish you and I were both ashore here stark naked;["][48] And he deposed that he never saw Joseph Swetser in Arms while he was aboard but he and Powell received about Twenty Five Pounds from the Quarter-Master. That the next Day after the Deponant was taken by Low, Joseph Swetser told him that he was a forced Man, and wished he had his Liberty as he had about Fourteen Months ago, and was resolved to run away from Low the first Opportunity he had.

Henry Barns deposed, that Joseph Swetser was very civil on board the Sloop *Ranger* to such Prisoners as was taken, and that they had no Engagement after the Deponant was on board, and that Joseph Libbey was Armed, and went on board several Vessels taken by them and plundered.

---

48 Historian Marcus Rediker has noted that this line was among those "suggestive shards" that helped fuel modern scholarly discussion about sexuality in pirate communities. He added: "In a homosocial and hypermasculine world, one that valued strength, stamina, toughness, courage and aggressiveness, the choice was for a sexual liberty that transgressed the polite standards of the day" (*Villains of all Nations*, 74–75).

Thomas Mumford, Indian (not speaking good English, Abishai Folger was sworn Interpreter) deposed, that Thomas Powell, Joseph Libbey and Joseph Swetser were all on board of Low the Pirate, that he saw Powell have a Gun when they took Vessels, but never saw him Fire; he saw him go on board of a Vessel once, but brought nothing from her as he saw, he [did] see him once strike a Negro but never a White Man. And he saw Joseph Libbey once go on board a Vessel by them taken and brought away from her one pair of Stockings. And that Joseph Swetser cook'd [*] on board with him some time, and sometime they made him bend the Sails;[49] once he saw the said Swetser clean a gun but not fire it: and Swetser once told him that he wanted to get ashore from among them and said if the Man of War should take them they would hang him; and in the Engagement of the Man of War Swetser sat unarm'd in the Range of the Sloop's mast, and some little time before the said Engagement he asked Low to let him have his Liberty and go ashore, but was refused.

Capt. Peter Solgard, Commander of the *Grey-hound* Man of War, deposed, that all the Prisoners now at the Bar were by him taken on board the *Ranger* on the Tenth of June last, in manner as aforesaid, and that he had seven Men Wounded in the Engagement.

Edward Smith, Lieut. of the said Man of War, deposed the same.

After the Witnesses were severally examin'd as aforesaid, the Court told the Prisoners if they had anything to say in their defense they might speak.

Thomas Powell said, he was taken by Lowther in the Bay of Honduras in the Winter 1721[–]2, and by him turned on board of Low, and detained by force ever since.

Joseph Libbey said, he was a forced Man, and was detained by Low, and produced an Advertisement of it.[50]

Joseph Swetser says he was taken by Lowther about a Year ago, and forced on board of Low, and detained there against his Will ever since, that he never shared with them, but had of the Quarter Master about Twelve Pounds, and to prove his being forced produced an Advertisement.[51]

Advocate General: ["]May it please your Honours, The Prisoners, not withstanding their Plea of not Guilty, don't deny the Facts, but insist upon their having done them, not by their own will and choice, but by constraint and necessity.

["]But it is evident, That Powell & Libbey were first Rate pirates, the former acting as Gunner on board the Sloop. And tho' Swetser has produced some Witnesses as to [his?] Innocency [from?] conversation before he met with and was forced by the Pirates, He can't be ignorant that he is not questioned for any of his Good but Evil

49 To bend the sails "is to affix them to the yards" (James, *Naval History*, I:xx)
50 See the entries in this chapter from the *Boston News-Letter* of 25 June–2 July and 2–9 July 1722. Despite the "ad of force," Libbey would be found guilty because testimony introduced in court portrayed him as an active member of the pirate crew. For more on the subject of forcing, see Leeson, *Invisible Hook*, 134–155.
51 See the entry in this chapter from the *Boston News-Letter* of 11–18 June, 1722.

Deeds. Probably at the first he might act with some reluctancy, 'till by the Repetition of his Crimes he became hardened into vicious habits (*nemo repente pessimus:*)[52] And, it is in proof, that he had a Gun, received part of the Spoils, and assisted in rowing when the Sloop engag'd the Man of War, all, or any of which Acts conducing to the main end, involves him in the same Guilt (*Facinus, quos inquinat Aequat.*)[53] The Attacking [of] His Majesties ship was a Notorious Piracy, tho' the Pirates were overcome, and taken by the Captain, who might have done Justice upon them himself by hanging them all up at the Yard Arm.

["]The plea of Necessity is dangerous in the Latitude us'd by the Prisoners: and may after this rate, be extended to palliate the breach of the Ten Commandments.["]

Then the Prisoners being taken away and all withdrawn but the Register.

The Court maturely weighed and considered the Evidences and the Cases of the Prisoners, and by an Unanimous Voice found the said Thomas Powell and Joseph Libbey guilty of the Piracies, Robberies and Felonies exhibited against them, and by a considerable Plurality of Voices found the said Joseph Swetser, not guilty.

Then the Prisoners were brought to the Bar, and the President acquainted Thomas Powell and Joseph Libbey that they were by an Unanimous Voice found guilty of the Piracies, Robberies and Felonies exhibited against them, and asked them if they had any thing to say, why Sentence of Death should not pass upon them for their Offences.

And the Prisoners offering nothing material, the President pronounced Sentence against them in the following Words,

["]You Thomas Powell and Joseph Libbey are to go from hence to the Place from whence you came, and from thence to the Place of Execution, and there you and each of you, are to be hanged by the Neck until you are Dead. And the Lord have Mercy upon your Souls.["]

And the President Pronounced the said Joseph Swetser, not guilty.

Adjourned to Two of the Clock in the Afternoon.

[Trial of Thomas Hazel, John Bright, John Fletcher, Thomas Child, and Patrick Cunningham]

The Court Met and Opened according to Adjournment [by Proclamation?], and Ordered Thomas Hazel, John Bright, John Fletcher, Thomas Child and Patrick Cunningham to be brought to the Bar, who were ordered to attend to the Articles read against them, for Piracies, Robberies, and Felonies.

Which were read by the Register in the same Words as to Joseph Libbey.

---

52   Sometimes rendered as *Nemo fit repente pessimus*: "No one becomes worst at first" (Adams, *Works*, I:249).
53   This might be translated as: "Guilt makes those it stains equal."

To which the said Prisoners severally pleaded, Not Guilty.

Advocate General: ["]May it please your Honours, The Prisoners before you have been Arraigned, have pleaded not guilty, and are the last of the miserable Crew to be tried – If I make out their Guilt, I shall not question your Justice.["]

The King's Evidences being called, Sworn and Interrogated, deposed as follows.

John Welland, late Master of the Ship *Amsterdam Merchant*, deposed, that on the Eighth Day of May last he was taken off of Cape Antonio by Low and Company, Pirates, in two Sloops, the *Fortune* and *Ranger*, and after he had been some time on board the *Ranger*, he was sent on board the *Fortune* where Low was, where he had his right Ear cut off, and was wounded very much with a Cutlass, and turn'd down the Hatches, where he lay bleeding for two or three Hours with a Centinel over him; at last he asked Patrick Cunningham (who he tho't was the means of saving his Life), a Prisoner now at the Bar, for to get him a Dram, for he was almost spent, and Patrick Cunningham got him some Water; then he asked him for the Doctor, and Cunningham went and brought the Doctor to him, and help'd the Doctor dress him, and said, they were so cruel they could not subsist long. And said Welland also deposed, that he saw John Bright and Thomas Hazel on board the *Ranger*, and Thomas Hazel was harnessed with a Gun.

John Ackin, late Mate of the said Ship *Amsterdam Merchant*, deposed, he saw Thomas Hazel, now a Prisoner at the Bar, on board the *Ranger* at the Time and Place aforesaid.

John Mudd, late Carpenter of said Ship, deposed that while he was a Prisoner on board the *Ranger*, he saw Thomas Hazeal, John Bright and John Fletcher, and that Thomas Hazel was harnessed.

William Marsh deposeth, that when he was on board the Pirate Low by whom he was taken (as afore deposed), he saw Thomas Hazeal on board the Schooner, and John Fletcher, now Prisoner at the Bar, a Boy.

John Kencate deposed, that Thomas Hazeal, John Bright and Patrick Cunningham, Prisoners at the Bar, received Shares on board the Pirate Sloop, and Hazeal and Bright went on board several Prizes and Plundered, that Thomas Child was in Arms with the rest in the Engagement with the *Grey-hound* Man of War, but that John Fletcher was as a Boy on Board, and no[t] otherwise.

Henry Barns deposed, that Thomas Hazeal was harnessed in the Engagement with the *Grey-hound* Man of War, and John Bright was the Drummer, and beat upon his Drum on the Round-House[54] in the Engagement, and that Patrick Cunningham had a Pistol in his hands at the said Time.

---

54 "A name given in East Indiamen and other large merchant ships, to square cabins built on the after-part of the quarter-deck, and having the poop for its roof; such an apartment is frequently called the coach in ships of war. Round, because one can walk round it. In some trading vessels the round-house is built on the deck, generally abaft the main-mast" (Smyth, *Lexicon*, 581).

John Wilson deposed, that John Bright was as brisk as any of them on board the *Ranger*, and beat the Drum on the Round House the Day they engaged the Man of War, and that John Fletcher was as a Boy on Board the Sloop, and no[t] otherwise.

Joseph Swetser deposed, that John Bright was Drummer, and beat upon the Round-House in the Engagement with the Man of War; that Thomas Hazeal had a Pistol at that time, and that Thomas Child came on board the *Ranger* from the *Fortune* but about three or four Days before the said Engagement and rowed in the time of the Engagement.

Thomas Jones deposed, that on the Day they engaged the *Grey-hound* Man of War, he saw Thomas Hazel bring his arms out of the Gun-Room, and saw and heard John Bright the Drummer beat the Drum upon the Round-House, and Thomas Child employed at an Oar in Rowing.

Captain Peter Solgard, commander of His Majesty's Ship *Grey-hound*, deposed, that all the Prisoners now at the Bar were by him taken on board the Sloop *Ranger* on the Tenth of June last after some hours Engagement in manner aforesaid and that he had seven Men wounded in the Engagement.

Edward Smith, Lieut. of the *Grey-hound* Man of War, deposed the same that Captain Solgard did.

After the Witnesses were severally Examined as aforesaid, the Court told the Prisoners if they had any thing to say in their Defence they might speak, and they should be heard.

Thomas Hazel said, he was taken from the Bay of Honduras about Twelve Months ago by Low, and forced on board, that he had got from one and another whilst aboard about Forty or Fifty Pounds, and that he had never been in the Bay since.

John Bright said he was a Servant to one Hester at the Bay and there taken by Low and Company about Three or Four Months ago, and forced away to be their Drummer.

Patrick Cunningham said that about Twelve Months ago he was taken in a Fishing Schooner by Low and Company, and forced away by them, and that at Newfoundland he endeavoured to get away from them but was stopped and detained by them ever since.

John Fletcher says, that he was a Boy on Board the *Sycamore* Galley, one Scot Commander, and he was taken out of her Low and Company at Bonavist, because he could play upon a Violin, and forced to be with them.

Thomas Child said that the beginning of March last he was taken out of Capt. Gilbert at the Bay of Honduras by Low and Company, and was forced to go with them, they gave him a Gun (which he never used) and about Fourteen or Fifteen Pounds as near as he can remember, and one double double Loon.[55]

---

55 The "double *doublon*, or four *pistole* piece," a *pistole* being worth about £0.86 by 1702 (McCusker, *Money and Exchange*, 6, 11).

Advocate General: ["]May it please your Honours, I will not detain you with any particular reflections on the Evidence, or upon the Prisoners' Cases differently Circumstanc'd. The Court I doubt not will duly weigh, and consider them, tempering Justice with Mercy, which sometimes is the true way to Justice.["]

Then the Prisoners were taken away from the Bar, and all Persons withdrawn from the Court save the Register.

The Court having deliberately and maturely weighed and considered the Evidences given against the Prisoners, by an Unanimous Voice found the aforesaid Thomas Hazel, John Bright, and Patrick Cunningham Guilty of the Piracies, Robberies and Felonies Exhibited against them at this Court.

And John Fletcher and Thomas Child not Guilty.

Then the Prisoners being brought to the Bar, the President told Thomas Hazel, John Bright and Patrick Cunningham, [t]hat they were by an Unanimous Voice found Guilty of the Piracies, Robberies and Felonies Exhibited against them; and asked them if they had anything to say, why Sentence of Death should not pass upon them for their Offences.

And the Prisoners offering nothing Material, the President pronounced Sentence against them in these following Words,

["]You Thomas Hazeal, John Bright, and Patrick Cunningham, are to go from hence to the place from whence you came, and from thence to the place of Execution, and there you and each of you are to be hanged by the Neck until you are Dead. And God in his Infinite Mercy Save your Souls.["]

And then the President pronounced John Fletcher and Thomas Child, not Guilty.

[Low's Articles]

The Articles of Agreement between Capt. Low and his Company[56]

I   The Captain shall have Two full Shares, the Master a Share and a half, the Doctor, Mate, Gunner, Carpenter, and Boatswain a Share and quarter.

II He that shall be found Guilty of Striking or taking up any unlawful Weapon either aboard of a Prize, or aboard the Privateer, shall suffer what Punishment the Captain and majority of the Company shall think fit.

III He that shall be found Guilty of Cowardice in the Time of Engagement, shall suffer what Punishment the Captain and the majority of the Company shall think fit.

---

56   A similar list of articles was published in the *Boston News-Letter*, 1–8 August 1723, 2. Their resemblance to those of George Lowther (as given in Schonhorn, ed., *General History*, 307–308), suggests they may have originated with his company.

IV   If any Jewels, Gold or Silver is found on board of a Prize to the Value of a Piece of Eight, and the finder do not deliver it to the Quarter-Master in Twenty-Four Hours Time, shall suffer what Punishment the Captain and majority of the Company shall think fit.

V   He that shall be found Guilty of Gaming, or playing at Cards, or Defrauding or Cheating one another to the Value of a Royal[57] of Plate, shall suffer what Punishment the Captain and majority of the Company shall think fit.

VI   He that shall be Guilty of Drunkenness in the Time of an Engagement, shall suffer what Punishment the Captain and majority of the Company shall think fit.

VII   He that hath the Misfortune to loose any of his Limbs in the Time of an Engagement in the Companies service, shall have the Sum of Six Hundred Pieces of Eight, and kept in the Company as long as he pleases.

VIII   Good Quarters to be given when Craved.[58]

IX   He that sees a Sail first shall have the best Pistol, or Small Arm aboard of her.

X   And lastly, No Snapping of Arms in the Hold.

John Kencate Declared, The above Articles to be the Articles agreed upon between Low and Company; to the best of his remembrance, having often seen them whilst with Low.

Before

Richard Ward, Register.

[List of Those Executed]

The Names, &c. of the Pyrates that were Executed on Friday, July the 19th 1723, at Newport on the Rhode-Island, at a Place called Bulls Point, within the Flux and Reflux of the Sea.

Names	Age	Places of Birth
Charles Harris[59]	[–]	[–]
Thomas Linnicar	21	Lancaster Engl.
Daniel Hyde	23	Virginia.

---

57   The "ryal" or real, part of a Spanish colonial peso.

58   Note also that Philip Ashton (see the following chapter) wrote that in Low's company "it was one of their Articles, Not to Draw Blood, or take away the Life of any Man, after they had given him Quarter, unless he was to be punished as a Criminal." Given the terrible treatment to which Low and his men subjected some prisoners, it is probable that articles like this were followed selectively. "Much has been made of pirate codes, and some historians have elevated them to the status of a holy writ. It seems more likely that they were guidelines, the basic tenets by which the pirates could ensure that their shipmates lived together without too much rancor" (Konstam, *Blackbeard*, 54–55).

59   Harris was 25, from London (Schonhorn, ed., *General History*, 330).

Stephen Mundon	29	London.
Abraham Lacy	21	Devonshire Eng.
Edward Lawson	20	Isle of Man.
[John Tomkins]	21	Gloucester Eng.
Francis Laughton	39	New York.
John Fitz-Gerrald	21	C.Limb. Ireland.
William Studfield	40	Lancaster Engl.
Owen Rice	27	South Wales
William Read	35	Lond derry E.
William Blades	28	Rhode-Island.
Thomas Hugget	24	London.
Peter Cues	32	Exon in Devon.
William Jones	28	London.
Edward Eaton	38	Wreaxham.
John Brown	29	Coun. Der.
James Sprinkly	28	Suffolk.
Joseph Sound	28	Westmin.
Charles Church	21	Marg. Par. Westmin.
John Waters	35	County of Devon.
Thomas Powell	21	Wethersfield Con.
Joseph Libbey	[–]	[–]
Thomas Hazel[60]	[–]	[–]
John Bright[61]	[–]	[–]

FINIS

[**Editor's Note:** Newspaper coverage in the aftermath of the trial at Newport included accounts of the execution of Harris and those convicted along with him. Reports also came in of new acts of piracy, some of which were attributed to Low and also Lowther; there were also mentions of other active rovers such as John Fenn and John Phillips.]

[*Boston News-Letter*, 11–18 July 1723, 2]

Canso,[62] July 1. The Pirates were the last Week at Whitehead[63] 6 Leagues Westward of us, and 11 of them in a Perryaugur took 2 French Shallops, abused the Men, Slit one of their Noses, Cut another over his Cheek with a Cutlass, and broke the Nose of the third with the back of the same, and let them go, who came in and made their complaint to the Major, &c.

---

60   Hazel or Hazeal was 50 (Schonhorn, ed., *General History*, 330).
61   Bright was 25 (Schonhorn, ed., *General History*, 330).
62   Fishing port in Nova Scotia.
63   Fishing settlement in Nova Scotia.

And last Thursday one of our Bank Sloops[64] met with them in a Sloop with 150 Men on Board, they ask'd them some Questions, Who was at Canso, Inquired after most of the Notedest Men, and left them without abuse; they did not know the Master's Name, but say most of them were West Country-men.[65] His Majesty's Ship *Sea Horse*[66] came in the same Day and left the New York Man of War[67] at Cape Sambrough,[68] and the next Day went in Quest of them on the Banks; the Pirate stood to the Eastward, and 'tis supposed to be Low.

Customs-House, Rhode Island, July 12. Entered Inwards, John Draper from Nevis, Joseph Sanford from Bahamies, Joseph Briant from Martinico, John Carr, Wm. Potter, Abraham Borden, and Peter Coggeshall from Barbadoes, by whom we are inform'd, That there was a Vessel arrived at Barbadoes from Antigua a little before he Sail'd, who gave an account, That His Majesty's Ship the *Feversham*,[69] the Station Ship for Antigua, had taken 8 Pirates on the Island of Tabego, and had carried them to Antigua in order to be tryed, which said 8 Pirates is supposed had some difference with the rest of their Company, deserted, but were discovered by the Man of War's Company. [. . .]

ooooo

[*Boston News-Letter*, 18–25 July 1723, 2]

New-Port, Rhode Island, July 19. On Wednesday last the 17th Instant, Three of the Condemned Pirates in our Prison by some means or other, got off their Irons; and when the Goal-Keeper, with a lusty young Man his Servant, and his Daughter open'd the Door where the Prisoners were, in order to give them their Breakfast, the said three Prisoners knock'd down the Goal-keeper with their Irons, got out of the Goal and ran a little way to the out Skirts of the Town, but were speedily pursued and soon apprehended, carryed back to the Goal and committed to the Dungeon.

---

64   A vessel operating from or near the Grand Banks (or Great Bank) of Newfoundland, sometimes referred to as a Banker (Falconer, *Universal Dictionary*, n.p.).

65   The south-western counties of England, such as Bristol, Cornwall, Devon, Dorset and Somerset.

66   HMS *Seahorse* was a 94-foot long sixth rate warship of 20 guns, built at Portsmouth and launched in 1712. Its first captain, James Falzell, died in a 14 September 1712 engagement with a privateer. HMS *Seahorse* later cruised in the Leeward Islands, the North Sea and the Baltic Sea. Sent to Newfoundland in 1719, it went on station in New England the next year (Winfield, *British Warships 1714–1792*, 245).

67   There was no HMS *New York*; this presumably refers to a warship based at New York, possibly HMS *Greyhound*.

68   Cape Sambro, Nova Scotia.

69   HMS *Faversham* was a 118–foot long, 40–gun, fifth rate warship launched and commissioned in 1712. It began operating from Barbados under Captain Charles Brown early in 1721 (Winfield, *British Warships 1714–1792*, 164). Those captured in this episode included the one-handed pirate Captain John Fenn, former gunner and then-consort to pirate Captain Thomas Anstis, who escaped. According to the *General History*, however, the vessel involved was HMS *Winchelsea* (Schonhorn, ed., 295–296). The latter vessel was a 108–foot long ship originally designated a 36–gun fifth rate warship, later reduced to 20 guns and sixth rate status. It saw action against French privateers in 1709, and began its tenure in the West Indies in 1718. It would be broken up in 1735 (Winfield, *British Warships 1714–1792*, 188).

My last gave you an Account of a Court call'd here on the 10th Instant for the Tryal of Pirates; and that on the 11th and 12th, 36 Men were brought before the Court, accused of Piracy, who all pleaded to their Indictment, Not Guilty. The Principal Evidence for the King then were Capt. Peter Solgard, and his Lieutenant, of his Majesty's Ship *Grayhound*, Capt. Welland of Boston, and some of his Company; of which 36 Men 28 of them were found Guilty of Piracy, two whereof are confined to Goal, and reprieved for 12 Months, eight were cleared paying their Prison Fees, the other 26 were Sentenced to be Executed.

The Court also Directed that the Hon. Samuel Cranston, Esq; Governour of this Colony,[70] and one of the Judges, next to the President, should take care that the said 26 Pirates should be Executed this Day; the Place within the Seamark,[71] and manner of Execution being left to His Honour to see it performed. And accordingly between the Hours of Twelve and Two the said 26 Pirates were Executed under their own deep Blew Flagg which was hoisted up on their Gallows, and had pourtraid on the middle of it, an Anatomy with an Hour-glass in one hand and a dart in the Heart with 3 drops of Blood proceeding from it, in the other.[72]

ooooo

[*Boston News-Letter*, 25 July–1 August 1723, 2]

New Port, Rhode Island, July 26. Some of the Pirates that were Executed here the 19th Instant, delivered what they had to say in Writing, which was read, or the Substance of it recited; and most of them said something at the Place of Execution; advising all People, and especially Young Persons, to beware of the Sins which they had been guilty of, that had brought them into such unhappy Circumstances, and to so sad an end, viz. Disobedience to Parents, profaning the Lord's Day, Swearing, Drinking, Gaming, Unchastity, and neglecting the Means of Grace, by absenting themselves from the Publick Worship of God, &c. The Rev. Mr. Bass went to Prayer with them, and some time after, the Rev'd. Mr. Clap concluded with a short Exhortation to them. Their Flag (mentioned in our last) was affixed at one Corner of the Gallows; which Flag they call'd *Old Roger*,[73] and often us'd to say they would live and die under it.

---

70 Samuel Cranston (b. 1659) was governor of Rhode Island from 1698 until his death in 1727. Shortly after he assumed office, Rhode Island became the target of increased scrutiny and criticism by English officials displeased at irregularities in the granting of privateer commissions and the treatment of pirates. Lord Bellomont, governor of New York, Massachusetts, and New Hampshire, was an especial critic until his own death in 1701 (Hawes, *Off Soundings*, 49–52).

71 "*Sea-Mark*, a point or conspicuous place distinguished at sea. Sea-marks are of various kinds, as steeples, promontories, piles of ruins, groups of trees, &c. and are very necessary to direct vessels on the coast of their situation" (Falconer, *Universal Dictionary*, n.p.).

72 Low and Francis Spriggs also employed the same basic design; Bartholomew Roberts at one point had a similar flag (Schonhorn, ed., *General History*, 234, 352).

73 Marcus Rediker noted that the authorities' display of the Jolly Roger at the place of execution was meant to send a message about the flag's symbolism: "Sail under it, they said, and you will die under it" (*Villains of All Nations*, 12). When a Royal Navy warship captured Captain James Skyrm's pirate ship (consort to Bartholomew Roberts), "The Colours were thrown over-board, that they might not rise in Judgment, nor be display'd in Triumph over them" (Schonhorn, ed., *General History*, 240).

ooooo

[*Boston News-Letter*, 1–8 August 1723, 2]

Custom House, Rhode Island, Aug. 1.

. . . The abovesaid [Captain Joseph] Rhodes from Nevis, informs, That Seven of the Pirates brought from Tabago to Antigua, by His Majesty's Station Ship, were executed there, and Finn their Captain hung up in Gibbets;[74] One or Two were Cleared. [. . .]

An exact Account of the Vessels taken by the Pirates during the time John Walters (one of those lately Executed at Rhode Island) was with them:[75]

Two Ships from Lisbon bound to St. Michael's,[76] Chandler and Roach (French) Commanders.

A Pink bound to said place, Commander's Name forgotten.

Two English Ships from Liverpoole, both bound to Jamaica from Barbadoes, Scot and Golden Masters.

A Sloop from Barbadoes bound to Jamaica, Roberts Master.

A Sloop trading among the Cape de Verde Islands,[77] James Pease Master.

Two Portugueze Sloops bound for Brazil, Commanders *Incognito*.

A Ship from London & Maderas,[78] bound to Jamaica, James Adlington Master.

A Sloop bound to Sancta Cruz.

Three Sloops from St. Thomas[79] bound to Curaso,[80] Wm. Lillie, Staples and Simpkins Masters.

A Sloop from Bermudas.

A Snow from New-York to Curacoa, Robert Leonard Master.

A Sloop from the Bay bound to New-York, Craige Master.

A Snow from London & Jamaica bound to New-York.

---

74 See the earlier entry from the *Boston News-Letter*, 11–18 July 1723.

75 John Waters or Walters, 35, of Devon, had been quartermaster on Harris's vessel (Schonhorn, ed., *General History*, 330). This text, originally in one long paragraph, has been reformatted.

76 São Miguel, in the Azores.

77 Group of islands off Africa's west coast.

78 Madiera is one of a group of Portuguese islands off the northwest coast of Africa.

79 A Danish colony in the Virgin Islands.

80 "Querisao [Curaçao] is the only Island of Importance that the Dutch have in the West-Indies. It is about 5 Leagues in length, and may be 9 or 10 in circumference: the Northernmost point is laid down in North lat. 12 d. 40 m. and it is about 7 or 8 Leagues from the Main, near Cape Roman. On the South side of the East-end is a good Harbour, call'd Santa Barbara; but the chiefest Harbour is about 3 Leagues from the S.E. end, on the South-side of it where the Dutch have a very good Town, and a very strong Fort. . . . At the East end are two Hills, one of them is much higher than the other, and steepest towards the North-side. The rest of the Island is indifferent level; where of late some rich Men have made Sugar-works; which formerly was all Pasture for Cattle: there are also some small Plantations of Potatoes and Yams, and they have still a great many Cattle on the Island; but it is not so much esteemed for its produce, as for its Situation for the Trade with the Spaniard" (Dampier, *New Voyage*, 40–41).

A Pink from Jamaica to Boston burnt, Andrew Delbridge Master.

Six Sloops taken in the Bay of Honduras, Tuthill, Norton, Medberry, Sprafort, Clark & Parrot Commanders.

A Spanish Briganteen burnt.

Two Snows from Jamaica bound to Liverpool.

A Snow from Jamaica to London, Bridds Master.

A Ship from Biddiford[81] to Jamaica and London, John Pinkam Commander.

Two Sloops bound from Jamaica to Virginia.

Three Ships from Jamaica to New-England, Eastwick, Wyling & Bunington Masters.

A Sloop from Jamaica to New-York or Amboy.

A Ship from Carolina to Biddiford, John Loverigne Commander.

Two Briganteens from Carolina to London, Robinson, &c. Commanders.

A Sloop from Virginia to Barmudas.

A Ship from Glasgow to Virginia.

A Scooner from New-York to South Carolina.

A Pink from Virginia to Dartmouth,[82] Pitman Commander.

A Sloop from Philadelphia to Surranam, Greeman Commander.

A Boat taken under Boneviss.[83]

And the Ships wherein Walters was taken.

In the whole, Forty-five Vessels Taken, beside the Boat.

John Walters. [. . .]

Advertisements

Boston, Aug. 7th 1723.

Whereas Capt. Richard Stanny, Master of the Brigantine *John and Elizabeth* of Boston, New-England, John Mountgomery, Mate, and William Martindale, Mariner, These Deponents Testify and say, That in their passage from Dover to Boston, They were taken on the 5th Day of July last in the Latitude of 42 deg. About [100?] Leagues to the Eastward of the Banks of Newfoundland, by a Pirate Sloop, Commanded by one George Lowther, Manned with about Twenty Men, having Seven Guns Mounted; the said Pirates broke open the Hatches of the said Brigantine, and took out of her divers Goods and Merchandizes, and having so Robbed the said Brigantine, and Plundered the Company, they did by Force & Violence carry away Two of the said Brigantine's company on board the said Pirate, Namely, Ralph Kendale of Sunderland, in the

---

81 Port in York County, Maine.
82 Port on Halifax Harbor, Nova Scotia.
83 Possibly Cape Bonavista in Newfoundland; alternately Boa Vista is one of the Cape Verde islands.

County of Durham, and Henry Watson of Dover, aforesaid, and very barbarously Whipt & Beat the said Kendale and Watson.

Suffolk ss. Boston, July 31, 1723.

Then Personally appeared Richard Stanny, John Mountgomery and William Martindale, and made solemn Oath to the Truth of their Declaration, Before me, J. Willard, Secr. & Just. Pea.

ooooo

[*Boston News-Letter*, 12–19 September 1723, 1]

Having lately received a very particular & exact Account of the Piracies & Murthers committed this Summer at Canso, we shall communicate it as it was sent in a Letter from thence to a Gentlemen in Boston.

Canso, August 1. 1723.

In my last Letter to you, I inform'd you of the mischief the Pirates had done on the French at Whitehead, 6 Leagues Westward of this Harbour; and now I proceed to say, that they went to the Eastward, and took a Sloop belonging to this Harbour, but treated them very kindly, and dismiss'd them without harm. The next News we heard of them was, that they had taken another Vessel, Capt. Job Prince Commander; they order'd them on Board, but Capt. Prince had no Boat, wherefore they only detain'd him about an hour and dismiss'd him without doing him any Damage. The next Vessel they took was one of Capt. Robinson's, whom they divested of their Arms, Ammunition and Silver Buckels, and then dismiss'd them. They had then in their Custody four French Ships, which they Plundered, used the men very Barbarously, and sent them, in a Vessel belonging to Canso, to Cape Briton.[84] They took Mr. Hood belonging to Boston, in a large Fishing Scooner, when they first came on the Banks from Boston; but that was another Pirate, who also forced away three of his Men. The latter Sloop, which is known to be Low, uses the English very Kindly; but the French find but little Mercy at his hand; they cut off some of their Ears and Noses, and treated them with all the Barbarity imaginable. One of the French Commanders desired him only to give him a Line from under his hand, that he had taken away some Casks of his Wine and Brandy, that his Owners might not suspect he had Dishonestly Sold them; upon which Low told him he would fetch him one, and accordingly brought up two Pistols, presenting one at his Bowels, he told him there was one for his Wine, and Discharg'd it; and there, says he (presenting the other at his Head in the same manner) is one for your Brandy; which said, he discharg'd that also. We hear they have since Taken near 40 French Fishing Vessels, and are gone towards Newfoundland. This is all that is Remarkable concerning these Enemies to Mankind in General. [. . .]

---

84 Cape Breton Island.

[**Editor's Note**: Another pirate captain active at the time, John Phillips, seems to have shared some of Low's demeanor towards captives, threatening one (as noted below) with mutilation. In this case, the threat was made to ensure the forcing of a sailor received public notice.]

[*Boston News-Letter*, 3–10 October 1723, 2]

Advertisements

Francis Palmer & Philip Stokes, Mariners, late belonging to the Scooner *Nymph* of the Harbour of St. Peters in Newfoundland, Jethro Furber late Master; Severally declare and say; That on the Sixth Day of September last, the said Scooner lying at an Anchor in the Harbour Briton in Newfoundland aforesaid, a Scooner came into the said Harbour, Commanded by John Phillips a Pirate,[85] Manned with nine Men; and surprised and took the said Scooner *Nymph* & Company; and by Force & Violence compelled John Burrell of Boston in New-England, Mariner (then belonging to the said Scooner *Nymph*), to go with the said Pirate Phillips; contrary to the said Burrell's Will, who was under great concern of Mind & Distress when Forc'd away by the said Pirate.

And the said John Phillips ordered the said Furber to declare upon his return home, that the said Burrell was a Forc'd Man: And that if the said Furber should neglect to do it, when he met with him again he would Cut off his Ears.[86]

Francis Palmer.

Philip Stokes.

Suffolk, ss. Boston, October 9th, 1723.

Then appeared the above written Francis Palmer and Philip Stokes, and made Oath to the Declaration above.

Before me, J. Willard, Sec. and Just. Pac.

Robert Ford Mariner, Declareth & saith, That on the Eighteenth Day of September last, he was taken in the Briganteen *Mary*, John Moore Master, by one John Phillips, a Pirate, who then Commanded a Scooner; that he saw on board the said Scooner John Burrell, who was called a Forc'd Man, who was very Kind to this Declarant, and gave him his Hat again, which had been taken from him by a French Boy.

Robert Ford.

---

85 Phillips' first stint at piracy occurred after he was forced (as a carpenter) into pirate Captain Thomas Anstis' crew, which he eventually joined willingly and stayed with until they broke up at Tobago. His return to England was cut short by news that some of his companions had been arrested there. He signed aboard a ship to Newfoundland, where in August 1723 he and several others seized a vessel and went "upon the piratical Account." He died in a revolt of prisoners aboard his pirate ship in April 1724 (Schonhorn, ed., *General History*, 341–351).

86 The same page of the same issue of the *Boston News-Letter* included a notice that: "Capt. Moore arrived here from Holland on Saturday last, who was taken on the Banks of Newfoundland, on the 8th of Sept. past, in the Lat. of 43 & 45, by a Pirate sloop Commanded by one Phillips, with 19 Men, 12 of whom they said were forced."

[**Editor's Note:** At the end of July 1723, according to Captain Johnson's *General History*, "Low took a large Ship, called the *Merry Christmas*, and fitted her for a Pyrate, cut several Ports in her, and mounted her with 34 Guns. Low goes aboard of this Ship, assumes the Title of Admiral, and hoists a black Flag, with the Figure of Death in red, at the Main-Top-Masthead, and takes another Voyage to the Western Islands [Azores], where he arrived the Beginning of September."[87] Subsequent reports (as noted below) indicated Low had supposedly reunited with George Lowther in the Azores. The truth of this is unclear, but Lowther was cruising in the Caribbean by early 1724; he would meet his end on La Blanquilla, shooting himself to avoid capture by pirate hunters. Not long after, rumors and reports began spreading of the possible fate of Low himself.]

[*Boston News-Letter*, 10–18 October 1723, 2]

Rhode-Island, Octob. 10. [. . .] We are inform'd by Capt. Philip Tillingheast of this Port, lately arrived from Fyal,[88] That Low & Lowder, Pirates, were at Fyal, and had a Ship there with 5 or 6 other Vessels in company which they had taken; they barbarously used several Persons taken by them, by cutting off their Ears, &c. 'Tis thought they went to the Cape DeVerde islands. The Porteguize were greatly inraged against the Pirates for abusing their People, and taking their Vessels. When the said Tillingheast was going in to Fyal the People there thought him to be a Pirate, fired divers shot at his Vessel, upon which he was oblig'd to lower his Sail and come too,[89] and so got ashore with a few hands; he was carryed before Authority and afterward sent to Goal; and orders were given to go on board his Vessel and search; his Chest and Papers were brought ashore, his Letters broke open, and perused by some English Merchants and other Gentlemen, but finding nothing whereby they might accuse him of Piracy, he was cleared and set at liberty. [. . .]

Boston, October 18. [. . .] On Tuesday last came hither by the way of Rhode-Island, Capt. Maccarty's Mate, who with their Company were taken by a French Pirate of 12 Guns and 24 Hands, as they were bound into Jamaica; they set the Master and Men ashore, but carried away the Boy, and Vessel.

ooooo

[*Boston News-Letter*, 19–27 March 1724, 2]

Boston, March 27. [. . .] From Curcoa to New-York it's said [. . .] that another Pirate had taken Low, burnt his Sloop, and put him and his Crew upon a Maroon Island.

---

87 Schonhorn, ed., *General History*, 335.
88 Faial, a volcanic island in the Azores.
89 Coming-To, or Trying, is "the situation in which a ship lies nearly in the trough or hollow of the sea in a tempest, particularly when it blows contrary to her course. In trying . . . the sails are always reduced in proportion to the increase of the storm" (Falconer, *Universal Dictionary*, n.p.).

And from St. Thomas that the Assiento Company[90] had setled a Factor[91] there. That Nicola, a French Pirate in a two Mast Boat and 13 hands, keeps at the Virgin Islands. That an Assiento Sloop found Lowder the Pirate Careening at Blanco Island near Curacoa;[92] whereupon he and his Men, about 40, left their Sloop, & ran into the Bushes, which the Assiento Sloop took; and a little after, Lowder's Doctor and seven of his Men surrender'd themselves as forced Men, and were carry'd Prisoners to St. Thomas.

ooooo

[*Boston News-Letter*, 30 April–7 May 1724, 2]

Our Merchants have Advice, That the *Delight*, Captain Hunt, and the *Squirrel*, Captain Stevenson, have been taken on the Coast of Guinea by Lowe the Pirate.[93]

ooooo

[London *Daily Courant*, 12 June 1724, 1][94]

St. Christopher's March 24. On the 11th of this Month 16 Pyrates were tryed here, their Names are, John Churchill, Edward MacDonald, Nicholas Lewis, Richard West, Samuel Levercott, Robert White, John Shaw, Andrew Hunter, Jonathan Delve, Matthew Freebairn, Henry Watson, Roger Grange, Ralph Cander, Robert Willis, Robert Corp, and Henry Wynn. Andrew Hunter, Jonathan Delve, and Robert Willis, were acquitted, the other 13 were found Guilty, two of which were recommended to Mercy by the Court of Admiralty, and accordingly pardoned, the other 11 were executed on the 20th Instant.[¶]

The said Pyrates were taken in the following Manner: The Sloop *Eagle* of Barbadoes, commanded by Walter Moore, being upon a Voyage to Comena,[95] on the Spanish Continent of America, and seeing on the 5th Day of October last, at the Island of Blanko, where Traders do not commonly use, it being uninhabited, a Sloop, which he supposed to be a Pyrate, coming nearer he found the said Sloop just careen'd, with her Sails unbent and her great Guns on Shore; so he took that Advantage to attack

---

90 Put very briefly, Asiento refers to non-Spanish business syndicates involved in importing slaves to the New World. See Carswell, *South Sea Bubble*, 47–8, 65–67.

91 This being "an agent, deputy, or representative" (*Oxford English Dictionary*, V:654).

92 The sloop was the Barbados-based *Eagle*, commanded by Walter Moore, owned by the South Sea Company (Schonhorn, ed., *General History*, 316).

93 According to the *General History*: "Low took his old Tour to the Canaries, Cape de Verd Islands, and so to the Coast of Guiney; but nothing extraordinary happened till they arrived near Sierraleon in Africa, where they met with a Ship called the *Delight*, Captain Hunt Commander; this Ship they thought fit for their own Purpose, for she had been a small Man of War, and carry'd 12 Guns; however, they mounted 16 on board her, mann'd her with 60 Men, and appointed one Spriggs, who was then their Quarter-Master, to be Captain of her; who, two Days after, separated from the Admiral, and went to the West-Indies a Pyrating, upon his own, and particular Company's Account . . . " (Schonhorn, ed., 336).

94 © British Library Board (The London *Daily Courant*, 12 June 1724, 1). Used with permission.

95 Cumana, Venezuela.

the said Sloop, after having hoisted his Colours and fired a Gun at the Head of the other Sloop, to oblige her to shew her Colours, which she answered with hoisting a St. George's Flag at the Top Mast Head, and fired at the Sloop *Eagle*; but when they found Moore and his Crew resolved to board their Sloop, they cut their Cables and hawled[96] their Stern on Shore, which obliged the *Eagle* to come to an Anchor athwart their Hause,[97] where she engaged them until they called for Quarter and struck. At which time George Lowther, who was the Captain on board the said Pyrates, with about 10 or 12 of his Crew, made their Escape out of the Cabin Window, and then the Master of the *Eagle* got the Sloop off, secured her, and went on Shore with 25 Men, where they remained five Days and Nights in pursuit of the said Lowther and Company, but they could not take more than five of them, and then proceeded with the said Sloop and Pyrates to Comena aforesaid.[¶]

Being arrived there, the Master of the *Eagle* informed the Governour that he had taken a Pyrate Sloop, upon which the Governour sent a Guard on board the same, and after having tryed and condemned the pyratical Sloop, delivered her to the Sloop *Eagle*'s Company that took her, and then the said Governour sent a small Sloop to the Island of Blanko, with about 25 Hands in pursuit of the Pyrates that were left there, which took four of the said Pyrates with seven small Arms or thereabouts, leaving behind them the Captain, three Men and a little Boy, which they could not take, and Three of the Four they took were condemned for Life to be Galley Slaves, and the other to the Castle of Arraria. The Master of the *Eagle* was afterwards informed, that George Lowther, the Captain of the said Pyrate Sloop, had shot himself on the said Island of Blanko, and was found dead with his Pistol burst by his Side.[¶]

We do not hear that there are any more Pyrates, except a Ship commanded by one Edward Lowe, with about 50 Pyrates in his Crew. The most of the Pyrates lately exe-cuted here, were formerly with him. One of them named Nicholas Lewis, was his Quarter-Master, who gave a most terrible Relation of his Barbarity; that particularly in the Bay of Honduras he murthered 45 Spaniards in cold Blood about 12 Months past;[98] and that some time before, he took a Portuguese Ship bound Home from Brazil, the Master of which had hung 11,000 Moydores[99] of Gold in a Bag out of the Cabin Window, and as soon as he was taken by the said Lowe, cut the Rope and let them drop into the Sea, for which Lowe cut off the said Master's Lips, and broiled them before his Face, and afterwards murthered him with the whole Crew, being 32

---

96 "To Haul . . . an expression peculiar to seamen, implying to pull a single rope, without the assistance of blocks, or other mechanical powers: when a rope is otherwise pulled, as by the application of tackles, or the connection with blocks, &c. the term is changed into bowsing" (Falconer, *Universal Dictionary*, n.p.).

97 "Hause, or Hawse, is generally understood to imply the situation of the cables before the ship's stern, when she is moored with two anchors out from forward, viz. one on the starboard, and the other on the larboard bow. Hence it is usual to say, She has a clear hause, or a foul hause. It also denotes any small distance ahead of a ship, or between her head and the anchors employed to ride her; as, 'He has anchored in our hause; the brig fell athwart our hause,' etc." (Falconer, *Universal Dictionary*, n.p.).

98 See the 11 May 1723 entry from the *British Journal* above.

99 The Portuguese *moidore* or *moeda*, a common gold coin in the New World. It was worth about £1.37 in 1702 (McCusker, *Money and Exchange*, 5, 6, 12).

Persons. This Lowe is notorious also for his Cruelties even to British subjects who have fallen into his Hands.

ooooo

[*Boston News-Letter*, 8–15 October 1724, 1–2]

They write from Barbadoes, May 17, That some Men belonging to a Sloop of that Island were arrived there, having been taken by Lowe the Pirate, off of St. Lucia, they reported that Lowe had but 30 Hands on board, and hoped he was by that Time taken by, or at least driven from that Coast by a French Man of War, that was sent from Martinico in pursuit of him.

[**Editor's Note:** The *Boston News-Letter* of 4–11 February 1725 included on page 2 an item from Newport citing sailor Jonathan Barlow, who Low had captured off Guinea and forced into his crew, and who eventually escaped. After recounting brutal treatment at the hands of Low, Barlow related: "That a great difference falling out between Low and his Men, they had discarded him, and sent him away with two other Pirates, and some small matter of Provisions, in a French Sloop they had taken about Martinico, and since have heard nothing of him." According to one version of events, a French ship from Martinique – perhaps the one referred to in the last article transcribed above – subsequently captured Low and his loyalists. "[A]fter a quick trial by the French, he and his companions received short shrift on a gallows erected for their benefit."[100] Under any circumstances, Low stands out for reprehensible cruelty, even in the rogues' gallery of pirate history.]

---

100 Dow and Edmonds, *Pirates of the New England Coast*, 217; Ellms, *Pirates' Own Book*, 250–251.

8

"Such bad Company" – Edward Low and Francis Spriggs as seen by prisoners Philip Ashton and Nicholas Merritt (1722–1724)

Philip Ashton was master of the schooner *Milton* and his "kinsman" Nicholas Merritt master of the shallop *Jane* in mid-June 1722 when pirate Edward Low captured them off Nova Scotia. Presumably because the two fishermen from Marblehead, Massachusetts were skilled sailors, Low forced them into his flotilla and tried several times, unsuccessfully, to make them sign his company's articles. The pair eventually escaped in separate attempts; each overcame enormous difficulties to return home.

In 1725, they jointly published accounts of their time served as Low's prisoners. Ashton – who included details of his *Robinson Crusoe*-like experiences on Roatán Island in the Bay of Honduras after his escape – did portray Low's ferocity in making threats, yet neither he nor Merritt corroborated the blood-curdling newspaper reports of Low's treatment of captives. Low was depicted as capable of great anger, yet also able to burst into tears at the thought of his child left behind in Boston. Ashton also recounted Low's refusal to force married men into his crew, and how only "Low's merry Air" once saved him and fellow captives from the wrath of quartermaster Farrington (or Francis) Spriggs.

Like Low, Spriggs apparently began his career under George Lowther's command. According to the *General History*, Low eventually put Spriggs, with eighteen men, in charge of a prize taken off the Guinea coast. Instead of keeping pace with Low's vessel as expected, Spriggs changed course in the night and set sail for the West Indies, where he and his crew embarked on their own reign of terror. It lasted until some point in 1725, when they ran afoul of the sloop HMS *Spence* in the Bay of Honduras. The warship forced the pirates ashore; its crew burned Spriggs' vessel while he and his men hid in the woods.[1] Little seems certain about Spriggs after this, though a report circulated in 1726 that his crew had marooned him.[2]

Regardless, the accounts of Ashton and Merritt offer candid glimpses of some of the most dreaded pirates of the Golden Age. While a large part of Ashton's tale

---

1 Schonhorn, ed., *General History*, 352–357. HMS *Spence* was a 64-foot long sloop launched at Deptford in 1723. It carried 80 sailors, eight three-pounder cannon and four half-pounder swivel guns. It served in Jamaica and the West Indies in the 1720s, and was broken up at Deptford in 1730 (Winfield, *British Warships 1714–1792*, 296).
2 Dow and Edmonds, *Pirates of the New England Coast*, 287, citing the *New England Courant*, 30 April 1726.

addressed his castaway status once fleeing his captors, the latter were never far from his fears. And though his surroundings might be seen as naturally idyllic, for him they were clearly not Paradise. He also documented his own encounter with latter-day *boucaniers*, a group of hunters operating in the Bay of Honduras, who in Ashton's eyes were little better than the pirates he had fled.

Merritt's story is shorter but no less dramatic. His escape from Low's company came about due to a successful revolt of forced men aboard a prize sloop. Before he could get home, however, he would spend months in prison on the Portuguese island of São Miguel, with the horrors of smallpox added.

ooooo

From John Barnard, compiler, *Ashton's Memorial. An History of the Strange Adventures and Signal Deliverances of Mr. Philip Ashton, Who, after he had made his Escape from the Pirates, liv'd alone on a Desolate Island for about Sixteen Months, &c. with A short Account of Mr. Nicholas Merritt, who was taken at the same time. To which is added A Sermon on Dan. 3.17[3]* (Boston: Samuel Gerrish, 1725).

[. . .]
Ashton's Memorial.
An History of the Strange Adventures, and Signal Deliverances of
Mr. Philip Ashton, Jun.[4]
of Marblehead.

Upon Friday, June 15th, 1722, After I had been out for some time in the Schooner *Milton*, upon the Fishing grounds, off Cape Sable Shoar, among others, I came to Sail in Company with Nicholas Merritt, in a Shallop, and stood in for Port Rossaway, designing to Harbour there, till the Sabbath was over; where we Arrived about Four of the Clock in the Afternoon. [¶]

When we came into the Harbour, where several of our Fishing Vessels had arrived before us, we spy'd among them a Brigantine which we supposed to have been an Inward bound Vessel, from the West Indies, and had no apprehensions of any Danger from her; but by that time we had been at Anchor two or three Hours, a Boat from the Brigantine with Four hands, came along side of us, and the Men Jumpt in upon

---

3 "If it be so, our God whom we serve, is able to Deliver us from the Burning Fiery Furnace, and He will Deliver us out of thine Hand, O King" (as quoted on page 45 of Barnard's monograph).

4 "Ashton was the son of Philip and Sarah (Hendly) Ashton, and was born in Marblehead, Aug. 12, 1702. He married, first, Jane or Jean Gallison, Dec. 8, 1726, who bore him a daughter Sarah, baptized Dec. 3, 1727, in the First Church, the mother dying a week later. On July 15, 1729, he married, second, Sarah Bartlett and they had Eliza, baptized Oct. 25, 1730; Philip, baptized May 28, 1732; William, baptized Oct. 20, 1734; Thomas, baptized Apr. 17, 1737 and Jean, baptized Aug. 15, 1742. The date of his death is not known" (Dow and Edmonds, *Pirates of the New England Coast*, 221).

A pirate armed with pistols and cutlass (Howard Pyle).

our Deck, without our suspecting any thing but that they were Friends, come on board to visit, or inquire what News; till they drew their Cutlashes and Pistols from under their Clothes, and Cock'd the one and Brandish'd the other, and began to Curse & Swear at us, and demanded a Surrender of our Selves and Vessel to them. It was too late for us to rectify our Mistake, and think of Freeing ourselves from their power: for however we might have been able (being Five of us and a Boy) to have kept them at a Distance, had we known who they were, before they had boarded us; yet now we had our Arms to seek, and being in no Capacity to make any Resistance, were necessitated to submit our selves to their will and pleasure. In this manner they surprised Nicholas Merritt, and 12 or 13 other Fishing Vessels this Evening.

When the Boat went off from our Vessel, they carried me on board the Brigantine, and who should it prove but the Infamous Ned Low, the Pirate, with about 42 Hands, 2 Great Guns, and 4 Swivel Guns. You may easily imagine how I look'd, and felt, when too late to prevent it, I found my self fallen into the hands of such a mad, roaring, mischievous Crew; yet I hoped, that they would not force me away with them, and I purposed to endure any hardship among them patiently, rather than turn Pirate with them.

Low presently sent for me Aft, and according to the Pirates' usual Custom, and in their proper Dialect, asked me, If I would sign their Articles, and go along with them. I told him, No; I could by no means consent to go with them, I should be glad if he would give me my Liberty, and put me on board any Vessel, or set me on shoar there. For indeed my dislike of their Company and Actions, my concern for my Parents, and my fears of being found in such bad Company, made me dread the thoughts of being carried away by them; so that I had not the least Inclination to continue with them.

Upon my utter Refusal to joyn and go with them, I was thrust down into the Hold, which I found to be a safe retreat for me several times afterwards. By that time I had been in the Hold a few Hours, they had compleated the taking [of] the several Vessels that were in the Harbour, and the Examining of the Men; and the next Day I was fetched up with some others that were there, and about 30 or 40 of us were put on board a Schooner belonging to Mr. Orn of Marblehead, which the Pirates made use of for a sort of a Prison, upon the present occasion; where we were all confined unarm'd, with an armed Guard over us, till the Sultan's[5] pleasure should be further known.

The next Lord's Day about Noon, one of the Quarter Masters, John Russel by Name, came on board the Schooner, and took six of us (Nicholas Merritt, Joseph Libbie,[6] Lawrence Fabins, and myself, all of Marblehead, the Eldest of us, if I mistake not, under 21 Years of Age, with two others), and carried us on board the Brigantine; where we were called upon the Quarter Deck, and Low came up to us with Pistol in hand, and with a full mouth demanded, ["]Are any of you Married Men?["] This short and unexpected Question, and the sight of the Pistol, struck us all dumb, and not a Man of us dared to speak a word, for fear there should have been a design in it, which we were not able to see thro'. Our Silence kindled our new Master into a Flame, who could not bear it, that so many Beardless Boyes should deny him an Answer to so plain a Question; and therefore in a Rage, he Cock'd his Pistol, and clapt it to my Head, and cryed out, ["]You D-g! why don't you Answer me?["] and Swore vehemently, he would shoot me thro' the Head, if I did not tell him immediately, whether I was Married or no.

I was sufficiently frightned at the fierceness of the Man, and the boldness of his threatning, but rather than lose my Life for so trifling a matter, I e'en ventured at length to tell him, I was not Married, as loud as I dar'd to speak it; and so said the rest of my Companions. Upon this he seemed something pacified, and turned away from us.

It seems his design was to take no Married Man away with him, how young soever he might be, which I often wondred at; till after I had been with him some considerable time, and could observe in him an uneasiness in the sentiments of his Mind, and the workings of his passions toward a young Child he had at Boston (his Wife being Dead, as I learned, some small time before he turned Pirate) which upon every lucid interval from Revelling and Drink he would express a great tenderness for, insomuch that I have seen him sit down and weep plentifully upon the mentioning of it; and then I concluded, that probably the Reason of his taking none but Single Men was, that he might have none with him under the Influence of such powerful attractives,

---

5   "The Arabic word *sultan* is used to denote power, might, and authority, or the possessor of such power, a ruler" (Esposito, ed., *Oxford Encyclopedia of the Modern Islamic World*, IV:135).

6   Joseph Libbey would be found guilty of piracy after testimony in court described him as an active member of Low's company (see preceding chapter).

as a Wife & Children, lest they should grow uneasy in his Service, and have an Inclination to Desert him, and return home for the sake of their Families.[7]

Low presently came up to us again, and asked the Old Question, Whether we would Sign their Articles, and go along with them? We all told him No; we could not; so we were dismissed. But within a little while we were call'd to him Singly, and then it was demanded of me, with Sterness and Threats, whether I would Joyn with them? I still persisted in the Denial; which thro' the assistance of Heaven, I was resolved to do, tho' he shot me. And as I understood, all my Six Companions, who were called in their turns, still refused to go with him.

Then I was led down into the Steerage, by one of the Quarter-Masters, and there I was assaulted with Temptations of another kind, in hopes to win me over to become one of them; a number of them got about me, and instead of Hissing, shook their Rattles, and treated me with abundance of Respect and Kindness, in their way; they did all they could to sooth my Sorrows, and set before me the strong Allurement of the Vast Riches they should gain, and what Mighty Men they designed to be, and would fain have me to joyn with them, and share in their Spoils; and to make all go down the more Glib, they greatly Importuned me to Drink with them, not doubting but this wile would sufficiently entangle me, and so they should prevail with me to do that in my Cups, which they perceived they could not bring me to while I was Sober: but all their fair and plausible Carriage, their proffered Kindness, and airy notions of Riches, had not the Effect upon me which they desired; and I had no Inclination to drown my Sorrows with my Senses in their Inebriating Bowls, and so refused their Drink, as well as their Proposals.

After this I was brought upon Deck again, and Low came up to me, with his Pistol Cock'd, and clap'd it to my Head, and said to me, ["]You D-g you! if you will not Sign our Articles, and go along with me, I'll shoot you thro' the Head["]; and uttered his Threats with his utmost Fierceness, and with the usual Flashes of Swearing and Cursing. I told him, That I was in his hands, and he might do with me what he pleased, but I could not be willing to go with him: and then I earnestly beg'd of him, with many Tears, and used all the Arguments I could think of to perswade him, not to carry me away; but he was deaf to my Cryes, and unmoved by all I could say to him; and told me, I was an Impudent D-g, and Swore, I should go with him whether I would or no. So I found all my Cryes, and Entreaties were in vain, and there was no help for it, go with them I must, and as I understood, they set mine and my

---

7 Economist Peter Leeson placed Low among the "minority of pirates [who] were also simply psychopaths," but observed that he "didn't brutalize everyone he encountered. Rather, he often reserved his perverse passions for times when unleashing them could profit him. . . . Low released English prisoners he captured with whom he had no axe to grind. More generally, Low seems to have recognized the importance of not overindulging his sadistic desires. Doing so would undermine his crew's ultimate goal – to take prizes with as little resistance as possible" (*Invisible Hook*, 132–133).

Townsmen's Names down in their Book, tho' against our Consent. And I desire to mention it with due Acknowledgments to God, who withheld me, that neither their promises, not their threatnings, nor blows could move me to a willingness to Joyn with them in their pernicious ways.

Upon Tuesday, June 19th, they changed their Vessel, and took for their Privateer, as they call'd it, a Schooner belonging to Mr. Joseph Dolliber of Marblehead, being new, clean, and a good Sailer, and shipped all their hands on board her, and put the Prisoners, such as they designed to send home, on board the Brigantine, with one _____, who was her Master, and ordered them for Boston.

When I saw the Captives were likely to be sent Home, I thought I would make one attempt more to obtain my Freedom, and accordingly Nicholas Merritt, my Townsman and Kinsman, went along with me to Low, and we fell upon our Knees, and with utmost Importunity besought him to let us go Home in the Brigantine, among the rest of the Captives: but he immediately called for his Pistols, and told us we should not go, and Swore bitterly, if either of us offered to stir, he would shoot us down.

Thus all attempts to be delivered out of the hands of unreasonable Men (if they may be called Men) were hitherto unsuccessful; and I had the melancholly prospect of seeing the Brigantine sail away with the most of us that were taken at Port-Rossaway, but my self, and three Townsmen mentioned, and four Isle of Shoal[8]-men detained on board the Schooner, in the worst of Captivity, without any present likelyhood of Escaping.

And yet before the Brigantine sailed, an opportunity presented, that gave me some hopes that I might get away from them; for some of Low's people, who had been on shoar at Port-Rossaway to get water, had left a Dog belonging to him behind them; and Low observing the Dog a shoar howling to come off, order'd some hands to take the Boat and fetch him. Two Young Men, John Holman, and Benjamin Ashton,[9] both of Marblehead, readily Jumpt into the Boat, and I (who pretty well knew their Inclination to be rid of such Company, & was exceedingly desirous my self to be freed from my present Station, and thought if I could but once set foot on shoar, they should have good luck to get me on board again) was geting over the side into the Boat; but Quarter Master Russel spy'd me, and caught hold on my Shoulder, and drew me in board, and with a Curse told me, Two was eno', I should not go. The two Young Men had more sense and virtue than to come off to them again, so that after some time of waiting, they found they were deprived of their Men, their Boat, and their Dog; and they could not go after them.

---

8   A group of small islands off the New Hampshire/Maine coast.
9   It is unstated whether Philip Ashton was related to Benjamin Ashton, who like the John Holman mentioned here hailed from Philip Ashton's hometown of Marblehead, Massachusetts.

When they saw what a trick was play'd them, the Quarter Master came up to me Cursing and Swearing, that I knew of their design to Run away, and intended to have been one of them; but tho' it would have been an unspeakable pleasure to me to have been with them, yet I was forced to tell him, I knew not of their design; and indeed I did not, tho' I had good reason to suspect what would be the event of their going. This did not pacifie the Quarter-Master, who with outragious Cursing and Swearing clapt his Pistol to my Head, and snap'd it; but it miss'd Fire: this enraged him the more; and he repeated the snapping of his Pistol at my Head three times, and it as often miss'd Fire; upon which he held it over-board, and snap'd it the fourth time, and then it went off very readily. (Thus did God mercifully quench the violence of the Fire, that was meant to destroy me!) The Quarter-Master upon this, in the utmost fury, drew his Cutlash, and fell upon me with it, but I leap'd down into the Hold, and got among a Crowd that was there, and so escaped the further effects of his madness and rage. Thus, tho' God suffered me not to gain my wished-for Freedom, yet he wonderfully preserved me from Death.

All hopes of obtaining Deliverance were now past and gone; the Brigantine and Fishing Vessels were upon their way homeward, the Boat was ashore, and not likely to come off again; I could see no possible way of Escape; and who can express the concern and Agony I was in, to see myself, a Young Lad not 20 Years Old, carried forcibly from my Parents, whom I had so much reason to value for the tenderness I knew they had for me, & to whom my being among Pyrates would be as a Sword in their Bowels, and the Anguishes of Death to them; confined to such Company as I could not but have an exceeding great abhorrence of; in Danger of being poisoned in my morals, by Living among them, and of falling a Sacrifice to Justice, if ever I should be taken with them. I had no way left for my Comfort, but earnestly to commit my self and my cause to God, and wait upon Him for Deliverance in his own time and way; and in the mean while firmly to resolve, thro' Divine Assistance, that nothing should ever bring me to a willingness to Joyn with them, or share in their Spoils.

I soon found that any Death was preferable to being link'd with such a vile Crew of Miscreants, to whom it was a sport to do Mischief; where prodigious Drinking, monstrous Cursing and Swearing, hideous Blasphemies, and open defiance of Heaven, and contempt of Hell it self, was the constant Employment, unless when Sleep something abated the Noise and Revellings.

Thus Confined, the best course I could take, was to keep out of the way, down in the Hold, or where ever I could be most free from their perpetual Din; and fixedly purpose with my self, that the first time I had an opportunity to set my Foot on shore, let it be in what part of the World it would, it should prove (if possible) my taking a final leave of Low and Company.

I would remark it now also (that I might not interrupt the Story with it afterwards) that while I was on board Low, they used once a Week, or Fortnight, as the Evil Spirit

"Noise and Revellings" on deck such as Ashton described (19th century engraving, artist unknown).

moved them, to bring me under Examination, and anew demand my Signing their Articles, and Joyning with them; but Blessed be God, I was enabled to persist in a constant refusal to become one of them, tho' I was thrashed with Sword or Cane, as often as I denyed them; the fury of which I had no way to avoid, but by Jumping down into the Hold, where for a while I was safe. I look'd upon myself, for a long while, but as a Dead Man among them, and expected every Day of Examination would prove the last of my Life, till I learned from some of them, that it was one of their Articles, Not to Draw Blood, or take away the Life of any Man, after they had given him Quarter, unless he was to be punished as a Criminal; and this emboldned me afterwards, so that I was not so much affraid to deny them, seeing my Life was given me for a Prey.

This Tuesday, towards Evening, Low and Company came to sail in the Schooner, formerly called the *Mary*, now the *Fancy*, and made off for Newfoundland; and here they met with such an Adventure, as had like to have proved fatal to them. They fell in with the Mouth of St. John's Harbour in a Fogg, before they knew where they were; when the Fogg clearing up a little, they spy'd a large Ship riding at Anchor in the Harbour, but could not discern what she was, by reason of the thickness of the Air, and concluded she was a Fish-Trader; this they look'd upon as a Boon Prize for them, and thought they should be wonderfully well accommodated with a good Ship under Foot, and if she proved but a good Sailer, would greatly further their Roving Designs, and render them a Match for almost any thing they could meet with, so that they need not fear being taken.

Accordingly they came to a Resolution to go in and take her; and imaging it was best doing it by St[r]atagem, they concluded to put all their Hands, but Six or Seven, down in the Hold, and make a shew as if they were a Fishing Vessel, and so run up along side of her, and surprise her, and bring her off; and great was their Joy at the distant prospect how cleverly they should catch her. They began to put their designs in Execution, stowed away their Hands, leaving but a few upon Deck, and made Sail in order to seise the Prey; when there comes along a small Fisher-Boat, from out of the Harbour and hailed them, and asked them, from whence they were? They told them, from Barbadoes, and were laden with Rhum and Sugar; then they asked the Fisherman, What large Ship that was in the Harbour? who told them it was a large Man of War.

The very Name of a Man of War struck them all up in a Heap, spoil'd their Mirth, their fair Hopes, and promising Design of having a good Ship at Command; and lest they should catch a Tartar, they thought it their wisest and safest way, instead of going into the Harbour, to be gone as fast as they could; and accordingly they stretched[10] away

---

10   "A word frequently used instead of *tack*; as, 'We shall make a good stretch.' – *To stretch*. To sail by the wind under a crowd of canvas" (Smyth, *Lexicon*, 662).

An 18th century English warship, or Man-of-War (artist unknown).

farther Eastwards, and put into a small Harbour, called Carboneur,[11] about 15 Leagues distance; where they went on Shoar, took the Place, and destroyed the Houses, but hurt none of the People; as they told me, for I was not suffered to go ashore with them.

The next Day they made off for the Grand Bank, where they took seven or eight Vessels, and among them a French Banker,[12] a Ship of about 350 Tuns, and 2 Guns; this they carried off with them, and stood away for St. Michael's.[13]

Off of St. Michael's they took a large Portugueze Pink, laden with Wheat, coming out of the Road, which I was told was formerly call'd the *Rose*-Frigat. She struck to the Schooner, fearing the large Ship that was coming down to them; tho' all of Low's Force had been no Match for her, if the Portugueze had made a good Resistance. This Pink they soon observed to be a much better Sailer than their French Banker, which went heavily; and therefore they threw the greatest part of the Wheat overboard, reserving only eno' to Ballast the Vessel for the present, and took what they wanted out of the Banker, and then Burnt her, and sent the most of the Portugueze away in a large La[u]nch they had taken.

---

11 Carbonear. An early 19th century work described "Carbonier, formerly Carboniero, or Collier's Harbour," as having "a spacious harbor" though exposed "to the easterly winds" (Anspach, *History of Newfoundland*, 299).
12 A ship operating from or near the Grand Bank of Newfoundland.
13 São Miguel, in the Azores.

Now they made the Pink, which Mounted 14 Guns, their Commodore,[14] and with this and the Schooner Sailed from St. Michael's, to the Canaries, where off of Tenerife they gave Chase to a Sloop, which got under the Command of the Fortress, and so escaped falling into their Hands; but stretching along to the Western end of the Island, they came up with a Fishing Boat, and being in want of Water, made them Pilot them into a small Harbour, where they went a shore and got a supply.

After they had Watered, they Sailed away for Cape de Verde Islands, and upon making the Isle of May,[15] they descry'd a Sloop, which they took, and it proved to be a Bristol-man, one Pare or Pier Master; this Sloop they designed for a Tender, and put on board her my Kinsman Nicholas Merritt, with 8 or 9 hands more, and Sailed away for Bonavista, with a design to careen their Vessels.

In their Passage to Bonavista, the Sloop wronged[16] both the Pink and the Schooner; which the Hands on board observing, being mostly Forced Men, or such as were weary of their Employment, upon the Fifth of September, Ran away with her and made their Escape.[17]

When they came to Bonavista, they hove down the Schooner, and careen'd her, and then the Pink; and there they gave the Wheat, which they had kept to Ballast the Pink with, to the Portugueze, and took other Ballast.

After they had cleaned and fitted their Vessels, they steered away for St. Nicholas,[18] to get better Water: and here as I was told, 7 or 8 hands out of the Pink went ashore a Fowling, but never came off more, among which I suppose Lawrence Fabins was one, and what became of them I never could hear to this Day. Then they put out to Sea, and stood away for the Coast of Brasil hoping to meet with Richer Prizes than they had yet taken; in the Passage thither, they made a Ship, which they gave chase to, but could not come up with; and when they came upon the Coast, it had like to have proved a sad Coast to them: for the Trade-Winds blowing exceeding hard at South East, they fell in upon the Northern part of the Coast, near 200 Leagues to the Leeward of where they designed; and here we were all in exceeding great Danger, and for Five Days and Nights together, hourly feared when we should be swallowed up by the violence of the Wind and Sea, or stranded upon some of the Shoals, that lay many Leagues off from Land. In this time of Extremity, the Poor Wretches had nowhere to go for Help! For they were at open Defiance with their Maker, & they could have but little comfort in the thoughts of their Agreement with Hell; such

---

14 Flagship.
15 Or Maio.
16 "To outsail a vessel by becalming her sails is said to wrong her" (Smyth, *Lexicon*, 739).
17 See Merritt's memoir below.
18 A newspaper placed this island about 30 leagues from the Isle of May, or Maio, and 24 leagues from St. Antony ("London. Part of a letter from Hamburg, July 9," *London Chronicle, or Universal Evening Post*, 22–24 July 1762, 88).

mighty Hectors[19] as they were, in a clear Sky and a fair Gale, yet a fierce Wind and a boisterous Sea sunk their Spirits to a Cowardly dejection, and they evidently feared the Almighty, whom before they defied, lest He was come to Torment them before their expected Time; and tho' they were so habituated to Cursing and Swearing, that the Dismal Prospect of Death, & this of so long Continuance, could not Correct the Language of most of them, yet you might plainly see the inward Horror and Anguish of their Minds, visible in their Countenances, and like Men amazed, or starting out of Sleep in a fright, I could hear them ever[y] now and then, cry out, ["]Oh! I wish I were at home.["]

When the Fierceness of the Weather was over, and they had recovered their Spirits, by the help of a little Nantes,[20] they bore away to the West Indies, and made the three islands call'd the Triangles, lying off the Main about 40 Leagues to the Eastward of Surinam. Here they went in and careened their Vessels again; and it had like to have proved a fatal Scouring to them.

For as they hove down the Pink, Low had ordered so many hands upon the Shrouds,[21] and Yards, to throw her Bottom out of Water, that it threw her Ports, which were open, under Water; and the Water flow'd in with such freedom that it presently overset her. Low and the Doctor were in the Cabbin together, and as soon as he perceived the Water to rush in upon him, he bolted out at one of the Stern-Ports, which the Doctor also attempted, but the Sea rushed so violently into the Port by that time, as to force him back into the Cabbin, upon which Low nimbly run his Arm into the Port, and caught hold of his Shoulder and drew him out, and so saved him.[22] The Vessel pitched her Masts to the Ground, in about 6 Fathom Water, and turn'd her Keel out of Water; but as her Hull filled, it sunk, and by the help of her Yard-Arms, which I suppose bore upon the Ground, her Masts were raised something out of Water: the Men that were upon her Shrouds and Yards, got upon her Hull, when that was uppermost, and then upon her Top-Masts and Shrouds, when they were raised again. I (who with other light Lads were sent up to the Main-Top-Gallant[23] Yard) was very difficultly put to it to save my Life, being but a poor Swimmer; for the Boat which

19 The Trojan warrior Hector figures prominently in Homer's *Iliad*.
20 Wine (Stephens, *Captured by Pirates*, 223, 238).
21 *Shrouds* are "a range of large ropes extended from the mast-heads to the right and left side of the ship, to support the masts, and enable them to carry sail, &c" (Falconer, *Universal Dictionary*, n.p.).
22 It is unknown if this "Doctor" was the same "Surgeon" with whom Low, at some point in his captaincy, had an altercation. According to the *General History*, a crewman accidentally struck Low with an edged weapon "upon his under Jaw, which laid the Teeth bare; upon this the Surgeon was called, who immediately stitched up the Wound; but Low finding fault with the Operation, the Surgeon being tollerably drunk, as it was customary for every Body to be, struck Low such a Blow with his Fist, that broke out all the Stitches, and then bid him sew up his Chops himself, and be damned; so that Low made a very pitiful Figure for some Time after" (Schonhorn, ed., 324).
23 The topgallant sail is the "third sail above the deck on a man-o'-war, or where single topsails are carried, but the sail next above the upper topsail on a vessel carrying double topsails. Some large merchant vessels divide the top-gallant sail in the same manner as the topsail, thus having double topgallant sails, named in the same way as the topsails – upper and lower" (Patterson, *Illustrated Nautical Dictionary*, 187).

picked the Men up refused to take me in, & I was put upon making the best of my way to the Buoy,[24] which with much ado I recovered, and it being large I stayed my self by it, till the Boat came along close by it, and then I called to them to take me in; but they being full of Men still refused me; and I did not know but they meant to leave me to perish there; but the Boat making way a head very slowly because of her deep load, and Joseph Libbie calling to me to put off from the Buoy and Swim to them, I e'en ventured it, and he took me by the hand and drew me in board. They lost two Men by this Accident, viz. John Bell, and one they called Zana Gourdon. The Men that were on board the Schooner were busy a mending the Sails, under an Auning, so they knew nothing of what had happened to the Pink, till the Boat full of Men came along side of them, tho' they were but about Gun-Shot off[25] and We made a great out-cry: and therefore they sent not their Boat to help take up the Men.

And now Low and his Gang, having lost their Frigate, and with her the greatest part of their Provision and Water, were again reduced to their Schooner as their only Privateer, and in her they put to Sea and were brought to very great straits for want of Water; for they could not get a supply at the Triangles, and when they hoped to furnish themselves at Tobago, the Current set so strong, & the Season was so Calm, that they could not recover the Harbour, so they were forced to stand away for Grand Grenada, a French Island about 18 Leagues to the Westward of Tabago, which they gained, after they had been at the hardship of half a pint of Water a Man for Sixteen Dayes together.

Here the French came on board, and Low having put all his Men down, but a suffi-cient number to Sail the Vessel, told them upon their Enquiry, Whence he was, that he was come from Barbadoes, and had lost his Water, and was oblig'd to put in for a recruit; the poor People not suspecting him for a Pyrate, readily suffered him to send his Men ashoar and fetch off a supply. But the Frenchmen afterwards suspecting he was a Smugling Trader, thought to have made a Boon Prize of him, and the next day fitted out a large Rhode-Island built Sloop of 70 Tuns, with 4 Guns mounted, and about 30 Hands, with design to have taken him. Low was apprehensive of no danger from them, till they came close along side of him and plainly discovered their design, by their Number and Actions, and then he called up his hands upon Deck, and having about 90 Hands on board, & 8 Guns mounted, the Sloop and Frenchmen fell an easy prey to him, and he made a Privateer of her.

---

24 "A floating shape anchored to the bottom to mark out a channel; also floated over a shoal, or near a rock, as a warning to mariners" (Patterson, *Illustrated Nautical Dictionary*, 32).

25 This could have referred variously to a cannon's point-blank or long-range distance. Point-blank range depended on factors such as shot weight and powder charge; the point-blank range of a cannonball shot from a four-pounder was about 500 yards (Frayler, "Armed to the Teeth," 2). From another source: "*Gun-shot* implies, says Falconer, 'the distance of the point-blank range of a cannon-shot.' With submission, we take a gun-shot distance to mean long, and not point-blank range: if this be correct, a ship is within gun-shot of another when she is within a mile or a mile and a quarter of her" (James, *Naval History of Great Britain*, I:xxii).

After this they cruised for some time thro' the West Indies, in which excursion they took 7 or 8 Sail of Vessels, chiefly Sloops; at length they came to Santa Cruz,[26] where they took two Sloops more, & then came to Anchor off the Island.

While they lay at Anchor here, it came into Low's Head, that he wanted a Doctor's Chest, & in order to procure one, he put four of the Frenchmen on board one of the Sloops, which he had just now taken, & sent them away to St. Thomas's, about 12 Leagues off where the Sloops belonged, with the promise, that if they would presently send him off a good Doctor's Chest, for what he sent to purchase it with, they should have their Men & Vessels again, but if not, he would kill all the Men & burn the Vessels. The poor People in Compassion to their Neighbours, & to preserve their Interest, readily complied with his Demands; so that in little more than 24 Hours the four Frenchmen returned with what they went for, & then according to promise, they & their Sloops were Dismissed.[27]

From Santa Cruz they Sailed till they made Curacao, in which Passage they gave Chase to two Sloops that outsailed them & got clear; then they Ranged the Coast of New Spain, and made Carthagena, & about mid-way between Carthagena and Port-Abella,[28] they descry'd two tall Ships, which proved to be the *Mermaid* Man of War,[29] & a large Guinea-Man. Low was now in the Rhode-Island Sloop, & one Farrington Spriggs, a Quarter-Master, was Commander of the Schooner, where I still was. For some time they made Sail after the two Ships, till they came so near that they could plainly see the Man of War's large range of Teeth, & then they turned Tail to, and made the best of their way from them; upon which the Man of War gave them Chase & overhalled[30] them apace. And now I confess I was in as great terrour as ever I had been yet, for I concluded we should be taken, & I could expect no other but to Dye for Companies sake; so true is what Solomon tells, a Companion[s] of Fools shall be destroyed.[31] But the Pirates finding the Man of War to overhale them, separated, &

---

26 Saint Croix, in the Virgin Islands.
27 Edward Teach made a similar demand for a chest of medicines. See the entry from the *Boston News-Letter*, 30 June–7 July 1718 in Chapter 4.
28 Portobello, which Morgan sacked in 1668, lay in "latitude 10° north, some forty leagues from the Gulf of Darien and eight leagues west of Nombre de Dios. With the exception of Havana and Cartagena, it is the strongest city which the King of Spain possesses in all the West Indies. Two strong forts stand at the entrance of the bay, protecting the town and harbour. These forts are always manned by a garrison of 300 soldiers, and not a single vessel can enter the bay without consent. Four hundred families have their permanent residence in the city, but the merchants only stay there when there are galleons in port, as the place is very unhealthy on account of the mountain vapours. The merchants reside in Panama, but have their warehouses in Porto Bello, kept up by their servants. Silver is brought from Panama on pack-mules ready for the arrival of the galleons, or the ships of the slave trade, delivering Negroes" (Exquemelin, *Buccaneers of America*, 134–135).
29 HMS *Mermaid* was a 36–gun ship rebuilt at Chatham in 1706–1707 as a 108–foot long vessel. It was specially sheathed in June 1720 for its voyage to the West Indies. Its captain in 1720 at Jamaica was Digby Dent; he was succeeded in October 1722 by Joseph Lawes, who commanded the warship until 1724 (Winfield, *British Warships 1714–1792*, 188).
30 "*Overhaul*, to examine; also to overtake a ship in chase" (James, *Naval History of Great Britain*, I:xxii).
31 Proverbs 13:20.

Low stood out to Sea, & Spriggs stood in for the Shoar. The Man of War observing the Sloop to be the larger Vessel much, and fullest of Men, threw out all the Sail she could, & stood after her, and was in a fair way of coming up with her presently: But it hapened there was one Man on board the Sloop, that knew of a Shoal Ground there-abouts, who directed Low to run over it; he did so; and the Man of War who had now so forereached him as to sling a Shot over him, in the close pursuit ran a Ground upon the Shoal, and so Low and Company escaped Hanging for this time.

Spriggs, who was in the Schooner, when he saw the Danger they were in of being taken, upon the Man of War's out sailing them, was afraid of falling into the hands of Justice; to prevent which, he, and one of his Chief Companions, took their Pistols, and laid them down by them, and solemnly Swore to each other, and pledg'd the Oath in a Bumper of Liquor, that if they saw there was at last no possibility of Escaping, but that they should be taken, they would set Foot to Foot, and Shoot one another, to Escape Justice and the Halter. As if Divine Justice were not as inexorable as Humane!

But, as I said, he stood in for the Shoar, and made into Pickeroon Bay,[32] about 18 Leagues from Carthagena, and so got out of the reach of Danger. By this means the Sloop and Schooner were parted; and Spriggs made Sail towards the Bay of Honduras, and came to Anchor in a small Island called Utilla, about 7 or 8 Leagues to Leeward of Roatan,[33] where by the help of a small Sloop he had taken the Day before, he haled down, and cleaned the Schooner.

While Spriggs lay at Utilla, there was an Opportunity presented, which gave occasion to several of us to form a design, of making our Escape out of the Pirates' Company; for having lost Low, and being but weak handed, Spriggs had determined to go thro' the Gulf, and come upon the Coast of New-England, to encrease his Company, and supply himself with Provision; whereupon a Number of us had entred into a Combination, to take the first fair advantage, to Subdue our Masters, and Free our selves. There were in all about 22 Men on board the Schooner, and 8 of us were in the Plot, which was, That when we should come upon the Coast of New-England, we would take the opportunity when the Crew had sufficiently dozed themselves with Drink, and had got sound a Sleep, to secure them under the Hatches, and bring the Vessel and Company in, and throw ourselves upon the Mercy of the Government.

But it pleased God to disappoint our Design. The Day that they came to Sail out of Utilla, after they had been parted from Low about five Weeks, they discovered a large Sloop, which bore down upon them. Spriggs, who knew not the Sloop, but imagined it might be a Spanish Privateer, full of Men, being but weak handed himself, made

32 From the Spanish word *picarón*. "A swindler or thief. Also, a piratical vessel" (Smyth, *Lexicon*, 526).
33 Utila and Roatán are islands in the Bay of Honduras.

the best of his way from her. The sloop greatly overhaled the Schooner. Low, who knew the Schooner, & thought that since they had been separated, she might have fallen into the hands of honest Men, fired upon her, & struck her the first Shot. Spriggs, seeing the Sloop fuller of Men than ordinary (for Low had been to Honduras, & had taken a Sloop, & brought off several Baymen, & was now become an Hundred strong), & remaining still ignorant of his old Mate, refused to bring to, but continued to make off; and resolved if they came up with him, to fight them the best he could. Thus the Harpies[34] had like to have fallen foul of one another. But Low hoisting his Pirate Colours, discovered who he was; and then, hideous was the noisy Joy among the Piratical Crew, on all sides, accompanied with Firing, & Carousing, at the finding [of] their Old Master, & Companions, & their narrow Escape: and so the design of Crusing upon the Coast of New-England came to nothing. A good Providence it was to my dear Country, that it did so; unless we could have timely succeeded in our design to surprise them.

Yet it had like to have proved a fatal Providence to those of us that had a hand in the Plot; for tho' our design of surprising Spriggs and Company, when we should come upon the Coast of New-England, was carried with as much secrecy as was possible (we hardly daring to trust one another, and mentioning it always with utmost privacy, and not plainly, but in distant hints), yet now that Low appeared, Spriggs had got an account of it some way or other; and full of Resentment and Rage he goes aboard Low, and acquaints him with what he called our Treacherous design, and says all he can to provoke him to Revenge the Mischief upon us, and earnestly urged that we might be shot. But God who has the Hearts of all Men in His own Hands, and turns them as He pleases, so over ruled, that Low turned it off with a Laugh, and said he did not know, but if it had been his own case, as it was ours, he should have done so himself; and all that Spriggs could say was not able to stir up his Resentments, and procure any heavy Sentence upon us.

Thus Low's merry Air saved us at that time; for had he lisped a Word in compliance with what Spriggs urged, we had surely some of us, if not all, have been lost. Upon this he comes on board the Schooner again, heated with Drink, but more chafed in his own Mind, that he could not have his Will of us, and swore & tore like a Mad-man, crying out that four of us ought to go forward, & be shot; and to me in particular he said, ["]You D-g, Ashton, deserve to be hang'd up at the Yards-Arm, for designing to cut us off.["] I told him, I had no design of hurting any man on board, but if they would let me go away quietly I should be glad. This matter made a very great noise on board for several Hours, but at length the Fire was quenched, and thro' the Goodness of God, I escaped being consumed by the violence of the Flame.

---

34   A *harpy* was a demonic and foul-smelling bird-woman creature from Greek mythology (Nardo, *Greek Mythology*, 50–51).

The next Day, Low ordered all into Roatan Harbour to clean, and here it was that thro' the Favour of God to me, I first gained Deliverance out of the Pirates' hands; tho' it was a long while before my Deliverance was perfected, in a return to my Country, and Friends; as you will see in the Sequel.

Roatan Harbour, as all about the Gulf of Honduras, is full of small Islands, which go by the General Name of the Keys. When we had got in here, Low and some of his Chief Men had got ashoar upon one of these small Islands, which they called Port-Royal Key, where they made them Booths, and were Carousing, Drinking, and Firing, while the two Sloops, the Rhode-Island, and that which Low brought with him from the Bay, were cleaning. As for the Schooner, he loaded her with the Logwood which the Sloop brought from the Bay, & gave her, according to promise, to one John Blaze, and put four men along with him in her, and when they came to Sail from this Place, sent them away upon their own account, and what became of them I know not.

Upon Saturday the 9th of March, 1723, the Cooper[35] with Six hands in the Long-Boat were going ashore at the Watering place to fill their Casks; as he came along by the Schooner I called to him and asked him, if he were going ashoar? [H]e told me Yes; then I asked him, if he would take me along with him; he seemed to hesitate at the first; but I urged that I had never been on shoar yet, since I first came on board, and I thought it very hard that I should be so closely confined, when every one else had the Liberty of going ashoar at several times, as there was occasion. At length he took me in, imagining, I suppose, that there would be no danger of my Running away in so desolate uninhabited a Place, as that was.

I went into the Boat with only an Ozenbrigs[36] Frock and Trousers on, and a Mill'd Cap upon my Head, having neither Shirt, Shoes, not Stockings, nor any thing else about me; whereas, had I been aware of such an Opportunity, but one quarter of an Hour before, I could have provided my self something better. However thought I, if I can but once get footing on Terra-Firma, tho' in never so bad Circumstances, I shall count it a happy Deliverance; for I was resolved, come what would, never to come on board again.

Low had often told me (upon my asking him to send me away in some of the Vessels, which he dismissed after he had taken them) that I should go home when he did, and not before, and Swore that I should never set foot on shoar till he did. But the time for Deliverance was now come. God had ordered it that Low and Spriggs, and almost all the Commanding Officers, were ashoar upon an island distinct from Roatan, where the Watering place was; He presented me in sight, when the

---

35 "A rating for a first-class petty officer, who repairs casks, &c." (Smyth, *Lexicon*, 212).
36 Ozenbrig was a "tough, coarse linen woven in Osnabruck, Westphalia," and which colonial-era Americans "made up into nearly everything from breeches and entire suits to sheets, table covers, and carpetbags" ("Habiliments and Habits").

Long Boat came by (the only opportunity I could have had), He had moved the
Cooper to take me into the Boat, and under such Circumstances as rendred me least
liable to Suspicion; and so I got ashoar.

When we came first to Land, I was very Active in helping to get the Cask out of the
Boat, & Rowling them up to the Watering place; then I lay down at the Fountain &
took a hearty Draught of the Cool Water; & anon, I gradually strol'd along the Beech,
picking up Stones & Shells, & looking about me; when I had got about Musket Shot[37]
off from them (tho' they had taken no Arms along with them in the Boat) I began to
make up to the Edge of the Woods; when the Cooper spying me, call'd after me, &
asked me where I was going; I told him I was going to get some Coco-Nuts, for there
were some Coco-Nut Trees just before me. So soon as I had recovered the Woods,
and lost sight of them, I betook my self to my Heels, & ran as fast as the thickness of
the Bushes, and my naked Feet would let me. I bent my Course, not directly from
them, but rather up behind them, which I continued till I had got a considerable way
into the Woods, & yet not so far from them but that I could hear their talk, when they
spake any thing loud; and here I lay close in a very great Thicket, being well assured,
if they should take the pains to hunt after me never so carefully they would not be
able to find me.

After they had filled their Cask and were about to go off, the Cooper called after me to
come away; but I lay snug in my Thicket, and would give him no Answer, tho' I plainly
eno' heard him. At length they set a hallooing for me, but I was still silent: I could
hear them say to one another, ["]The D-g is lost in the Woods, and can't find the way
out again;["] then they hallooed again; and cried, ["H]e is run-away and won't come
again["]; the Cooper said, if he had thought I would have served him so, he would not
have brought me ashoar. They plainly saw it would be in vain to seek for me in such
hideous Wood, and thick Brushes. When they were weary with hallooing, the Cooper
at last, to shew his good Will to me (I can't but Love and Thank him for his Kindness),
call'd out, ["]If you don't come away presently, I'll go off and leave you alone.["] But all
they could say was no Temptation to me to discover my self, and least of all that of
their going away and leaving me; for this was the very thing I desired, that I might be
rid of them, and all that belonged to them. So finding it in vain for them to wait any
longer, they put off with their Water, without me; and thus was I left upon a desolate
Island destitute of all help, and much out of the way of all Travellers; however this
Wilderness I looked upon as Hospitable, and this Loneliness as good Company, compared with the State and Society I was now happily Delivered from.

When I supposed they were gone off, I came out of my Thicket, and drew down to
the Water side, about a Mile below the Watering place, where there was a small run

---

37   A smoothbore musket was "accurate at 40–60 yards for the average marksman, 100 yards or more for the highly
     skilled. Effective range 200–250 yards, maximum range 400–500 yards" (Little, *Sea Rover's Practice*, 251).

of Water; and here I sat down to observe their Motions, and know when the Coast was clear; for I could not but have some remaining fears lest they should send a Company of Armed Men after me; yet I thought if they should, the Woods and Bushes were so thick that it would be impossible they should find me. As yet I had nothing to Eat, nor indeed were my Thoughts much concerned about living in this Desolate Place, but they were chiefly taken up about my geting clear. And to my Joy, after the Vessels had stayed five Dayes in this Harbour, they came to Sail, and put out to Sea, and I plainly saw the Schooner part from the two Sloops, and shape a different Course from them.

When they were gone and the Coast clear, I began to reflect upon my self, and my present Condition; I was upon an island from whence I could not get off; I knew of no Humane Creature within many scores of Miles of me; I had but a Scanty Cloathing, and no possibility of getting more; I was destitute of all Provision for my Support, and knew not how I should come at any; every thing looked with a dismal Face; the sad prospect drew Tears from me in abundance; yet since God had graciously granted my Desires, in freeing me out of the hands of the Sons of Violence, whose Business 'tis to devise Mischief against their Neighbour, and from whom every thing that had the least face of Religion and Virtue was intirely Banished (unless that Low would never suffer his Men to work upon the Sabbath, it was more devoted to Play, and I have seen some of them then sit down to Read in a good Book), therefore I purposed to account all the hardship I might now meet with, as Light, & Easy, compared with being Associated with them.

[**Editor's Note**: Ashton recounted many hardships in the months spent alone on uninhabited Roatán, "which I suppose is some 10 or 11 Leagues Long, in the Latitude of 16 deg. 30 min. or thereabouts." His principal need was food, but he also feared a return visit by Low's company. While Ashton was able to swim to a nearby key, which he found more pleasant than Roatán itself, he suffered injuries to his feet from walking barefoot. Over nine months he sank into illness and melancholy, until in November 1723 he spotted a canoe approaching from offshore. Its occupant was a hunter from "North-Britain, a Man well in Years, of a Grave and Venerable Aspect, and of a reserved Temper." Though this later *boucanier* had lived among the Spanish for two decades, he had for some reason fallen foul of them, and fled to Roatán. "He seemed very kind & obliging to me, gave me some of his Pork, and assisted me all he could; tho' he conversed little," Ashton wrote. Their companionship was brief. After three days, the man went off in his canoe to hunt, a sudden storm blew up, and Ashton never saw him again. The hunter had left behind (among other things) some pork, a knife, and flint for starting fires, which enabled Ashton to subsist easier.

Using an abandoned canoe, Ashton briefly visited Bonacco, "an Island of about 4 or 5 Leagues long, and some 5 or 6 Leagues to the Eastward of Roatan," where he narrowly eluded hostile Spaniards. Returning to Roatán and his "small island" just off it, he spent another seven months alone until June 1724, when a group of "Bay men" – hunters operating in the Bay of Honduras – came to Roatán. While overjoyed to have human contact, Ashton became wary of his new friends, who like his earlier visitor were a throwback to the *boucaniers*.]

And when I was so thorowly come to my self as to converse with them, I found they were Eighteen Men come from the Bay of Honduras, the chief of which were, John Hope, and John Ford. The occasion of their coming from the Bay was, a Story they had got among them, that the Spaniards had projected to make a descent upon them by Water, while the Indians were to assault them by Land, and cut off the Bay; and they retired hither to avoid the Destruction that was designed.[38] This John Hope and Ford had formerly, upon a like occasion, sheltred themselves among these Islands, and lived for four Years together upon a small Island called Barbarat,[39] about two Leagues from Roatan, where they had two Plantations, as they called them; and being now upon the same design of retreating for a time for Safety, they brought with them two Barrels of Flower, with other Provisions, their Fire-Arms, Ammunition and Dogs for Hunting, and Nets for Tortoise, and an Indian Woman to dress their Provision for them. They chose for their chief Residence a small Key about a quarter of a Mile Round, lying near to Barbarat, which they called the Castle of Comfort, chiefly because it was low, and clear of Woods and Bushes, where the Wind had an open passage, and drove away the pestering Muskettoes and Gnats. From hence they sent to the other Islands round about for Wood and Water, and for Materials, with which they Built two Houses, such as they were, for Shelter.

And now I seemed to be in a far more likely way to Live pretty tollerably, than in the Sixteen Months past; for besides the having Company, they treated me with a great deal of Civility, in their way; they Cloathed me, and gave me a large sort of Wrapping Gown to lodge in a[t] Night[s] to defend me from the great Dews, till their Houses were Covered; and we had plenty of Provision. But after all they were Bad Company, and there was but little difference between them and the Pirates, as to their Common Conversation; only I thought they were not now engaged in any such bad design as rendred it unlawful to Joyn with them, nor dangerous to be found in their Company.

In process of time, by the Blessing of God, & the Assistance I received from them, I gathered so much Strength that I was able sometimes to go out a Hunting with them. The Islands hereabouts, I observed before, abound with Wild Hogs and Deer, and Tortoise. Their manner was to go out a number of them in a Canoe, sometimes to one Island, sometimes to another, and kill what Game they could meet with, and

---

38 "The hunters' life . . . was not one of revelry and ease. On the one side were all the insidious dangers lurking in a wild, tropical forest; on the other, the relentless hostility of the Spaniards" (Haring, *The Buccaneers*, 79).
39 Barbareta.

Firk[40] their Pork, by beginning at one end of a Hog and cutting along to the other end, and so back again till they had gone all over him, and flee the flesh in long strings off from the Bones; the Venison they took whole or in quarters, and the Tortoise in like manner; and return home with a load of it; what they did not spend presently, they hung up in their House a smoak drying; and this was a ready supply to them at all times.

I was now ready to think my self out of the reach of any danger from an Enemy, for what should bring any here? [A]nd I was compassed continually with a Number of Men with their Arms ready at hand; and yet when I thought myself most secure, I very narrowly escaped falling again into the hands of the Pirates.

It happened about 6 or 7 Months after these Bay-men came to me, That three Men and I took a Canoo with four Oars, to go over to Bonacco, a Hunting and to kill Tortoise. While we were gone the rest of the Bay-men haled up their Canooes, and Dryed and Tarred them, in order to go to the Bay and see how matters stood there, and to fetch off their Effects which they had left behind them, in case they should find there was no safety for them in tarrying. But before they were gone, we, who had met with good Success in our Voyage, were upon our return to them with a full load of Tortoise and Firkt Pork. As we were upon entring into the Mouth of the Harbour, in a Moon-light Evening, we saw a great Flash of Light, and heard the report of a Gun, which we thought was much louder than a Musket, out of a large Periagua, which we saw near our Castle of Comfort. This put us into a great Consternation, and we knew not what to make of it. Within a Minute or two we heard a Volley of 18 or 20 small Arms discharged upon the shoar, and heard some Guns also fired off from the shoar. Upon which we were satisfied that some Enemy, Pirates or Spaniards were attacking our People, and being cut off from our Companions, by the Periaguas which lay between us and them, we thought it our wisest way to save our selves as well as we could. So we took down our little Mast and Sail, that it might not betray us, and rowed out of the Harbour as fast as we could; thinking to make our Escape from them undiscovered, to an Island about a Mile and [a] half off. But they either saw us before we had taken our Sail down, or heard the noise of our Oars as we made out of the Harbour, and came after us with all speed, in a Periagua of 8 or 10 Oars. We saw them coming, & that they gained ground upon us apace, & therefore pull'd up for Life, resolving to reach the nearest shoar if possible. The Periagua overhaled us so fast that they discharged a Swivel Gun at us, which over-shot us; but we made a shift to gain the shoar before they were come fairly within the reach of their small Arms; which yet they fired upon us, as we were getting ashoar. Then they called to us, and told us they were Pirates, and not Spaniards, and we need not fear, they would give

40 A form of preserving meat akin to that of the earlier *boucaniers*. The verb *firk* may have been intended as *jerk* or *jirk*, meaning "To cure (meat, esp. beef) by cutting it into long thin slices and drying it in the sun" (*Oxford English Dictionary*, VIII:216).

us good Quarters; supposing this would easily move us to surrender our selves to them. But they could not have mentioned any thing worse to discourage me from having any thing to do with them, for I had the utmost dread of a Pirate; and my first aversion to them was now strengthened with the just fears, that if I should fall into their hands again, they would soon make a Sacrifice of me, for my Deserting them. I therefore concluded to keep as clear of them as I could; and the Bay-men with me had no great inclination to be medling with them, and so we made the best of our way into the Woods. They took away our Canoo from us, and all that was in it; resolving if we would not come to them, they would strip us, as far as they were able, of all means of Subsistance where we were. I who had known what it was to be destitute of all things, and alone, was not much concerned about that, now that I had Company, and they their Arms with them, so that we could have a supply of Provision by Hunting, and Fire to dress it with.

This Company it seems were some of Spriggs' Men, who was Commander of the Schooner when I Ran-away from them. The same Spriggs, I know not upon what occasion, had cast off the Service of Low, and set up for himself as the Head of a Party of Rovers, and had now a good Ship of 24 Guns, and a Barmuda Sloop of 12 Guns, under his Command, which were now lying in Roatan Harbour, where he put in to Water and Clean, at the place where I first made my Escape.[41] He had discovered our People up on the small Island, where they Resided, and sent a Periagua full of Men to take them. Accordingly they took all the Men ashoar, and with them an Indian Woman and Child; those of them that were ashoar abused the Woman shamefully. They killed one Man after they were come ashore, and threw him into one of the Baymens' Canooes where their Tar was, and set Fire to it, and burnt him in it. Then they carried our People on Board their Vessels, where they were barbarously treated.

One of the Baymen, Thomas Grande, turned Pirate; and he being acquainted that Old Father Hope (as we called him) had hid many things in the Woods, told the Pirates of it, who beat poor Hope unmercifully, and made him go and shew them where he had hid his Treasure, which they took away from him.

After they had kept the Bay-men on board their Vessels for five Days, then they gave them a Flat of about 5 or 6 Tons[42] to carry them to the Bay in, but they gave them no Provision for their Voyage; and before they sent them away, they made them Swear

---

41 Off Sierra Leone, Low's company had taken the ship *Delight*, armed with 12 guns, which the pirates added more cannon to and incorporated into their flotilla. "Spriggs took Possession of the Ship with eighteen Men, left Low in the Night, and came to the West-Indies. This Separation was occasioned by a Quarrel with Low, concerning a Piece of Justice Spriggs would have executed upon one of the Crew, for killing a Man in cold Blood, as they call it, one insisting that he should be hang'd, and the other that he should note." (Schonhorn, ed., *General History*, 336, 352).

42 Perhaps a form of the *periagua* mentioned in the 1815 edition of William Falconer's maritime dictionary: "a flat-bottomed boat or barge for shallow water, occasionally fitted with two masts" (quoted in Schonhorn, ed., *General History*, xlvii).

to them, not to come near us, who had made our Escape upon another Island. All the while the Vessels rode in the Harbour, we kept a good look out, but were put to some difficulties, because we did not dare to make a Fire to dress our Victuals by, least it should discover whereabouts we were, so that we were forced to live upon Raw Provision for five Days. But as soon as they were gone, Father Hope with his Company of Bay-men (little regarding an Oath that was forced from them; and thinking it a wicked Oath, better broken, than to leave four of us in such a helpless Condition), came to us, and acquainted us who they were, and what they had done.

Thus the watchful Providence of God, which had so often heretofore appeared on my behalf, again took special care of me, and sent me out of the way of danger. 'Tis very apparent that if I had been with my Companions, at the usual Residence, I had been taken with them; and if I had, it is beyond question (humanely speaking) that I should not have escaped with Life, if I should the most painful and cruel Death, that the Madness and Rage of Spriggs could have invented for me; who would now have called to mind the design I was engaged in while we were parted from Low, as well as my final Deserting of them. But Blessed be God, who had designs of favour for me, and so ordered that I must at this time be absent from my Company.

Now Old Father Hope and his Company are all designed for the Bay; only one John Symonds, who had a Negro belonging to him, purposed to tarry here for some time, and carry on some sort of Trade with the Jamaica Men upon the Main. I longed to get home to New-England, and thought if I went to the Bay with them, it was very prob- able that I should in a little while meet with some New-England Vessel, that would carry me to my Native Country, from which I had been so long a poor Exile. I asked Father Hope, if he would take me in with him, and carry me to the Bay. The Old Man, tho' he seemed glad of my Company, yet told me the many Difficulties that lay in the way; as that their Flat was but a poor thing to carry so many Men in for near 70 Leagues, which they must go before they would be out of the reach of Danger; that they had no Provision with them, and it was uncertain how the Weather would prove, they might be a great while upon their Passage thither, & their Flat could very poorly endure a great Sea; that when they should come to the Bay, they knew not how they should meet with things there, and they were Daily in Danger of being cut off; and it may be I should be longer there, [even] in case all was well, than I cared for, e'er I should meet with a Passage for New-England; for the New-England Vessels often Sailed from the Bay to other Ports: so that all things considered, he thought I had better stay where I was, seeing I was like to have Company; whereas rather than I should be left alone he would take me in.

On the other hand, Symonds, who as I said designed to spend some time here, greatly urged me to stay and bear him Company. He told me that as soon as the Season would permit, he purposed to go over to the Main to the Jamaica Traders, where I might get a Passage to Jamaica, and from thence to New-England, probably quicker, and undoubtedly much safer than I could from the Bay; and that in the mean while I should fare as he did.

I did not trouble my self much about faring, for I knew I could not fare harder than I had done; but I thought, upon the Consideration of the whole, that there seemed to be a fairer Prospect of my getting home by the way of Jamaica, than the Bay; and therefore I said no more to Father Hope about going with him, but concluded to stay. So I thanked Father Hope and Company for all their Civilities to me, wished them a good Voyage, and took leave of them.

And now there was John Symonds, and I, and his Negro left behind; and a good Providence of God was it for me, that I took their Advice and stayed; for tho' I got not home by the way of Jamaica as was proposed, yet I did another and quicker way, in which there was more evident Interpositions of the Conduct of Divine Providence, as you will hear presently.

Symonds was provided with a Canoo, Fire-Arms, and two Dogs, as well as a Negro; with these he doubted not but we should be furnished of all that was necessary for our Subsistence; with this Company I spent between two and three Months, after the usual manner in Hunting and Ranging the Islands. And yet the Winter Rains would not suffer us to hunt much more than needs must.

When the Season was near approaching for the Jamaica Traders to be over at the Main, Symonds proposed the going to some of the other Islands that abounded more with Tortoise, that he might get the Shells of them, and carry to the Traders, and in Exchange furnish himself with Ozenbrigs and Shoes and such other necessaries as he wanted. We did so, and having got good store of Tortoise Shell, he then proposed to go first for Bonacco, which lies nearer to the Main than Roatan, that from thence we might take a favourable Snatch to run over.

Accordingly we went to Bonacco, and by that time we had been there about Five Days there came up a very hard North [wind], which blew exceeding Fierce, and lasted for about three Days; when the heart of the Storm was over, we saw several Vessels standing in for the Harbour; their number and largeness made me hope they might be Friends, and now an opportunity was coming in which Deliverance might be perfected to me.

The Larger Vessels came to Anchor at a great Distance off; but a Brigantine came over the Shoals, nearer in against the Watering place (for Bonacco as well as Roatan abounds with Water) which sent in her Boat with Cask for Water: I plainly saw they were Englishmen, and by their Garb & Air, and number, being but three Men in the Boat, concluded they were Friends, and shewed my self openly upon the Beech before them: as soon as they saw me they stop'd rowing, and called out to me to know who I was. I told them, and enquired who they were. They let me know they were honest Men, about their Lawful Business. I then called to them to come ashoar, for there was no Body here that would hurt them. They came ashoar, and a happy meeting it was for me. Upon enquiry I found that the Vessels were the *Diamond*[43] Man of War, and a Fleet under his Convoy, bound to Jamaica (many whereof she had parted with in the late Storm), which by the violence of the North [wind] had been forced so far Southward; and the Man of War wanting Water, by reason of the Sickness of her Men which occasioned a great Consumption of it, had touched here, and sent in the Brigantine to fetch off Water for her. Mr. Symonds, who at first kept at the other end of the Beech, about half a Mile off (lest the three Men in the Boat should refuse to come ashoar, seeing two of us together), at length came up to us and became a sharer in my Joy, and yet not without some very considerable reluctance at the Thoughts of Parting. The Brigantine proved to be of Salem[44] (within two or three Miles of my Father's House), Capt. Dove Commander, a Gentleman whom I knew. So now I had the prospect of a Direct Passage Home. I sent off to Capt. Dove, to know if he would give me a Passage home with him, and he was very ready to comply with my desire; and upon my going on Board him, besides the great Civilities he treated me with, he took me into pay; for he had lost a hand and needed me to supply his place. The next Day the Man of War sent her Long Boat in, full of Cask, which they filled with Water, and put on Board the Brigantine, who carried them off to her. I had one Difficulty more to encounter with, which was to take leave of Mr. Symonds, who Wept heartily at parting; but this I was forced to go thro' for the Joy of getting Home.

So the latter end of March 1725, we came to Sail, and kept Company with the Man of War, who was bound to Jamaica: the first of April we parted, and thro' the good hand of God upon us came safe thro' the Gulf of Florida, to Salem-Harbour, where we Arrived upon Saturday-Evening, the first of May: Two Years, Ten Months and Fifteen Days, after I was first taken by the Pirate Low; and Two Years, and near two Months after I had made my Escape from him upon Roatan Island. I went the same Evening to my Father's House, where I was received, as one coming to them from the Dead, with all Imaginable Surprise of Joy.

Thus I have given you a Short Account, how God has Conducted me thro' a great variety of Hardships and Dangers, and in all appeared Wonderfully Gracious to me. And I cannot but take notice of the strange concurrence of Divine Providence all along, in saving me from the Rage of the Pirates, and the Malice of the Spaniards, from the Beasts of the Field, and the Monsters of the Sea; in keeping me alive amidst so many Deaths, in such a lonely and helpless Condition; and in bringing about my Deliverance: the last Articles whereof as peculiarly Remarkable as any; – I must be

---

43   HMS *Diamond* was a 124--foot long, 40-gun warship commissioned in August 1723 under Captain James Windham and sent to Jamaica (Winfield, *British Warships 1714–1792*, 166).

44   Port city to the north of Boston.

just then gone over to Bonacco; a Storm must drive a Fleet of Ships so far
Southward; and their want of Water must oblige them to put in at the Island where I
was; – and a Vessel bound to my own Home must come and take me in. – Not unto
Men and means, but unto thy Name, O Lord, be all the Glory! Amen.

Philip Ashton, Jun.

ooooo

**A Short Account
of Mr. Nicholas Merritt's[45]
Escape from the Pirates, and his
Sufferings, till his Return
Home.**

I Was taken by the Pirate Low, in at Port-Rossaway; at the same time my Kinsman
Philip Ashton was; and while I continued under Low's Custody was used much as he
was; and all my entreaties of him to free me were but in vain; as you have seen
something of in the foregoing History: So that I shall not enlarge in telling how it
fared with me under the Pirates' hands, but only give some short Account of the
manner of my Escape from them, and what I met with afterwards till I Arrived at
Marblehead, where I belong.

Low had with him the *Rose* Pink, the Scooner, and a Sloop taken from one Pier of
Bristol, and was standing away for Bonavista. I who was on board the Scooner had
been greatly abused by an old Pirate, whom they called Jacob, but what his Sirname
was I know not: I desired some that were upon occasion going on board Low, to
acquaint him how much I was beat and abused by old Jacob: they did so; and Low
ordered me to be put on board the Sloop. Thus the Foundation of my Escape was
lay'd, and my Sufferings proved the means of my Deliverance.

On board the Sloop there were Nine hands (one of them a Portugue), whom Low
had no Suspicion of, but thought he could trust them as much as any Men he had;
and when I came on board I made the Tenth Man. We perceived that the Sloop
greatly wronged both the Pink and Scooner; and there were Six of us (as we found by
sounding one another at a distance) that wanted to get away. When we understood
one another's minds pretty fully, we resolved upon an Escape. Accordingly the Fifth of
September, 1722, a little after break of Day, all hands being upon Deck, three of us

---

45   "Nicholas Merritt, tertius, the son of Nicholas and Elizabeth Merritt, was born in Marblehead and baptized Mar.
29, 1702 in the First Church. He married Jane or Jean Gifford in December, 1724, which may account for the
name of the shallop *Jane*, which he commanded when taken, although he had a sister Jane, and also a sister
Rebecca who married Robert Gifford, who was taken but released at Port Roseway" (Dow and Edmonds, *Pirates of
the New England Coast*, 270).

Six went forward, and three aft, and one John Rhodes, who was a Stout hand, step'd into the Cabbin and took a couple of Pistols in his hands, and stood in the Cabbin Door, and said, If there were any that would go along with him, they should be welcome, for he designed to carry the Sloop home, and Surrender himself; but if any Man attempted to make resistance, he Swore he would shoot down the first Man that stirred. There being five of us that wanted to gain our Liberty, he was sure of us; and as for the other four they saw plainly it was in vain for them to attempt to oppose us. So we haled close upon a Wind, and stood away.

When we parted with Low, we had but a very little Water aboard, and but two or three pieces of Meat among us all; but we had Bread eno'. We designed for England; but our want of Water was so great, being put to half a Point[46] a Man, and that very muddy and foul, from the time we parted with Low, and meeting with no Vessel of whom we could beg a Supply, that it made us come to a Resolution to put in at the first Port: so we Steered for St. Michael's, where we Arrived September 26.

So soon as we got in, we sent a Man or two ashoar, to inform who we were, and to get us some Provisions & Water. The Consul, who was a French Protestant, with a Magistrate, and some other Officers came on board us, to whom we gave an Account of our selves, and our Circumstances. The Consul told us, there should not a Hair of our Heads be hurt. Upon which we were all carri'd ashoar, and examined before the Governour; but we understood nothing of their Language, and could make him no Answer, till one Mr. Gould, a Linguistor[47] was brought to us; and upon understanding our Case, the Governour cleared us. But the Crusidore, a sort of Superintendant over the Islands, whose power was Superiour to the Governour's, refused to clear us, and put us in Jayl, where we lay 24 Hours.

The next Day we were brought under Examination again, and then we had for our Linguistor one Mr. John Curre, who had formerly been in New-England. We gave them as full and distinct [an] Account as we could, where, and when, we were sever-ally taken, and how we had made our Escape from the Pirates. They brought several Witnesses Portaguese against us, as that we had taken them, and had Personally been Active in the Caption[48] and Abuse of them, which yet they agreed not in; only they generally agreed that they heard some of us Curse the Virgin Mary, upon which the Crusidore would have condemned us all for Pirates. But the Governour, who thought we had acted the honest part, interposed on our behalf, and said, that it was very plain, that if these Men had been Pirates, they had no need to have left Low, and under such Circumstances, and come in here, and resign themselves, as they did; they could have stayed with their Old Companions, and have been easily eno'

---

46 Presumably a typographical error for *pint*, although similar renderings (*poynt, poyntt*) could be found in the 1500s (*Oxford English Dictionary*, XI:880).

47 Interpreter, translator.

48 Capture.

supplied with what they wanted; whereas their taking the first opportunity to get away from their Commander, and so poorly accommodated, was a proof to him, that we had no Piratical designs; and if he (the Crusidore) treated us at this rate, it was the way to make us, and all that had the unhappiness to fall into Pirates' hands, turn Pirates with them. Yet all he could say would not wholly save us from the Angry Resentments of the Crusidore, who we thought was inflamed by the Portague that was among us. So he committed us all to Prison again; me with three others to the Castle, the rest to another Prison at some considerable distance off: and so much pains was taken to Swear us out of our Lives, that I altogether despaired of Escaping the Death of a Pirate; till a Gentleman, Capt. Littleton (if I mistake not), told me it was not in their power to hang us, and this comforted me a little.

In this Prison we lay for about four Months, where, at first we had tolerable allowance of such as it was, for our Subsistance; but after three Months time they gave us only one Meal a Day, of Cabbage, Bread, and Water boiled together, which they call Soop. This very scanty allowance put us out of Temper, and made us resolve rather than Starve, to break Prison, and make head against the Portuguese, and get some Victuals; for Hunger will break thro' Stone Walls. The Governour understanding how we fared, told the Crusidore that we should stay in his Prison no longer, as the Castle peculiarly was; and greatly asserted our Cause, and urged we might be set at Liberty; but the Crusidore would not hearken as yet to the clearing us, tho' he was forced to remove us from the Castle, to the Prison in which our Comrades were, where after they had allowed us about an hour's converse together, they put us down into close Confinement; tho' our allowance was a small matter better than it had been.

Under all this Difficulty of Imprisonment, short allowance, and hard fare, false Witnesses, and fear lest I should still have my Life taken from me (when I had flattered my self, that if I could but once set Foot upon a Christian shoar, I should be out of the reach of Danger), I had a great many uneasy Reflections. I thought no bodies case was so hard as mine: first to be taken by the Pirates, and threatned with Death for not Joyning with them; to be forced away, and suffer many a drubbing Bout among them for not doing as they would have me; to be in fears of Death for being among them, if we should be taken by any Superiour force; and now that I had designedly, and with Joy, made my Escape from them, to be Imprisoned and threatned with the Halter. Thought I, When can a Man be safe? [H]e must look for Death to be found among Pirates; and Death seems as threatning, if he Escapes from them; where is the Justice of this! It seemed an exceeding hardship to me. Yet it made me Reflect, with Humility I hope, on the Justice of God in so Punishing of me for my Transgressions; for tho' the tender Mercies of Man seemed to be Cruelty, yet I could not but see the Mercy and Goodness of God to me, not only in Punishing me less than I deserved, but in preserving me under many and sore Temptations, and at length delivering me out of the Pirates' hands: and I had some hope that God would yet appear for me, and bring me out of my distress, and set my Feet in a large place.

I thought my Case was exceedingly like that of the Psalmist; the Meditation on some Verses in the XXXV. Psalm, was a peculiar support to me: I thought I might say with him, *False Witnesses did rise up; they laid to my charge things that I knew not; they rewarded me evil for good. But as for me, when they were taken* (tho' I dont remember I had ever seen the Faces of any of them then) *I humbled my self, and my Prayer returned into my own bosom; I behaved my self as tho' they had been my friends, I bowed down heavily, as one that mourneth for his mother; but in my adversity they rejoyced, and gathered themselves together against me; yea, they opened their mouth wide against me, – they gnashed upon me with their teeth, and said Aha, Aha, our eye hath seen it, – so would we have it. But Lord how long wilt thou look on? [P]reserve my Soul from their Destruction, let not them that are mine Enemies wrongfully rejoyce over me, – stir up thy Self and awake to my Judgment, even unto my cause, my God and my Lord, and let them not rejoyce over me – and I will give thee thanks in the great Congregation, my tongue shall speak of thy Righteousness, and thy Praise all the day long.*

In the midst of all my other Calamities, after I had been in this Prison about two Months, I was taken down with the Small-Pox, and this to be sure was a very great Addition to my Misery. I knew well how we dreaded this Distemper in my own Country: and thought I, how can I possibly escape with Life? To be seised with it in a Prison, where I had no Help, no Physician, nor any Provision suitable therefor; only upon my first being taken I sent word of it to the Consul, who was so kind as to send some Bundles of Straw for me to lye upon, instead of the hard Stones which as yet had been my Lodging, and the Portuguese gave me some Brandy, and Wine & Water to drive out the Pock. I was exceedingly dejected, and had nothing to do but to commit my self to the Mercy of God, and prepare myself for Death, which seemed to have laid hold upon me; for which way soever I looked, I could see nothing but Death in such a Distemper, under such Circumstances; and I could see the Portuguese how they stared upon me, looked sad, and shook their heads; which told me their apprehensions, that I was a Dead Man. Yet I had this comfort, that it was better to Die thus by the hand of God, than to Die a vile Death by the hand of Man, as if I had been one of the worst of Malefactors.

But after all it pleased God in His Wonderful Goodness so to order it, that the Pock came out well, and filled kindly, and then I had the comfort of seeing the Portuguese look more pleasant, and hearing them say, in their Language, that it was a good sort. In about five or six Days the Pock began to turn upon me, and then it made me very Sick, and at times I was something out of my Head; and having no Tender or Watcher, I got up in the Night to the Pail of Water to drink, which at another time, and in another place, would have been thought fatal to me;[49] but God in infinite Mercy prevented my receiving any hurt thereby, and raised me up from this Sickness.

After I recovered of this Illness, I was but in a weak Condition for a long time, having no other Nourishment and Comfort, than what a Jayl afforded, where I still lay for near three Months longer. At length, sometime in June, 1723, I was taken out of Jayl, and had the Liberty of the Consul's House given me, who treated me kindly, and did not suffer me to want any thing that was necessary for my Support.

While I was at Liberty, I understood there was one John Welch, an Irishman, bound to Lisbon, whom I desired to carry me thither. And in the latter end of June I set Sail in him for Lisbon, where we Arrived about the middle of July, after we had been 21 Days upon the Passage. When I had got to Lisbon, being almost Naked, I apply'd my self to the Envoy, told him my Condition, and desired him to bestow some old Cloaths upon me. But he (good Man!) said to me, that as I had Run away from the Pirates, I might go to Work for my Support, and provide my self with Cloaths as well as I could. And I found I must do so, for none would he give me. I had nothing against Working, but I should have been glad to have been put into a Working Garb; for I was sensible it would be a considerable while before I could purchase me any Cloaths, because Welch play'd me such an Irish trick, that he would not release me, unless I promised to give him the first Moidore I got by my Labour; tho' I had wrough[t] for him all the Passage over, and he knew my poor Circumstances: however when I came to Sail for New-England, Welch was better than his Word, and forgave me the Moidore, after I had been at the Labour of unloading his Vessel.

I spent some time in Lisbon; at length I heard there was one Capt. Skillegorne bound to New-England, in whom I took my Passage home; who Clothed me for my Labour in my Passage. We touched in at Madara, and Arrived at Boston upon Wednesday, September, 25, 1723. And I at my Father's House in Marblehead the Saturday after.

So has God been with me in six troubles, and in seven.[50] He has suffered no evil to come nigh me. He has drawn me out of the Pit, Redeemed my Life from Destruction, and Crowned me with Loving Kindness and Tender Mercies: unto Him be the Glory for ever. Amen.

Nicholas Merritt, Jun.

---

49 Fever sufferers were sometimes denied water in the belief that it would harm them. "We have no doubt but hundreds of our readers painfully remember hours of terrible agony, while burning with fever-heat, craving a draught of clear, cool water. But it was denied them! Water would, in nine cases out of ten, have quenched the raging thirst, reduced the jumping pulse, and quieted the throbbing brain. But, no. The poor dying patient must literally 'burn up alive;' and, to increase the heat and aggravate the pain, fresh fuel must be added, in the shape of calomel, to increase the flame. The patient dies – unless, by some mere accident, or neglect on the part of the doctor, he rejects his doses, bribes a child, obtains water, rest, and – recovers!" (from *The Water-Cure Journal and Herald of Reforms Devoted to Physiology, Hydropathy, and the Laws of Life* [New York], XVII:3 [March 1854], 57).

50 Job 5:19.

9

"Hung up in Chains" –William Fly and the end of the Golden Age (1726)

William Fly, about 27 when he died, reportedly took two turns going "on the account" during his lifetime.[1] What is known of his pirate career involves his second purported stab at it – a short, brutal cruise in 1726, the facts of which were recorded for posterity in a Boston courtroom. Through this he became the last of the sea robbers documented in the *General History*'s second volume, issued in 1728. As the *General History* can be seen as defining much of piracy's so-called Golden Age, Fly's execution and hanging in chains helped mark the end of that era.

The removal of a comparatively minor pirate such as Fly was not decisive of itself in bringing the period to a close. More important was the fact that European navies had used the time of relative peace after the Treaty of Utrecht to become more active against pirates.[2] And as the later 18th century was, in the words of Angus Konstam, "marked by a near-constant string of wars," corresponding calls for privateers put many of those likely to turn to piracy into government employment.[3] Later acts of maritime crime would occur in American waters, but piracy would not return to Golden Age levels until the 1810s and 1820s, when it accompanied the rise of poorly regulated privateering in the Latin American revolutions against Spain.

Fly, according to Captain Charles Johnson, the author of the *General History*, was an experienced seaman who, having survived an earlier career in piracy, "had an Opportunity of repenting his former Crimes, and, as a Fore-Mast Man, or petty officer, of getting his Bread in a warrantable Way." Instead, while serving as boatswain aboard the Bristol-based snow *Elizabeth*, bound from Jamaica to the Guinea coast late in May 1726, he engineered a mutiny with the intention of taking the vessel on a pirate cruise.[4] Captain John Green (who Fly later accused of having abused the crew) was dragged on deck, denied time to say his prayers, and then heaved overboard. Green managed to

---

1   Fly's estimated age is given in Mather, *Vial Poured Out Upon the Sea*, 5.
2   It has been estimated that there were about 4,000 pirates active between 1716–1726. Their activity peaked in 1719–1722, when somewhere between 1,800 and 2,400 operated. The number rapidly dropped to 500 by 1724, and less than 200 in 1725–1726 (Rediker, *Villains of All Nations*, 29–30).
3   Konstam, *Piracy*, 272–273.
4   The snow was functioning "probably as an illicit slaver" (Baer, *British Piracy*, III:231).

hang onto a piece of rigging, from which a mutineer wielding an axe dislodged him. Shortly afterward mate Thomas Jenkins received similar treatment.[5]

Having renamed the snow the *Fame's Revenge*, Fly and his crew began robbing vessels along the Atlantic coast of North America. Late in June, having sent several of his fellow pirates aboard a prize ship, and relying on forced men to work his own craft, Fly's prisoners overpowered their captors. They then sailed the *Fame's Revenge* to Great Brewster island off Boston Harbor, where they turned Fly and three others over to the authorities.[6] As a formality, all of those aboard the pirate vessel were charged with piracy, Fly's former prisoners being quickly acquitted. The court convicted Fly and three others: Henry Greenville, Samuel Cole, and George Condick, the last being reprieved.

The report from which the following is excerpted details the trial and includes appendices that, according to scholar Manuel Schonhorn, "contained detailed depositions which [the *General History*'s author] put in coherent order."[7] As a primary source it helps document how an era of maritime crime reached its conclusion.

ooooo

From *The Tryals of Sixteen Persons for Piracy, &c. Four of which were found Guilty, And the rest Acquitted. At a Special Court of Admiralty for the Tryal of Pirates, Held at Boston within the Province of the Massachusetts-Bay in New-England, on Monday the Fourth Day of July, Anno Dom. 1726. Pursuant to His Majesty's Commission, Founded on an Act of Parliament, made in the Eleventh and Twelfth Years of the Reign of King William the Third, Intitled; An Act for the more Effectual Suppression of Piracy. And made Perpetual by an Act of the Sixth of King George* (Boston: Joseph Edwards, 1726.)

[Trial of William Atkinson]

[Editor's Note: The trial opened on 4 July 1726, presided over by Massachusetts Lt. Gov. William Dummer, who had also sat on the courts that tried the survivors of Samuel Bellamy's company in 1717, and Charles Harris and his crew in 1723. Notary Samuel Tyler served as Register; the prosecuting attorney was Robert Auchmuty, who had been defense counsel at the 1717 trial of Bellamy's men. The "Honourable Commissioners" also included an individual Joel H. Baer described as "perhaps the most despised man in Boston at the time, Captain James Cornwall of the station ship HMS *Sheerness*. Only a few days before the trial, Cornwall had refused to go out in search of pirates and had fired four rounds at a ship the Lieutenant-Governor had hired for the purpose, damaging its sails. . . . He may have received a disquieting welcome, for he did not attend the next day's session . . . ."[8]

---

5 Schonhorn, ed., *General History*, 606–608; Mather, *Vial Poured Out Upon the Sea*, 21, 48.
6 Schonhorn, ed., *General History*, 613.
7 Schonhorn, ed., *General History*, 695.
8 Baer, *British Piracy*, III:447.

The first phase of the trial involved the examinations of Fly's former captives aboard the *Fame's Revenge*, who appear to have been tried (and acquitted) as a matter of routine. The first of them brought into court was Captain William Atkinson, an experienced navigator who had been a passenger on the sloop *John & Hannah*, captained by John Fulker. Fly had captured the sloop on 3 June en route from North Carolina to Boston, ran it aground at Cape Hatteras, and forced Atkinson to serve aboard the *Fame's Revenge*.

The indictment read out against Atkinson consisted of three articles, each accusing him of having been part of Fly's crew during three different acts of piracy. The first was the capture, on or about 7 June 1726, of the ship *John & Betty*, captained by John Gale, from which the pirates took £100 worth of equipment and clothing. The second was an 11 June episode off Delaware Bay in which Fly's crew took the sloop *Rachel*, captained by Samuel Harris, and forced a member of Harris's crew, one James Benbrook, aboard the pirate vessel. The third was the 23 June taking, near Browns Bank (a shoal off the coast of Plymouth, Massachusetts), of the fishing schooner *James*, George Girdler master, after which Fly put six men aboard the *James* and sent it off to chase other prizes, keeping Girdler and two others prisoner aboard the *Fames' Revenge*. To all three articles, Atkinson pleaded Not Guilty.]

Then the said Robert Auchmuty made the following Speech to the Court.

["]May it please Your Honours, and the Honourable the Commissioners,

["]William Atkinson stands Articled against for Acts of Piracy & Robbery perpetrated & done upon the High Seas, within the Jurisdiction of the Admiralty of Great Britain, & has pleaded, Not Guilty.

["]How Dear & Tender the Lives, Liberties, and Properties of His Majesty's Good Subjects are unto Him clearly appears in His wise equal & Benign Administration: And therefore such as are Honoured by Special Commission to Prosecute in His Name, ought not therewith to put an Edge on their Fancy & Words, to the cutting down of the Innocent; for the Aquittal of the Guiltless is always most Acceptable to Our Gracious Prince, and highly Satisfactory to Your Honours.

["]I therefore Articled the Gentleman on Tryal, not with the prospect of Conviction, but that the Laws may be Complied with. And now he has an Opportunity of Manifesting his Innocency before Your Honours, whose Wisdom and Justice will render his Acquittal much more Honourable, if by you judged Not Guilty.[9]

---

9 "Since there is nothing in 11–12 Will. III, c.7 [the 1700 law under which pirates were then tried in the British colonies] that explicitly requires piracy commissioners to indict anyone, we may conclude that the Advocate-General of Massachusetts was following the commission's desire to clear Atkinson's reputation and publicly honour the courage of those who captured Fly so that other seamen might follow their example. (Of course, he was also preparing the eleven to act as bona fide witnesses against Fly and his men.) . . . No other colonial court treated men who claimed to have been forced into piracy with less hostility or even suspicion." (Baer, *British Piracy*, III:231).

["]And without further Trespassing upon Your Honours, I shall proceed to the Examination of the King's Evidence.["]

Afterwards, at the Motion of the Advocate-General, the Witnesses for the King were called, namely George Girdler, late Master of the aforesaid Schooner, named the *James*, Joseph Marshall, and William Ferguson, Marriners, belonging to the said Schooner, who being Sworn, Testified, That the said Schooner was taken on the 23d of June last, as she lay too, a Fishing on Browns-Banks, so called, by a Snow called the *Fame's Revenge*, one William Fly Master; who caused a Black Flagg to be hoisted, and fired a great Gun at her; but the Witnesses when they went on Board the Snow did not see the Prisoner Armed; that soon after they were taken, they saw another Schooner, whereupon the said William Fly sent Six of his Crew in pursuit of her in the Schooner which they had taken; and while they were in Chase of the other Schooner, the said William Atkinson the Prisoner at the Bar, with Three others on Board the Snow, seized the said William Fly, and put him in Irons, and also secured Three other Pirates on Board, now in His Majesty's Goal in Boston, namely Samuel Cole, Henry Greenvill, and George Condick, and brought the said Snow into the Harbour of Boston, where she now is. And no Witnesses appearing against the Prisoner, and he having made a very good Defence, The Court was Ordered to be Cleared. And after the Court had duly weighed and Considered the Prisoner's Case in private, they Voted *Nemine Contradicente*;[10] that he was not Guilty.

Then the Court was Opened, and the Prisoner brought to the Bar again, and the President Pronounced him the said William Atkinson not Guilty: Whereupon he was Ordered to be Discharged, without paying any Fees, or Costs of Prosecution.

[Trial of Samuel Walker and Thomas Streaton]

[Editor's Note: The indictment read out against Samuel Walker and Thomas Streaton was essentially the same as that against Atkinson. To all three articles, Walter and Streaton pleaded Not Guilty.]

Then the King's Advocate[11] moved the Court, That the said William Atkinson, being now found Innocent of the Crimes wherewith he was Charged, might be admitted to give Evidence on His Majesty's behalf against the Prisoners at the Bar, which the Court consented to, and the said William Atkinson was accordingly Sworn.

And being Interrogated, saith, That he Agreed with Capt. John Fulker at North-Carolina, to come Passenger from thence to Boston in the Sloop *John & Hannah*, whereof the said Fulker was Master; But that on the Third of June last, as she lay at Anchor off

---

10 Nobody contradicting.
11 Robert Auchmuty.

Cape Hadderas Bar,[12] they saw a Snow standing in for the Harbour of Carolina, when the said Capt. Fulker, and the said Atkinson, with one other Passenger, namely Mr. Roan,[13] and Samuel Walker (one of the Prisoners at the Bar), who was Mate of the said Sloop, and one Bor, took the Sloop's Boat, and went on Board the said Snow, Imagining the Captain of her might be a Stranger, and wanted a Pilot to carry her safely into the Harbour of Carolina; But after they had been on Board some time, they understood by the People, they were Pirates, and that she was then Commanded by one William Fly (now a Prisoner in Boston Goal), and that he, with others on Board, had in the Night time, in the Month of May last, surprized the Captain of her, viz. John Green, and Thomas Jenkins the Mate, and thrown them overboard; But that Thomas Streaton, one of the Prisoners at the Bar, was in his Hammock, when the Fact was committed, and no ways consenting to the Murther, as the Deponent understood, and was by the Crew put in Irons, and that he, together with the said Samuel Walker, the other Prisoner, were treated as forced Men by the Pirates at the times of the several Captions[14] of divers Vessels which happened afterwards.

Then George Girdler, Joseph Marshall, and William Ferguson, who belonged to the aforesaid Schooner, were called and Sworn. And being asked as to the Prisoners' Behaviour when the said Schooner was taken, They Declared, the Prisoners at that time Affirmed that they were forced Men, and were two of the Men that afterwards seized & subdued the said William Fly, and the Three other reputed Pirates before-named.

Then the Court was Cleared and in Private. And after the Evidences produced had been duly considered, The Court Unanimously Voted, That the said Prisoners, namely Samuel Walker and Thomas Streaton, were not Guilty.

Whereupon they being brought to the Bar again, the President Pronounced them not Guilty. And the Court Ordered them to be Discharged without paying any Fees.

Then the Court was Adjourned to Three a'Clock Post Meridiem.

[Trial of John Cole, John Brown, Robert Dauling, John Daw, James Blair, Edward Lawrence (or Laurence), Edward Apthorp, and James Benbrook]

[**Editor's Note:** Six of the men named in the two articles of indictment addressed here were forced from the ship *John & Betty* when Fly captured it on 6 or 7 June; the exceptions were James Benbrook or Benbrooke (forced off the sloop *Rachel* on 11 June), and Edward Apthorp (forced off the sloop *John and Hannah* along with Atkinson at Cape

---

12   Cape Hatteras, North Carolina.
13   Originally "Richard Ruth," corrected as per the errata.
14   I.e., captures.

Hatteras, North Carolina, on 3 June). Benbrook was not charged in the first article of indictment, which concerned the taking of the *Rachel*. He was, however, included in the second article, regarding the capture of the fishing schooner *James*. All eight pleaded Not Guilty.]

Then the Witnesses for Our Sovereign Lord the King were called, and Sworn, namely Capt. William Atkinson, Samuel Walker, Thomas Streaton, George Girdler, Joseph Marshall, and William Ferguson.[15] And upon their Examination, it came out in Proof, That on the Sixth Day of June last, the said John Cole, John Brown, Robert Dauling, John Daw, James Blair, & Edward Lawrence (Six of the Prisoners at the Bar) were taken in the Ship *John and Betty*, John Gale Commander, off the Capes of Virginia, by the aforenamed William Fly, then Commander of the said Snow, by him called the *Fame's Revenge*, and detained on Board her, contrary to their wills: And that the said Edward Apthorp, one other of the Prisoners, belonged to the Sloop *John and Hannah*, John Fulker late Master, and went on Board the said Snow, with the said Fulker, Capt. Atkinson, and others, in order to Pilot her into Carolina; And that James Benbrooke (the other Prisoner at the Bar) was afterwards, viz. on the Eleventh of June last, taken by the said William Fly, and his Crew on Board the Sloop *Rachel*, whereof Samuel Harris was Master, in her Passage from New York to Philadelphia. And all the King's Evidences before-named Testified, That the Prisoners were not active with the Pirates, in taking any Vessels, but were declared by the Pirates to be forced Men, and disapproved of their Piratical Acts: And it also Evidently appeared to the Court, that the said James Benbrooke was one of the Men that seized the said William Fly, and took his Sword from him, and broke it. And no other Witnesses appearing against the Prisoners, they were directed to make their Defence: Which accordingly they did; And the King's Advocate thereupon Concluded the Prosecution by summing up the Evidence, and submitting the same to the Consideration of the Court. Afterwards the Court was Cleared; And having duly weighed and Considered the Matters Alledged, as well by the King's Witnesses, as by the Prisoners for them-selves; the Court were of Opinion that they were not Guilty.

Whereupon the said John Cole, John Brown, Robert Dauling, John Daw, James Blair, Edward Laurence, Edward Apthorp, and James Benbrooke, were again brought to the Bar, and the President, in the Name of the Court, Pronounced them not Guilty, And they were Ordered to be Discharged, without paying any Fees.

[Trial of Morrice Cundon]

[**Editor's Note:** Auchmuty evidently was more certain of the guilt of Morrice Cundon than of those previously called to the bar. A native of Cork, Ireland, Cundon had served

---

15   Girdler, Marshall and Ferguson had been aboard the *James*.

with Fly aboard the snow *Elizabeth* and survived the mutiny Fly led aboard it. Thus he had been with Fly from the start of his piratical cruise. The six articles of indictment against him were preceded by the observation that Cundon had acted "not having the Fear of God before his eyes, but being Instigated by the Devil."[16]

The six articles accused Cundon of complicity in the 27 May mutiny aboard the *Elizabeth* and of having a hand in the murder of Green and Jenkins; the actual seizure of the *Elizabeth*, and its cargo; the 3 June seizure of the sloop *John & Hannah*; the 6 or 7 June capture of the *John and Betty*; the 11 June capture of the *Rachel*; and the 23 June taking of the *James*. Cundon pleaded Not Guilty to all charges.]

The Witnesses on behalf of His Majesty were Sworn, namely Capt. William Atkinson, Thomas Streaton, and Samuel Walker. And it appeared by their respective Testimonies, That the said Morrice Cundon belonged to the said Snow while called the *Elizabeth*, and Commanded by Capt. Green, and that he was at Helm when Capt. Green, and his Mate, were thrown over-board by William Fly, and several others of the said Snow's Company; But that the said Cundon was no ways Acting or Consenting thereto, or to any of the Acts of Piracy, and Robberies, afterwards committed; And therefore the said Fly talk'd of dismissing the Prisoner, the first Vessel he took, and of getting another Man in his room. And further the Witnesses Deposed, that when the said Snow was taken by Capt. Atkinson, and others, the said Cundon exprest his Joy thereat. And in his own Defence, declared to the Court, that he never suspected the least design in any of the Snow's Company, to Murder the said Capt. Green, and his Mate, before Fly came to him while at Helm, and threatned to blow out his Brains, if he stirr'd from the Helm: And then it was not in his power to prevent their Executing their wicked design, because most of the Snow's Company were at that time upon Deck, Assisting in, or Consenting to the throwing of the said Capt. Green, and his Mate over-board: and it would have been a Rash Attempt, in him alone, to oppose them.

The Advocate-General Concluded this Prosecution, in Observing to the Court, That the Prisoner by no Act, discovered his Disapprobation of the Proceedings of such as were actually Concerned in the said Murther; and was therefore by Law, a Principal,[17] and Pray'd Judgment accordingly.

Upon which the Court was Cleared, and in Private; And after mature Deliberation, and Consideration of what the King's Witnesses Deposed, and the Prisoner offered in his Defence, as also the Replication of the Advocate-General, The Court Voted, That the said Morrice Cundon is not Guilty.

---

16   Joel H. Baer interpreted this remark as being "used here to inform the commissioners that the prosecutor believes that this defendant is, in fact, a pirate" (*British Piracy*, III:447).

17   A "*principal* is, in criminal law, a person who actually or constructively commits a crime" (Nolfi, *Legal Terminology Explained*, 303).

Whereupon the Prisoner being brought again to the Bar, the President Pronounced him not Guilty; And the Court Ordered him to be Discharged without paying any Fees.

Then the Court was Adjourned to Tuesday the 5th Day of July Instant, at Nine a-Clock, before noon.

[Trial of William Fly]

[**Editor's Note:** The proceedings of 5 July began with Fly being brought to court, where he was read essentially the same articles of indictment as Cundon. Fly pleaded Not Guilty to all charges.]

[. . .] The King's Advocate thereupon made a Speech to the Court, in the words, or to the Effect following, viz.

["]May it please Your Honour, Mr. President, and the Honourable the Commissioners, William Fly stands Articled against, for Acts of Piracy, Murder, Felony, and Robbery, committed upon the High Seas, and within the Jurisdiction of the Admiralty of Great Britain, Contrary to the Statues in this case made and provided, and to the Peace of our Lord the King, His Crown and Dignity; to which he has pleaded, Not Guilty.

["]I shall not Trespass upon Your Honours' Patience in opening the Nature of Piracy, a Crime of the first Magnitude in the Catalogue of Capital Offences; this has been the work of others more Equal to the Performance. What I conceive necessary to offer, is the Consideration of that Hackney Defence made by every Pirate upon Trial, namely, That he was a forced Man, and in order to Strike the Passions they represent in moving terms, what dangers they encounter'd, as the Risque of having their Brains blow'd, and what Severities they underwent, as Sweating[18] & the like before they departed from their native Integrity. All which, if prov'd, will not, strictly speaking, amount to an Exemption from Punishment; For neither Necessity, *Major Vis*,[19] or Self-Preservation, can legally justify the Commission of an Act, *Malum in se*.[20] But unmask these Dreggs of Mankind, and then they will appear Blaspheming their Creator, Coining of Oaths, Embrewing their Hands in Innocent Blood, and [Racking?] their Hellish Inventions for unheard of Barbarities.["]

---

18 "The Manner of a Sweat is thus: Between the Decks they stick Candles round the Mizen-Mast, and about twenty five Men surround it with Points of Swords, Penknives, Compasses, Forks, &c. in each of their Hands: Culprit enters the Circle; the Violin plays a merry Jig, and he must run for about ten Minutes, while each Man runs his Instrument into his Posteriors" (*British Journal*, 8 August 1724, reproduced in Baer, *British Piracy*, I:312).

19 Latin for "a greater force, a *vis major* is an unpredictable force of nature that may be a superseding cause . . ." (Nolfi, *Legal Terminology Explained*, 219).

20 Distinguished from *malum prohibitum* (wrong because it is prohibited), *malum in se* is Latin for wrong by itself, "because it is inherently dangerous or evil" (Nolfi, *Legal Terminology Explained*, 300). The concept of *malum in se* "applies to acts, like murder or rape, that are illegal by definition. But the law did not treat all homicides as murder; homicide in self-defence, even when the victim is innocent, might be justifiable . . . Such inflamed rhetoric would not be controlled until the accused's lawyers were allowed to make objections and mount a thorough defence" (Baer, *British Piracy*, III:447–448).

["]This in a great measure will Turn out to be the dreadful Case of the Prisoner at the Bar, and Providence seems to point out his punishment (which I pray God may be only Humane), not only in the wonderful manner of subduing him, but in that he is to be Try'd by your Honours, whose great Justice & Judgment, has been sufficiently Experienced, not to be imposed upon by the most subtil Prosecution, to Convict the Innocent, or by the most Artful Pretences to acquit the Guilty. I shall therefore proceed to Examine the King's Evidences which will Invincibly prove the Articles against him, and thereupon doubt not of your Justice to His Majesty, this Province, and to the Prisoner's Demerits in declaring him Guilty.["]

Then Morrice Cundon and Thomas Streaton, Witnesses in behalf of His Majesty, were Called and Sworn.

And first, the said Morrice Cundon Declared, That on the 27th Day of May last, about One a-Clock in the Morning, while he was at Helm, William Fly, then Boatswain of the Snow called the *Elizabeth* (belonging to His Majesty's Subjects in Bristol in Great Britain), after he had been sometime forward with several sailors on Board the said Snow, came abaft,[21] with some of them, viz. one Alexander Mitchell, and others, and said to the Deponent, while at Helm these words, viz. ["]Damn you, you Dog, if you stir Hand or Foot, or speak a Word, I'll blow your Brains out.["] And immediately thereupon the said Fly went into the Cabbin, where Captain Green was in Bed, and Alexander Mitchell follow'd him, and while they were there, the Deponent heard the said Captain Green Cry out, ["W]hat's the matter?,["] and they soon hawled him upon Deck, and were about to throw him into the Sea; when the said Capt. Green applied himself to the said Fly the Boatswain, saying, ["]For God's sake, Boatswain, don't throw me overboard, for if you do I shall go to Hell.["] Then the said Fly bid the Captain say after him these words, viz. "Lord have Mercy upon my Soul.["] And soon after he was thrown overboard.

And the said Morrice Cundon, and Thomas Streaton both Deposed, that some Days after the Master and Mate were Drowned, they met a Ship called the *Pompey*, which came from Jamaica in Company with the Snow, when the Captain of the Ship hail'd the Snow, and ask'd how Captain Green did; and Fly being upon Deck, made Answer, ["V]ery well, at your Service Sir.["]

Afterwards Capt. William Atkinson, Samuel Walker, Edward Apthorp, John Cole, Robert Dauling, John Brown, George Girdler, & James Benbrooke, Witnesses for the King, were called and Sworn; and Testified, that they were all taken by the said Snow, and that the said William Fly Acted as Captain, when the several Vessels (mention'd in the Articles) to which they respectively belonged, were taken; And at such times ordered

---

21 "This word, generally speaking, means behind, inferred relatively, beginning from the stem and continuing towards the stern, that is, the hinder part of the ship" (Smyth, *Lexicon*, 11).

the Black Flagg to be hoisted, and Encouraged the Pirates when they were backward, to go on Board the said Vessels. And the said William Atkinson particularly Deposed, That soon after the Caption of the Schooner, named the *James*, whereof the said George Girdler was Master, they discovered another Schooner, whereupon the said Atkinson Advised the said Fly to Man the said Schooner *James* with some of his Hands & go in Chase of the said Vessel, as before exprest by the said Atkinson, in his Defence made upon his Tryal; which the said Fly accordingly did; And some short time afterwards the said Atkinson discovering other Vessels forward, diverted the said Fly from his Arms, which lay on the Quarter-Deck; And while he was looking with his Glass to take sight of said Vessels, the said Atkinson and others, Overcame and subdued him, and Three other Pirates, as before is set forth.

After the Witnesses had been fully heard, the said William Fly was Informed by the Court, that then was his time to offer what he had to say in his own Defence; which he did, by Denying any hand in the Murther, and several other Facts Sworn to by the King's Witnesses: And thereupon the Advocate-General summ'd up and Enforc'd the Evidence, and gave the Law upon the Facts: and Concluded, that the Prisoner at the Bar was Legally Guilty of Murther, Piracy, Felony and Robbery, according to the Articles.

Afterwards the Court was Cleared, and in Private. And upon Deliberate Consideration of the several matters and things by the Witnesses Sworn to against the Prisoner, as also the Law thereupon; the Court Voted, That the said William Fly is Guilty of the several Articles Exhibited against him.

Then he was brought to the Bar again, when the President in the Name of the Court Pronounced the said William Fly Guilty. Upon which the Advocate, in behalf of His Majesty, demanded Sentence against the Prisoner. Who was thereupon ask'd if he had anything to say why Sentence of Death should not be given against him; and shewing no sufficient Reason to the contrary The President pass'd Sentence against him accordingly in the words following, viz. "You William Fly are to go from hence to the Place from whence you came, and from thence to the Place of Execution, there to be Hang'd up by the Neck until you be Dead, And the Lord have Mercy upon your Soul."

Then the Prisoner was Remanded to Goal; and the Marshall of the Admiralty Directed to keep him in safe Custody.

[Trial of Samuel Cole, George Condick and Henry Greenville]

[Editor's Note: The indictment against Samuel Cole, George Condick, and Henry Greenville involved the same six articles Cundon and Fly had already faced. All pleaded Not Guilty to all charges.]

[. . .] Then the Witnesses on His Majesty's behalf, Namely Morrice Cundon, and Thomas Streaton, Marriners, which Sail'd from Jamaica in the said Snow, were Called and Sworn.

And first, the said Morrice Cundon, Testified, That Samuel Cole, and Henry Greenvill,[22] were both of them upon Deck, with others, when Capt. Green, and the Mate were thrown overboard, on the Twenty-seventh of May last before Day.

And the said Thomas Streaton Deposed, That as he lay in his Bed in the Morning of that Day, between One & Two of the Clock, he heard Samuel Cole, one of the Prisoners at the Bar, say to Jenkins the then Mate, ["]Come out of your Cabbin, you Dog,["] and presently after he was haul'd out of his Bed upon Deck, and the Deponent heard some Body fall upon the Deck, which he believ'd to be Jenkins, and soon after one Winthrop told him, that he should go over-board after his Captain; and he was soon thrown into the Sea, where he called to the Doctor earnestly several times to hand him a Rope, but by that time the Doctor was put in Irons.

Afterwards William Atkinson, Samuel Walker, Edward Apthorp, and John Cole, were Sworn, and Testified, That the Prisoners were reputed Pirates when the several Vessels mentioned in the said Articles were Taken and Robbed; and upon all Occasions acted as such, never pretending to the contrary in the Deponents' hearing; only the Deponents said, that Samuel Cole, the Quarter-Master, was put in Irons by Fry's Order for Mutiny, and so was continued in Irons while the two last Vessels mentioned in the said Articles were taken; and that Condick[23] was commonly the worse for Drink, and not able to bear Arms when several of the Vessels were taken; and for the most part was serviceable to the Pirates as their Cook.

Then the Prisoners were heard what they had to say for themselves: And the said Samuel Cole, and Henry Greenvill, deny'd that they had any hand in Murthering the said Capt. Green, and his Mate; but said they had both of them been cruel to the Men, and therefore they had agreed to rise upon them, and put them on shoar the first Land they made. And the said Cole and Greenvill also owned that they were with others upon Deck when the Captain and his Mate were thrown overboard; and the said Condick confess'd in like manner that he was consenting to the said Capt. Green, and his Mate's, being put on shoar, but deny'd that he had any hand in their being Murthered, alledging that he was then in his Hammock asleep. Upon whom the Advocate Replied, That by Law the Prisoners Confederating and Consenting to do an Unlawful Act in Rising against their Commander (which by the Statute is declared

---

22   Samuel Cole was "about Thirty Seven years of Age, having a Wife and seven Children"; Henry Greenville (or Greenvill) was "a married Man about forty seven years of age." Cole told Cotton Mather that a few days before the revolt aboard Fly's pirate ship, Fly put him in irons and beat him severely every day (Mather, *Vial Poured Out Upon the Sea*, 5, 50).

23   Condick was "a Youth of Twenty, or thereabouts" (Mather, *Vial Poured Out Upon the Sea*, 5).

Piracy) and forcibly pretending to put him on shoar, and Death ensuing, they were severally Guilty of Murther, if there were no other Evidence against the Prisoners: but the Advocate also summ'd up the Evidence against them in Support of all the other Articles, and Concluded in Demanding Judgment.

Whereupon Orders were given to Clear the Court: The Court being in Private, fully and deliberately weighed & Considered the Evidences against the Prisoners, and also the Defense made by them respectively, and the Advocate-General's Replication, and Voted, as follows, Viz.

1st. That the said Samuel Cole, is Guilty of all the four first Articles Exhibited against him, but not Guilty of the two last Articles.

2ndly. That the said George Condick is not Guilty of the first Article of Murther Exhibited against him, but of the other five Articles the Court Voted him to be Guilty.

3dly. That the said Henry Greenvill is Guilty of all the Six Articles Exhibited against him.

Then the Court being Open'd, The said Samuel Cole, George Condick, & Henry Greenvill were again brought to the Bar, when the President in the Name of the Court Pronounced them severally Guilty as aforesaid. And then the Advocate-General in His Majesty's behalf demanded Judgment against them.

Whereupon they were ask'd, what they had to say, why Sentence of Death should not be given against them. And they offering no sufficient Reason to the contrary, The President Pronounced Sentence against them in the words following, viz.

"You Samuel Cole, George Condick, & Henry Greenvill, are to go from hence to the place from whence you came, and from thence to the place of Execution, and there to be Hanged up by the Neck, until you and each of you be Dead, And the Lord have Mercy upon your Souls."

Then the Prisoners were Remanded to Prison, and the Marshall caution'd to take strict Charge of them. After which the Court was Adjourned to Six a Clock Post Meridiem.

The Court met according to the said Adjournment.

And in Consideration that the beforenamed George Condick was commonly Intoxicated with Liquor, and an Ignorant Man, about Twenty Years of Age, having no hand (as appeared) in the Murther of the Captain, or Mate, and seldom taking up Arms at the Caption of any of the Vessels, but mostly was imployed as Cook on board the Snow; The Court Voted, That the said George Condick be Recommended to His

Honour the Lieutenant Governour & Commander in Chief of this Province, for a Reprieve for Twelve Months, that so His Majesty's Pleasure by or before that time may be known concerning him the said Condick.

Afterwards, The Court proceeded to Consider when the Sentence against the said William Fly, Samuel Cole, & Henry Greenvill, should be put in Execution. And Voted, That they should be Executed on Tuesday the [29th][24] Day of July Instant, at the usual place for the execution of Pirates, in or near Charles-River, so called, between the Hours of Ten & Four of the Clock: And that the said William Fly, being the Chief Leader of them, his Dead Body should be carried from the Place of Execution to an Island called Nick's-Mate,[25] near the Entrance of the Harbour of Boston, and there be Hung up in Chains. And His Honour the President was Desired by the Court to Sign the Dead Warrant, Commanding the Marshall of the Admiralty to put the aforesaid Sentences against them in Execution on the said [29th] Day of July accordingly.

APPENDIX

[Statement of William Atkinson]

Here follows a Copy of the Declaration of Capt. *William Atkinson*, taken by the Notary, upon his Arrival at Boston, in the Snow *Elizabeth*, otherwise called the *Fame's Revenge* (lately Commanded by William Fly), on the 28th of June 1726. And also Copies of the Examinations of several Persons on Board the Snow, taken before Samuel Checkley and Habijah Savage Esqrs; Two of His Majesty's Justices for the County of Suffolk, on the 29th Day of the said Month, by Order of His Honour the Lieut. Governour, and His Majesty's Council of the Province of the Massachusetts-Bay.

The Declaration of *William Atkinson*, late Commander of a Brigantine called the *Boneta*. This Declarant saith, That he left the said Brigantine at North-Carolina, and took his Passage in the Sloop whereof Capt. John Fulker was Master, bound from Carolina aforesaid to Boston; And on the 3d of June Instant, as the said Sloop lay at Anchor off Cape-Hadderas Bar, they discovered a Snow standing in for the Harbour of Carolina; the said Capt. Fulker, his Mate, and the Declarant with one other Passenger, and a Boy, took the Sloop's Boat, and went on Board the Snow, supposing that the Master of her wanted a Pilot. When they came on Board, Capt. Fulker and the other Passenger was sent for by the Captain of the said Snow, whose Name was William Fly; and afterwards the said Atkinson was sent for and went down the Cabbin to the said Fly, who entertained him civilly; but after some short time the said Atkinson heard the said Captain Fly say, they, viz. (he and his Company) were Gentlemen of Fortune (meaning they were Pirates as the Declarant understood). And upon further Enquiry, the Declarant understood that the said Snow was called the *Elizabeth*,

---

24   Originally "Twelfth"; corrected as per the errata.
25   Also known locally as Nixes Mate or Nixes Island; today part of the Boston Harbor Islands National Recreation Area.

belonging to His Majesty's Subjects in Bristol in Great Britain, and was Commanded by Capt. Green, who had Fifteen Men on Board, that the said Fly was Boatswain, and in the Night about the 27th of May last, he with the rest of the Men rose, and hawled the Captain and Mate from their Beds [and threw them overboard];[26] and confined the Gunner, Doctor, and Carpenter.[¶]

Some few hours after,[27] the said Snow came to Anchor about three Miles from the Sloop. The said Fly and Company told Capt. Fulker they must have his Sloop if she sailed better than the Snow; and accordingly the said Fly sent the said Fulker with five or six of the said Fly's Men on Board the Sloop in her Boat, in order to fetch her along-side the Snow; but the Wind being contrary they could not bring her off, which Fly perceiving, in a great passion, he Swore he would burn her, if they did not bring her out. He ordered Capt. Fulker to the Geers,[28] and caus'd him to be whip'd severely. Afterwards the Boat's Crew labour'd to bring the Sloop to the Snow, and they carried her out as far as the Bar, but there she bilged and sunk; then the Pirates tryed to set her on fire, as Fulker's Mate told the Declarant, but the fire did not take.[¶]

Afterwards when the Snow was about to Sail, the said Fulker and his Passengers, & Men, intreated the said Fly for to give them their Liberty, who promised them they should have their Liberty the first Vessel they took, and not before; so on the fifth of June they sailed from Carolina, and on the sixth Day of said Month, they saw a Ship called the *John and Betty*, Commanded by John Gale, bound from Barbados to Virginia, and gave her Chase some considerable time, but finding the Ship out-sail'd the Snow, the said Fly hoisted a Jack at the Maintopmast head in Token of Distress, but Capt. Gale sailed from 'em notwithstanding. So the said Fly continued the Chase till next Morning, when he hoisted the Black Flagg, and fired several Guns at the Ship, and came up with her, there being then but little Wind, and then the said Gale struck his Colours, and Fly Manned his Long-Boat with a Pateraro,[29] and the said Fly's Crew went on Board the Ship with their Muskets, Pistols, and Cutlashes, and having made the Men Prisoners sent them to Capt. Fly on Board the Snow. And after they had robbed the Ship of several of her Sails, and some Cloaths and Small Arms, and detained 'em about two days, they let them go, and also gave the said Capt. Fulker and his other Passenger Mr. Roan,[30] together with Capt. Green's Doctor, liberty to go with the said Capt. Gale, but they still detained the Declarant. And the said William Fly told the Declarant that he should be their Pilot on the Coast of New-England, or else he would blow his Brains out.[¶]

---

26 Text added as per the errata page.
27 I.e., after the conversation in the Cabin.
28 *Jeers*, "an assemblage of strong tackles by which the lower yards are hoisted up along the mast, or lowered down, as occasion requires . . ." (Smyth, *Lexicon*, 409).
29 "*Paterero*. A kind of small mortar sometimes fired for salutes or rejoicing, especially in Roman Catholic countries on holidays" (Smyth, *Lexicon*, 520).
30 Changed from "Mr. Ruth" per the errata.

"They set all sail, and there was a fine sea-chase" (George Varian).

Then they stood for this Coast, and off Deleware-Bay they met a Sloop Commanded by one Harris bound from New-York to Pensilvania, having about Fifty Irish and Scots Passengers on Board, and the Pirate again hoisted his Black Flagg, and ordered the Sloop to strike, which she did; And the Declarant was sent on Board the Sloop (tho' without Arms) with three of the Pirate[s] Armed, to take possession of her; the Declarant being Ordered to Navigate her, and keep her by the Snow; which three Pirates Ransackt the Vessel; and one of her Company, namely James Benbrooke, being a lusty Fellow, as they call'd him, was forced on Board the Pirate. And after they had detained the said Sloop about twenty-four hours they let the Captain and all his Men go in the said Sloop on their Voyage, except the said Benbrooke.[¶]

After this the said Fly Ordered the Snow to be carried into Martha's Vinyard, but the Declarant purposely mist that Place. And the said Fly finding his Expectation frustrated, was angry with and threatned to kill the Declarant, a little beyond Nantucket. And on the 23d Day of June Instant they stood from thence Eastward, and met with a Fishing Schooner on Brown's Banks, so called (the Master is now on Board the Snow) and the said Fly hoisted his Black Flagg, and fired a Great Gun after himself, and told the People he would sink her, if they did not bring their Boat on Board, so they came on Board; and Fly told the Master he must have the Schooner, unless he could tell him where he might get another that would Sail better; so after he had receiv'd what Information he could get, the Pirates set Sail after another Schooner which about Twelve a-Clock that day appeared in sight, and the said Capt. Fly sent the Scooner with Seven Hands, viz. six Pirates, and one George Tasker, after the other

Scooner; and he the said Fly with Three more Pirates (one of them being in Irons for Mutiny) remained on Board the Snow, with fifteen others, who were taken and detained by the said Fly, viz. the said Declarant, and Capt. Fulker's Mate, and two of his Boys, the Carpenter, and Gunner of Capt. Green, six of Capt. Gale's Men, the aforesaid Benbrooke, who belonged to Capt. Harris, and three of the Fisher-men belonging to the Scooner.[¶]

And while the Pirates on Board the Scooner were gone in Chase as aforesaid, several other Fishing Vessels appeared in sight a-head of the Snow, when the said Fly was on the Quarter-Deck, with two Small Arms loaded, and a sword, and the said Atkinson took notice to him, that he espied some Vessels forward, and thereupon Fly went forward, and as he set on the Windless[31] with his Prospective-Glass,[32] the Declarant Secured his Arms, and Walker and Benbrooke by the Declarant's Direction took hold of the said Fly, and put him in Irons; And the said Atkinson, with his Mates, soon confined the other Pirates, and made themselves Masters of the Snow, the rest of the People on Board standing Neuter or unactive, not being made privy to the Design of taking the Pirates. And on the Day of the date hereof the said Snow was brought up to the Great Brewster near the Light-House, where the four Pirates are kept in irons under the Guard of the People on Board her. And further the Declarant saith not.

William Atkinson
Boston, June 28th, 1726
Attest. Samuel Tyler, N-Publicus

[Statement of Morrice Cundon]

Morrice Cundon, Native of Cork, saith, That he was Ship'd on Board the Snow called the *Elizabeth*, belonging to Merchants in Bristol in Great Britain, Capt. John Green of Bristol, Commander, and Sailed from Jamaica in her last April bound for Guinea: But in the Prosecution of the Voyage, viz. on the 27th of May, about One a Clock in the Morning, when the Examinant was at Helm, the Boatswain, namely William Fly, was forward (having the Charge of the Captain's Watch) about an hour, with several other of the Men, Then the Boatswain came aft, and said to the Examinant, that he would go & look on the Hour Glass, in the Cabbin, to see what a Clock it was: And after a few Minutes he came up again and went forward. About a Quarter of an Hour after he came aft with Alexander Mitchel, Henry Hill, Samuel Cole, Thomas Winthrop, and others of the Sailors; And the said William Fly spoke softly to the Examinant at Helm, saying, ["]Damn you, if you stir hand or foot, or speak a word, I'll blow your Brains out["]; and then he hawl'd up his Shirt, so that the Deponent saw his naked Arm, and went down again into the Cabbin, with some Instrument in his hand, and Alexander

---

31 *Windlass*, the crank-operated winch, usually located towards the bow of a vessel, used to lift heavy objects and also to let out and haul in the anchor cable (Smyth, *Lexicon*, 733).

32 I.e., a perspective glass or telescope.

Mitchel follow'd him, and presently the Examinant heard the Captain say, ["]What's the matter[?"]; and they two soon brought the said Capt. Green upon Deck, who (as 'tis thought) perceiving they were about to fling him over-board, Applied himself to the Boatswain, saying ["]For God's sake, don't throw me overboard, for if you do I shall go to Hell.["] Then the Boatswain bid him say after him, "Lord have Mercy upon my Soul.["] And he, with Mitchell and Winthrop flung him overboard, And soon after, the Examinant heard Winthrop make his boast that he had cut the Captain's Hand off with a Cooper's broad Ax, as he hung by the Main-Sheets; Afterwards others went and secured Thomas Jenkins the Mate, and brought him upon Deck, and then Winthrop told him he should go over after his Commander; And accordingly they threw him over, just afore the Main-Shrouds, having first cut him down the Shoulder with a broad Ax, as Mitchel, Winthrop and Cole afterwards declared: The Mate after he was thrown over, Cryed out to the Doctor, for God's sake, to give him a Rope, then Fly went to the Doctor's Cabbin and secured him, as he lay in his Bed, and put him in Irons; and placed one John Fitz-Herbert at Helm, and the Examinant with the Carpenter, viz. Thomas Streaton were laid in Irons; the said Herbert seemed to be sorry for what was done.[¶]

Then after some Consultation together they steered their Course for North Carolina; and came in sight of a Sloop at Anchor off Carolina within the Bar, And Capt. John Fulker the Master, Capt. William Atkinson, Mr. Roan, another Passenger, with Samuel Walker, Fulker's Mate, and a Young Lad, went on Board the said Snow, in order to Pilot her in; when the said Fly told them he was come with a Cargo from Jamaica, but the Examinant being confined in the Steeridge[33] did not hear what else passed between then. They sent away the Boat, in order to bring the Sloop over the Bar, but the Tide not serving, they could not bring her out; And upon their return, by the said Fly's Order, the said Fulker was severely Whip'd.[¶]

The next Morning they sent away the Boat to bring the Sloop out, and as they were bringing her off, she run on shoar and Bilged. So upon the Boat's return, the Snow weighed Anchor, and set Sail for Martha's Vinyard to Water as they gave out: And in their way, off the Capes of Virginia, they met a Ship which proved to be a Bristol Ship under Capt. John Gale's Command; They took some Sails and other things out of her; And after they had detained him about Twenty-four Hours, they suffered the Doctor of the Snow, viz. Richard Ruth, and Capt. Fulker, one of his Passengers, and a Servant Boy, to go in the Ship. And afterwards in June, off the Capes of Deleware, the said Fly took a Sloop that had about 50 Passengers on Board, the Snow having a Black Flagg hoisted, and detained her some time, and took one James Benbrooke out of her, who is now on Board the Snow; And then set the Sloop and Passengers at Liberty, having first taken out of her some Small Arms, and a Barrel of Cyder. Afterwards they pur-

---

33   *Steerage*, "A large space below deck . . . which in some merchant ships was used for crew accommodation . . . . In the days when sailing ships carried passengers the steerage was that part of the ship next below the quarterdeck and immediately before the bulkhead of the great cabin" (Dear and Kemp, *Oxford Companion*, 561).

posed, as they gave out, to Water, at Martha's Vinyard, and then go to the Coast of Guinea, but the Pilot missing the place, went to Brown's Banks, so called, Eastward, and there on Thursday last they took a Scooner, one George Girdler Master, the Snow's Black Flagg flying: And the Pirates put six of the Snow's Company in her, who with one Man more sail'd after another Scooner that appeared in sight; And while they were absent the said Atkinson and others surprized and seized the said Fly: But the Examinant being then Sick in his Hammock, can give no further Account of the matter, save only, that the Snow being afterwards Chased by the said Scooner, and another Scooner that the six Pirates had taken, the Examinant, tho' Sick, was so well disposed that he help'd to load the Snow's Great Guns and Small Arms to defend her from the Pirates. And on the 28th of June he came to Boston in the said Snow. The Pirates when they met with the aforesaid Vessels fired upon them.

The Examinant adds, that after the said Fly and his Crew had killed the Captain and Mate of the Snow, they met the Ship *Pompy*, which came out from Jamaica in Company with the Snow, and the Captain of the Ship hailed the Snow, and ask'd how Capt. Green did, and Fly answered, ["]Very well, at your Service Sir.["]And further the Examinant saith, That John Cole, and six other of Capt. Gale's Men were made Prisoners, and put in Irons, who are all aboard the Snow, except the Carpenter, namely George Tasker, who was left on Board the Scooner with the six Pirates.

his mark
Morrice Cundon

[Statement of Thomas Streaton]

Thomas Streaton, late Carpenter of the Snow called the *Elizabeth*, a Native of London, Declares and saith, That he ship'd himself on board the said Snow at Jamaica, under Capt. John Green's Command, to proceed a Voyage to Guinea; But in the Prosecution of the Voyage, viz. on the 27th of May last, between One and Two of the Clock in the Morning, he heard Samuel Cole say, to the Mate Thomas Jenkins; ["]Come out of your Cabbin you Dog["]; and the Mate cried out soon after, saying ["]For the Lord's sake, save my Life["]; but they hawl'd him out of his Cabbin, and carried him upon Deck; And the Examinant heard some Body fall upon the Deck, which he believed to be the Mate: And afterwards he was thrown overboard; And while he was in the Water he called to the Doctor, and desired him to hand him a Rope. But by that time the Doctor was put in Irons. Afterwards the Examinant got out of his Hammock, & was looking up the Hatches, Intending to go upon Deck, but one of the Snow's Company told him if he did not keep in his Cabbin, he would blow his Brains out: About two days after they met one of the Ships that came out in Company with the said Snow, viz. the Ship *Pompy*, and some Person on board hailed the Snow, & ask'd, how Capt. Green did, to which Fly Answer'd, very well. The said Fly & his Company consulted together, whether they had best Attack the said Ship, but 'twas alledged that they had not Hands eno' to mann her; and so they left her, &

steer'd their course for Carolina; and came in sight of a Sloop at Carolina, when Capt. Fulker the Master of her, & others, came on Board the Snow, in order to Pilot her in. They Attempted to bring the said Sloop over the Bar, but run her on shoar on the Bar, where [she Bilged?]. Then the said Snow set sail designing for Martha's Vinyard, to Water, as the Pirates [said?], & off the Capes of Virginia they met a Bristol Ship, Capt. Gale Commander, out of which they took some things & gave the said Capt. Gale an Anchor & other things by way of Exchange; the Pirates kept the Ship about twenty four hours, & then permitted her to go, & gave leave to the Doctor of the Snow, & Capt. Fulker, with one of said Fulker's Passengers, & a Servant, to go with them in the Ship. And afterwards in this present Month of June off the Capes of Deleware they took a Sloop that had about fifty Passengers on board, kept her some time, & then left her, only took out of her one James Benbrooke, some Small Arms, & other things. Afterwards they sailed for Martha's Vinyard, but missing the Place, they arrived at Browns Bank to the Eastward, where on Thursday last they took a Scooner Commanded by one Girdler, & put six of the Pirates on Board, who went in pursuit of other Vessels then in sight, and while they were absent Capt. Atkinson with the Examinant, & others, surprized & subdued the said Fly, & three more of his Crew, who were put in Irons. The Examinant further saith, that the six Pirates in the Scooner took another Scooner, and stood after the Snow, but could not come up with her, and in the Night they left her, and made the best of their way for Boston, where they arrived the 28th of June Instant.

The said Examinent saith further, That John Cole, John Brown, Robert Dauling, John Daw, James Blair, Edward Laurence, & George Tasker, were taken out of Capt. Gale's ship & put in Irons, who were all on Board the Snow, except the Carpenter, viz. Tasker, who was left on board the Scooner with the six Pirates.

his mark
Thomas Streaton

[Statement of Samuel Walker and Edward Apthorp]

Samuel Walker, late Mate of the Sloop *John & Hannah*, whereof John Fulker was Commander, and *Edward Apthorp*, Marriner, being Examined, say, That on or about the Third Day of June last, as the said Sloop lay at Anchor off Cape Hadderas Bar in North Carolina, they espied a Snow, and the said Fulker, Mr. Roan, Capt. Atkinson, with the Examinant[s], and a Boy, took the Boat and went on Board the Snow in order to Pilot her in; and after they had been on Board some time they understood the Men on Board the Snow were Pirates: And they Ordered the said Walker and others to go in the Boat & bring the Sloop along of the Snow, but they run her on Shoar, and she bilged on the Bar; The Pirates then Attempted to set the Sloop on Fire twice, but the Fire went out: After they came on Board the Snow, they set Sail for the Coast of New England; And about two or three Days after the said Fly & Company took a Ship whereof John Gale was Master, belonging to Bristol, and carried away Seven of his

Men, and put them in Irons, namely James Blair, John Brown, John Cole, Robert Dauling, John Daw, Edward Lawrence, & George Tasker, and all of them are now on Board the Snow, except George Tasker: And the Pirates permitted Capt. Fulker, the said Roan, and his Boy, and the Doctor of the Snow to go away in the said Gale's Ship. Then they stood away for Deleware-Bay, where they met a Sloop with about Fifty Irish and Scots Passengers on Board bound to Philadelphia, and took out of her one James Benbrooke, now in the Snow. From thence the said Fly and Company designed to Martha's Vinyard, as they gave out, but missed the Place: Capt. Atkinson was their Pilot, who carried them to Browns Bank Eastward, where they took a Scooner, one George Girdler Master, and put on Board her Capt. Gale's Carpenter, viz. the said George Tasker, and six Pirates, who went in pursuit of another Scooner; and while they were gone, the said Capt. Atkinson, & the said Walker, with the said Benbrook & Thomas Streaton, rose up against the said Fly, & three other Pirates on Board the Snow, and brought her to Boston the 28th of June Instant.

Samuel Walker
Edward Apthorp

[Statement of John Cole, John Brown, James Blair, Edward Lawrence, Robert Dauling, and John Daw]

John Cole, *John Brown*, *James Blair*, *Edward Lawrence*, *Robert Dauling*, & *John Daw*, being Examined, say, That on the Sixth of June Instant, John Gale, Captain of the Ship *John & Betty*, was taken off the Capes of Virginia by one William Fly, Master of the Snow called by the Pirates the *Fame's Revenge*, formerly called the *Elizabeth*; who Robb'd the said Ship of a Foretop-Gallant-Sail,[34] a Mizen-stay-Sail, and sundry other [things?], and gave the said Capt. Gale an Anchor and some Cask, and permitted the Doctor of the Snow, Capt. Fulker, and three others to go in the said Gale's Ship, but detained the Examinants on board the Snow, & put them in Irons. And further the Examinants affirm to the Truth of what relates to the Pirates taking the Sloop off Deleware, and the Scooner, as is above Declared by Samuel Walker & Edward Apthorp.

Signed by John Cole, & the other persons abovenamed.

[Statement of James Benbrook]

James Benbrook of Dublin, a Passenger bound from New York to Philadelphia, in the Sloop *Rachel*, Capt. Samuel Harris of New London Master, Declares and saith, that the said Sloop was taken on the Eleventh of June [illegible] six Leagues East from Cape May, by Wm. Fly, Commander of the Snow, Called the *Elizabeth*, after the *Fame's Revenge*, who plundered the said Sloop and took the Examinant, & put him in

---

34 The uppermost sail on the mast nearest the front (fore) of the vessel (*Mast* entry, Falconer, *Universal Dictionary*, n.p.).

Irons on board the said Snow, and on the 12th Day of the said Month they dismiss'd Capt. Harris and his Company, having first taken all the Sloop's Colours, Capt. Harris's Instruments, and some of his Cloaths. Then they sailed to the Coast of New-England and on Thursday last, took a Schooner on Browns Bank, and put Seven Men on board, six of them Pirates, who were in pursuit of another Vessel; and in the mean time Capt. Atkinson with the Examinant and two others, viz. Thomas Streaton and Samuel Walker, having projected how they should surprise the said Fly, took this opportunity, and seized him, and put him in Irons, with three more Pirates on aboard, and [illegible] Sail for Boston, where they arrived the 28th of June Instant.

James Benbrook

[Statement of George Girdler, Joseph Marshall, and William Ferguson]

George Girdler of Marblehead, late Master or Skipper of the Scooner called the *James*; *Joseph Marshall*, and *William Ferguson*, both lately belonging to the said Scooner, being Examined, say, That on Thursday last the 23d of June Instant, as the said Scooner lay too on Brown Banks [illegible], there bore down upon 'em a Snow with English Colours; And when they came near to Windward they hoisted a Black Flagg, and fired at the Scooner, and bid 'em lower their Sails, and bring their Boat on Board; and when the Examinants went on Board they perceived the Snow was Commanded by William Fly, a Pirate, who made Prisoners of the Examinants; Then they put Six Pirates and another Man, viz. George Tasker, on Board the Scooner, who, with Three Young Men more taken in her, viz. Thomas Sango, Richard Girdler and William Girdler, went in Quest of and took another Scooner in sight of the Snow, and while they were gone Capt. Atkinson and three others, surprized Capt. Fly; and made a Prisoner of him and Three more Pirates then onboard the Snow, namely, Samuel Cole, George Condick, and Henry Greenvill.

George Girdler

Joseph Marshall

his Mark
William Ferguson

Attest. Samuel Tyley, N-Publicus

[**Editor's Note**: Puritan clergyman Cotton Mather, who ministered to the convicted men in prison, found Fly obstinate, "a most uncommon and amazing Instance of Impenitency and Stupidity." Mather noted that "The Sullen and Raging Mood, into which he fell, upon his being first Imprison'd, caused him to break forth into furious Execrations, and Blasphemies too hideous to be mention'd; and not eat one morsel of any thing, but subsist only upon a little Drinking, for almost all the remaining part of his Life."

According to Mather, Fly went unrepentant to his execution, "with a Nosegay in his hand, and making his Complements, where he thought he saw occasion." At the gallows with Greenville and Cole, Fly even helped adjust his own noose, having "reproached the Hangman, for not understanding his Trade." His only remark to the crowd, according to Mather, was to "advise the Masters of Vessels to carry it well to their Men, lest they should be put upon doing as he had done." While Cole and Greenville prayed, "Fly look'd about him unconcerned."

But Mather also wrote that "it was observed and is affirm'd, by some Spectators, that in the Midst of all his affected Bravery, a very sensible Trembling attended him; His hands and his Knees were plainly seen to Tremble – And so we must leave him for the Judgment to come."[35]]

---

35 Mather, *Vial Poured Out Upon the Sea*, 47–49.

Bibliography

An Abridgment of the English Military Discipline. Printed by Especial Command, for the Use of His Majesties Forces (London: John Bill, Henry Hills, Thomas Newcomb, 1685).

Adams, Thomas, *The Works of Thomas Adams*, Vol. 1 (Edinburgh: James Nichol, 1861).

Adler, Eric, *Valorizing the Barbarians: Enemy Speeches in Roman Historiography* (Austin, TX: University of Texas Press, 2011).

A Full and Exact Account of the Tryal Of all the Pyrates, Lately taken by Captain Ogle, On Board the Swallow *Man of War, on the Coast of Guinea* (London: J. Roberts, 1723).

Allen, John, *Inquiry into the Rise and Growth of the Royal Prerogative in England* (London: Longman, Brown, Green and Longmans, 1849).

An Account of the Pirates, with Divers of their Speeches, Letters, &c. And A Poem Made by One of them: Who were Executed at Newport, on Rhode-Island, July 19th, 1723, (Boston?: "Re-Printed in the Year 1769").

An Interesting Trial of Edward Jordan, and Margaret his Wife, who were Tried at Halifax, N.S. Nov. 15th, 1809, for the Horrid Crime of Piracy and Murder . . . (Boston: 75 State Street and 52 Orange Street, 1809).

Anspach, Lewis Amadeus, *A History of the Island of Newfoundland . . .* (London: T and J. Allman, 1819).

Appleby, John C., "Women and Piracy in Ireland: From Gráinne O'Malley to Anne Bonny," in Margaret MacCurtain and Mary O'Dowd, eds., *Women in Early Modern Ireland* (Edinburgh: Edinburgh University Press, 1991), 53–68 (reprinted in Pennell, ed., *Bandits at Sea*, 283–298).

Ayres, Philip, compiler, *The Voyages and Adventures of Capt. Barth. Sharp and Others, in the South Sea: Being a Journal of the Same. . . .* (London: Philip Ayres, 1684) [also reproduced in Baer, *British Piracy*, I:109–280].

Baer, Joel H., ed., *British Piracy in the Golden Age: History and Interpretation, 1660–1730*, 4 vols. (London: Pickering and Chatto, 2007).

Berckman, Evelyn, *Victims of Piracy: The Admiralty Court, 1575–1678* (London: Hamilton, 1979).

Bialuschewski, Arne, "Daniel Defoe, Nathaniel Mist, and the *General History of the Pyrates*," *Papers of the Bibliographical Society of America*, 98 (2004), 21–38.

Bingham, Hiram, "Potosí," *Bulletin of the American Geographical Society*, 43:1 (1911), 1–13.

Bizzarro, Salvatore, *Historical Dictionary of Chile*, 3rd ed. (Lanham, MD: Scarecrow Press, 2005).

Black, Clinton V., *Pirates of the West Indies* (Cambridge, UK: Cambridge University Press, 1989).

Blackmore, H.L., *The Armouries of the Tower of London: The Ordnance*, Vol. 1, (London: H.M. Stationery Office, 1976).

Bolster, W. Jeffrey, *Black Jacks: African American Seamen in the Age of Sail* (Cambridge: Harvard University Press, 1998).

Boyd, Julian P., ed., *The Papers of Thomas Jefferson*, Vol. 1 (1760–1776), (Princeton, NJ: Princeton University Press, 1950).

Bracewell, Wendy, "Women among the Uskoks: Literary Images and Reality," *MOST* (Zagreb) 2, 1988, 44–51 (reprinted in Pennell, ed., *Bandits at Sea*, 321–334).

Bradbury, Jim, *The Medieval Archer* (New York: Barnes and Noble, 1985).

Bradford, Gershom, *The Mariner's Dictionary* (New York: Weathervane Books, NY, 1952).

Bradlee, Francis B.C., *Piracy in the West Indies and its Suppression* (Salem, MA: Essex Institute, 1923).

Breverton, Terry, *Admiral Sir Henry Morgan: King of the Buccaneers* (Gretna, LA: Pelican, 2005).

Brown, Vera Lee, "The South Sea Company and Contraband Trade," *American Historical Review* 31 (July 1926), 662–678.

Burford, Robert, *Description of a View of the City of Lima, and the Surrounding Country* (London: T. Brettell, 1836).

Burg, B.R., *Sodomy and the Perception of Evil: English Sea Rovers in the Seventeenth-Century Caribbean* (New York: New York University Press, 1983).

Cahill, Robert Ellis, *Finding New England's Shipwrecks and Treasures* (Salem, MA: Old Saltbox Publishing, n.d.).

————, *New England's Pirates and Lost Treasures* (Salem, MA: Old Saltbox Publishing, n.d.).

Carlova, John, *Mistress of the Seas* (New York: Citadel, 1964).

Carswell, John, *The South Sea Bubble* (London: Cresset, 1961).

Chapelle, Howard I., *The History of the American Sailing Navy: The Ships and Their Development* (New York: W. W. Norton, 1949).

Cicero, Marcus Tullius, *De Officiis*, Walter Miller translator (Cambridge, MA: Harvard University Press, 1997).

————, *Pro Publio Quinctio; Pro Publio Sexto Roscio Amerino; Pro Quinto Roscio Comoedo; De Lege Agraria*, John Henry Freese translator (Cambridge, MA: Harvard University Press, 1984).

Clifford, Barry, *Expedition Whydah* (New York: Harper Collins, 1999).

Cohen, Saul, ed., *Columbia Gazetteer of the World*, 3 vols. (New York: Columbia University, 2008).

Coke, Sir Edward, *Third Part of the Institutes of the Laws of England . . .* 4th ed., (London: Crooke et al., 1669).

Colledge, J.J., and Ben Warlow, *Ships of the Royal Navy* (Newbury, UK: Casemate, 2010).

Cordingly, David, *Under the Black Flag: The Romance and the Reality of Life Among the Pirates* (New York: Harcourt Brace, 1995).

Cox, John, "The Adventures of Capt. Barth. Sharp, And Others, in the South Sea," in Philip Ayres, compiler, *Voyages and Adventures of Capt. Barth. Sharp*, 1–114.

Dampier, William, *Memoirs of a Buccaneer: Dampier's New Voyage Round the World, 1697* (Mineola, NY: Dover, 1968).

Dear, I.C.B., and Peter Kemp, eds., *The Oxford Companion to Ships and the Sea* (Oxford: Oxford University Press, 2005).

De Souza, P., *Piracy in the Graeco-Roman World* (Cambridge, UK: Cambridge University Press, 2002).

Dow, George Francis, *Every Day Life in the Massachusetts Bay Colony* (Bowie, MD: Heritage Books, 2002).

Dow, George Francis, and John Henry Edmonds, *The Pirates of the New England Coast, 1630–1730* (Mineola, NY: Dover, 1996).

Earle, Peter, *The Sack of Panamá: Captain Morgan and the Battle for the Caribbean* (New York: Thomas Dunne, 1981).

Eltis, David, *The Military Revolution in Sixteenth-Century Europe* (New York: Barnes and Noble, 1995).

Ellms, Charles, *The Pirates Own Book* (New York: Dover, 1993).

Esposito, John, ed., *The Oxford Encyclopedia of the Modern Islamic World*, 4 vols. (Oxford: Oxford University, 1995).

Exquemelin, Alexandre O., *The Buccaneers of America*, Alexis Brown translator (Mineola, NY: Dover, 2000).

Falconer, William, *An Universal Dictionary of the Marine . . .* 2nd ed. (London: T. Cadell, 1771) [also available as a Gale ECCO facsimile reprint].

Ffoulkes, Charles, *The Gun-Founders of England* (Cambridge: Cambridge University Press, 1937).

Findlay, Alexander George, *A Directory for the Navigation of the Pacific Ocean*, Vol. 1 (London: R.H. Laurie, 1851).

Forester, C. S., *The Age of Fighting Sail* (Garden City, NY: Doubleday, 1956).

Frayler, John, "Armed to the Teeth" [informational staff memo] (Salem, Mass.: Salem National Maritime Historic Site, March 16, 2001).

Frohock, Richard, "Exquemelin's Buccaneers: Violence, Authority, and the Word in Early Caribbean History," *Eighteenth-Century Life*, 34:1 (Winter 2010), 56–72.

Garrison, James D., *Pietas From Vergil To Dryden* (University Park, PA: Penn State Press, 1988).

Gibbs, Joseph, *Dead Men Tell No Tales: The Lives and Legends of the Pirate Charles Gibbs* (Columbia, S.C.: University of South Carolina Press, 2007).

——————, *On the Account: Piracy and the Americas, 1766–1835* (Brighton, UK: Sussex Academic Press, 2012).

Goodwin, Joshua Michael, "Universal Jurisdiction and the Pirate: Time for an Old Couple to Part," *Vanderbilt Journal of Transnational Law*, 39 (2006), 973–1011.

Gosse, Philip, *The Pirates' Who's Who* (Glorieta, N.M.: Rio Grande Press, 1988).

Guilmartin, John F. Jr., "The Earliest Shipboard Gunpowder Ordnance: An Analysis of Its Technical Parameters and Tactical Capabilities," *The Journal of Military History* 71:3 (July 2007), 649–669.

Grotius, Hugo, *On the Law of War and Peace*, Stephen C. Neff ed. (Cambridge: Cambridge University Press, 2012).

Grose, Francis, *Classical Dictionary of the Vulgar Tongue*, 2nd edition (London: Hooper, 1788).

"Habiliments and Habits," http://www.chroniclesofamerica.com/colonial_folkways/habiliments_and_habits.htm, accessed 4 July, 2013.

Hainsworth, Roger, and Christine Churches, *The Anglo Dutch Naval Wars, 1652–1674* (Phoenix Mill, Gloucestershire: Sutton, 1998).

Hakluyt, Richard, *The Principal Navigations, Voyages, Traffiques and Discoveries of the English Nation*, Edmund Goldsmid ed., 16 vols. (Edinburgh: E. & G. Goldsmid, 1890).

Hardy, John, *A Chronological List of the Captains of His Majesty's Royal Navy . . .* (London: T. Cadell, 1784).

Haring, Clarence Henry, *The Buccaneers in the West Indies in the XVII Century* (New York: Dutton, 1910).

Harland, John, *Seamanship in the Age of Sail* (Annapolis, MD: Naval Institute Press, 2003).

Hawes, Alexander Boyd, *Off Soundings: Aspects of the Maritime History of Rhode Island* (Chevy Chase, MD: Posterity Press, 1999).

Hazel, John, *Who's Who in the Roman World* (Routledge: London, New York, 2001).

Hill, Christopher, "Radical Pirates?" in *The Collected Essays of Christopher Hill*, Vol. 3 (Amherst, MA: University of Massachusetts Press, 1985), 161–187.

Hill, S. Charles, "Episodes of Piracy in Eastern Waters, 1519–1851," entry xv, *Indian Antiquary* 49 (1920), 1–10.

Hornblower, Simon and Tony Spawforth, eds., *Who's Who in the Classical World* (Oxford: Oxford University Press, 2000).

Howse, Derek, and Norman J. W. Thrower, eds., *A Buccaneer's Atlas: Basil Ringrose's South Sea Waggoner* (Berkeley: University of California Press, 1992).

Hume, David, *The History of England from the Invasion of Julius Caesar to the Revolution of 1688* (London: Robinson, 1833).

James, Charles, *A New and Enlarged Military Dictionary, or, Alphabetical Explanation of Technical Terms . . .* 2nd ed. (London: T. Egerton, 1805).

James, William, *The Naval History of Great Britain*, 6 vols., (London: Bentley, 1837).

Justice, Alexander, *General Treatise of the Dominion and Laws of the Sea* (London: Executors of J. Nicholson, 1710).

Justinus, Marcus Junianus, *Justini Historiae Philippicae*, annotated by Karl Benecke (Leipzig: Hartmann, 1830).

Kemp, Peter, *The History of Ships* (New York: Barnes & Noble, 2002).

Kinkor, Kenneth J., "Black Men Under the Black Flag," in Pennell, ed., *Bandits at Sea*, 195–210.

Knight, Stephen, *Robin Hood: A Mythic Biography* (Ithaca, New York: Cornell University Press, 2003).

Konstam, Angus, *Blackbeard: America's Most Notorious Pirate* (New York: Wiley, 2006).

——————, *The History of Pirates* (New York: Lyons Press, 1999).

——————, *Piracy: The Complete History* (London: Osprey, 2008).

Lane, Kris E., *Pillaging the Empire: Piracy in the Americas, 1500–1750* (Armonk, NY: Sharpe, 1998).

Lambert, Andrew, *War at Sea in the Age of Sail, 1650–1850* (London: Cassell, 2000).

Lavery, Brian, *The Arming and Fitting of English Ships of War, 1600–1815* (London: Conway, 1987).

——————, *Royal Tars: The Lower Deck of the Royal Navy, 875–1850* (London: Conway, 2010).

Leeson, Peter T., *The Invisible Hook: The Hidden Economics of Pirates* (Princeton: Princeton University Press, 2009).

Lenfesty, Thompson, and Tom Lenfesty Jr., *Dictionary of Nautical Terms* (New York: Facts on File, 1994).

Lever, Darcy, *The Young Sea Officer's Sheet Anchor* (Mineola, NY: Dover, 1998).

Linebaugh, P., and Marcus Rediker, "The Many-Headed Hydra: Sailors, Slaves, and the Atlantic Working Class in the Eighteenth Century," *Journal of Historical Sociology*, 3 (1990), 225–252.

Little, Benerson, *How History's Greatest Pirates Pillaged, Plundered, and Got Away with It* (Beverly, MA: Fair Winds, 2011).

——————, *The Sea Rover's Practice: Pirate Tactics and Techniques, 1630–1730* (Washington, DC: Potomac, 2005).

Lloyd, Christopher, "Bartholomew Sharp, Buccaneer," *The Mariner's Mirror*, 42–43 (1956), 291–301.

Long, Edward, *The History of Jamaica*, 3 vols., (London: Lowndes, 1774).

Lucie-Smith, Edward, *Outcasts of the Sea: Pirates and Piracy* (New York: Paddington Press, 1978).

MacDonald, Michael, "The Secularization of Suicide in England, 1660–1800," *Past and Present* 111 (May 1986), 50–100.

Malte-Brun, M., *A System of Universal Geography, or a Description of All the Parts of the World on a New Plan*, Vol. 2 (Boston: Samuel Walker, 1834).

Maraist, Frank L., *Admiralty in a Nutshell* (St. Paul, MN: West Publishing, 1988).

Mather, Cotton, *The Converted Sinner: The Nature of a Conversion to Real and Vital Piety: And the Manner in Which it is to be Pray'd & Striv'n for* (Boston: Belknap, 1724).

——————, *Instructions to the Living, from the Condition of the Dead* (Boston: Allen, 1717).

——————, *The Vial Poured Out Upon the Sea* (Boston: Belknap, 1726).

McCusker, John J., *Money and Exchange in Europe and America, 1600–1775* (Chapel Hill: University of North Carolina, 1978).

Merriam-Webster's Biographical Dictionary, rev. ed. (Springfield, MA: Merriam-Webster, 1995).

Merriam-Webster's Collegiate Dictionary, 10th ed. (Springfield, MA: Merriam-Webster, 1999).

Merriam-Webster's Geographical Dictionary, 3rd ed. (Springfield, MA: Merriam-Webster, 2001).

Meide, Chuck, "The Development and Design of Bronze Ordnance, Sixteenth through Nineteenth Centuries" (Williamsburg, VA: College of William and Mary, November 2002).

Mohr, Ralph S., *Governors for Three Hundred Years, 1638–1954, Rhode Island and Providence Plantations* (Providence: State of Rhode Island, Graves Registration Committee, August 1954).

Murray, Dian, "One Woman's Rise to Power: Cheng I's Wife and the Pirates," in R.W. Guisso and S. Johannesen, eds., *Women in China: Current Directions in Historical Scholarship* (Youngstown, NY: Philo Press, 1981), 147–161.

Nardo, Don, *The Monsters and Creatures of Greek Mythology* (Mankato, MN: Compass Point Books, 2012).

Nicholson, Edward, *Men and Measures: A History of Measures, Ancient and Modern* (London: Smith, Elder & Co., 1912).

Nolfi, Edward A., *Legal Terminology Explained* (London: McGraw-Hill, 2009).

Pack, James, *Nelson's Blood: The Story of Naval Rum* (Annapolis, MD: Naval Institute Press, 1982).

Patterson, Howard, *Patterson's Illustrated Nautical Dictionary* (New York: 9 and 101 Fourth Ave., n.d.).

Pennell, C. R., ed. *Bandits at Sea: A Pirates Reader* (New York: New York University Press, 2001).

Phillips, Edward, *The New World of English Words, or A General Dictionary* (London: E. Tyler for Nath. Brooke, 1662).

Pope, Dudley, *Harry Morgan's Way: The Biography of Sir Henry Morgan, 1635–1684* (Cornwall: Stratus, 2001).

Powell, George, "A Pirate's Paradise," *The Gentleman's Magazine*, 276:52 (Jan-June 1894), 20–36.

Preston, Diana and Michael, *A Pirate of Exquisite Mind: Explorer, Naturalist, and Buccaneer: The Life of William Dampier* (New York: Berkley, 2004).

Rediker, Marcus, *Between the Devil and the Deep Blue Sea: Merchant Seamen, Pirates and the Anglo-American Maritime World, 1700–1750* (Cambridge: Cambridge University Press, 1989).

—————, *The Slave Ship: A Human History* (New York: Penguin, 2007).

—————, *Villains of All Nations: Atlantic Pirates in the Golden Age* (Boston: Beacon, 2004).

Richards, Stanley, *Black Bart* (Llandybie, Carmarthenshire: Christopher Davies, 1966).

Ringrose, Basil, *Bucaniers of America. The Second Volume. Containing The Dangerous Voyage and Bold Attempts of Captain Bartholomew Sharp, and others; performed upon the Coasts of the South Sea, for the space of two years, &c.*, (London: William Crooke, 1685) [also available as an EEBO (Early English Books Online) Editions reprint].

Ritchie, Robert C., *Captain Kidd and the War Against the Pirates* (Cambridge, MA: Harvard University Press, 1986).

Rogers, Clifford J., "The Military Revolutions of the Hundred Years' War," *The Journal of Military History* 57:2 (April 1993), 241–278.

Rogers, Woodes, *A Cruising Voyage Round the World . . .* (London: A. Bell, 1712).

Room, Adrian, *Alternate Names of Places* (Jefferson, N.C.: McFarland, 2009).

Rowland, Donald, "Spanish Occupation of the Island of Old Providence, or Santa Catalina, 1641–1670," *The Hispanic American Historical Review*, 15:3 (August 1935), 298–312.

Sanders, Richard, *If a Pirate I Must Be . . . : The True Story of "Black Bart," King of the Caribbean Pirates* (New York: Skyhorse Publishing, 2007).

Schonhorn, Manuel, ed., *A General History of the Pyrates* (Mineola, NY: Dover, 1999).

Seitz, Don C., *Under the Black Flag* (London: Stanley Paul, 1927).

Shales, Melissa, *Barbados* (London: New Holland Publishers, 2007).

Silverman, Kenneth, *The Life and Times of Cotton Mather* (New York: Welcome Rain Publishers, 2001).

Simpson, A., and E.S.C. Weiner, eds., *Oxford English Dictionary*, 2nd ed., 20 vols. (Oxford: Clarendon, 1989).

Sluiter, Engel, "Dutch-Spanish Rivalry in the Caribbean Area, 1594–1609," *Hispanic American Historical Review* 28 (May 1948), 165–196.

Smyth, W. H., *The Sailor's Lexicon* (New York: Hearst, 2005).

Snow, Edward Rowe, *Pirates and Buccaneers of the Atlantic Coast* (Boston: Yankee Publishing, 1944).

Sobel, Dava, *Longitude: The True Story of a Lone Genius Who Solved the Greatest Scientific Problem of His Time* (New York: Walker and Co., 2007).

Stanley, Jo, ed., *Bold in Her Breeches: Women Pirates Across the Ages* (London: Pandora, 1996).

Starkey, David J., E. S. van Eyck van Heslinga, and J. A. De Moor, eds. *Pirates and Privateers: New Perspectives on the War on Trade in the Eighteenth and Nineteenth Centuries* (Exeter: University of Exeter Press, 1997).

Stephen, Thomas, *The Book of the Constitution of Great Britain* (Glasgow: Blackie & Son, 1835).

Stephens, J.R., ed., *Captured by Pirates: Twenty-two Firsthand Accounts of Murder and Mayhem on the High Seas* (New York: Barnes and Noble, 2006).

Stevens, Harm, *Dutch Enterprise and the VOC, 1602–1799* (Amsterdam: Stichting Rijksmuseum, 1998).

Stevens, Michael E., and Steven B. Burg, *Editing Historical Documents: A Handbook of Practice* (London: Sage, 1997).

Stone, Jon R., *Latin for the Illiterati: Exorcizing the Ghosts of a Dead Language* (New York: Routledge, 1996).

Talty, Stephan, *Empire of Blue Water: Captain Morgan's Great Pirate Army, the Epic Battle for the Americas, and the Catastrophe That Ended the Outlaws' Bloody Reign* (New York: Broadway Paperbacks, 2007).

Thomas, Hugh, *The Slave Trade: The History of the Atlantic Slave Trade 1440–1870* (New York: Simon & Schuster, 1997).

The Trials of Major Stede Bonnet and Thirty-three Others, at the Court of Vice-Admiralty, at Charles-Town, in South-Carolina, for Piracy: 5 George I A.D. 1718, as contained in Cobbett, William, T.B. Howell, and T.J. Howell, compilers, *A Complete Collection of State Trials and Proceedings for High Treason and Other Crimes and Misdemeanors . . .* 33 vols. (London: T.C. Hansard and others, 1809–1826), XV:1231–1302.

Tucker, Jonathan B., *Scourge: The Once and Future Threat of Smallpox* (New York: Grove Press, 2001).

Tucker, Spencer, *Handbook of 19th Century Naval Warfare* (Stroud: Sutton, 2000).

Turley, Hans, *Rum, Sodomy and the Lash: Piracy, Sexuality, and Masculine Identity* (New York: New York University, 1999).

Uden, Grant, and Richard Cooper, *A Dictionary of British Ships and Seamen* (Harmondsworth: Allen Lane, 1980).

Updike, Wilkins, *Memoirs of the Rhode Island Bar* (Boston: Thomas H. Webb & Co., 1842).

Vanderbilt II, Arthur T., *Treasure Wreck: The Fortunes and Fate of the Pirate Ship Whydah*, 2nd ed., (Atglen, PA: Schiffer Publishing, 2007).

Wafer, Lionel, *A New Voyage and Description of the Isthmus of America* (Cleveland: Burrows Brothers, 1903).

Watson, George, "*Nahuatl* Words in American English," *American Speech*, 13:2 (April 1938), 108–121.

Warren, Charles, *History of the Harvard Law School and of Early Legal Conditions in America* (New York: Lewis, 1908).

Weir, Alison, *Henry VIII: The King and His Court* (New York: Ballantine, 2001).

Wheelwright, Julie, "Tars, Tarts, and Swashbucklers," in Jo Stanley, ed., *Bold in Her Breeches*, 176–200.

The Wigmaker in Eighteenth-Century Williamsburg (Colonial Williamsburg Foundation: Williamsburg, VA: 1904).

Williams, Neville, *Captains Outrageous* (London: Barrie and Rockliff, 1961).

Willis, Sam, *Fighting at Sea in the Eighteenth Century: The Art of Sailing Warfare* (Woodbridge: Boydell & Brewer, 2008).

Winfield, Rif, *British Warships in the Age of Sail, 1603–1714* (Barnsley, Yorkshire: Seaforth, 2010).

——————, *British Warships in the Age of Sail, 1714–1792* (Barnsley, Yorkshire: Seaforth, 2007).

Woodard, Colin, *The Republic of Pirates: Being the True and Surprising Story of the Caribbean Pirates and the Man Who Brought Them Down* (New York: Harvest, 2007).

Index

abaft, 216
about, 37
Abraham (aboard the *Samuel*), 125
Abram Trepassé (Trepassey Bay), 128
account, going on the, viii, 21–22
accumulative crimes and evidence, 76, 78
Ackin, John, 150, 154, 158, 159, 163
Act of Grace, 103, 112, 125, 130
Act of Parliament, 87
Adams, Abigail, 75
Adams, John, 75
Adams, John Q., 75
Adlington, James, 170
Adventure (taken by Bradish), 125
Adventure (Teach's sloop), 117
affidavit, 77
Africa, 122, 124, 126, 170, 175
aggravating circumstances, 71
albecatos, 34
Alexander, John, 47
Allen, Richard, xi
Amboy, 117, 171
Amsterdam, 64, 85, 87
Amsterdam Merchant, 145, 148, 150, 154, 159, 163
Andreas (Kuna captain), 23
Andreas (Kuna emperor), 23, 24, 25, 36
Anguilla, 53, 67
animus depradandi, 60
Anne (Queen of England), 106
Anomabu, 122
Anstis, Thomas, 168, 173
Antigua, 53, 76, 105, 114, 120, 155, 168, 170
Apthorp, Edward, 212–213, 216, 218, 226–227
Archer, John Rose, 103
Archipélago Juan Fernández, 43, 44, 45
Argandona, Don Thomas de, 39
Arica, 41, 43, 45–46, 47, 48
Arraria, castle of, 176
Arthur, Capt., 106
Ash, Isle of (Isla Vaca/Île à Vache), 7–8
Ashton, Benjamin, 183
Ashton, Philip, 138, 142, 143, 179–203
Asiento, 175
Athens, 58
Atkins, John, 30

Atkinson, William, trial of, 209–21; as witness at
    Fly trial, 213, 214, 216, 217, 218, 220–223,
    224, 225, 226, 227, 228
Auchmuty, Robert, at trial of survivors of
    Bellamy's company, 57; at Fly trial, 209,
    210–211, 213, 214, 215, 216, 217, 218–219
Azores (Western Islands), 129, 144, 170, 174,
    187
Aztecs, 34

Baer, Joel H., xiii, 6, 12, 16, 22, 26, 35, 37, 38, 39,
    47, 50, 57, 63, 67, 69, 76, 80, 84, 126, 133,
    134, 137, 148, 149, 208, 209, 210, 214, 215
Bahamas, 54, 65, 79, 129, 131, 168
Baker, Thomas, 73; trial of, 57–71; statement of,
    81–83; and Mather, 87, 88–89; at execution,
    100
Baltic Sea, 113, 168
banana wine, 30
bank, 27
bank vessels, 168, 187
bar, 108
Barbacoa, 14
Barbados, 3, 52, 71, 81, 103–104, 106, 111, 112,
    113, 114, 126, 128, 129, 132, 142, 151, 168,
    170, 175, 177, 190, 221
Barbareta, 197
Barbary Coast, 145
barcos de la armadilla, 28
Barlow, Jonathan, 177
Barns, Henry, 148, 150, 153, 155, 158, 160
bark or barque, 17, 28
Barro Colorado, 14
Bass, Rev., 169
batalia, 15
Bay (or Gulf) of Honduras, 106, 107, 138, 144,
    155, 156, 161, 164, 171, 176, 178, 179, 192,
    193, 194, 197, 200–201
Bay of Biscay, 120, 128
Bay of Guayacán, 40
Bay of Manta, 50
Bay of Panamá, 34
Bay of Snakes, 48
bear away, 29, 51
bear up, 29, 51

beat, 120
Bedhampton, 83
Bedlow, Capt., 109
Beeching, Jack, 1, 6, 7
beer, 113
Beer, Captain, 54–55
Bell, John, 190
Bellamy, Samuel, xi, 54–56, 62–68, 72, 73, 75–78, 80–82, 84–86, 101, 108, 109, 148, 209
Bellomont, Lord, 53, 169
Benbrooke or Benbrook, James, 210, 212–213, 216, 222, 223, 24, 226, 227–228
bend sails, 161
Bermuda, 12, 111, 112, 145, 170, 171
Berry Islands (Bahamas), 132
Besneck, John, 135–136
Biddiford, 171
Bilbao, 120
bilge, 39
Biscay, Bay of, 120, 128
bit (coin), 156
Blackbeard (see Teach, Edward)
Blades, William, 153, 154, 155, 157, 167
Blair, James, 212–213, 226, 227
Blanco/Blanko/Blanquilla, 54, 65, 75, 78, 80, 83, 110, 138, 174, 175, 176
Blaze, John, 194
Block Island (Rhode Island), 55, 85, 106, 146, 151
Bloodworth, Capt., 106
Boa Vista, 171
boatswain, 85
Bold in Her Breeches (Jo Stanley), 130, 134
Bolivia, 17
Bolster, W. Jeffrey, 119
bomkins, 37
Bonacco, 196, 198, 201, 203
Bonaire, 152
Bonavista, 164, 171, 188, 203
Boneta, 220
Bonnet, Stede, xi, 103–104, 109, 112–114
Bonny, Ann, xi, xii, 130–137
Bonny, James, 130
Book of Common Prayer, 64
boot-topping, 39; *see also* breaming, careening, graving
Bor (sailor), 212
Borden, Abraham, 168
Boston (Lincolnshire), 62, 85, 87
Boston (Massachusetts), 17, 53, 57, 64, 71, 73, 81, 101, 108, 114, 117, 119, 126, 138, 141, 150, 169, 171, 172, 173, 178, 181, 207, 210, 211, 220, 225, 226, 227
Boston News Letter, discussed, 55, 101
Boston Town House (Old State House), 57
boucan, 1
boucan de tortue, 36
boucaniers (*see* buccaneers)

Boure, Louis de (*see* La Bouche/La Buse, Olivier De)
Bowls, Capt., 126
bowsprit, 64
Boydel, John, 144
Bradish, Joseph, 125
Bradley, Joseph, 11, 13
Brand, Ellis, 109, 119
brass ordnance, 17
Brazil, 110, 122, 170, 176, 188
breaming, 33; *see also* boot-topping, careening, graving
Brett, John, 65, 66, 73, 76, 77
Breverton, Terry, 6
Briant, Joseph, 168
Bridds, Capt., 171
brig and brigantine, 29
Bright, John, 162–165, 167
bring to, 63
Bristol (England), 50, 67, 75, 76, 80, 81, 83, 85, 101, 105, 114, 126, 168, 188, 203, 208, 216, 221, 223, 224, 226
Bristol (Speightstown), 126, 129
Bristol milk (wine), 30
Brooker, Capt., 110
Brown, Capt., 114
Brown, Charles, 168
Brown, John (I: Bellamy's company), trial of, 57–71; statement of, 79–80; and Mather, 87, 92–94; at execution, 100
Brown, John (II: "The Tallest," in Charles Harris' company), 153, 155, 156, 157, 167
Brown, John (III: "The Shortest," in Charles Harris' company), 153, 155, 156, 157, 167
Brown, John (IV: forced from *John and Betty*), 212–213, 216, 226, 227
Browns Bank, 211, 222, 225, 226, 227, 228
Bucaniers of America, 3, 6, 20; *see also* Exquemelin, Alexandre
buccaneers, x, 54, 138, 179, 196–197, 198; background on, 1–6; vessels described, 6; diversity of, 14; armament of, 25; and authority, 36, 44, 46, 52; *see also* Cox, John; Dampier, William; Exquemelin, Alexandre; Morgan, Henry; Sharp, Bartholomew; Ringrose, Basil; Wafer, Lionel
Budger, Capt., 105
bulge, 39
Bull, Capt., 120
Bunington, Capt., 171
buoy, 190
burden or burthen, 33
Burg, B.R., ix
Burrell, John, 173

cable's length, 38
Cabo Corrientes, 80
Cabo Lorenzo, 50

Cagway, 7
callaloo, 35
Cambridge, 125
Campos y Espinosa, Don Alonzo de, 10
Canary Islands, 7, 9, 10, 30, 129, 175, 188
Canary wine, 30
Cander, Ralph, 175
canoes, described, 23
Canso, 167, 172
cantaloon, 144
Cap Haïtien (Cape Francois), 81, 84
Cape Antonio, 150, 151, 154, 160, 163
Cape Blanco, 40
Cape Breton Island, 172, 173
Cape Cod, 56, 64, 81, 82, 86–87, 110, 147
Cape de Verde, 144, 156, 158, 170, 171, 174, 175, 188
Cape Fear, 114
Cape Francois (Cap-Haïtien), 81, 84
Cape Hatteras, 210, 212–213, 220, 226
Cape May, 227
Cape Nicholas, 84
Cape Passaro, 37, 50
Cape Race, 128
Cape Roman, 170
Cape Sable, 143, 156, 179
Cape Sambro, 168
Cape St. Francisco, 37, 49
capital crime, 75
captain's journal, 125
Caracas, 37, 85
Carbonear, 187
careening, 33, 48, 140; see also boot-topping, breaming, graving
Caribbean, viii, x, 1, 7, 8, 31, 53, 74, 79, 82, 83, 128, 129, 138, 144, 174
Carmanthenshire, 71, 83
Carr, John, 168
Carry, Samuel, 124, 125, 126
Cartagena, 9, 10, 12, 191, 192
Carty, Patrick, 135
Catherine (Queen of England), 43
caulking, 44
Cavallo, 47
Caverly, Richard, 55
Cayman Islands, 8
Chagres, castle of, 11, 13–14, 19
Chamo, 45
Chandler, Capt., 170
Channel Islands, 125
Charles I, 48
Charles II, 6, 22, 43
Charles River, 220
Charleston, 108
Charlestown, 71, 141, 142, 144
chase guns, 107
Chatha, 191
Checkley, Samuel, 220

Checkley, Thomas, 65–66
Chepillo, 28, 30
Child, Thomas, 162–165
Chile, 40
Chira, 47
Church of England, 64
Church, Charles, 153, 154, 156, 157, 167
Churchill, John, 175
Cicero, Marcus Tullius, 41, 59
Ciudad de los Reyes (Lima), 19
Clap, Rev., 169
claret, 30
Clark, Capt., 108
Clark, Jeremiah, 154, 171
Clarke, Simon, 136
Codd, Capt., 105
Coggeshall, Peter, 168
Cohier, James, 132
Coiba, 26, 34–35, 36
Coke, Sir Edward, 59
Cole, John (I: witness at trial of Bellamy's surviving men), 64, 66
Cole, John (II: forced from John and Betty), 212–213, 216, 218, 225, 226
Cole, Samuel, 209, 211, 217–220, 223, 224, 225, 228, 229
Collier, Edward, 8, 9, 11, 12, 15
Collier's Harbour, 187
Collyer, John, 143, 144
Colombia, 37
Combs, Capt., 113–114
comets, 31
coming to, 174
compos mentis, 100
Condick, George, 209, 211, 217–220, 228
Connecticut, 117, 167
Constanta, Donna Joanna, 50
constructive evidence, 76
Cook, Edward or Edmund, 33, 36, 45
cooper, 194
Coquimbo, 40, 42, 43
coram, 10
coram me, 142
coram nobis, 144
Cordingly, David, xi–xii, 7, 82, 117, 119, 124–125
Cordoba, 14
Cork, 85, 213, 223
Cornelian, Peter, 135–136
Cornelison, Capt., 83
Cornelius, John, 68
Corner, Richard, 135
Corney, John, 76
Cornwall, 52, 124, 168
Cornwall, James, 209
Corp, Robert, 175
County Derry, 167
County Limerick, 167
Cowes, 110

Cox, John, 20, 22; on Kuna, 23; on Coxon, 31; on loot from Spanish vessel, 32; on unrest following Sawkins' death, 36; on capture of Spanish vessel, 39; on water shortage, 41; on battle near Ilo, 42; on attempt to burn buccaneer ship, 43; on Sharp's removal, 44; Sharp on, 44; on Arica, 45, 46, 48; on modification to buccaneer vessel, 47; on Ringrose, 48; on capture of *El Santo Rosario*, 50; on end of Sharp's voyage, 52–53
Coxon, John, 22, 24, 26, 28, 31–32
Craig, Capt., 108
Craige, Capt., 170
Cranmer, Thomas, 64
Cranston, Samuel, 148, 169
Crocus Bay, 67
Cromwell, Oliver, 48
Crowley, 108
Crumpsley, Andrew, 62, 64, 83, 84, 85
crusidore, 204
Cuba, 7, 8, 11, 65, 80, 145
Cuba, Marcus De, 9–10
Cues, Peter, 153, 155, 157, 167
Culliford, Robert, 44
Cumana, 175
Cundon, Morrice, 213–215, 216, 217, 218, 223–225
Cunningham, Patrick, 162–165
Curaçao, ix, 3, 106, 170, 174, 175, 191
Curre, John, 204
cutlass or cutlash, 62

Dampier, William, 12, 20, 46; on New Panamá, 26; and Coxon, 31; on Pueblo Nova, 35; on Gorgonia, 36; on Cape St. Francisco and Cape Passaro, 37; on Isle of Plate, 38; on Juan Fernández/Queen Catherine's island, 43; on buccaneers, 44; on Sharp's removal, 44; on Arica, 45; on Blanco/La Blanquilla, 75; on Curaçao, 170
Danwell (pirate), 160
Darién, 20, 22, 23, 26, 191
Dartmouth, 171
Dauling, Robert, 212–213, 216, 226, 227
Davis Land, 52
Davis or Davies, John, 132, 135
Davis, Howell, 122
Davis, Thomas, 87; trial of, 71–79; statement of, 83
Daw, John, 212–213, 226, 227
Dear, I.C.B., 29, 33, 35, 39, 44, 51, 62, 224
Defoe, Daniel, 55, 178
Delander, Robert, 11, 14
Delaware, 106, 210, 222, 224, 226, 227
Delbridge, Andrew, 171
Delight, 175, 199
Delve, Jonathan, 175
Demelt, Abraham, 119

Demilt, Capt., 106
Dent, Digby, 191
Deptford, 145, 178
derrotero, 21, 50
Devon, 54, 167, 168, 170
Devonshire, 167
Dillon, Thomas, 135, 136
Discovery Bay, 135
Dispensa, 47
Doan or Dunn, John, 64, 66
Dodman Head, 113
dollar, 32
Dolliber, Joseph, 183
Dolphin, 8
Dorset, 168
doubloon, 156; double doubloon, 164
Dove, Capt., 202
Dover, 171, 172
Dow, George Francis, 75, 177, 178, 179, 203
Downing, Capt. Thomas, 112
Drake, Sir Francis, 38, 39, 40, 45, 49, 69
Drake's Island, 38
Draper, John, 168
driving, 47
Dry Harbour Bay, 135, 136
Dublin, 62, 65, 105, 227
Duke de Palata, 19
Duke of York's Harbour, 49
Dummer, William, 57, 148, 209
Dunavan, James, 62, 64–65
Dunbar, James, 52
Dunn or Doan, John, 64, 66
Durham, 171–172

Eagle, 175, 176
Earl, Thomas, 135
Earle, Peter, 4, 6, 8, 10, 14, 25
East Indiamen, 163
Eastham, 64, 66, 86, 87
Eastwick, Capt., 150, 154, 171
Eaton, Edward, 153, 154, 156, 157, 167
ebb tide, 27
Edmonds, John Henry, 75, 177, 178, 179, 203
Edward III, 59
Edward or Edwards, Capt. (alias for Stede Bonnet), 112, 114
Edwards, Capt. (commander of prize to Low/Harris), 155
Eger, Capt., 155
El Santo Rosario, 21, 50
Elizabeth (shallop), 143
Elizabeth (snow), 208, 214, 216, 220, 223, 225, 227
Ellms, Charles, see *Pirates Own Book*
England, Edward, 65
English Channel, 125
English Civil War, 7
Essex County, 143
Eustatis (St. Eustatis), 3, 72, 109

Every, Henry, xii, 54, 63
Exeter, 167
Exquemelin, Alexandre, 20, 138; on buccaneers, 3; on Morgan, 6; on Panama, 11; on assault of Panamá, 17; on division of loot, 19; on recall of Modyford and Morgan, 19; on buccaneers' firearms, 25; on Portobello, 191

Fabins or Phabens, Lawrence, 143, 181, 188
factor, 175
Faial, 174
Falconer, William, 9, 10, 11, 13, 17, 23, 27, 29, 30, 33, 35, 36, 37, 38, 39, 40, 43, 47, 48, 51, 55, 62, 63, 64, 81, 85, 107, 108, 121, 125, 136, 143, 144, 159, 168, 169, 174, 176, 189, 190, 199, 227
fall down, 47
Falzell, James, 168
Fame's Revenge, 209, 210, 211, 213, 220, 227
Fancy, 186
Farmer, Capt., 106
fathom, 13
Featherstone, George, 132, 135, 136
Fells (passenger on *Sparrow Hawk*), 64
felones de se, 149
Fenn, John, 168, 170
Ferguson, William, 211, 212, 213, 228
fetch, 40
filibuster, 1
firearms, discussed, 25, 62
firk, 198
fish gig, 51
Fisher, Archibald, 151, 158
Fitz-Gerrald, John, 148, 152, 153, 167, 224
Fitzgerald, Thomas, 62–64, 70
flat, 199
flaw, 43
Fletcher, John, 162–165
flood tide, 27
Florida, 111, 131, 202
Flucker, James, 141, 142, 144
flush deck, 47
Flushing (Vlissingen), 62, 81, 87
Fly, William, xi, 148, 208–229
flying jib-boom, 64
Ford, John, 197
Ford, Robert, 173
fore-and-aft rigging, 35
foremast, 65
foretop gallant sail, 227
forlorn, 14, 26
Forms of Prayer, 93
Fortune, 141, 145, 150, 151, 160, 163, 164
four-pistole piece, 164
Fox (or Fawkes), Thomas, 73, 77
Frayler, John, 47, 190
Freebairn, Matthew, 175
freebooter, 1

French, John, 76
frigate, 11
frigate-built, 11, 55
Fulford, Ann (alias for Ann Bonny), 132
Fulker, John, 210, 211, 212, 213, 220, 221, 223, 224, 226, 227
Furber, Jethro, 173
fusil (musket), 25

Galápagos Islands, 36
Gale, John, 210, 213, 221, 223, 224, 225, 226, 227
galley-built, 11, 55
Galliardena, 9
Gallo, 36, 37
Galoone, John, 12
Gambia Castle, 141
gambling, 39
Gardiners Island, 106
Gatchel, Benjamin, 113
General History of the Robberies and Murders of the Most Notorious Pyrates (Capt. Charles Johnson), viii, xiii, 55, 56, 67, 81, 101–103, 106–107, 108, 109, 112, 114, 122, 124, 125, 126, 128, 130–131, 133–134, 138, 141, 144, 145, 165, 166, 167, 168, 169, 170, 173, 174, 175, 178, 189, 199, 208, 209
George I, 106, 118, 125, 130
Ghana, 122
Gibson, Andrew, 132
Gift, 12
Gilbert, Capt., 164
Gilespy, Henry, 125
Gilford, Robert, 143, 144
Girdler, George, 210, 211, 212, 213, 216, 217, 225, 226, 227, 228
Glamorgan, 7
Glasgow, 171
Gloucester, 167
Glyn, Thomas, 73, 75, 76
goal (archaic rendering of gaol – i.e., jail), 57
Goelet, Capt., 106
going on the account, viii, 21–22
Gold Coast, 126
Golden Age of Piracy, defined, viii, 208
Golden Cap (Kuna king) 23, 24, 25
Golden Island, 22
Golden, Capt., 170
Golfo Dulce, 48, 49
Gordon, George, 113, 117
Gorgonia, 36, 37
Gosse, Philip, 38
Gould (translator), 204
Gourdon, Zana, 190
Grand or Great Bank (Newfoundland), 129, 168, 171, 172, 187
Grande, Thomas, 199
Grange, Roger, 175
grape shot, 44

Graves, Capt., 126–127
graving, 48; *see also* boot-topping, breaming, careening
Great Brewster, 209, 223
Greeman, Capt., 171
Green Island, 81
Green, John, 208–209, 212, 214, 216, 218, 221, 223, 224, 225
Greenville or Greenvill, Henry, 209, 211, 217–220, 228, 229
Grenada, 128
grenades or grenadoes, 13, 62
Grigg, Capt., 105
Grinnaway, Capt., 111
Guayacán, Bay of, 40
Guayaquil, 39, 40, 49
Guinea, 126, 155, 175, 177, 208, 223, 225
Guineaman, 126
Gulf of Florida, 202
Gulf of Mexico, 29
Gulf of Nicoya, 47
Gulf of Panamá, 33
Gulf of San Miguel, 22
Gulpho Dolce, 45
gun-shot (distance), 190
gunner, 159
Guzmán, Don Juan Pérez de, 10, 13, 14, 17

Hacke, William, 52
Haiti, 1, 8, 81
Halifax Harbor, 171
halliards, 121
Ham, John, 132
Harbor Island, 135
Harmonson, John, 12
Haro, Don Francisco De, 16
harpy, 193
Haring, Clarence Henry, 1, 3, 17, 20, 197
Harris, Charles, xi, 125, 138, 141, 142, 148, 152, 166, 170, 209, 222, 223
Harris, Peter, 24, 28
Harris, Samuel, 210, 227–228
Harrison, Thomas, 11
Harwood, Noah, 135
haul, 176
hause, 176
Havana, 11, 79, 84, 191
Hawes, Alexander Boyd, 145, 169
Hawkins, Sir John, 69
Hazel or Hazeal, Thomas, 162–165, 167
head sail, 64
hearsay, 78
heave to, 63
Hector (*Iliad*), 189
helm, 63
Henry VIII, 64
Hester, ———, 164
Hill, Henry, 223

Hilliard, John, 44
Hispaniola, 36, 66, 80, 81, 85, 135
HMS *Berwick*, 145
HMS *Burford*, 151
HMS *Diamond*, 202
HMS *Eltham*, 151
HMS *Faversham*, 168
HMS *Greyhound*, 141, 145, 147, 148, 151, 155, 158, 161, 163, 164, 168, 169,
HMS *Lowestoffe*, 117
HMS *Lyme*, 109, 113, 119
HMS *Mermaid*, 191
HMS *Pearl*, 113, 117, 119, 120
HMS *Richmond*, 52
HMS *Scarborough*, 109, 110
HMS *Seahorse*, 168
HMS *Sheerness*, 117, 209
HMS *Spence*, 178
HMS *Squirrel*, 57
HMS *Swallow*, 124, 125
HMS *Wakefield*, 52
HMS *Winchelsea*, 168
hogshead, 112
hold, 64
Holman, John, 183
Homer, 189
Honduras, Bay (or Gulf) of, 106, 107, 138, 144, 155, 156, 161, 164, 171, 176, 178, 179, 192, 193, 194, 197, 200–201
Hood, Mr., 172
Hoof, Peter Cornelius, trial of, 57–71; flogged for trying to escape, 81; statement of, 83–84; and Mather, 87, 94–95; at execution, 100
Hope, John, 197, 199, 200, 201
Hornigold, Benjamin, 54, 56, 79, 80, 84, 101
hostis humani generis, 149
Howard, William, 118
Howell, John, 132, 135
Huantajaya, 45
Huasco, 46
Hugget, Thomas, 153, 153, 157, 167
Hume, Francis, 109, 110
Hunt, Capt., 175
Hunter, Andrew, 175
Hurst, Capt., 109
Hyde, Daniel, 148, 152, 153, 166
Hyde, Mr. (navy officer), 120

icebergs, 51
Iliad (Homer), 189
Île à Vache/Isla Vaca/Isle of Ash, 7–8
Ilo, 40, 43, 47
Incas, 19
indentured servants, 105, 106
Iquique, 45
Ireland, 122, 126
Isaacs, Capt., 132
Isla del Caño, 47, 48

Isla del Gallo, 36, 37
Isla Perico, 33
Isla Robinson Crusoe, 43
Isla Vaca/Île à Vache/Isle of Ash, 7–8
Islas Los Testigos, 78, 83, 85
Isle of Ash (Isla Vaca/Île à Vache), 7–8
Isle of Man, 167
Isle of Pines, 65, 66, 80, 84
Isle of Plate, 37, 38, 49
Isle of Shoals, 143, 183
Isle of Wight, 110
Isola del Cavallo, 47

jack, 144
Jackson, John, 117
Jacob (pirate), 203
Jacobite Rebellion, 76, 106
Jamaica, 3, 4, 6, 7, 8, 9, 10, 11, 19, 35, 53, 54, 67, 72, 75, 76, 79, 80, 85, 87, 106, 107, 111, 113, 131, 135, 170, 171, 174, 178, 200, 201, 202, 208, 216, 218, 223, 224, 225
James, 210, 211, 213, 214, 217, 228
Jane, 178
jeers, 221
Jenkins, Thomas, 209, 212, 214, 218, 221, 224, 225
Jennings, Henry, 111
jerked or jirked meat, 1, 198
Jersey (Channel Islands), 125
Jesuits Bark, 80
jib, 64, 120, 121
John and Betty, 210, 212, 213, 214, 221, 227
John and Elizabeth, 171
John and Hannah, 210, 211, 212, 213, 214, 26
Johnson, Captain Charles, 55, 101–103, 124, 130–131, 133–134, 145, 174, 208, 209
Johnson, Humphrey, 117
Jolly Roger, 56, 82, 125, 141, 169; *see also* piracy and pirates: flags
Jones (Bartholomew Roberts' company), 124
Jones, Capt. (pirate commander), 113–114
Jones, Thomas, 150, 153, 155, 157, 158, 160
Jones, William, 153, 154, 155, 157, 167
Jordan, Edward, 21
Juan Fernandez island (Archipélago Juan Fernández), 43, 44, 45
Julian, John, 75, 81

Kemp, Peter, 29, 33, 35, 39, 44, 51, 62, 224
Kencate, John, 157–158, 159–160, 163, 166
Kendale, Ralph, 171–172
Kennedy, Walter, 122, 126
Kent, 24, 125
Kidd, William, xii, 53, 54, 125
King Charles Harbour, 48–49, 52
King, Capt., 142
King's Islands, 29
Kingston, 133

Kingston, Capt., 79
Konstam, Angus, 3, 7, 8, 79, 85, 101, 103, 105, 106, 111, 118, 127, 129, 131, 133, 166
Kuna, 20, 23, 26

La Bouche/La Buse ("The Buzzard"), Olivier De, 54, 56, 65, 66, 67, 68, 72, 75, 80, 82, 83, 84, 85, 109–110
La Concorde, 106
La Rochelle, 84
La Santissima Trinidád, 31
La Serena, 42
Lacy, Abraham, 148, 153, 167
Laja reef, 14
Lambeth (pilot), 81
Lancaster, 166, 167
Land of Promise, 107
Land's End, 124
Las Cruces, 14
latitude, 35, 51
Laughton, Francis, 148, 153, 152, 167
Lawes, Joseph, 191
Lawes, Sir Nicholas, 136, 137
Lawrence or Laurence, Edward, 212–213, 226, 227
Lawson, Edward, 148, 152, 153, 167
Lawson, Henry, 113
Layal, Capt., 155
Le Cerf Volant, 8, 11
Le Couter, Michael, 125
league, 15
Lechmere, Edmund, 113
Leeson, Peter, xi, 103, 119, 182
leeward, 35
Leeward Islands, 29, 52, 53, 109, 144, 168
Leonard, Robert, 170
letter of marque, 1
Levasseur, Olivier (*see* La Bouche/La Buse, Olivier De)
Levercott, Samuel, 175
Lewis, Nicholas, 145, 175, 176
Libbey or Libbie, Joseph, 141, 142, 143, 158–162, 167, 181, 190
lie (nautical term), 63
Lillie, William, 170
Lily, 11
Lima, 12, 19, 32
limes, in wine, 30
Linnicar, Thomas, 148, 152–153, 166
Linsey, Capt., 105
Lisbon, 170, 207
Little, Benerson, 1, 6, 9, 12, 14, 20, 21, 22, 24, 25, 30, 32, 36, 41, 42, 53, 54, 62, 135, 195
Little Bristol (Speightstown), 126, 129
Littleton, Capt., 205
Liverpool, 105, 111, 170, 171
Liverpool Merchant, 156
livre, 84
Llanrhymney, 7

Lloyd, Capt., 145
Lloyd, Christopher, 20, 21, 22, 50, 53
log board, 125
log book, 125
logwood, discussed, 79
London, 6, 54, 80, 105, 108, 126, 138, 167, 171, 225
Londonderry, 167
Long, Capt., 144
Long Island (Bahamas), 78, 80
Long Island (New York), 106, 125, 145, 151, 160
longitude, 35, 51
Loverigne, John, 171
Low, Edward, xi, 82, 138–177, 178–194, 196, 199, 200, 202, 203, 204; use of term *privateer* in Low's company, 165, 183, 190
Lowther or Lowder, George, 138, 140, 141–142, 145, 154, 155, 161, 165, 167, 171, 174, 175, 176, 178
Lucy, Peter, 57
Ludbury, Richard, 12
Lycurgus, 58
Lyne, Philip, ix

MacCarty, Capt., 174
MacDonald, Edward, 175
MacDowell, Capt., 110
MacGlenan, Capt., 114
machete, 135
Mackonachy, Alexander, 62, 63, 64, 65
Madiera, 30, 81, 105, 170, 207
Magellan, Ferdinand, 44
Magellanic Clouds, 37, 40
Maine, 143, 183
mainsail, 35
Maio (Isle of May), 188
Mairee, Capt., 114
major vis, 215
Majorca, 10
malum in se, 215
malum prohibitum, 215
mamey apple, 34
Manta, 38, 50
Manwaring, Capt., 114
manzanilla de la muerte (poisonous apple), 52
Maraca, 80
Maracaibo, 11
Marblehead, 143, 178, 179, 181, 183, 203, 207, 228
Margarita, 75, 83
Mark, Mr., 108
Markcos or Marquess, Jacobus, 47–48
marooning, 67, 82, 83, 174
Marsh, William, 152, 155, 159, 163
Marshall, Joseph, 211, 212, 213, 228
Martha's Vineyard, 147, 222, 224, 225, 226, 227
Martindale, William, 171–172
Martinique, 3, 141, 168, 177
Mary (brigantine), 173

Mary (schooner), 143, 186
Mary and Sarah, 135, 136
Mary Anne (pink; Bellamy prize), 56, 57, 62, 64, 65, 66, 68, 70
Mary Anne (sloop; commanded by Bellamy), 85
Masco, 43
Massachusetts, xiii, xiv, 54, 57, 62, 71, 125, 147, 148, 149, 169, 178, 183, 209, 210
matchlocks, 9
Mather, Cotton, xi; and survivors of Bellamy's company, 86–100; and John Rose Archer, 103; and Fly and his convicted crew, 228–9
Mayflower, 11
Maynard, Lt. Robert, 103, 117–121
Medberry, Capt., 171
Mediterranean, 145
Menzies or Meinzies, John, 148
Mercy, Capt., 155
meridians, 51
Merritt, Nicholas, 141, 142, 143, 174, 178, 179, 180–181, 183, 188, 203–207
Merry Christmas, 174
Messon, Charles, 141, 142
Mexico, 202
Milan, 10
Milton, 178, 179
Mindanao, 12
Minnens, Hugh, 125
Mitchell, Alexander, 216, 223–224
mizen or mizzen mast, 65
Modyford, Sir Thomas, 3, 4, 6, 7, 8, 15, 19
moidore, 176
Moleene, Dego ("Diego the Mulatto"), 12
Moll, Herman, 52
Monck, George, 7
Montecristi, 37, 38, 50
Montego (foodstuff), 35
Montego Bay, 8, 35
Montgomery, Capt., 81
Montgomery, Robert, 39
Moor, Capt., 76
Moore, John, 173
Moore, Walter, 175, 176
Mora de Sama, 45, 47
Morgan, Bledry, 15
Morgan, Edward, 7
Morgan, Henry, x, 4–19, 20, 21–22, 69
Morgan, Thomas, 7
Morris, Isaac, 73–74, 77
Morris, John, 8, 12, 15
Morris, Owen, 72, 75
Mountgomery, John, 171–172
Mudd, John, 151, 154, 158, 159, 163
Mumford, Thomas, 142, 153, 154, 155, 156, 157, 161
Mundon, Stephen, 148, 153, 167
musket (fusil), 25; musket shot (distance), 195
Myngs, Christopher, 7, 8, 12

Nahuatl (Aztec language), 34
Nantasket, 62, 65
Nantes, 62, 84, 87, 189
Nantucket, 62, 142, 147, 156, 222
Nassau, 79, 130, 132
Nauset island, 64
nemine contradicente, 211
nemo fit repente pessimus, 162
Nevis, 49, 52, 53, 109, 168, 170
New Hampshire, 143, 169, 183
New Jersey, 117
New London, 227
New Panamá, 26
New Providence, 129, 131, 132, 135
New York, 17, 52, 57, 62, 81, 84, 87, 106, 110,
    112, 120, 145, 167, 168, 169, 170, 171, 174,
    213, 227
Newfoundland, xi, 124, 128, 129, 164, 168, 171,
    172, 173, 186, 187
Newport, 55, 141, 145, 148, 154, 167, 168, 169,
    177
Newton, Thomas, 107, 108
Nichols, William, 143
Nicoya, 47, 48, 52
Nixes Mate, 220
Nombre de Dios, 191
Norman, Moses, 66
Norman, Richard, 11, 14
Norris, William, 135
North Britain, 125, 196
North Carolina, 109, 112, 114, 117, 118, 120, 210,
    211, 212, 213, 220, 224, 226
North Sea, 113, 168
Norton, Capt., 171
notary public, 77
Nova Scotia, 143, 144, 167, 168, 171
Noyes, Oliver, 76
Nymph, 173

Ocracoke, 120
offen or offing, 32
Old State House (Boston), 57
Oliver, John, 113
Orkney, Earl of, 116
Orn, Capt., 181
Osgood, Peter, 76
Osnabruck, 194
Ouidah, 54, 127
overhaul, 191
Ozenbrig, 194

Pacific Ocean, 15
Pack, James, 113
Paita, 33, 36, 40, 49
Palata, Duke de, 19
Palisse, Montigny De, 129
Palma, 10
Palmer, Francis, 173

Panamá, x, 4, 6, 20, 22, 26, 28, 30, 31, 33, 34, 35,
    49, 50, 191; Morgan's campaign against,
    7–19; description of, 11
Pare (or Pier), Capt., 188
Parrot, Capt., 171
paterero, 221
Patterson, Howard, 27, 35, 37, 39, 40, 44, 63, 189,
    190
Patrick, Noah, 132
Pearl, 12
Pearl Islands, 29
Pease, James, 170
Peeke, John, 6, 19
Peko, 45
pendant or pennant, 144
Pennell, C.R., viii-ix, xii
per curium, 144
Peralto, Don Francisco, 31
periagua, described, 29; "flat," 199
Perico, 33
Peroz, Lucas, 10–11
Peru, 10, 17, 19, 31, 33
Peso, value of, 32
Petit Goâve, 66, 81, 84
Phabens or Fabins, Lawrence, 143, 181, 188
Philadelphia, 105, 106, 110, 112, 113, 171, 213,
    227
Philippa, 127
Philippines, 12
Phillips, John, 103, 173
piastra, value of, 32
picarón, 192
Pickeroon Bay, 192
piece of eight, value of, 32
Pier, Capt., 203
pikes, 16
pilot, 9
pineapple wine, 30
pink, 62
Pinkentham, Capt., 111
Pinkham, John, 171
pinnace, 107
pipe, 105
piracy and pirates: articles, 3, 141, 155, 156, 158,
    165–166, 186; black pirates, discussed, 119;
    definitions and legal discussions, x, 58–60,
    68–69, 71–72, 149, 210, 215, 218–219;
    democratic elements, 103, 122, 130;
    estimated numbers of pirates active in early
    1700s, 208; flags, ix, 56, 82, 107, 111, 125,
    128, 141, 146, 150, 151, 169, 174, 176, 211,
    221, 222, 224, 225, 228; forcing captives to
    join, xi, 82–86, 111–112, 126, 141–143, 152,
    155, 156, 158, 161, 164, 171–172, 173, 178,
    180, 181, 182, 183, 186, 213, 215, 221, 222;
    plans for suicide if caught, 125, 146, 159,
    192; royal pardons, 22, 79, 103, 109, 112,
    125, 130

piracy trials, 21–22, 52, 53, 134, 141; of survivors of Bellamy's company, 57–79; of Bonny and Read, 135–137; of Charles Harris and company, 148–167, 169; of William Fly and crew, 208–220

Pirates Own Book (Charles Ellms), 128, 131, 177

Piscataqua (Portsmouth, New Hampshire), 113, 117, 143, 150, 154

pistole (coin), 156, 164

Pitman, Capt., 171

Pizarro, Francisco, 19

Plantain Island, 28

plantain wine, 30

Plummer, Capt., 126

plying, 40

Plymouth (England), 113

Plymouth (Massachusetts), 148, 210

Pochet Island, 64

Point Borrica, 49

Point of Mangroves, 37

Point St. Helena, 39

Pompey, 216, 225

Pope, Dudley, 6, 8, 9, 11, 12, 14, 15, 19

Port Maria, 135

Port Roseway or Rossaway (Shelburne, Nova Scotia), 142, 179, 183, 203

Port Royal, 3–4, 7, 12, 14, 26, 36, 133

Port Royal Key, 194

Porto, 105

Portobello, 4, 12, 14, 20, 22, 83, 84, 191

Portsmouth (England), 52, 83, 168

Portsmouth (Piscataqua), 113, 150

Postillon, 85

Potosí, 17

Potter, William, 168

Powell, Richard, 9

Powell, Thomas, 158–162, 167

paxaros niños, 51

Prince, Job, 172

Prince, Lawrence (buccaneer), 12, 15

Prince, Lawrence (*Whydah* captain), 72, 80–81, 82, 83, 85

principal (legal term), 214

Príncipe, 122

privateers and privateering, x, 1, 3, 4, 8, 9, 11, 12, 22, 31, 36, 44, 54, 101, 111, 112, 113, 159, 168, 169, 192, 208; use of term *privateer* among Low's company, 165, 183, 190

Protestant Caesar, 106–108

Providence (island), 12, 13, 14, 15

Providence, 156

Provincetown, 54

Puebla Nova or Nuevo, 34, 35

Puerto Rico, 10

Punta Mala, 34

Pyne, John, 12

quadrant, 35

quartermaster, role of, 81, 130

Queen Anne's Revenge, 106, 107, 109

Quelch, John, 148

quinine, 80

Quintor, Hendrick, trial of, 57–71; statement of, 85; and Mather, 87, 96–97

Quito, 31

Rachel, 210, 213, 214

Rackam, Jack, xii, 130–136

Raleigh, Sir Walter, 69

Ramillies wigs, 101

Ranger (Bartholomew Roberts), 127

Ranger (Charles Harris), 138, 145, 150, 151, 154, 155, 156, 158, 159, 160, 161, 163, 164

rapier, 32

Raritan Bay, 117

re infecta, 13

Read, Capt., 114

Read, Mary, xi, xii, 130–137

Read, William, 148, 152, 153, 167

real (coin), 156

Real de Sancta Maria (El Real), 22

Rebecca, 141, 143, 144

Red Sack wine, 30

Rediker, Marcus, xi, 105, 125, 126, 131, 160, 169, 208

reefing, 63

Resto, 47

Réunion island, 65

Revenge (Bonnet), 104, 105, 109

Rhenish wine, 30

Rhode Island, 55, 64, 66, 106, 108, 111, 112, 114, 117, 126, 141, 148, 149, 167, 168, 169, 190, 194

Rhodes, John, 204

Rhodes, Joseph, 170

Rice, Owen, 148, 153, 167

Rich, Richard, 142

Richardson, Joseph, 105

Richards, Capt., 72, 73, 76, 80, 82, 85

Rimac valley, 19

Ringrose, Basil, 20, 28; on Kuna, 26; on loot from Spanish vessel, 32; on Arica, 45; on paxaros niños, 51; on allegedly enchanted island, 52

rinigado, 35

Rìo de la Hacha, 9

Ritchie, Robert C., 53, 106, 125

Rivera Pardal, Manoel, 8–9

Roach, Capt. (vessel from Barbados), 132

Roach, Capt. (French), 170

road (nautical term), 36

Roan (passenger), 212, 221, 224, 226, 227

Roatán, 107, 192, 194, 196, 197, 199, 201, 202

Roberts (sloop captain), 170

Roberts, Bartholomew, viii, xi, 122–129, 159, 169

Robin Hood, 66
Robinson (I), Capt., 171
Robinson (II), Capt., 172
Robinson Crusoe (Daniel Defoe), 178
Rogers, Capt. (of Barbados), 126–127, 129
Rogers, Francis, 30
Rogers, Thomas, 12
Rogers, Woodes, 28, 79, 130, 132
Rolland, Capt., 106
Rose, 187, 203
Rotherhithe, 113
round house, 163
Rowan, Capt. Dr., 132
Royal Fortune, 124, 127
rum, 113
Russel, John, 181, 183, 184
Ruth, Richard, 224

s.s. (*scilicet*), 115
Saba island, 72
sack wine, 30
Sailing Bay, 128
Salem, 202
Salter, Thomas, 143
Samuel (prize to Bartholomew Roberts), 122, 124–129
Samuel (schooner), 143
San Blas Islands, 31
San Pedro y la Fama, 8, 9
San Tiago river, 49–50
Sancta Cruz/St. Croix, 80, 84, 85, 170, 191
Sancta Maria del Darién, 22
Sandford, Capt., 106
Sandy Hook, 106
Sanford, Joseph, 168
Sango, Thomas, 228
Santa Barbara (Curaçao), 170
Santa Catalina, 12, 14
Santa Maria, 22, 25, 26
Santa Marta, 22
Santander, 144
Santo Rosario, 21, 50
Sâo Miguel (St. Michael's), 170, 179, 187, 188, 204
sapota, 34
Satisfaction, 11
Savage, Habijah, 220
savannah, 15
Sawkins, Richard, 26, 27, 28, 31, 32, 35
Schonhorn, Manuel, xiii, xiv, 55, 67, 133, 209; see also *General History of the Robberies and Murders of the Most Notorious Pyrates*
schooner, 136
scilicet, 115
Scot, Andrew, 156, 158, 164, 170
Scotland, 125
Sea King, 129
Sea Nymph, 105, 106

seaman, defined, 10
sea mark, 169
Second Anglo-Dutch War, 22
Second Dutch War, 7
Segovia, 22
Seville, 10
Sewall, Stephen, 144
shallop, 143
Sharp, Bartholomew, viii, x, 20–53
Shaw, John, 175
Sheerness, 109
Shelburne (Port Roseway or Rossaway), 142, 179, 183, 203
Sherrall, Henry, 51
Sherry sack wine, 30
ship, defined, 55
shoal, 36
Shrimpton, Samuel, 76
shrouds, 189
Shuan, John, trial of, 57–71; statement of, 84; and Mather, 87, 97–98
Shute, Samuel, 56, 57, 87
Sierra Leone, 175, 199
Simmons, Clement, 12
Simpkins, Capt., 170
Simson, Capt., 84
Sipkins, Capt., 106
Skiff, Nathan, 147
Skillegorne, Capt., 207
Skyrm, James, 169
slaves and slavery, xi, 14, 17, 54, 55, 72, 75, 106, 119, 122, 126, 129, 175, 176, 191, 200, 201, 208
sloop, 33
Slut's Bush, 64, 65
small shot, discussed, 44
smallpox, 154, 179, 206, 207
Smart, Thomas, 57
Smith, Edward, 151, 155, 158, 161, 164
Smith, James, 57–61, 68–69, 71–72, 77–79
Smith, John, 141, 142
Smith, Seth, 73
Smith, William, 64
Smyth, W.H., 21, 27, 36, 38, 40, 51, 64, 65, 120, 126, 132, 146, 163, 186, 188, 192, 194, 216, 221, 223
Snake Island, 53
Snakes, Bay of, 48
snow, 62
Solgard, Peter, 145, 146, 147, 149, 151, 155, 158, 161, 164, 169
Solon, 58
Somerset, 168
Sound, Joseph, 153, 154, 156, 157, 167
South Carolina, 54, 55, 109, 132, 171
South Sea Company, 175
South Seas, 12, 15, 17, 24, 26, 27, 31, 36, 50, 175

South, Thomas, 87; trial of, 57–71; later testimony, 72–73; statement of, 85
Spanish Armada, 39
Spanish Main, defined, 8
Spanish Town, 67, 85, 132, 135
Sparrow Hawk, 64
Sparta, 58
Speightstown (Little Bristol), 126, 129
Spenlow, Thomas, 135, 136
spelter, 44
Spice Islands, 125
Spike's Bay, 52
spiking cannon, 19
spinster, as legal term, 131
Spofford, Capt., 105
Spotswood, Alexander, 114–116, 117
Sprafort, Capt., 171
Spriggs, Francis or Farrington, 138, 169, 175, 178, 191, 192, 193, 194, 199, 200
Springer's Key, 31
Sprinkly, James, 153, 156, 157, 167
spritsail, 51
square-rigging, 35
Squirrel, 175
St. Andero, 144
St. Antony, 188
St. Catherine (Jamaican parish), 133
St. Christopher's (St. Kitts), 109, 110, 111, 141, 142, 175
St. Croix/Sancta Cruz, 80, 84, 85, 170, 191
St. Eustatis (Eustatis), 3, 72, 109
St. George's Banks, 62
St. Jago (Santiago, Cuba), 7, 9
St. Jago de la Vega, 135; *see also* Spanish Town
St. John (or *St. Jean*), 12
St. John's Harbor, 186
St. Kitts (St. Christopher's), 109, 110, 111, 141, 142, 175
St. Lucia, 177
St. Michael, 72, 73, 75
St. Michael (Sâo Miguel), 170, 179, 187, 188, 204
St. Nicholas, 188
St. Peter's Harbor, 173
St. Thomas, 53, 84, 174, 191
St. Vincent, 109
stand, 30
Stanley, Jo, 130, 134
Stanny, Richard, 171–172
Staples, Capt., 170
stay, 39
steelyards, 144
steerage, 224
stem, 146
Stephens, William, 52
Stevenson, Capt., 175
Stokes, Philip, 173
Stoner, John, 65

Straits of Magellan, 44, 51
straits, or streights, 44
Streaton, Thomas, 211–212, 213, 214, 216, 218, 224, 225–226, 227, 228
stretch, 186
strike, 62
Stuart dynasty, 106
Studfield, William, 148, 153, 167
Suffolk, 167
Suffolk County, 57, 220
sultan, 181
Sultana, 72, 73, 75, 77
Summersett, 126–127
Sunderland, 171
Suriname, 120, 171, 189
swan shot, 44
Swan, Charles, 12
sweating, 215
Swetser or Sweetser, Joseph, 141, 142, 158–162, 164
swivel gun, 132
Sycamore Galley, 156, 158, 164
Symonds, John, 200, 201, 202

Taboga, 33, 168, 170, 190
tack, 37, 186
Talty, Stephan, 4, 8, 10, 11, 12, 14,
Tanner, 65
Tasker, George, 226, 227, 228
Teach or Thatch, Edward ("Blackbeard"), x, 73, 79, 101–121, 125, 159, 191
Teneriffe, 188
tercio, 15
Terra Australis, 52
tertia, 15
tertiation, 15
Testigos (Islas Los), 78, 83, 85
Tew, Thomas, xii, 54
Thames river, 125
Thomas, Capt. (alias for Stede Bonnet), 114
Thomas, Capt., 120
Thomas, Dorothy, 134, 135, 137
Tierra firme, 8, 10
Tillingheast, Philip, 174
Tobago, 127, 173
Tomaco harbour, 37
Tomkins, John, 148, 153, 167
topgallant, 189
topsail, 63
Topsail Inlet, 109
Tortuga, 3, 7
Tosor, Capt., 80, 82, 85
Tower of London, 19
treason, piracy as a form of, 59
Treaty of Utrecht, 54, 79, 101, 208
Trefry, Thomas, 143, 144
Trepassey Bay, 128
Triangles (islands), 189, 190

triangular trade, 126; *see also* slaves and slavery
Trinity, 31
Troy, 189
Tryals of Captain John Rackam, 133, 135–137
trying, 174
Turneffe islands, 107
turtle, as foodstuff, 36
tutenag, 44
Tuthill, Capt., 171
Tyburn, 138
Tyler, Samuel, 209, 223

Universal Dictionary of the Marine (*see* Falconer, William)
Utila, 192

Valentine, John, at trial of Thomas Davis, 71, 75–77; at trial of Charles Harris and crew, 148–150, 152, 153–154, 157, 161–162, 163, 165
Van Vorst, Simon, trial of, 57–71; statement of, 84–85; and Mather, 87, 89–92; at execution, 100
Vane, Charles, viii, xii, 130, 132, 133
Venezuela, 152, 175
Venta Cruce (Venta de Cruces), 13, 14, 19
Verses Composed by Captain Henry Every… , 63
Vincent (Marshal of the Court of Admiralty), 71
Virgin Islands, 54, 80, 84, 170, 191
Virginia, 63, 72, 77, 81, 83, 103, 105, 106, 109, 112, 113, 114, 115, 116, 117, 119, 120, 166, 171, 213, 221, 226
vis major, 215
viva voce, 77
Vlissingen (Flushing), 62, 81, 87

Wafer, Lionel, 20, 23, 52; on warree, 24; on mamey apple, 34
Waldron, John, 145
Walker, Samuel, 211–212, 213, 214, 216, 218, 224, 226–227, 228
War of the Spanish Succession, 54, 79, 101, 111
Ward, Richard, 148
warree, 24–25
watch, 63
Waters or Walters, John, 153, 154, 156, 157, 167, 170–171
Watling, John, 31, 43, 44, 46
Watson, Henry, 172, 175
weather (nautical term), 39
Weekham, Benjamin, 154

Welch, John, 207
Welland, John, 148, 150, 152, 154, 157, 159, 163, 169
Wentworth, Sir Thomas (Lord Strafford), 76
West Indies, ix, 1, 30, 120, 126, 144, 145, 152, 155, 156, 168, 170, 175, 178, 179, 191, 199
West, Richard, 175
Western Islands (Azores), 129, 144, 170, 174, 187
Westminster, 138, 167
Westphalia, 194
Wethersfield, 167
wheel (maneuver), 16
Wheelwright, Julie, 133, 134, 136, 137
White, Robert, 175
Whitehead, 167, 172
Whydah (port of Ouidah), 54, 127
Whydah, 54–56, 56, 57, 60, 61, 62, 64, 65, 66, 71, 75, 77, 78, 80, 83, 84, 85, 86, 91
Wickham, Benjamin, 158
Willard, J., 142, 172, 173
William, 132
Williams, James, 67, 72, 73, 75, 80, 82, 83, 85
Williams, Glyndwr, 52
Williams, Neville, x, xi, 1, 103, 122
Williams, Paulsgrave, 54, 55, 65, 80, 81, 85
Williamsburgh, 116
Willis, Robert, 142, 175
Willis, Sam, 44
Wills, Henry, 12
Wilson, John, 148, 153, 158, 160, 164
Windham, James, 202
windlass, 223
windward, 35, 40
Windward Islands, 106
wine types, 30; from Nantes, 189
Winfield, Rif, 52, 109, 113, 145, 168, 178, 191, 202
Winthrop, Thomas, 218, 223, 224
Wolcot, Joseph, 144
Woodard, Colin, 55, 57, 65, 72, 75, 79, 101, 103, 106, 108, 111, 112, 114, 115, 117, 118, 132
Wragg, Samuel, 108
Wreaxham, 167
wrong (nautical term), 188
Wyer, William, 106–108
Wyling, Capt., 171
Wynn, Henry, 175

yard, 35
York County, 171
Young, Capt., 145

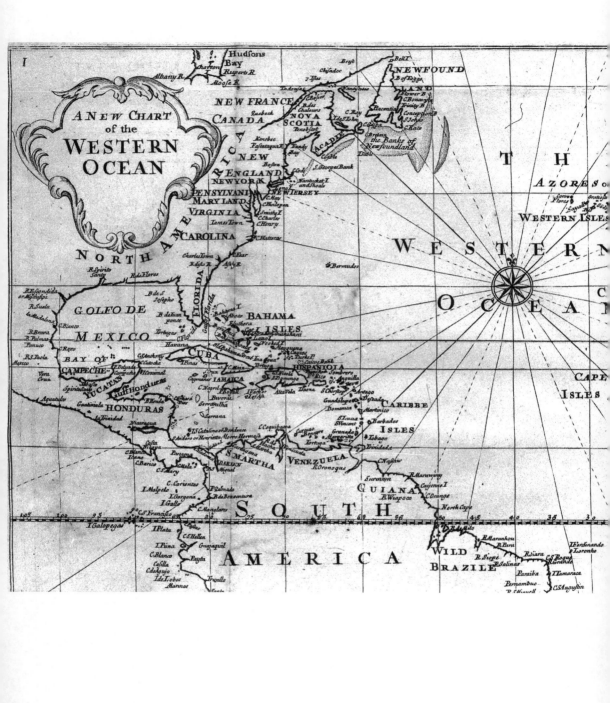

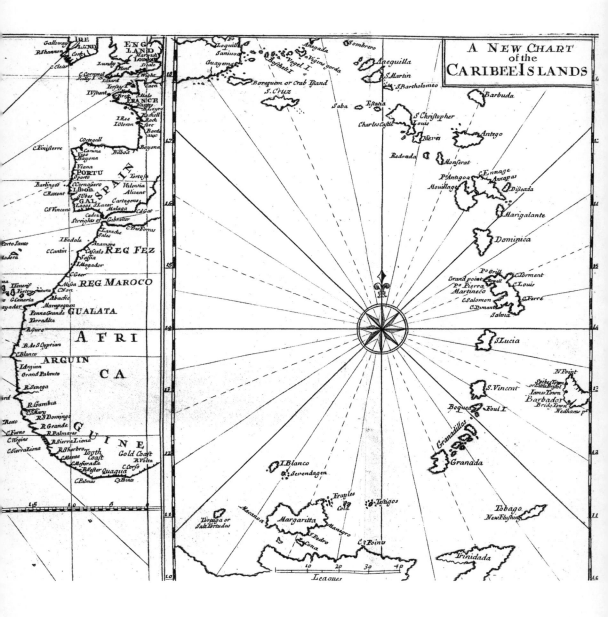